The 25 Sitcoms That Changed Television

The 25 Sitcoms That Changed Television

TURNING POINTS IN AMERICAN CULTURE

Laura Westengard and Aaron Barlow, Editors

 PRAEGER™

An Imprint of ABC-CLIO, LLC

Santa Barbara, California • Denver, Colorado

Library of Congress Cataloging-in-Publication Data
Names: Westengard, Laura, editor. | Barlow, Aaron, 1951– editor.
Title: The 25 sitcoms that changed television : turning points in American
   culture / Laura Westengard and Aaron Barlow, editors.
Other titles: Twenty five sitcoms that changed television
Description: Santa Barbara, California : Praeger, [2018] | Includes index.
Identifiers: LCCN 2017032208 (print) | LCCN 2017047059 (ebook) |
   ISBN 9781440838873 (ebook) | ISBN 9781440838866 (hard copy : alk. paper)
Subjects: LCSH: Situation comedies (Television programs)—United States. |
   Television broadcasting—Social aspects—United States.
Classification: LCC PN1992.8.C66 (ebook) | LCC PN1992.8.C66 A16 2018 (print) |
   DDC 791.45/617—dc23
LC record available at https://lccn.loc.gov/2017032208

ISBN: 978-1-4408-3886-6 (print)
      978-1-4408-3887-3 (ebook)

22 21 20 19 18   1 2 3 4 5

This book is also available as an eBook.

Praeger
An Imprint of ABC-CLIO, LLC

ABC-CLIO, LLC
130 Cremona Drive, P.O. Box 1911
Santa Barbara, California 93116-1911
www.abc-clio.com

This book is printed on acid-free paper ∞

Manufactured in the United States of America

For my television family: Angela, Christine, Douglas, and Georgia. Created by: George and Mildred

For Jan

Contents

Introduction

Laura Westengard and Aaron Barlow

What is television today, toward the end of the second decade of the 21st century? What is television, at the end of its seventh decade as the glue holding together American popular culture? Is it simply the box that has grown from grainy black-and-white beneath rabbit ears in the living room into myriad sizes and shapes with increasing definition and colors? Or is it now a part of us, something we take wherever we go—not because of the hardware but because of what we have seen and will see?

The things that have changed television have changed us; the things that have changed us change television. Situation comedies, the focus of this collection of essays, are often entwined with our earliest memories, defining the ways we look back on our childhood and setting the terms of how generations see themselves. Baby boomers are united by memories of *Leave It to Beaver* and *I Love Lucy* as members of Generation X are by *The Cosby Show* and *Seinfeld*. It is almost possible to pinpoint when an American was born by simply asking what the most important sitcom of their childhood was. True, after the 1960s, sitcoms were no longer directed at the entire family, but it is the children and the young who still take them most to heart and are most clearly defined by them. And, of course, those children grow up.

There is no way to define the 25 sitcoms that have changed television without defining how they have changed us, the generations of audiences who have grown up with these shows. This makes choosing the sitcoms for a list of the 25 most influential impossible—or at least impossible to do so in a way that pleases everyone. Influence depends on time (in one's personal life and in the broader culture) and audience as much as on quality or originality. Influence may have little to do with initial popularity, and influence can change as the culture changes, a once-forgotten show becoming relevant to a new era for reasons of politics or even technology. At the same time, what once was a looming giant can fade into irrelevancy, seeming dated and a dead end. Though the artifact may stay the same, how we see it is in continual flux.

To create this volume, we asked a range of scholars and writers to think about the sitcoms that were most important to them. We asked if they could make a case for particular ones as sparks for or reflections of change. We deliberately didn't ask much more than that and made clear that our own list of suggestions was nothing more than tentative. If someone could make a convincing case for a sitcom we had not considered, then by all means give it a try.

The 25 sitcoms on the list presented here, then, were not assembled by any single person or group working in concert and making decisions for everyone else but by individual interests stitched together by the editors to create what we think is a whole that, although not comprehensive (that would be impossible) or accurate in any impartial sense (another impossibility), does reflect today's broad vision of what Americans see as the sitcoms that helped make American television and American culture what they are today. Some of the essays do this through individualistic perspectives; others go for the broad sweep. Both approaches are appropriate because television is both individualistic and a group phenomenon—like American culture itself.

This is especially true today. In the 1950s, there were essentially three national networks along with a scattering of independent or public stations. Everyone watched from a small menu if they watched television at all. In the 1970s, that really started to change, the result of two factors. First, cable television created national stations (led by Chicago's WGN and Atlanta's WTCG) and new networks not dependent on feeds to local stations. The sudden increase in demand for programming was partly met by syndication of older programming, resulting in a tremendous expansion of available "reruns" and bringing older shows (and movies) back into public consciousness. The second was the development of the cheap videocassette recorder, which allowed people to record television shows for later viewing or to purchase (or rent) programs and movies at will for viewing and reviewing at leisure.

Over the decades since, the breadth of available programming has expanded tremendously—in the quality of the shows, in the technical sophistication of reproduction, and in the number and types of venues available for viewing. Today, a television show can be a hit without the majority of Americans even knowing it exists—for it might appear only on subscription channels such as HBO. Though there are still network hits in the sitcom world such as *Modern Family*, there are also hits on cable channels that define success more narrowly such as *Broad City* and *The Boondocks* on the

Comedy Central cable network and Adult Swim, respectively, and *Grace and Frankie* on the subscription service Netflix.

One advantage of the expansion of venues and possibilities for sitcoms is that target audiences can be narrower without sacrificing the success of the program. In traditional television (and even on most cable networks), ratings rule everything, and specific demographics rule the ratings. Advertisers interested in narrower demographic models had to hope that they could reach them within the broader ratings or in tandem with "gold standard" demographics such as "males, 18 to 54." Such advertisers can now change their strategies more easily than in the past, looking at networks and even individual shows that do not attempt to reach the broadest possible audience (or the gold standard ones) but are designed for specific niches. *Broad City*, of course, doesn't really expect a huge baby boomer audience or try to attract it. Advertisers wishing to reach millennials will be tempted to focus their advertising there rather than paying for larger numbers, including people beyond the particular intended market. This isn't a new pattern, of course, having long ago been successfully explored by the magazine industry. It was not really possible in television, however, until the variety of venues had reached a certain critical mass. Today, *The Boondocks* can assume a predominately African American audience without sacrificing success. As a show relying on a subscription service and not advertising, *Grace and Frankie* can focus on a demographic perhaps underrepresented by the existing customer base—in this case, suburban Americans in their 60s and older—in an attempt to expand that base. Sitcoms that are among the first taking advantage of these changes and similar ones are often more influential than others that have had greater popular success.

As we considered this growth in television and its sitcoms, we realized we had better establish a few terms or we could be swamped by the rising waters of television possibilities. Most of what we came up with is standard for television but repeating them does help frame this project. Most important was the word "sitcom" itself. An American situation comedy—or sitcom—we knew, is a half-hour comedy generally airing on a weekly basis with recurring cast and location. Though its genesis can be found in radio of the 1920s and 1930s and before that vaudeville, the sitcom is really a television feature, the very name arising in the 1950s with shows like *I Love Lucy* and *The George Burns and Gracie Allen Show* (both of which had roots in radio) and *Life with Elizabeth* (arguably one of the first half-hour situation comedies on television), defining the genre for the new medium.[1]

Sitcoms are predicated on what Marshall McLuhan would have called a "cool medium"[2] premise—that is, they depend on viewer involvement with characters carrying over from episode to episode even when (as they usually are) plots are more or less independent each episode. Changes in characters and situations have to be made with care, the confidence viewers have developed in character personality a fragile trust. Producers discovered this early on when they substituted actors in one role—the most famous early example being *Bewitched* (1964–1972), with actor Dick Sargent replacing Dick York after five seasons. On Broadway, replacements were (and are) a fact of life—but Broadway is a "hot" medium of once-off productions that are meant to be self-contained. In sitcoms, identification with characters is part of what drives viewers from one episode to the next. Messing with that can mean messing with the success of the show.

Sitcoms, in part because of "cool" media associations between the medium and the audience, tend to be self-limiting. Most of the time, changes in characters and locations signal attempts to salvage a show once ratings begin to sag. These are often efforts to revitalize audience interest and identification with shows whose casts have been depleted or whose story lines have grown stale. This is generally where a series ends, though dreams of renewed profits sometimes lead to a show "jumping the shark," a phrase taken from a stunt pulled on *Happy Days* (1974–1984) in which Fonzie (Henry Winkler) jumps over a shark while on water skis wearing his signature motorcycle jacket.

Limitations also arise from the sitcom's fundamental relationship with commerce. Sitcoms have always served to sell products—witness stars such as Lucille Ball and Desi Arnaz selling cigarettes in ads during their own show. Originally sponsored by a single corporate interest, the "sole sponsorship" model that resulted in the Ball and Arnaz type of ads was soon replaced by a "magazine concept" in which shows were divided into segments so that a several advertisers could feature their products—a concept whose artifacts we know (and love to hate) as "commercials."[3] This relationship with capital and sales means that even though sitcoms frequently address important developments in culture, history, and politics, their radicalism can only go so far—far enough to generate a publicity buzz, remain fresh and relevant, and keep ratings high but not so far as to alienate viewers or shed negative light on the advertisers who have paid for their segment of airtime. Perhaps it is this push and pull—this playing the line—that captures the imagination of each generation and continues to invite nostalgia once a show's initial time has passed.

What is a sitcom? Even the genre definition we previously gave is fairly nebulous. Does a situation comedy have to be all about the jokes? According to Sioned Wiliams (controller of comedy at British network ITV), not necessarily.[4] Should it reflect reality? Well, no, in fact sitcoms often showcase "actorly" performances and feature artificiality for the sake of amusement and entertainment (recall Fonzie jumping that shark).[5]

For the purposes of this collection, our definition of the genre is also a bit freeform. A tighter definition may have been possible 50 years ago when television itself was a narrower concept; today, both television and the sitcom range far from what once were rigid constraints. True, the traditional definition of a sitcom as "a half-hour series focused on episodes involving recurrent characters within the same premise" and in which each episode is "generally closed off, explained, reconciled, solved at the end of the half hour" generally holds true as the dominant structure of the shows we feature here.[6] However, there are certainly some that challenge that traditional structure and aesthetic. Ultimately, generic definitions are fluid and ever shifting, especially as they interact with changing market forces and media forms, and our list reflects that flexibility.

As we have hinted, the development of new media forms—from radio to television, network to cable, and now the Internet—has certainly shaped and reshaped sitcoms over the years. Our chapters feature sitcoms from various media platforms, and our contributors consider the implications of these venues. For examples, look at how cable allowed for the more risqué content of *Sex and the City* on HBO and how *Broad City* began its run on Comedy Central with a fan base already in place from its roots as a Web series.

The book is organized by decade, generally by initial air date, and features a postscript that shifts our gaze to the present and future of television. Throughout the chapters, each show's content and influence take center stage, and attention is paid to the development of the sitcom, its predecessors and successors, and how the show addresses the major issues of its time and place. Each chapter makes an argument about the show's impact on both television and the broader culture. Often the shows featured here are deemed influential because of their popularity (the "viral" hits of their time), but some of the shows appear because they were the first to do something, were historically resonant, or had unanticipated influence on media more broadly. If the book had been arranged thematically, we could easily have included sections featuring race and class (*The Jeffersons*, *The Boondocks*, *The Fresh Prince of Bel-Air*, *All in the Family*), gender and sexuality (*Will and Grace*; *Sex and the City*; *Modern Family*; *Mary Hartman, Mary Hartman*; *One Day at a Time*; *Broad City*), domesticity and marriage (*I Love Lucy*, *The Honeymooners*, *Leave It to Beaver*, *Modern Family*), and the workplace (*Get Smart*, *The Mary Tyler Moore Show*, *Murphy Brown*, *The Office*), among others. But, of course, there are slippages and overlaps in any show's content, and these sitcoms are, perhaps unexpectedly, complex, tending to defy any single thematic categorization. Therefore, we did not try to force a conceptual framework on the volume aside from the roughly chronological, and we trust the readers to see the thematic threads that weave between the shows featured, whether they pick up just a chapter or two or read all 25.

NOTES

1. "Betty White on Life with Elizabeth," *Pioneers of Television*, n. d., http://www.pbs.org/wnet/pioneers-of-television/video/betty-white-on-life-with-elizabeth, retrieved April 12, 2017.

2. Marshall McLuhan, *Understanding Media: The Extensions of Man*, Berkeley, CA: Gingko Press, 2003, 39–44.

3. Darrell Y. Hamamoto, *Nervous Laughter: Television Situation Comedy and Liberal Democratic Ideology*, New York: Praeger, 1989, 5.

4. Quoted in Brett Mills, *TV Genres: Sitcom*, Edinburgh: Edinburgh University Press, 2009, 24.

5. Ibid., 27.

6. Lawrence E. Mintz, "Situation Comedy," pp. 114–115 in *TV Genres: A Handbook and Reference Guide*, edited by Brian Rose, Westport, CT: Greenwood Press, 1985.

PART 1

The Fifties and Sixties

1

I Love Lucy: An Appreciation

Aaron Barlow

I Love Lucy *(1951–1957) established much about how we understand sitcoms today. In "I Love Lucy: An Appreciation," Aaron Barlow argues that* Lucy *offered a unique blend of innovation and cliché, knowing intuitively just how much past, present, and future to integrate into the show to create lasting magic. With no need to argue for its influence per se, Barlow focuses on several iconic episodes that frequently appear on "top" lists so he can examine the importance of the show on several fronts—from its unparalleled comedic performances to its technical innovations and continuing legacy.*

What other television star has not only had a statue made of her but also *been* a statue? Appropriately enough, sculptor Dave Poulin chose a pose from the popular episode "Lucy Does a TV Commercial" for a statue commissioned privately for display in Celoron, New York, where Lucille Ball lived when she was young. The statue was installed in 2009 but has since been nicknamed "Scary Lucy" because it shows a demonic woman with a bottle of what looks like medicine and a spoon about to reach into a child's mouth. Rather than showing the revolutionary figure Ball actually was, this statue makes her look reactionary, like someone forcing on us something we know we have never liked. Even the artist calls it "by far my most unsettling sculpture."[1]

Would "Revolutionary Lucy" be more fitting? We all know the answer to that, which is partly why Poulin's statue fails. After all, if we were going

3

to create a statue of Lucille Ball, we would more likely base it on a statue she literally created. In the last episode of *I Love Lucy* in its original configuration, "The Ricardos Dedicate a Statue" (first aired on May 6, 1957), Lucy poses as a statue of a Revolutionary War soldier, replacing one she has accidentally destroyed—a fitting tribute to the woman who revolutionized television, destroying whatever expectations anyone had about it before.

Outside of Charlie Chaplin and Walt Disney, no figure in the history of entertainment has had anything like Lucille Ball's power or influence over the future of their media—or impact on American culture in general. For any figure other than these three, an argument can always be made for a substitute, for someone else of equal stature. Not so for the creations of these three artists—the "Little Tramp," Mickey Mouse, and Lucy Ricardo— and certainly not for Lucy when it comes to television. There has never been *anyone* like her on TV, and there never will be, given her particular place in the early development of the medium. Her place in history is secure; her influence continues unabated today. She's the colossus looming over every ship entering television's harbor and one that no earthquake could possibly destroy.

No one will argue that *I Love Lucy* is not the most influential sitcom ever. Not "possibly," not "one of" but "the." One day, of course, another program may come along whose influence is as obvious and ubiquitous but it, too, will have grown in importance under the shadow of Lucy.

As Lori Landay, writing in 2001, claims, the influence of *I Love Lucy* extends far beyond television:

> The Lucy phenomenon is a triumph of commodification, the television series, the merchandise, and the character are all aspects of one of the most successful products television and postwar American society has ever manufactured. Today, Nick at Nite reruns, websites, fan conventions, collectibles, television specials, books, videotapes, laserdiscs, the merchandising, and the recent popular vote to put Lucy on a U.S. postage stamp commemorating the 1950s are all evidence of the contemporary Lucy phenomenon.[2]

I Love Lucy has become an indelible feature of American culture and commerce. Fifteen years after Landay wrote about it, the phenomenon continues and will do so for the foreseeable future.

Significantly, though she was quite clearly an original, one of the many rather odd and remarkable things about Lucille Ball is that she was *no* original—at least not in terms of comedic ideas. She constantly sponged up the past, wringing it out and into her new routines for the new medium. Like all first-rate comedians, she was a student of all of those who had successfully told jokes or acted out skits before her—and she reused what had worked in one situation, altering it for the needs of the next. Her own originality lay primarily in transforming herself and the comedic material she had mastered, making it suitable for the small black-and-white screen. She reworked the slapstick of vaudeville and early silent movies, recognizing that its exaggerations were perfect for the fuzzy images of television's first decade.

Other people, of course, were involved in this (including Ball's husband and costar, Desi Arnaz), for television is never a solo enterprise, but it was clearly Lucille's touch that formed and controlled the show.

The originality of Lucille Ball lies in a vision of the past, the medium, its audience, and its future. No one else at the time of *I Love Lucy* was able to "see" all of these at once—and perform so deftly. She was also, to use the cliché, the right person in the right place at the right time, ready to turn to television from radio and bringing a vast experience in film also to bear. As Alexander Doty writes,

> while Lucy Ricardo of "I Love Lucy" borrows most immediately from . . . [her] radio character [in *My Favorite Husband*], a closer examination reveals that the televisual star image developed for (and to some extent by) Ball is actually the result of her complex and contradictory film image becoming a palimpsest upon which the character of the domestic screwball is layered. What emerges is a creation that is both conventional sitcom character and variety show performer—simultaneously "Lucy Ricardo" and "Lucille Ball" (the composite film image). In "I Love Lucy," elements of Ball's earlier film personalities are strategically camouflaged by Lucy's house dresses, aprons, and hostess pants.[3]

Lucille's past media performances would remain a critical component of what made her successful each Monday night at 9:00 p.m. throughout most of the 1950s.

Why? Aside from experience, what made Lucy so right for the time—and so influential?

More than a decade before Marshall McLuhan's *Understanding Media* was published, Ball had already come to understand the distinction that McLuhan would make between "hot" and "cool" media. The former is totally engaging, and the latter is less immediately engaging but demands more activity over the long run on the part of the audience. She knew she had to keep things simple if she were to succeed on "cool" television and to make audiences feel as though they were, in some way, direct participants in the show so they would tune in each week. She had to create patterns that quickly became apparent to audiences, to create a community of viewers, and to narrow focus to a few identifiable locales. In her own way, Ball was a theorist of television, but one who was able to put her ideas into practice.

Having succeeded in hot film and radio, Ball was able to pirate aspects of each that could be transformed into this new and different medium. She recognized that TV wasn't simply movies writ small or radio with pictures. She saw that something else was developing and recognized that she had the tools needed for success within it. The result was not only a show that molded a genre but also a series of sophisticated renderings of past comedy and style into the new medium.

Take, for example, the episode "Lucy and Ethel Buy the Same Dress" from season three. This is one of the episodes that would make my own top-10 list of all her shows and for several reasons. The episode not only builds to an expected climax—though with a twist—but also makes use of Lucy's own film past, adapting it appropriately to the small screen. In the episode, Lucy and Ethel perform the Cole Porter song "Friendship" from *Du Barry Was a Lady*. This happens to be the one song in which audiences hear Lucy's singing voice in the 1943 movie version of the 1939 musical. In the movie, she duets with Red Skelton and is eventually joined by Gene Kelly, Virginia O'Brien, and others (including Zero Mostel). The background is a large stage. In the TV show, she duets with Vivian Vance and is joined at the end by Desi and William Frawley (who pull the two singers offstage to end the episode). The background is a closed stage curtain. In the TV show, the song is a reprise of an earlier "rehearsal" of the song, the finale becoming a parody of the earlier performance. The in-joke of Lucy's prior movie performance of the song doesn't even matter—but those who got it would have felt a special connection to Lucy and insider knowledge because she does not trumpet (or even mention) her old performance of the song.

More significantly, Lucy does not reprise her movie performance but instead transforms the presentation to one of exaggerated facial expressions and broad physical motions that, while vaguely reflecting the dance steps of the movie, are clearly of the simplified sort one might expect from an amateur performance—not steps simplified for the needs of television (though, in fact, that's what is going on). There's even a mention early in the episode that "Friendship" is an "old" Cole Porter song, later referred to as "corny"—but nothing at all connects it directly to Ball. As she did so often, she deftly transforms a movie performance appropriately for *I Love Lucy* and for television, perhaps doing so for the first time quite deliberately and thus successfully.

Lucille understood that her own past minor stardom would not suffice for continuing success in the cool medium of television where identity and not glamour would be the cornerstone of success. Taking a cue from the Iowa farmer who said he used every part of the pig except its squeal to the extreme of even using the squeal, Lucille even made this understanding of the place of Hollywood and the role of glamour a part of her schtick, making her character almost constantly starstruck while using her Hollywood connections to recruit guest stars playing themselves as straight men and women to her comic.

THE POWER OF *LUCY*

Even those who never loved *I Love Lucy* or its successor, *The Lucy-Desi Comedy Hour*, have to admit to the power of the shows, which ran from October 15, 1951, to April 1, 1960, dying only because of the collapse of the marriage of Lucille and Desi. Though that's only about a third of the time *The Simpsons* has lasted, not even the animated sitcom can overshadow the older show.

I Love Lucy also didn't last nearly as long as *The Adventures of Ozzie and Harriet*, which premiered almost exactly a year after but continued as a half-hour sitcom until 1966 and its 425th episode (half-hour *I Love Lucy* episodes ended in 1957 with the 180th episode). But who remembers the Nelsons? Only the musical success of son Ricky (and some of his children) has kept the family from disappearing almost completely from public view. Lucille, as Lucy, on the other hand, doesn't even need a last name—not even today.

It wasn't simply the popularity of *I Love Lucy* that made the show last. In fact, the show wasn't initially a blockbuster. For the 1951–1952 season, it ranked third, barely beating out *The Red Skelton Show*. The next year, of course, it was the runaway leader, but its share went down the year after that (though it was still number one). In 1954–1955, the rating once again dropped, though the show easily bested number two, *The Jackie Gleason Show*. The next year, down once again, it was bested by a game show. In its last year, though it once again achieved the number one position, *I Love Lucy*'s ratings once again declined. What made *Lucy* so important was that audiences continued to remember her—a fallout of her understanding of the needs of a "cool" medium—and that other sitcoms looked to *Lucy* for leadership almost from the start.

Of course, part of that leadership came from Desi, who was responsible for incorporating relatively new and unusual production strategies that soon became standard or at least influential for television sitcoms. These included using film as the primary recording and storage medium (rather than relying on live broadcasts followed by kinescopes for rebroadcast), recording in front of live audiences, and using three cameras at once—a time-saver that also granted a great deal of flexibility to the production. Desilu, the production company owned by Arnaz and Ball, soon became a television powerhouse (and eventual owner of the studio RKO General) and production home to many of the more successful sitcoms of the 1950s and

1960s, including *Make Room for Daddy, The Andy Griffith Show, My Three Sons, The Dick Van Dyke Show,* and *Hogan's Heroes.*

BEYOND IMPACT

Today's arguments about *I Love Lucy* and the subsequent Ricky and Lucy shows no longer concern the importance of the series but which episodes are "best," "favorite," or "most influential," all separate categories with different meanings even though they are often conflated. The first is supposed to be an absolute and objective rating (something of an impossibility), the second a subjective appreciation, and the third something of a negotiation between the first two.

There are 180 episodes of the 30-minute *I Love Lucy* plus 13 of the *Lucy-Desi Comedy Hour.* Compiling the information from eight top-10 lists of episodes,[4] we find that 38 appear on at least one or about 20 percent of the total have been selected as a top-10 episodes by at least one of these list makers. Even so, there isn't tremendous variation, especially at the top of the list. The top five, from all the lists taken together, appear somewhere on most of the lists. They are:

1. "Lucy Does a TV Commercial"
2. "Job Switching"
3. "Lucy's Italian Movie"
4. "Lucy Is Enceinte"
5. "Harpo Marx"

Overall, the top two are effectively tied and far outstrip the others. "Lucy Does a TV Commercial" and "Job Switching" both appear on seven lists and are ranked either first or second on six. Only "Lucy Thinks Ricky Is Trying to Murder Her" "The Great Train Robbery," "The Freezer," and "Lucy Is Enceinte" are also ranked at the first or second spot on any of the lists.

The people who made these lists were choosing favorites or the best as based on their own television aesthetics. They were not choosing episodes based on influence, a much more ephemeral and difficult task—and an almost impossible one in this particular case—because it is the body of work that makes *Lucy* so influential, not any particular episode.

The fact that concocting such lists remains so popular also demonstrates the fact of viewer identification with the show. This first resulted from the "immediacy of the new medium, broadcast into the home, representing a marriage and domestic life, a feedback loop of representation and domesticity, no matter how comically distorted,"[5] something Ball understood from her radio audience and which has resonated over the decades since. It is a reflection of fan feelings of "ownership" or identification with the characters.

In making my own list of top episodes, I have relied on how they illustrate the importance of *I Love Lucy*. "Lucy and Ethel Buy the Same Dress," as we have seen, shows how effectively Lucille Ball mined the past and converted it to television. However, that's not the only time that happened. In fact, it probably occurred more often than anyone realizes, for Lucy was mining her private home life almost as much as her past and public professional life. The barbecue Arnaz built at the couple's Desilu home (the name the couple chose for their company was one they had earlier used for christening their house and indicates their continual melding of personal and professional lives and roles and the critical fact that they were a married couple playing a married couple) in the early 1940s shows up, though in brick, in "Building a B-B-Q" in season six. The chickens that had become almost pets at about that same time at Desilu also show up in the television show in the two-part "Lucy Raises Chickens" and "Lucy Does the Tango," also in season six. If one looks hard enough, a relevant incident from Lucille's life can probably be found in the majority of *I Love Lucy* episodes—setting a pattern certainly taken advantage of by Larry David and Jerry Seinfeld almost 40 years later for *Seinfeld* but evident in development of almost every sitcom since *Lucy*. Joann Gardner comments on this:

> [The] blurring of identities between outer and inner levels of presentation, between actual and fictional roles, calls our attention to the artistic structure itself, and Lucy's constant attempts to infiltrate television stardom keep us aware of the implicit irony that we are watching the achievement of that dream: a television star who is performing in her own attempt to perform.[6]

Ball, of course, was completely aware of how this developed a complicity between her and her viewers, one further heightening the comedy and its impact on her audience.

LUCY AND LUCILLE

Season one's "Be a Pal," another of my favorites, makes subtle use of Lucille and Desi's real marital problems going back to the beginning of their relationship. This exchange, occurring near the end of the episode, encapsulates a great deal of their marital troubles:

> **Ricky:** Lucy, please, would you mind telling me what's going on?
> **Lucy:** We make everything nice like when you little boy in Cuba. You like?
> **Ricky:** No, I don't.
> **Lucy:** Oh, you don't?

Ricky: Now, look, would you please explain to me what is the idea of all this?

Lucy: Well, I thought you were getting tired of me and if our home reminded you of Cuba you might like me better.

Ricky: Oh, Lucy darling, if I wanted things Cuban I'd have stayed in Havana. That's the reason I married you because you're so different from anyone I've known in Cuba.

Lucy: Who did you know in Cuba?

Lucille's combined desire to please Desi and her jealousy, not to mention that she really was the one who knew what was going on in both their professional and personal lives (Desi's philandering did not get past Lucy), certainly comes through in this dialogue.

In season three's "The Black Wig," Ball returns to the jealousy theme, playing against her trademark red hair with a black wig so Lucy can test Ricky's fidelity. Ricky, of course, finds out about the ploy even before it is enacted, making for a hilarious bit of double role-playing on the street when the two "strangers" meet. For me, this becomes another of the greatest of the *I Love Lucy* episodes.

One of the continuing tropes of *I Love Lucy* is Lucy's fear of Ricky, something of a reversal of the situation in the Lucy–Desi relationship. It rarely appears as a fear of physical violence (except in "Lucy Thinks Ricky Is Trying to Murder Her," where the absurdity of the fear is part of the humor) but as fear based on the contemporary structure of marriage in American society in which the wife must act submissively out of fear her marriage will fall apart. Lucy is clearly committed to the Ricardo marriage (just as Lucille Ball was to the Arnaz one) and will do anything to ensure that Ricky is never so angry that he might walk away. Erin Lee Mock argues that this raises Lucy's fear of Ricky

> to [a] thematic, and therefore, hyperbolic level. The audience and the performers may laugh from the safety of that hyperbole. In this respect, however, Lucy is no different from the other housewives on 1950s television. In fact, she is the prototype. And, although Ricky's outbursts are written off as manifestations of his "Cuban temper," sitcom husbands with different ethnic markers—or seemingly none at all—are crafted after his raging model, with varying degrees of subtlety.[7]

Instead of a "raging model," Ricky's behavior is more the acceptance of the perceived norms of marriage than character—and Lucy's fear of him is more of a play on prevailing *American* norms than any reflection of their relationship, real or fictional, or of the stereotypes of Latin volatility (again, something played with but not accepted). Ricky is portrayed as the standard American husband and dad right down to his hobbies, skills, and friendships. Still, though he and Lucy certainly are television prototypes, the comedic depiction of marital violence (or its threat) goes back to the dawn of entertainment. That, however, does not reduce the influence of *I Love Lucy*, instead placing it once again at that point of change where technology allows a new manifestation of older tropes.

BRINGING IT FORWARD

Ball's great skill—her ability to turn personal experience into humor—was buttressed by an ability shared by every successful comedian. It was recognized in Ball by Buster Keaton, "the great stone face," one of the top film comics of the 1920s. He mentored her during her time at MGM and then at Columbia Pictures in the 1940s. This was the ability to learn from every other comic she encountered, adapting what she saw to her own particular comedic talents. In a 1960 interview with Herbert Feinstein, Keaton said about her:

> **Keaton:** Lucille Ball is my top. The greatest character comedienne, Marie Dressler. Light comedienne, Lucille Ball.
>
> **Feinstein:** What are your reasons for thinking so?
>
> **Keaton:** I mean of all time, as far as I can remember. Nothing Lucille can't do.
>
> **Feinstein:** You get the impression that she's a great sport, that she has a wonderful sense of humor, that she can kid herself.
>
> **Keaton:** Yeah, she can do anything.[8]

So time has proven.

THE FACE OF TELEVISION

Another episode I include in my list of the best is "Lucy and the Loving Cup," in which Lucy spends most of the episode with said cup stuck on her head, her comedy coming from body action of a sort probably learned at the knee of Buster Keaton. The episode serves as another example of understanding of the needs of a "cool" medium where the face and its smaller movements are of reduced importance. Yet by the time this episode aired in season six (on January 7, 1957), Lucy's face was one of the best known in the nation. By deliberately hiding it, she not only shows the extent of her own comedic skills but also sends the message that the laughs—and the show—are more important than the star, setting a sitcom ethos still influential today.

In season one's "The Freezer," much earlier than "Lucy and the Loving Cup," Ball shows that she understood from the start that the idea of her facial expression—and not necessarily her face itself—made people laugh. She probably learned this during her time on radio just before the development of *I Love Lucy* when she starred in *My Favorite Husband.* Performing before a live audience, Ball got laughs for faces she made that radio audiences, of course, could not see. She learned that what audiences imagine can be as powerful as what they actually see—and that audiences participate in cool-medium humor as much as they absorb it. "The Freezer," then, also becomes one of my top *I Love Lucy* episodes.

Lists of the "greatest" of anything are always subjective, based on the compiler's interests and needs. The "most popular," on the other hand, is much easier to judge because numerical criteria can be used—most watched, most rerun, most written about, and so on. With *I Love Lucy*, the problem of *judging* the show becomes almost insoluble—except in terms of popularity, where two episodes—"Lucy Does a TV Commercial" from season one and "Job Switching" from season two—are generally close to the top. Because Lucille Ball herself became such an icon, we tend to remember the shows that show *her* at her best, not necessarily the ones that are the best television.

CONCLUSION

In 2016, a new statue of Lucy by Carolyn Palmer replaced Dave Poulin's "Scary Lucy." The new statue shows Lucy walking, hand on hip and with a slight and knowing smile. It exhibits pride and even a hint of swagger, appropriate for this icon of television, the woman whose character became its most influential face.

The controversy over the Poulin statue, though something of an act of comedy itself (it even sparked a skit on *Saturday Night Live* on April 11, 2015—season 40, episode 18), shows the sustained power of Lucy. Ball's Lucy Ricardo has every bit the iconic power of Charlie Chaplin's tramp. The two are the major images of entertainment media of the 20th century, the tramp for the movies and the first half of the century and Lucy for television and the second half of the century. As I noted in the start of this chapter, the only other media figure of comparable strength is the cartoon character Mickey Mouse.

In 1951, the year *I Love Lucy* premiered, television in the United States was, according to a *Fortune* magazine article published at the time, "an amorphous mass, given over to fantastic complications, and vulnerable as only the very young (of whatever size) can be."[9] According to the piece, TV had already failed in the prophesy that radio would "shrivel away under the baleful glare of the video screen. Movies would follow their own victim, vaudeville, into limbo. National culture was to be displaced by national stupor."[10] At that time, according to the same article, there were only 107 TV stations in the country, serving 63 markets, 29 of which were served by only one station. There were some 15.5 million televisions nationwide for a population of some 152 million, about one for every 10 people. The first color broadcasts occurred that year, but it would be more than a decade later that color would come into its own on the small screen. And the screens were small; 12- and 16-inch screens were the most common.

Television has grown since then, to say the least. That it grew so fast and so successfully is due, at least in part, to the extraordinary talent and intelligence of Lucille Ball.

NOTES

1. Dave Poulin in "'Scary' Lucille Ball Artist Apologizes: It Is 'By Far My Most Unsettling Sculpture'" by Emmet McDermott, *The Hollywood Reporter*, April 6, 2015, http://www.hollywoodreporter.com/news/lucille-ball-statue-sculptor-apolog izes-786633.

2. Lori Landay, "Millions 'Love Lucy': Commodification and the Lucy Phenomenon," *NWSA Journal* 11(2) (Summer 1999), 25–47, 26.

3. Alexander Doty, "The Cabinet of Lucy Ricardo: Lucille Ball's Star Image," *Cinema Journal* 29(4) (Summer 1990), 3–22, 3–4.

4. Tyler Coats, "Decider Essentials: The 10 Best 'I Love Lucy' Episodes," August 6, 2014, http://decider.com/2014/08/06/decider-essentials-the-10-best-i -love-lucy-episodes; "Top 80 Best Episodes of 'I Love Lucy,'" IMDb, August 21, 2014, http://www.imdb.com/list/ls075532737; Lucille Barilla, "Wah! 10 Best I Love Lucy Episodes Ever," August 6, 2011, http://www.sheknows.com/entertainment /articles/838035/happy-100th-birthday-lucille-ball; Kristin, "10 Best 'I Love Lucy' Episodes," August 5, 2011, http://www.woolandwheel.com/2011/08/10-best-i-love -lucy-episodes.html; "The Best I Love Lucy Episodes," Ranker, no date, http://www .ranker.com/list/best-i-love-lucy-episodes/reference?var=3&utm_expid=16418821 -174.EbTIzGo1TBWiVK5QCBwtow.2&utm_referrer=https%3A%2F%2Fwww .google.com%2F; "Pick Me Results: The 10 Best Episodes of 'I Love Lucy,'" MeTV, November 24, 2015, http://www.metv.com/lists/pick-me-results-the-10-best -episodes-of-i-love-lucy; "Best 'I Love Lucy' Episodes," shareranks, no date, http:// shareranks.com/2948,Best-I-Love-Lucy-Episodes; "The Top 10 Best I Love Lucy Episodes of All Time," Culturalist, no date, https://www.culturalist.com/c/best-i -love-lucy-episodes-of-all-time-1399.

5. Lori Landay, "The Mirror of Performance: Kinaesthetics, Subjectivity, and the Body in Film, Television, and Virtual Worlds," *Cinema Journal* 51(3) (Spring 2012), 129–136, 132.

6. Joann Gardner, "Self-Referentiality in Art: A Look at Three Television Situation-Comedies of the 1950s," *Journal in Popular Culture* 11(1) (1988), 35–50, 36.

7. Erin Lee Mock, "The Horror of 'Honey, I'm Home!': The Perils of Postwar Family Love in the Domestic Sitcom," *Film & History*, 41(2) (Fall 2011), 29–50, 30.

8. Herbert Feinstein, "Buster Keaton: An Interview," *The Massachusetts Review* 4(2) (Winter 1962), 392–407, 400.

9. *Fortune*, August 1951.

10. Ibid.

BIBLIOGRAPHY

Brady, Kathleen. *Lucille: The Life of Lucille Ball*. New York: Hyperion, 1994.

Doty, Alexander. "The Cabinet of Lucy Ricardo: Lucille Ball's Star Image." *Cinema Journal* 29(4) (Summer 1990), 11.

Feinstein, Herbert. "Buster Keaton: An Interview." *The Massachusetts Review* 4(2) (Winter 1962), 392.

Gardner, Joann. "Self-Referentiality in Art: A Look at Three Television Situation-Comedies of the 1950s." *Journal in Popular Culture* 11(1) (1988), 35–43.

Landay, Lori. "Millions 'Love Lucy': Commodification and the Lucy Phenomenon." *NWSA Journal* 11(2) (Summer 1999), 25–47.

Landay, Lori. "The Mirror of Performance: Kinaesthetics, Subjectivity, and the Body in Film, Television, and Virtual Worlds." *Cinema Journal* 51(3) (Spring 2012), 129–136.

McDermott, Emmet. "'Scary' Lucille Ball Artist Apologizes: It Is 'By Far My Most Unsettling Sculpture.'" *Hollywood Reporter*, April 6, 2015, http://www.hollywoodreporter.com/news/lucille-ball-statue-sculptor-apologizes-786633.

Mock, Erin Lee. *Film & History*, 41(2) (Fall 2011), https://www.questia.com/library/journal/1P3-2531327481/the-horror-of-honey-i-m-home-the-perils-of-postwar.

2

The Honeymooners: American Dreaming Scaled Down to the Small Screen

Martin Kich

Though short-lived, The Honeymooners (1955–1956) carved out an enduring place in American television, Jackie Gleason's character Ralph Kramden was perhaps situation comedy's most enduring male icon (with his comedic partner Ed Norton not far behind). As Martin Kich shows here, the popularity of the show results from the characters falling short of the American dream but continually striving for it—unlike other sitcoms of the time where characters seemed to be living that dream to some degree. Though the show is laced with "problems"—jokes about Kramden's weight, threats (at least) of spousal abuse, and more—it teeters "on the thin line that separates deep laughter from genuine pathos," which is part of why it succeeds.

The Honeymooners features a small cast of ordinary characters interacting in a confined but ordinary setting. Most of the action takes place in the main living space of the Brooklyn apartment of Ralph Kramden, a bus driver played by Jackie Gleason, and his wife, Alice, played by Audrey Meadows. The only other major characters are the Kramdens' neighbors and closest friends, Ed and Trixie Norton. Played by Art Carney, Ed is a sewer worker; his wife, Trixie, is played by Joyce Randolph.

The Honeymooners helped establish many of the fundamental elements of the situation comedy. Although most of those elements did not originate with *The Honeymooners*, it is accurate to say that this series served as a prototype for many subsequent efforts in the genre. That paradox is just one of many when one tries to write perceptively about this series and its impact on the genre and, more broadly, on American culture.

These paradoxes are apparent in simply reporting on the history of *The Honeymooners*. As a "series," *The Honeymooners* ran for just a single season of 39 episodes originally aired in 1955 and 1956. The concept for the show evolved from sketches written for the television variety shows that Jackie Gleason hosted starting in 1951—*Cavalcade of Stars*, which aired on the DuMont Television Network, and *The Jackie Gleason Show*, which aired on CBS. The recurring sketches became so popular that, after receiving a new contract from CBS, Gleason decided to experiment with transforming them into a half-hour situation comedy that would provide the lead-in to an hour-long variety show. This transition appeared somewhat natural because many of the sketches had been as long as standard half-hour episodes. Nonetheless, after the 1955–1956 season, Gleason decided that producing a full season of half-hour episodes of the show was eventually—perhaps quickly—going to undermine their spontaneity and quality. In addition, reducing *The Honeymooners* to a recurring sketch on his variety show would allow him much more flexibility with the materials and allow the story ideas to determine the length of the sketches, some of which, however, did end up as long as or even longer than the half-hour episodes.

So someone unfamiliar with the show and its history might ask, why should a situation comedy that ran for a single season in the mid-1950s be remembered at all and why it had such enduring appeal and influence? Well, with considerable foresight for the time, Gleason decided to have the 39 episodes filmed so that they could be syndicated for rebroadcast. In addition to the rather lucrative long-term contract that he signed with the CBS television network, which was not unusual for the early "stars" of the new medium, he had also retained the rebroadcast rights to the shows that he not only starred in but also produced. So the 39 episodes that aired in 1955–1956 began to be broadcast in syndication the following year and have never been off the air since that time. (Gleason showed considerable foresight in filming the episodes and retaining initial syndication rights, but after several years he sold the syndication rights back to CBS for $1.5 million, a large sum at the time but a modest one given the many subsequent decades over which the show has continued in syndication[1]). Given that the series was initially broadcast relatively early in the history of television—at about the time that television sets began to be common in American homes—and given that most subsequently syndicated situation comedies have had more than 100 episodes, it is arguable that the 39 episodes of *The Honeymooners* have been among the most frequently watched episodes of any show in the history of American television.

After the 1956–1957 season, *The Jackie Gleason Show* went off the air for five years. Gleason returned to the air in 1962 with a variety show called *The American Scene Magazine*, which aired until 1966, and then with a new version of *The Jackie Gleason Show*, which aired until 1970, when CBS did a major overhaul of its prime-time programming in a determined effort to appeal to a younger and more progressive viewership. Nonetheless, for another 15 years, *Jackie Gleason Specials* aired regularly on the network, with each special including "new" sketches. Although all of the sketches aired in the 1960s, 1970s, and 1980s were in color and some had settings and situations far removed from the basic setting of the 39 episodes, some of the "new" sketches were actually remakes of the "lost" sketches from the variety shows of the 1950s.

Indeed, as baby boomers began to enter middle age and become nostalgic for the cultural artifacts of their youth, most of the "lost" episodes from the 1950s were "recovered" from where Gleason had been storing them all along—in his personal vaults—and were not only released on VHS tapes and then DVDs but also edited—combined or trimmed—to be aired in syndication as half-hour episodes. In the end, only a handful of the sketches had actually been lost, and it is probable that at least some of those have survived in other private collections.

Because no other situation comedy has had or is likely to have a comparable history, it is difficult to compare the longevity of *The Honeymooners* to that of other situation comedies. Moreover, several animated situation comedies have had unprecedented longevity whether measured in number of years or number of episodes broadcast. But several commentators, most notably Donna McCrohan in *The Honeymooners Companion*, have pointed out that, among the early situation comedies, only the various versions of Lucille Ball's eponymous shows had a cumulative run of original programming comparable to that of *The Honeymooners*.

In contrast to the ambiguities involved in delineating the history and determining the longevity of *The Honeymooners*, the critical stature that the series has achieved is much easier to demonstrate. In several polls conducted by *TV Guide*, television critics have ranked it among the most significant television shows, never mind situation comedies, of all time. In a 2002 poll, it ranked third among the "50 Greatest Television Shows of All Time."[2] By 2013, its ranking had slipped to 13th, but for a show that is now more than 60 years old, the ranking is not only respectable but also remarkable.[3] In a 1999 poll, Ralph Kramden ranked second and Ed Norton ranked 20th among the "100 Greatest TV Characters Ever!"[4] In a 2013 list, Ed Norton ranked second, and Ralph Kramden ranked 14th.[5] And in a 1997 poll,

"The $99,000 Answer" ranked sixth and "TV or Not TV" ranked 26th among the "100 Greatest Episodes of All Time."[6]

The enduring popularity of *The Honeymooners* demonstrates that although it is a product of the decade in which it was conceived, most notably in the social mores and gender roles accepted by the characters, it also has elements with a more timeless appeal. One of the most prototypical of those is the setting. Although a few episodes take the characters outside the small Brooklyn apartment in which Ralph and Alice Kramden live, most of the action occurs in the kitchen just inside the apartment's exterior door. Indeed, even in those episodes in which the action moves out of that room, the characters almost always return to it for the denouement. The centrality of the Kramdens' apartment has many parallels in later situation comedies, most notably in the Bunkers' living room in *All in the Family*. But in many later shows, the central setting—for example, Jerry's apartment in *Seinfeld* and the bar in *How I Met Your Mother*—is more of a base of operations for the characters' forays into the city and beyond than the setting in which most of the action occurs.

The Kramden kitchen provides a simple, seemingly straightforward setting. The furnishings are sparse. There is a window and a door that frame most shots. Along the left wall is the door to the bedroom and a chest of drawers. In the center of the room is a kitchen table and several chairs. And along the right wall is a bare sink, a stove, and a small pantry. Despite its apparent simplicity, this setting actually has many nuanced aspects. Although it is in many ways a prototypical setting for a situation comedy, it actually owes a great deal to the sets for vaudeville skits. There are just enough pieces of furniture and objects to suggest an actual space but not enough of either to hinder the performers or distract from their words and actions. Yet because the episodes and sketches of the 1950s were shot in black and white, they rather quickly suggested something almost documentary (the Korean War was the last American war documented primarily in black and white photographs and film) as all newer television programming began to shift to color. (This effect applies, of course, to shows other than *The Honeymooners* that have had great longevity in syndication. On the other hand, although I have not made any study to support this suggestion, I suspect that in the case of programs from the 1950s that have had less enduring appeal, their black-and-white nature has probably contributed to their seeming dated.) Such documentary reportage is at the far end of the spectrum from the gaudy affectations of vaudeville. Or perhaps another way of appreciating the impact of this setting is to think of it as a stage set for an expressionist drama (which certainly influenced the film noir of the first decade following World War II, almost all of which were shot in black and white) on which broad comedy is being performed.

The Honeymooners is a treatment of working-class life in the mid-1950s. It has commonly been regarded as offering a fairly pointed contrast to the more typical situation comedies of the 1950s and the early 1960s that focused on middle-class family life in expanding suburban neighborhoods around U.S. cities—for example, *Leave It to Beaver, The Adventures of Ozzie and Harriet, Father Knows Best, The Donna Reed Show, Dennis the Menace,* and *The Dick Van Dyke Show.* It has often been pointed out that the Kramdens are childless, unlike the married couples in those other situation comedies. But it has less frequently been noted that the Kramdens are also not middle class—not upwardly mobile. Indeed, the core premise of most of the show's storylines is that Ralph is continually scheming of ways to achieve the American Dream only to discover that he either does not have what is required or does not even have a clue about what is required. In one of the more enduringly popular episodes, "TV or Not TV," which happens to be the first of the "classic 39 episodes," the Kramdens do purchase a television set, but a home with a lawn remains well out of their grasp. Their horizon has been literally and figuratively confined by the wall of brick and windows beyond the fire escape that that can be seen just outside their apartment window. Their horizon—their future—is, in effect, a mirror image of their present. So, although they are not completely untouched by the consumerism that comes to define American society after the Second World War, they are representative of the folks for whom the American Dream will always be more a lingering, bittersweet fantasy than a tangible reality or even a reasonable possibility.

In "Hard Work Always Pays Off: Jobs, Families, and the Evolution of a TV Myth," Mary Ann Watson asserts that Ralph Kramden provides a negative example or cautionary take on the socioeconomic myth that most working-class situation comedies have reinforced:

> Unlike Chester Riley, though, his blue-collar prime-time contemporary, Ralph Kramden of *The Honeymooners,* was unwilling to invest honest sweat and patience in the American Dream. He was a driver for the Gotham Bus Company on the Madison Avenue line and resented every minute behind the wheel. During his long shifts he dreamt up get-rich-quick schemes. Ralph bought into a uranium mine in Asbury Park, marketed glow-in-the-dark shoe polish, and bought the formula for a phony hair restorer.
>
> All, of course, are hilarious failures. Ralph never learns that big ideas alone won't amount to anything. Imaginative enterprise, for some lucky risk-takers, can be a shortcut to financial independence—but it requires homework that Ralph can't be bothered with.[7]

Watson even ties the Kramdens' childlessness into her argument: "The underlying pathos of the series about a quintessential loser was that the Kramdens remain childless during the baby boom era."[8]

In an essay for *Cultural Anthropology*, George Lipsitz approaches working-class situation comedies from a strikingly different angle, one that allows a somewhat more generous or at least forgiving take on Ralph Kramden's limitations. Lipsitz frames his discussion of television series with a working-class focus by delineating the paradox that such series are, in fact, at odds with the consumer economy that provides the operating revenue for the networks:

> The presence of this subgenre of ethnic, working-class situation comedies on television network schedules seems to run contrary to the commercial and artistic properties of the medium. . . . The relative economic deprivation of ethnic working-class households would seem to provide an inappropriate setting for the display and promotion of commodities as desired by the networks and their commercial sponsors. Furthermore, the mass audience required to repay the expense of network programming encourages the depiction of a homogenized mass society, not the particularities and peculiarities of working-class communities. As an artistic medium, television's capacity for simultaneity conveys a sense of living in an infinitely renewable present—a quality inimical to the sense of history permeating shows about working-class life. Yet whether set in the distant past . . . , or located in the contemporaneous present, the subgenre of ethnic working-class situation comedies in early network television evoked concrete historical associations and memories in their audiences.[9]

Lipsitz suggests that the working-class situation comedies such as *The Honeymooners* appealed both to newly affluent middle-class Americans, most of whom had vivid memories of the extended economic hardships of the Great Depression, and the working-class Americans who were incrementally better off and had some prospect of being even better off if only because the rapidly expanding economy seemed to be helping everyone. Indeed, part of the continuing appeal of *The Honeymooners* may be that in the postindustrial era in which the distinctions between being working class and middle class have again become more marked, Ralph Kramden's faith in the American Dream seems all the more poignant, all the more bittersweetly nostalgic.

Much has been written about the stagnation of middle-class income and wealth over the last four-plus decades. The rise in Ed Norton's popularity may in part be due to the erosion of the working-class's position within the American economy. Although Ralph Kramden is itching with ambition or dissatisfaction, depending on how one frames it, Ed Norton is basically satisfied with his circumstances—glad to have his job in the sewers. Indeed, he often rises to a comically unexpected level of eloquence when commenting on his work. In one episode, he observes, "Like we say in the sewer, 'Time and tide wait for no man.'" But in several instances in which he speaks about the loss of his job, the comic effect of his remarks gives way to the much more poignant sense of his vulnerability and loss. In one episode, he tries to sympathize with Ralph, recalling when he was laid off from his job: "I know just how you feel because I went through the same thing two or three years ago when they laid me off from the sewer. I felt just like a fish out of water." Likewise, in another episode in which he is fired from his job, Norton says with as much bitterness and despair as he ever expresses, "Ol' Ed Norton, reliable ol' Ed Norton, working 17 years in the sewer. And now everything's down the drain!" Over the more than six decades since those episodes were filmed, there has been more, not less, reason to ask what kind of a country America has become when not even a job in the sewers is safe.

In the focal essay of a collection of essays in which Albert Camus attempts to explore the major features of existentialism, he suggests that the myth of Sisyphus offers the defining metaphor for the human condition. We are doomed to struggle against our circumstances even though we can never succeed in transcending them. Camus argues that the persistence of our efforts, despite our consciousness of the absurdity of our condition, is what sets us apart as a species—the one thing that ennobles us—if nobility is possible, if it has any meaning, in the context of the general absurdity of existence. This insight is actually not far removed from a common perception of labor (in particular, manual labor), which might seem conceptually far removed, even at the opposite end of the spectrum, from existentialism—namely, the perception that such labor can become a value in itself, especially when there are minimal economic rewards for doing it. So a coal miner takes pride in his ability to endure not just miserable but also dangerous conditions deep underground or for a steelworker to work not just year after year but decade after decade in the scorching heat and smothering dust of a mill. For a couple of decades immediately following the Second World War, those industries operated at peak employment and workers in those industries made a middle-class income from their work. In hindsight, though, the refrain in Tennessee Ernie Ford's song "Sixteen Tons" was not something that most of those workers ever permanently transcended: "Sixteen tons and what do you get. Another year older and deeper in debt."

Although Ralph Kramden and Ed Norton do not work in the same place or even have similar jobs, their personal friendship is clearly a major buffer against the broader world in which they are trying to earn a living. Much has been written about the singular importance of unit cohesion among soldiers on a battlefield; for them, the survival of fellow soldiers becomes just as important as and even more important than their own survival—and much more important than the strategic aims and broader course of the battle. When men spent—and could count on spending—their whole working lives working in a particular mine or mill, there was an analogous cohesion among the members of crews. More broadly, in the small communities that were built around the mines and mills, there was a strong sense of cohesion, of shared experience and common purpose—of "real" community. Beyond the engaging aspects of each of their personalities, a significant part of the enduring appeal of Ralph Kramden and Ed Norton's friendship is the suggestion of that sort of bond between them as working men. For instance, in episode eight of the "classic 39 episodes," Ralph and Ed's friendship is disrupted by a relatively minor misunderstanding over a gift, but when Ralph learns that Ed has been injured in an explosion in the sewers, he completely forgets about the misunderstanding and becomes consumed by his concern for his friend.

The paradox that the American Dream has often had the strongest hold on those for whom it seems always just out of reach is represented in Ralph Kramden's physical size and the contrast between his size and the small space in which he and Alice live. In most episodes, Ralph pushes Alice to wry exasperation by asserting in some manner or another that he is the "king of his castle" only to have her point out that great size does not equate with greatness and, in any case, his "castle" is tiny and modest by any measure.

In many ways, Ralph's size is the physical corollary to his unrealized ambitions. He is literally and figuratively a larger-than-life character who eats as compulsively as he schemes to get ahead. His great attraction as a character is that because his great size and his outsized ambitions border equally on the ridiculous and essentially benign, he seems always to be teetering on the thin line that separates deep laughter from genuine pathos. In one episode, Ralph is moved to a somewhat rare moment of introspection, and it leads to the following exchange with Ed Norton:

> **Ralph:** Me and my silly pride. Well, I promise you this, Norton. I'm gonna learn. I'm gonna learn from here on out how to swallow my pride.
>
> **Norton:** Well, that ought not to be too hard; you've learned how to swallow everything else.
>
> **Ralph:** GET OUT!

The relationship between the two works because of these kinds of exchanges. Ed Norton is not simply the foil who sets up Ralph's comical tirades of abuse. In many instances, this foil turns the tables and gets the punchline, even if he seems to do so spontaneously rather than deliberately. It is ironic that the frequent inversion of the informal hierarchical relationship between these two working-class friends is never replicated in their workplaces. The closest thing to it in their work is their occasional attempts to assert that they are not defined by their ordinary jobs, assertions that are undercut by their own awareness, as well as ours as viewers, of their great psychological as well as financial dependence on the jobs.

Over the last two decades, there has been some increasing criticism of *The Honeymooners* for its reinforcement of anachronistic sexist attitudes.[10] Although Ralph is in many ways a prototypical "loser" and Alice often punctures his bloated pretense of self-importance, she always seems to stop short of berating him in a hurtful way. Instead, she seems satisfied with maintaining a sort of equilibrium in their relationship in which he is the primary wage earner but she provides the repository of common sense that sustains their household and their relationship.

More specifically, critics of the show have pointed to the recurring physical threats that Ralph bombastically directs at Alice—threats that were expressed in several of the most popular catchphrases from the show: "Bang, zoom, bang!" and "To the moon, Alice!" Even though Ralph never acts on the threats and Alice never takes them seriously, we have become so conscious of spousal abuse that we have become rightly concerned about minimizing it in any way.

That said, this issue is analogous to the controversy surrounding the use of the "N-word" in *The Adventures of Huckleberry Finn*. It seems perfectly justifiable to point out that the work of fiction or the television series contains elements that are now considered not only anachronistic but also problematic. It does not seem justifiable, however, to expect that the creators of the works should have anticipated the shifts in our cultural and moral sensibilities, especially when the works seem largely to reinforce themes that we would currently embrace—an abhorrence of slavery in the case of the Twain novel and an appreciation for the pervasiveness of domestic violence against women in the case of *The Honeymooners*. It may be fair to say that although few young women today would want to be in Alice Kramden's marriage, a sizable percentage of them would find much to like and even admire in Alice herself.

A complex analysis of the series that bears on these issues, as well as some of the points made earlier in this essay, is provided by Virginia Wright Wexman in "Returning from the Moon: Jackie Gleason, the Carnivalesque, and Television Comedy." Wexman's analysis of the series is grounded thoroughly in critical theory. She takes a highly original approach in analyzing in depth *The Honeymooners* in relation to the variety show of which it was originally (and subsequently) an integral part and for which it provided a lead-in even when it was presented as a distinct series over the 1955–1956 television season:

> The contrast between the Gleason of *The Jackie Gleason Show* and the Gleason of *The Honeymooners* can thus be understood as a Bakhtinian opposition. As the star moves from the role of gracious host to that of harried bus driver, his body image changes from classical to grotesque. In particular, the smooth, finished appearance of Gleason the host is transformed in his portrayal of Ralph Kramden into ungainly clownishness. Though in his role

as host Gleason's sizable stomach is concealed by well-cut clothing, his corpulence is exaggerated by Ralph's bus driver's uniform, and it repeatedly makes Ralph the butt of the other characters' "fat" jokes. As host, Gleason's utterances are mellow and measured, but as Ralph his laugh often ends in loud, uncontrolled coughing. Ralph's eyes habitually bug out. He is frequently characterized as having "a big mouth," a description which contains literal as well as figurative truth, in view of the fact that his mouth is often agape as he roars in rage or pain. All of these elements position Ralph's body in Bakhtinian terms as one "in the act of becoming."[11]

About Alice's role, Wexman observes:

In some ways the image of Alice, as portrayed most famously by Audrey Meadows, echoes the classical model associated with Gleason the star. Neatly dressed, with her hands on her hips or thrust into her pockets, she presents a more modestly scaled image of a classical body. Like Gleason, she dominates her surrounding space, though in a less grandiose and more functional manner. Scenes are most often set in the Kramdens' kitchen, a room over which Alice exercises complete mastery (in contrast to Ralph, who is conspicuously ill at ease with all of its culinary appurtenances). Alice invariably stands her ground in the face of the inflated male egos with which she must cope. As the still presence around which her husband revolves, she is capable of calling a halt to his extravagant gestures simply by saying, "Now you listen to me, Ralph."

Alice's image differs most importantly from that of Gleason the star in that she participates in a narrative and therefore in a principle of orderly temporal progression. She is the one who customarily brings *The Honeymooners* to a harmonious conclusion by straightening out the errors of the men, thereby ordering the chaos they wreak and creating a story in time. Her goals are pragmatically conceived, and she usually manages to achieve them. By contrast, as we have seen, the two clowns are out of step with the progress of time: Norton is a laggard and Ralph is overly hasty. In this sense Alice's role suggests a version of the notion of historical progress which Bakhtin associates with his concept of the classical body.[12]

Although I find Wexman's analysis extremely compelling as well as original, I ultimately cannot help but feel that the distance between Bakhtin's theories and the dialogue of *The Honeymooners* might make the application of the theory to the show seem like something of a scholarly put-on. Likewise, although I can offer no basis for justifying jokes about spousal abuse, I do think that an equally strong case (but not one that I actually want to make) could be made for criticizing the show for its incessant jokes about Ralph's weight, for its being an extended exercise in fat shaming. (Several sources have acknowledged that Gleason himself occasionally complained that the writers whom he employed seemed inordinately fond of the jokes about his girth—even during those periods he had managed to lose quite a bit of weight.) Clearly, some subjects that were once staples of both stand-up routines and situation comedies have gone out of fashion. Dean Martin and Foster Brooks made such successful, long careers out of playing drunks that it was almost impossible to tell when they may have actually been at least somewhat inebriated while performing. But the attention to the human costs of alcoholism and, more specifically, those of driving while intoxicated have taken much of the humor out of drunkenness.

Even so, the line between comedy and pathos is often extremely thin and can depend simply on whether something is happening to you or to someone else or whether something hurts terribly for the moment or causes more extended pain or damage. In the end, there seems to no chicken-or-the-egg issue here: If something is funny, we can attempt to explain why it is funny or even why it is discomfiting or inappropriate that it is funny; on the other hand, no theory of what is or ought to be funny was ever a prerequisite or even a helpful corollary for being a successful comedian or comic actor. Many of us may be able to explain (with varying degrees of success) why Ralph and Alice Kramden and Ed and Trixie Norton have made us laugh. But almost none of us can actually learn how to provoke such laughter by way of that analysis. There is something spontaneous and inexplicable in what makes a great joke work.

Sometimes a joke contains an almost perfect balance of understatement and audacity. About a month after the 9/11 terrorist attacks on the World Trade Center towers, Gilbert Gottfried got booed off the stage at a Friars Club roast for making the following joke:

> I have to leave early tonight. I have to fly out to L.A. I couldn't get a direct flight. I have to make a stop at the Empire State Building.

The joke should go down as not only the best one ever made about a terrible moment in U.S. history but also as one of the most effective and even profound responses to that event. That Gottfried got booed off the stage at a Friars Club roast for making the joke simply provides an almost perfect frame for an almost perfect joke.

Such a joke would not have been written into *The Honeymooners*, of course. But there are parallels in having the audacity to make quiet jokes on the topics that usually produced the most bombastic outbursts. Earlier in the essay, in writing about the relationship between Ralph's size and the size of the set around which he had to move, I asserted that he seems always to be teetering on the thin line that separates deep laughter from genuine pathos. Sometimes, this tonal balance is captured almost perfectly in what might seem like a throw-away line of dialogue. In one episode, Ralph brings home a suitcase that someone had left behind on his bus. His mother-in-law has paid Alice a visit, and when Ralph enters the apartment carrying the suitcase, she asks dryly, "New lunchbox?"

It is a cruel thing to say but also extremely funny.

NOTES

1. Ron Simon, "Ralph Kramden and *The Honeymooners* Turn the Big 5-0—Sort of," *Television Quarterly* 36(1) (Fall 2005), 61.

2. Wikipedia, https://en.wikipedia.org/wiki/TV_Guide%27s_50_Greatest_TV _Shows_of_All_Time.

3. Bruce Fretts and Matt Roush, *"TV Guide Magazine*'s 60 Best Series of All Time," December 23, 2013, http://www.tvguide.com/news/tv-guide-magazine -60-best-series-1074962/.

4. "TV Guide's 50 Greatest TV Characters of All Time," IMDb, June 29, 2011; http://www.imdb.com/list/ls000999550/.

5. "TV Guide's 50 Greatest TV Characters of All Time," listal, May 13, 2013; http://www.listal.com/list/tv-guides-50-greatest-tv.

6. Wikipedia, https://en.wikipedia.org/wiki/TV_Guide%27s_100_Greatest _Episodes_of_All-Time.

7. Mary Ann Watson, "Hard Work Always Pays Off: Jobs, Families, and the Evolution of a TV Myth," *Television Quarterly* 36 (3–4) (Spring–Summer 2006), 33.

8. Ibid.

9. George Lipsitz, "The Meaning of Memory: Family, Class, and Ethnicity in Early Network Television Programs," *Cultural Anthropology* 1(4) (November 1986), 355–356.

10. Donna Gore, *"The Honeymooners* Was No Honeymoon . . . (When Nostalgia Is Not So Nice)," *Time's Up*, January 16, 2012; http://timesupblog.blogspot.com /2012/01/honeymooners-was-no-honeymoon-when.html; Gianna Palmer, "From Ralph Kramden to Chris Brown: How Much Progress?" *Wesleyan Argus*, March 29, 2009; http://wesleyanargus.com/2009/03/29/from-ralph-kramden-to -chris-brown-how-much-progress.

11. Virginia Wright Wexman, "Returning from the Moon: Jackie Gleason, the Carnivalesque, and Television Comedy," *Journal of Film and Video* (Special Issue on Stars and the Star System) 42 (4) (Winter 1990), 25.

12. Ibid., 29.

BIBLIOGRAPHY

Gore, Donna. *"The Honeymooners* Was No Honeymoon . . . (When Nostalgia Is Not So Nice)." *Time's Up*, http://timesupblog.blogspot.com/2012/01/honey mooners-was-no-honeymoon-when.html.

McCrohan, Donna. *The Honeymooners Companion*. New York: Workman, 1978.

Palmer, Gianna. "From Ralph Kramden to Chris Brown: How Much Progress?" *Wesleyan Argus*, March 29, 2009, http://wesleyanargus.com/2009/03/29 /from-ralph-kramden-to-chris-brown-how-much-progress/.

"Pow! Right in the Kisser!" Editorial, *The New York Times*, November 14, 1987, http://www.nytimes.com/1987/11/14/opinion/pow-right-in-the-kisser .html.

Simon, Ron. "Ralph Kramden and *The Honeymooners* Turn the Big 5-0—Sort of." *Television Quarterly* 36(1) (Fall 2005), 59–64.

Watson, Mary Ann. "Hard Work Always Pays Off: Jobs, Families, and the Evolution of a TV Myth." *Television Quarterly* 36(3–4) (Spring–Summer 2006), 32–39.

Wexman, Virginia Wright. "Returning from the Moon: Jackie Gleason, the Carnivalesque, and Television Comedy." *Journal of Film and Video* (Special Issue on Stars and the Star System) 42(4) (Winter 1990), 20–32.

3

Leave It to Beaver: The Long and Memorable Life of Eddie Haskell

Aaron Barlow

When considering the ideal of midcentury domestic perfection, a certain formulation dominates the popular imagination—a single-family house in the suburbs, white picket fence, nuclear family with working dad in suit and stay-at-home mom in pearls, and two (maybe 2.5) adorable children. Leave It to Beaver (1957–1963) almost single-handedly injected the American consciousness with this nostalgic vision of the 1950s. In "Leave It to Beaver: The Long and Memorable Life of Eddie Haskell," Aaron Barlow examines how the show's iconic status affected the lives of the actors who played those memorable roles. Focusing specifically on Barbara Billingsley (June Cleaver) and Ken Osmond (Eddie Haskell), Barlow presents a new reading of the lingering influence that iconic television shows can have, not just on television and media culture more broadly but also on their famous cast members.

In 1980, the millions of baby boomers who went to see the new movie *Airplane!* were in for a delightful shock. As June Cleaver, Barbara Billingsley had been part of boomers' early years and, in the 1960s, the butt of jokes about a strangling and staid American culture. Their image of her was a prim and proper woman vacuuming an immaculate living room in pearls and high heels. *Leave It to Beaver,* the show she was remembered for and which ran from October 4, 1957, to June 20, 1963 (the first season on CBS, the rest on ABC), had made an indelible impact on that generation's image of American suburban culture, and it later became a touchstone for those in rebellion against it.

Even the actors who appeared most frequently throughout the series were included, after the show had ended, in the rejection of the *Beaver* vision of the United States that grew into an influential counterculture over the decade after the show ended its run. Now, almost at the start of the Reagan era, Billingsley would turn the lingering distaste for the show (even as the country grew more conservative) on its head.

So great had been the growing aversion for the world of 'the Beav," as his brother Wally (Tony Dow) called Jerry Mathers's character Theodore Cleaver, that almost the entire cast disappeared from television for the rest of the 1960s after the show ended. Significantly, the show wasn't canceled because of poor ratings but because the child actors had grown so that the premise could not be continued. Over the next few years, Dow surfaced occasionally, as would Ken Osmond (Eddie Haskell), but their disappearance seemed complete to most young viewers whose attention was turning to other things, so much so that urban legends had it that Osmond or Mathers had died fighting in Vietnam.

It took Billingsley until the 1980s to return to television as a regular actor—probably thanks to that surprising turn in *Airplane!*

The exchange that reintroduced us to her, really just a short cameo, went like this (she plays "Jive Lady"):

Randy [stewardess]: Can I get you something?

Second Jive Dude: 'S'mofo butter layin' me to da' BONE! Jackin' me up . . . tight me!

Randy: I'm sorry, I don't understand.

First Jive Dude: Cutty say 'e can't HANG!

Jive Lady: Oh, stewardess! I speak jive.

Randy: Oh, good.

Jive Lady: He said that he's in great pain and he wants to know if you can help him.

Randy: All right. Would you tell him to just relax and I'll be back as soon as I can with some medicine?

Jive Lady: [to the Second Jive Dude] Jus' hang loose, blood. She gonna catch ya up on da rebound on da med side.

Second Jive Dude: What it is, big mama? My mama no raise no dummies. I dug her rap!

Jive Lady: Cut me some slack, Jack! Chump don' want no help, chump don't GET da help!

First Jive Dude: Say 'e can't hang, say seven up!

Jive Lady: Jive-ass dude don't got no brains anyhow! Shiiiiit.[1]

Nothing further from the suburban white-bread Cleaver household could have been imagined by contemporary audiences (as one might guess, few African Americans were ever even on the show)—unless Billingsley were to have appeared in full dominatrix leather and chains. It was liberating to see June Cleaver, well, liberated.

Billingsley's appearance in *Airplane!* was an unbridled success, but she was not the first choice for the part. Jim Abrahams, David Zucker, and Jerry Zucker, the writer and directors of the movie, had wanted Harriet Nelson of the much longer running *The Adventures of Ozzie and Harriet* (434 episodes as opposed to 234 for *Leave It to Beaver*) to play the role, but she turned it down out of concern for the language.[2] The writers and directors had not thought seriously about the relative impact of the two sitcom moms but only the point of the joke. That Nelson turned them down was just as well for the movie and for the future of the *Beaver* "franchise," for Billingsley, for sitcom veterans as a whole, the genre itself, and even American popular culture. After all, Billingsley was much more recognizable to baby boomers than Nelson (for reasons that are made clear below) and, because of that, was more successful as "Jive Lady" than Nelson ever could have been.

Through the jarring contrast between her cultural image and her lines, Billingsley showed there was a way to deal with the lingering fame from an old sitcom role without either simply exploiting the role or completely ignoring it, the Scylla and Charybdis of the sitcom afterlife.

The reaction to Billingsley's few short lines told sitcom producers that there could be a lot more to their shows in the future than they then thought possible, and much more could be done with the actors' images than they had generally imagined. She set a whole new level and type of aftermarket success based not on the fact that she was loved but that she was known—and on the fact that she was willing to poke fun at the image that had built up around her.

Yet, as we shall see, it is Osmond's Eddie Haskell, perhaps the most memorable character from the show, who is probably the best confirmation of the importance of the phenomenon Billingsley brought to light for both good and bad.

Al White, who played "Second Jive Dude" and helped coach Billingsley in the fictitious language of "Jive," speaks of how much he enjoyed working with her, in part because of who she was:

And as a matter of fact, my mother just loved *Leave It To Beaver*, and what I did was, I asked Barbara if she wouldn't mind speaking to my mother. That was the crowning moment, because I called my mother, and I said, "Mom, I have Barbara Billingsley here, and she'd actually like to speak to you." She was so excited, and Barbara was so gracious.[3]

The lack of black characters on *Leave It to Beaver* did not stop African Americans from watching, including not just White's mother but a young Oprah Winfrey, who, "in the absence of a cookie-baking mother, ... dreamed on his [Beaver's],"[4] a point about the lack of diversity within shows that production companies and advertisers were slow to pick up on, especially when the situation was reversed. Fact was, if they wanted to watch television during the 1950s and early 1960s, black viewers were going to have to watch whites (unless they wanted to stick solely with the infrequent shows featuring the stereotypes and almost blackface of shows like *Amos 'n' Andy* or even *Beulah*). The only African American who ever appeared in a role on *Leave It to Beaver* was Kim Hamilton, who played a maid on "The Parking Attendants" (season six, episode 17).[5] The audience affected by the likes of *Leave It to Beaver* extended far beyond the white suburban middle class, the show becoming something rural farm kids jumping from haylofts and stickball players from the inner cities could both understand, even if they didn't exactly identify *with* it. The plots, after all, centered on the children and their problems, something that crossed class, racial, and ethnic boundaries.

At almost the same time, *Leave It to Beaver* was becoming something young people in their growing disenchantment with mainstream American culture could focus their hate on, though with a certain affection as well. Hate it and love it they did for most of the 1960s and well into the 1970s. It wasn't until Billingsley demonstrated that the country was ready to embrace the Cleavers (or at least their image through her familiar face) that television was once again willing to feature the actors from the series.

Proof of this came just a year later when the idea for a sequel series was pitched. Most of the original cast was reassembled (Hugh Beaumont, who had played Ward Cleaver, had suffered a stroke and could not participate) for a made-for-TV movie. Probably in part because they had been able to find little work outside of Mayfield, the re-creation of the fictional town for *Still the Beaver* attracted all of the major cast members who could possibly make the time.

The success of *Still the Beaver* when it aired in 1983 led to a cable-only sitcom of the same name that found a home for its first season, 1984–85, on the Disney Channel and then, for three subsequent seasons, now renamed *The New Leave It to Beaver*, on Superstation WTBS (later TBS Superstation), Ted Turner's Atlanta station that had become one of the first national stations on cable. The show followed the now-adult children of the original show as they tried to negotiate lives as parents and professionals.

Later, Billingsley and Osmond (along with Frank Bank, who had played Lumpy Rutherford in both shows) appeared in cameo roles in a 1997 *Leave It to Beaver* film that attempted to re-create Mayfield for a new generation of viewers. The film, however, did not do well. It was the actors, not their characters without them, that audiences remembered and wanted to see. The roles were important, certainly, but it was the people who played them who, in this case, resonated most loudly with audiences.

The show's creators, Joe Connelly and Bob Mosher, after looking at structures of contemporary sitcoms, noted that the centers in the families presented from *The Adventures of Ozzie and Harriet* on were the parents and the children orbiting them. They knew that the kids in the audience weren't paying much attention to the adults but that adults, as parents, were perfectly willing to pay attention to children if the plots were not themselves overly childish. They decided to buck the trend and try to create a show that centered on the children but would still be interesting to adults, a critical point for advertising of the time. Connelly and Mosher had seen the success of animal–child pairings in dramas and sitcoms such as *Lassie* and *Circus Boy* and knew that a focus on adult characters wasn't absolutely necessary for success. "The stories would be told from the kids' point-of-view as Connelly and Mosher recalled it and observed it in their own children. Mosher was the father of two children and Connelly the parent of [seven]."[6] To that time, most American television shows that used a child's viewpoint were cartoons, and even precious few of those did so. Connelly and Mosher had both cut their teeth in advertising before writing for radio, *Amos 'n' Andy* being their most notable association.

One important point to remember about *Leave It to Beaver* itself is that it centered on the children—Wally, Beaver and their friends. The parents were more stereotypical and unchanging than the kids. Part of this was natural: Dow and Mathers couldn't help but physically grow over the six-year run. Part of it, though, developed through the nature of the plots, which were always kid-centered. Whether or not they liked the show, baby boomers understood it because the plots and main characters reflected their own childhood situations—even when class, race, and setting might differ. The characters were quickly imprinted on their group psyche and instantly recognizable for the rest of their lives. Thus, Billingsley, not Nelson, whose children were adjuncts to her and not the other way around (though her younger son, Ricky, would later become a teen-idol pop star), became the stereotypical sitcom mom in the eyes of the children of the time, instantly recognizable in 1980 where Nelson might have just seemed oddly familiar. Like all mothers of the time, Billingsley, after all, had always been somewhere nearby the more recognizable kids.

As television began to muscle radio aside (for sitcoms, at least), *Amos 'n' Andy* spun off a television version, Connelly and Mosher writing for it, as well, began using their knowledge of the needs of advertisers along with their experiences writing for radio in their efforts in the newer medium. To this, they added observation of their own children when creating *Leave It to Beaver.*

Other shows soon imitated the kid-centered format that Connelly and Mosher had created for *Leave It to Beaver,* including *Dennis the Menace* (almost immediately) and *The Many Loves of Dobie Gillis* (though these were high-school students) and eventually *The Brady Bunch* and *The Partridge Family,* among others. In this respect, *Leave It to Beaver* was an instant influence on the course of the sitcom, even though it was never a runaway ratings success. Its greatest influence, however, lies in showing just how important a role a sitcom can play in American culture and just how careful its creators and actors need to be as a result. The show demonstrated that a sitcom's place in popular culture, if it is an enduring success, needs to be carefully negotiated and even planned. Otherwise its legacy can take on an unexpected life of its own—something that somehow needs to be expected and prepared for as the afterlife of *Leave It to Beaver* demonstrates.

A great deal of attention began to be paid in the 1950s to secondary marketing and selling show-related paraphernalia whenever a program was a hit, particularly with children. *Leave It to Beaver* sparked a board game and quite a few books, including a Dell Comics series, a Little Golden Book, and several paperbacks. These confirmed the images of the characters and the actors who portrayed them in the minds of young Americans. A show with the endurance of *Leave It to Beaver* in the popular imagination can even be a long-term goldmine for its owners through syndication. Beyond that—and this was not quite as understood then as it is now—character images such as Billingsley's June Cleaver and Osmond's Eddie Haskell can take on lives of their own, carrying on in the popular imagination long after the show has receded into history.

Though June Cleaver and Eddie Haskell, who was portrayed as a bad boy who always played up to parents and authority figures with false compliments, were not as central to the show as Wally and the Beav, it is they who continue to be recognized most readily, for they quickly came to represent certain stereotypes in the broader American culture. They have become archetypes, cultural reference points, or markers for identifying traits all Americans have encountered. Creators of sitcoms today hope that their characters, too, can join the parade, and many of them plan for it and even try to abet it by judicious marketing—but only a few actually succeed. Thanks to Billingsley and Osmond, those who do now know how to handle it better.

Of course, stars have capitalized on their screen images since the infancy of film. Stuntman Yakima Canutt, a former rodeo champion, once was riding in a parade when he was heckled, "You can't ride like Tom Mix."[7] Of course, *he* had been doing the riding that the 1920s star Mix was known for. But Mix was the star and carefully cultivated the idea that he was the great horseman who appeared on screen. Roy Rogers, like Mix before him, capitalized on his screen "cowboy" image in countless personal appearances, particularly in the 1950s, as have hundreds of stars since in their own distinctive ways. The difference is that these stars jealously guarded the positive aspects of their images. Mix never liked that he could be upstaged by a stunt rider. In addition, in a time of Hollywood and then network moral censorship, stars for decades would work hard to keep their personal images as clean and wholesome as their presentations on screen.

What the actors from *Leave It to Beaver* discovered, however, was that being associated with a squeaky-clean show, even a successful one, didn't necessarily help their future employment. Beaumont found that he could not go back to playing heavies after becoming so well known as Beaver's wise and kindly father. His career dried up, and he moved home to Minnesota in the late 1960s to grow Christmas trees.[8] The other characters in the show had pretty much the same experience. Their situations were noted by others taking on sitcom roles. Experienced actors began to contemplate the effect a sitcom role could have on their subsequent careers in a manner quite different from simply a one-off movie or television appearance playing against type.

Again, actors in successful television shows generally have two choices: embrace the character you play or work hard and immediately to distance yourself from it in the public mind. Playing roles against type, of course, is the easiest road to the latter. Touring in costume and in character (as Roy Rogers did) takes one to the former. This was true in movies, too, where typecasting was also often a bête noir (or the savior of a career), but the small screen brought characters into the house on a weekly basis in recurring roles, achieving a household familiarity that the large screen could not manage. This could often be fine for the run of the show—but afterward?

Osmond writes:

> Typecasting doesn't really hit you all at once; it works on you slowly and subtly, eroding your spirit as you sit by the phone, waiting for the callback that never comes. I went on lots of auditions, and I had lots of rejections. Sometimes I would walk into the room and the casting agent would blurt out, "Hey, you're Eddie Haskell aren't you? Well, I'm afraid it won't work out, nobody can forget you."[9]

A role such as Eddie Haskell could have serious repercussions, especially when the broader culture was embroiled in dramatic change. For Osmond, it meant a hiatus of well over a decade in his acting career: "Hopelessly typecast, I was unable to secure anything other than bit parts in TV shows and films. I needed a steady job."[10] So, he became a Los Angeles police officer.

Osmond was eminently recognizable as the smarmy Eddie Haskell and, according to Mathers, "one of the most memorable *Leave It to Beaver* characters."[11] Osmond wrote in 1997 that "people don't 'Eddie' me so much in Los Angeles these days and I think that's fine."[12] That was after years of struggle with the image he could not shed. On the other hand, Frank Bank, who played another of Wally's friends, the semi–sad sack Lumpy, writes:

> On the show, whenever anyone called Clarence Rutherford by his nickname, he always replied, irritably, in that whiny voice of his:
> "Don't call me Lumpy."
> But I say:
> "Call me Lumpy."
> I say it proudly.[13]

According to Bank's memoir, *Call Me Lumpy: My Leave It to Beaver Days and Other Wild Hollywood Life*, he was able to cash in on his fame from the show, at least in terms of his relations with the opposite sex. Few of his fellow cast members could say the same thing, no matter the terms.

Even in the 1960s, when so many American youths were doing everything they could to disassociate themselves with what they saw as the stale American life of the previous decade, the memories of *Leave It to Beaver* were so strong with those born in the decade after World War II that connection with the show did remain a badge of some honor to the show's cast even though it had dried up further possibilities for work in film or television. Of course, success—especially success within mass media—always draws attention in America, if not everywhere. But *Leave It to Beaver* had become something other than simply a success in the minds of that generation as it started to get older. It had become a touchstone, a marker, or shared identity even though not one of fandom. It represented what their lives were supposed to have been but never were. The characters then remained famous, even if unwatched and even as other shows and their stars faded.

The show made Eddie Haskell (and to lesser degrees the other characters) into what we now call an "icon." As Osmond writes, "This was the singular role that would define me, for good and bad, for the rest of my life."[14] It wasn't meant to be that way. In fact, his role was initially a one-off and, though Osmond would appear in almost 100 episodes, he would never be paid on a seasonal contract. Even so, his character would become an integral part of the series: "Before long, Eddie Haskell would evolve from being merely a secondary character name, to a synonym for untrustworthy souls everywhere,,"[15] and he became an image, he said, he could never shake.

So pervasive and recognizable is the name and personality of Eddie Haskell that a psychologist can name the "Eddie Haskell effect" and be confident everyone will understand exactly what he is referring to. Ronald Riggio, who teaches at Claremont McKenna College, authored a short piece for *Psychology Today* that includes this passage:

> My 10-year-old daughter clearly understands the Eddie Haskell effect. She had often mentioned a girl at her school who was a bully. When I visited the campus a little girl greeted me warmly, "Hello, Mr. Riggio," she said sweetly. I noticed the look of disgust on my daughter's face. When I later commented on how polite she was, my daughter said, "Sure. She's like that to the adults, but she's the bully I've told you about."[16]

The article was published in 2011, some 50 years after the introduction of Eddie Haskell and at least two decades after the second Beaver show went off the air. Yet the phrase still resonates.

The irony of the Haskell image, and something that probably enhanced its impact, is the fact that "*Leave It to Beaver* offered an oasis and a safe harbor for those wanting to forget the evils and the frightening realities of the world at the time."[17] The assassination of John Kennedy, which happened just months after the end of the show, the violence of the reactions to the civil rights movements, and the increasing horror of the war in Vietnam— all shown on television in graphic detail—contributed to a growing sense that the world beyond the suburbs was one of constant danger. For all of his unpleasant traits, Haskell was ultimately constrained each episode by other characters in the show, making his "evil" much more palatable and less threatening than that of the real world. He could be despised without worry because his bullying was always made harmless by the actions, generally, of one member or another of the Cleaver family.

Yet there was worry for Osmond. The need to manage and protect the image of even a 'bad boy' like Haskell came clear to him when he was called in to the internal affairs office of the Los Angeles police department and all but accused of being a porn star on the side. It turned out that "John Holmes" (John Estes), who famously made pornographic films, looked a little like Osmond—and some of his movies were labeled as starring Osmond as Haskell. "Pretty soon, the word was out that Eddie Haskell had turned to doing porno."[18] Osmond spent years trying to legally pursue those who were labelling the films that way but was ultimately unsuccessful. He did so not so much to protect the Haskell image but to protect his own. After all, his very career had been threatened by the idea that it was, in fact, Osmond starring in the mislabeled Holmes films. Protecting one's image, Osmond was discovering, could be a lot more complicated than simply defending a character's reputation—or lack of it.

This was not the only time when the notoriety of the Haskell character led to a false pairing, though the other one was a lot less likely to affect Osmond's new life. The "shock rock" star of the 1970s, Alice Cooper (Vincent Furnier), who cultivated his own bad-boy image, was long rumored to actually be the actor who had also appeared as Eddie Haskell. Frustrated by the persistence of the story, Furnier even had a shirt made that proclaimed, "No, I am not Eddie Haskell." Osmond, in his police uniform, once introduced himself to Furnier as the "real" thing.[19]

We don't know how long Eddie Haskell or the other images and characters associated with *Leave It to Beaver* will live in the public imagination. But the impact on how sitcoms are perceived by those who make them will certainly remain. Osmond contrasts the life of *Leave It to Beaver* to the Soviet Union's satellite Sputnik, which was launched the same day the sitcom debuted. It "fell back to earth in just a couple of months and burnt up in the atmosphere. Over a half century later, Beaver is still broadcasting somewhere in the world. The show has been translated into Spanish, Japanese, and even Swahili."[20] That may be, though the comparison may be a bit of a stretch (Sputnik launched the space race leading to the U.S. moon landings), but the show's import remains, particularly in how sitcom characters are managed. Sputnik, however, certainly did its job, fascinating and worrying Americans before its life ended. *Leave It to Beaver* has yet to stop.

NOTES

1. Jim Abrahams, David Zucker, and Jerry Zucker, *Airplane!* (Paramount, 1980).

2. Will Harris, "Surely You Can't Be Serious: An Oral History of *Airplane!*" *A.V. Club*, April 17, 2015, http://www.avclub.com/article/surely-you-cant-be-serious -oral-history-airplane-218043.

3. Ibid.

4. Catlin Flanagan, "The Glory of Oprah," *The Atlantic*, December 2011, https://www.theatlantic.com/magazine/archive/2011/12/the-glory-of-oprah /308725/.

5. Carmel Dagan, "Actress Kim Hamilton Dies at 81," *Variety*, November 6, 2013, http://variety.com/2013/film/obituaries-people-news/actress-kim-hamilton -dies-at-81-1200803013/.

6. Peter Orlick, "Leave It to Beaver," *Museum of Broadcast Communications*, http://www.museum.tv/eotv/leaveittob.htm.

7. Yakima Canutt and Oliver Drake, *Stunt Man: The Autobiography of Yakima Canutt* (Norman, OK: University of Oklahoma Press, 1979), 68.

8. Ken Osmond and Christopher Lynch, *Eddie: The Life and Times of America's Preeminent Bad Boy* (Los Angeles: Ken Osmond, 2014), 97.

9. Ibid.

10. Ibid., 119.

11. Jerry Mathers, "Foreword." In Osmond and Lynch, op. cit., 1.

12. Ken Osmond, "Introduction." In Frank Bank, *Call Me Lumpy: My Leave It to Beaver Days and Other Wild Hollywood Life* (Lenexa, KS: Addax Publishing Group, 1997), 8.

13. Frank Bank, *Call Me Lumpy: My Leave It to Beaver Days and Other Wild Hollywood Life* (Lenexa, KS: Addax Publishing Group, 1997), 17. Though a fascinating memoir, this is not a book that should be relied on for factual confirmation. For example, Bank confuses Woolworth heir Lance Reventlow, who died in a plane crash, with Revlon heir Peter Revson, who died in a race-car crash. Both were famously wealthy and Formula One drivers but not the same person.

14. Osmond and Lynch, op. cit., 49.

15. Ibid., 53.

16. Ronald Riggio, "Bullies and the Eddie Haskell Effect," *Psychology Today*, January 27, 2011, https://www.psychologytoday.com/blog/cutting-edge-leadership /201101/bullies-and-the-eddie-haskell-effect.

17. Osmond and Lynch, op. cit., 68.

18. Ibid., 152.

19. Ibid., 170.

20. Ibid., 65.

BIBLIOGRAPHY

Bank, Frank. *Call Me Lumpy: My Leave It to Beaver Days and Other Wild Holly-wood Life*. Lenexa, KS: Addax Publishing Group, 1997).

Canutt, Yakima, and Oliver Drake. *Stunt Man: The Autobiography of Yakima Canutt*. Norman, OK: University of Oklahoma Press, 1979.

Dagan, Carmel. "Actress Kim Hamilton Dies at 81." *Variety*, November 6, 2013.

Flanagan, Catlin. "The Glory of Oprah." *The Atlantic*, December 2011.

Harris, Will. "Surely You Can't Be Serious: An Oral History of *Airplane!*" *A.V. Club*, April 17, 2015.

Orlick, Peter. "Leave It to Beaver." *Museum of Broadcast Communications*.

Riggio, Ronald. "Bullies and the Eddie Haskell Effect," *Psychology Today*, January 27, 2011.

4

Big Lessons from a Small Town:
The Andy Griffith Show

Cynthia J. Miller and Tom Shaker

Though approached with trepidation by many small-town residents when it first appeared, The Andy Griffith Show *(1960–1968) is steeped in rural storytelling traditions from the Appalachian Jack tales that Griffith himself had long mastered to resonances of the sly and dry wit of Will Rogers. The trepidation came from the source of the show—Hollywood. The delight came from the characters, the removal from politics and social change, and recognition of the story forms themselves—and it has led to a fan base that has made the annual "Mayberry Days" in Griffith's home town off Mt. Airy, North Carolina, a continuing hit, people traveling across the country to wander the little town's main street with people dressed as characters from the show. The "magic" of Mayberry, as Cynthia J. Miller and Tom Shaker call it, has never disappeared. Television, though it continually attempts to recapture it, rarely manages the feat.*

As part of television's "rural revolution," *The Andy Griffith Show* (CBS 1960–1968) followed the era's popular trend toward developing comedies that featured communities in the American heartland and their naïve but well-intentioned inhabitants, drawing on portrayals of "rubes" by early film stars such as Will Rogers in the 1920s and 1930s and front porch philosophers Lum and Abner in the 1940s and 1950s. The show spoke to audiences about down-home wisdom and simplicity, and it emphasized values of the American heartland in the face of increasing cultural sophistication,

Vietnam-era unrest, and rapid social change resulting from the civil rights movement.

The fictional town of Mayberry, North Carolina, served as the show's slow-moving, bucolic setting. Populated with rural archetypes—from Griffith's circumspect sheriff and Don Knotts's flighty and self-important deputy, to a gossiping barber, anxious spinsters, and an unrepentant town drunk—the town provided the backdrop for Sheriff Taylor to employ traditional folk wisdom to settle local disputes and humorously outwit arrogant "city slickers" passing through the town. Although portrayed as caricatures, Mayberry's residents also served as touchstones of small-town life: striving and yet content, wary and yet welcoming, proud and yet humble. As Gustavo Firmat observes, "[w]hat characterizes Mayberrians are not their ties to the soil . . . but their ties to the town and, hence, to one another."[1] Their relationships, as they helped each other through the ups and downs of everyday life, reinforced nostalgic mainstream values and social norms at a time when televised programming actively avoided treating controversial issues.

The lessons offered by The Andy Griffith Show provide a nostalgic curative for troubled times, promoting face-to-face relationships, social responsibility, and the pitfalls of material wealth, as well as "coming of age" lessons for all ages, such as self-acceptance, trust, accountability, and the nature of love. The show's audiences are positioned as "others" to the citizens of Mayberry—refugees from the bustling outside world seeking respite in the town's gently humorous everyday comings and goings—yet they are also drawn into the fold and embraced as Mayberry's own, encouraged to "take a load off," "set a spell," and feel at home amid fictive friends and relations with whom they share basic needs, values, experiences, and dreams. This appeal to and construction of a sense of shared humanity with viewers made The Andy Griffith Show an iconic part of American popular culture both during and after its eight-year run. As Geoffrey Campbell suggests, "The Andy Griffith Show is not so much a time capsule of what was, but a road map of what can continue to be."[2]

MEET ME AT THE FISHIN' HOLE

No show better illustrates the ideal of small-town life in rural America than The Andy Griffith Show, a series that has retained its popularity with fans for half a century. On October 30, 1960, the series premiered and immediately captured the imagination of the public. In fact, in an era when viewers had just three network choices (ABC, CBS, and NBC), ratings traditionally fell in the 20- to 30-percent range, The Andy Griffith Show debut ratings were 26.6 percent. Only the Bob Hope and Red Skelton shows ranked higher.[3] In its entire eight-season run, the show never fell out of the top-10 programs in the ratings. It went out a "winner" when, in its last year on the network, it was the top-rated television program in the country.

The series began as a spin-off of the popular *Danny Thomas Show*, which aired on ABC from 1953 to 1957 and on CBS from 1957 to 1964. Sheldon Leonard, who produced the Thomas show with Thomas himself, encouraged Griffith to transition to the new medium. Griffith was in the midst of a burgeoning film career, having starred in Elia Kazan's highly acclaimed *A Face in The Crowd* (1957) and Mervyn Leroy's *No Time For Sergeants* (1958), and he was starring on Broadway in *Destry Rides Again* when Leonard and Thomas offered to produce a pilot episode for him as part of Thomas's series. The plot would feature Thomas as a slick celebrity stuck in a rural town run by a hick sheriff.[4]

The episode "Danny Meets Andy Griffith" aired on February 15, 1960, and introduced America to the fictional town of Mayberry, North Carolina (which was modeled after Griffith's own hometown of Mt. Airy), an oasis of idiosyncratic characters whose lives intersect in the town's day-to-day activities. Although the pilot varied somewhat, the core cast of the series was Sheriff Andy Taylor (Griffith); his deputy, Barney Fife (Don Knotts); Taylor's five-year-old son, Opie ("Ronny" Howard); Aunt Bee (Frances Bavier); barber Floyd Lawson (Howard McNear); Otis Campbell (Hal Smith)[5]; and cousins Gomer and Goober Pyle (Jim Nabors and George Lindsey). Taylor does his best to keep peace and harmony, acting as both sheriff and father figure for all.

Griffith's down-home Southern charm, common sense, and humorous anecdotes were a natural fit for his role as sheriff. Although his character began as a "Southern clown," hamming it up on screen with an exaggerated drawl, Griffith felt his acting was "wooden" and was uncomfortable in the role. Only when he adopted the role of straight man for Knotts's deputy did the character of Sheriff Andy Taylor come into its own,[6] such as in this scene from "Barney's First Car":

Barney: The last big buy I made was my mom and dad's anniversary present.

Andy: What did you get them?

Barney: A septic tank

Andy: For their anniversary?

Barney: Yeah, oh they're really hard to buy for. Besides it was something they could really use. They were thrilled. Two tons of concrete, all steel reinforced.

Andy: You're a fine son, Barn.

Barney: I try[7]

Director Peter Baldwin recalled endless laughter during script readings, with Griffith doing the unthinkable for a comic: giving away funny lines "not just once or twice a script, but often. . . . It was really generous of him." But he knew that Knotts would make a funny line even funnier. Then Griffith's reaction, "a deadpan nod or subtle furrowing of the brow," would get another laugh.[8] In an interview for the Archive of American Television, Griffith admitted that by the second episode, "I knew . . . that Don should be the comic and I should play straight for him. That made all the difference."[9] He continued: "I loved playing the straight man to all these great comedic actors," and he noted that he actually played straight man to the whole town—from Floyd to Aunt Bee.[10] Despite his background as a stage actor, for Griffith it was the other comedic actors who "made it work."[11]

Griffith was probably never more effective than in his portrayals of the sheriff's relationship with his son, Opie. His slow, unruffled demeanor served as the perfect foil for the child actor's innocent comedy and modeled an easygoing parenting for adult viewers. Howard's Opie offered a complementary character with whom younger audience members could identify. In "Opie and The Spoiled Kid," for example, Opie makes a new rich friend who tries to teach him how to manipulate Andy into raising his allowance. Opie throws a fit, crying and holding his breath to get his way, and Andy patiently lets him go through the motions until the boy realizes how foolish his behavior is. When his friend, Arnold, finally gets punished for his bad behavior by his own father, Opie offers a humorous lesson in diplomacy:

Opie: Is Arnold going to get spanked?

Andy: Don't you think he deserves it?

Opie: I don't wanna say. After all, he is one of my own kind.[12]

The pair so successfully reinforced traditional family values for viewers that Andy Taylor was ranked number eight in *TV Guide*'s list of the "50 Greatest TV Dads of All Time."[13]

With 249 episodes, *The Andy Griffith Show* has long been considered a "classic," with fans, critics, and scholars alike citing the quality of the writing, the talent of the cast, and perhaps the most important, the crafting of the town itself as a character. From its rural topography to its simplistic architecture and visible lack of economic development, the town is an active agent in the show's nostalgic appeal. As show creator and executive producer Sheldon Leonard said, "The show should have been called *Mayberry*."[14] Unique among other rural television comedies of the era—such as *Green Acres* or *Petticoat Junction*—Mayberry is, as Richard Michael Kelly observes, a small world "filled with wonderful characters we can all understand and care about." The town is, as he suggests, "timeless."[15]

The show's iconic theme, the "Fishin' Hole" song, both captures and helps to create the down-home feel of the series through a sense of place. It is only whistled—the following original lyrics were discarded—but the soundscape it conveys is the same:

What a great place to rest your bones

And mighty fine for skippin' stones

Even without the lyrics, the whistled tune evokes for viewers images of simplicity and innocence that blend with the opening credits' small-town images to set the stage for the story to follow, creating a seamless narrative context for the series' episodes.

BEIN' NEIGHBORLY: FRIENDS, FAMILY, COMMUNITY

Mayberry was not just *any* small town; it was a carefully crafted community that consistently supported the show's life lessons. Although many communities have, as sociologists have long illustrated, "fuzzy boundaries"[16]—membership that is fluid and sometimes difficult to define—the confines of Mayberry's community are clear at the outset, and both regular and recurring characters are easily identified. Many of the recurring characters such as the "Fun Girls" from Mt. Pilot[17] and the backwoods hillbilly family the Darlings,[18] although not residents of the town itself still read as "local" for viewers and function as part of the community by fulfilling specific narrative roles. These two sets of characters represent opposite, but similar extremes when juxtaposed against true Mayberrians, helping to reinforce local norms and values: The Fun Girls, on one hand, are "city" girls, and the Darlings, on the other hand, are mountain folk. Both, however, represent wildness by Mayberry's standards and are the bearers of chaos and abandon whenever they visit the town. The Fun Girls, with their more sophisticated party-girl demeanors and overt sexuality, wreak havoc with Andy's love life (and the moral code of the town). The wayward women repeatedly descend on Mayberry with their sights set on romancing Andy and Barney, forcing the two lawmen into one compromising situation after another. The women receive their collective name when Helen and Thelma Lou cancel their dates with Andy and Barney for the local dance after witnessing "the boys" drive off with the provocatively dressed blonde strangers clinging to them: "Shouldn't be hard for you to get yourselves another date," Thelma Lou exclaims. "Why don't you take the two young ladies who were with you last night when you were 'working'? They look like *fun* girls!"

Similarly, the Darlings, stone-faced and silent, serve as a reminder about the consequences of a loss of propriety and social graces whenever they and their father, Briscoe Darling (Denver Pyle), come down from the hills. Making their debut in "Here Come the Darlings," the bluegrass-picking family (played by the Dillards, real-life musicians) unsuccessfully attempts to stay one step ahead of the law as family members break one law after another—sneaking into the local hotel through an upstairs window, hiding out in empty buildings—appealing to Andy's good nature but creating trouble wherever they go. Even the daughter of the clan, Charlene (Maggie Peterson), displays rough hillbilly upbringing as she flirts with Andy ("He shore is perty") and requests that her siblings play a "romantic" tune during their overnight in Andy's jail, suggesting "Salty Dog" as her song of choice. The Darlings, along with their fellow mountain man Ernest T. Bass, whose trademark rock throwing continually leads him into trouble, bring both color and commotion to the town.

Once in awhile, characters representative of the wider world also came to Mayberry. As early as the pilot, Sheriff Andy made his mark as a purveyor of rural philosophy to those outside the community, tutoring them (and the audience) in a simpler, gentler way of life. After the sheriff apprehends Danny Thomas's character (Danny Williams) for running a stop sign, he spots the entertainer's large wad of cash and raises the $5 fine to $100 or 10 days in jail. When publicly accused of fraud and corruption, the sheriff argues:

> It 'pears to me like a great big entertainer like Mr. Williams here influences a lot o' people. They look up to him, admire him . . . maybe even foller the example he sets. So the way I see it, a big man has got more of a responsibility to obey the law an' respect the folks who enforce it. Mr. Williams seemed to be in a powerful hurry. That may be why he didn't see that stop sign. Mr. Williams an' a whole lotta people like him seem to be in a big hurry, an' it's a pity.

He reminds Thomas and the "folks" at home that between his departure and his destination, there are "a lotta mighty good folks to meet, an' a lotta wonderful experiences to be had by a feller that'll take the time to 'preciate it"—a classic message to "stop and smell the roses" in a time of rapid social change.

The appeal of that message is also made apparent in episodes such as "Andy's English Valet," in which Malcolm Merriweather (Bernard Fox), an Englishman bicycling through America, makes a stop in town to ask for directions and gets into an accident. To work off his fine, he becomes Andy's "gentleman's gentleman." Merriweather's character develops an affection for the townspeople and their way of life and returns two more times to visit Mayberry and his newfound friends. The sense of difference created by characters such as this is palpable—all reside not only outside the geographic confines of Mayberry but also outside the moral and social confines, illustrating the notion that it is subjectivity that holds a community together: emotions, values, traditions.[19]

"Community," however, is self-perpetuating and self-preserving, so despite their differences, the townspeople of Mayberry attempted to draw many of these outsiders into the fold, even temporarily, not only to partake of their hospitality but also to reap the social and ideological benefits that their small, neighborly town has to offer. Andy and Barney demonstrate the value of "belonging" to the Darlings as they meet on common ground during front porch bluegrass jams, and the pair even attempt to help Ernest T. Bass find a mate ("My Fair Ernest T. Bass") or be proud of himself ("Ernest T. Bass Joins the Army"). These outsiders, as they visit more often, come to be treated like Mayberry's own.

However, being an "insider" is also a complicated role to negotiate. As with any small town, Mayberry's close-knit community has few secrets, and the line between "private" business and "community" business is often blurred or disappears entirely. On one hand, this often results in displays of solidarity and support for characters in times of need, but it also results in stereotypical nosy neighbors, meddling among friends, and, of course, gossip, as this exchange from "The Bookie Barber" illustrates:

> **Aunt Bee:** [talking about the new barber in town] Sarah tells me he's pretty popular with the ladies, too!
>
> **Andy:** Sarah over at the switchboard?
>
> **Aunt Bee:** Uh, huh; you know she doesn't talk much about people.
>
> **Andy:** Oh, Nooooooo . . .
>
> **Aunt Bee:** She just happened to overhear some of his phone calls. Do you know he's got girlfriends all the way from here to Morehead City?
>
> **Andy:** You think it's right for Sarah to listen in on his phone calls?
>
> **Aunt Bee:** No, of course not. And before she said one word I told her straight out she shouldn't do it. Gossiping is very rude.
>
> **Andy:** Good for you, Aunt Bee.
>
> **Aunt Bee:** And I'm not one to carry tales about people either . . . (long pause). . . . Well, don't you want to hear what she said?[20]

Despite the gossip and occasional good-natured envy and competitiveness, the townsfolk of Mayberry play roles that not only support each other but also ensure their place in the community. Even Otis Campbell, who embraces his status as town drunk by locking himself away in a cell to sleep off the effects of his latest binge, is a significant part of Mayberry's network of relationships.

Examples of similar communal nurturing abound. In "The New Housekeeper," the show's first episode, Aunt Bee tries everything to form a bond with Opie, who is distraught over the loss of his beloved housekeeper, Rose, who has married and left the Taylor household. Aunt Bee fails at all attempts to do what little boys like to do. When she finally decides to leave while Opie is sleeping, the boy sees his aunt with her bag packed outside. He runs out and starts pleading with his "Pa" to make her stay: "If she goes, what'll happen to her? She can't do anything—play ball, catch fish or frogs. She'll be helpless! That's why she's gotta stay so I can teach them to her!"[21] Similarly, in the classic episode "The Pickle Story," Aunt Bee makes inedible "kerosene" pickles, but neither Andy nor Barney has the heart to tell her how bad they are, so they praise her pickles and try to secretly discard them after she leaves:

Andy: Where we throw them?

[Barney goes to the wastebasket with his mouth full.]

Andy: No wait! She might find out and it'd break her heart.

Barney: Well, we've got to do something![22]

These humorous acts of kindness illustrate the use of comedy in the series, both as a form of relationship building within the narrative and as a means of "tutoring" audiences in down-home notions of family and community. The folk wisdom that informs those strategies, of course, is the foundation of *The Andy Griffith Show.*

FRONT PORCH PHILOSOPHY

This intimate sense of rural community had a strong resonance with television audiences, thanks to the strong tradition of humorous "front porch philosophers" in American popular culture in the first half of the 20th century. Harvey Bullock, one of the show's writers, once remarked, "I always regarded the show as set in the thirties, even though it played in the sixties."[23] From the vaudeville stage to radio, motion pictures, and television, beloved characters such as Will Rogers, Scattergood Baines, Longfellow Deeds, Jefferson Smith, and the team of Lum and Abner, like Sheriff Andy Taylor, served as guides for safe passage between the "good old days" and the new. Each brought a homey rural sensibility to an increasingly complicated world and tucked away inside each laugh a healthy dose of reassurance. Times changed, but these characters stayed the same, standing steady and unruffled in the face of rapid social change and representing "something fundamentally honest in human nature, something which, in the hectic movement of the passing time, we seem to be in danger of forgetting and eventually losing."[24]

All of these homespun philosopher-comics arose in eras when material improvement in the world around them was apparent—but so was moral decline, and Americans longed for a return to the halcyon days of country fairs and church socials, general stores, and station houses—a simpler, more satisfying, face-to-face world. Their lives and worlds were uncomplicated, secure, and sympathetic, embodying neighborliness and humanity, regardless of their roles. As one reviewer said of Will Rogers:

> There was always the quiet homely voice and the lovable smile to keep us in touch with the things we knew and understood . . . with an awkward grace readily comprehended. He was . . . open-handed, free and easy, loquacious, oddly philosophical, genuinely sentimental with a smile ever within reach of one of the boys.[25]

Those same words could have easily been used by any viewer to describe Sheriff Andy Taylor. Griffith's character, along with his family and friends, presented a vision of rural idealism that brought warm laughter to bear in the face of uncertainties and offered up a remedy: images of a simpler, safer life sheltered from a world of rapid social and economic change.

Mayberry's homespun wisdom also resonates with scholarly and social scientific research of the era. Sociologists in midcentury America suggested that a significant value of the community as an entity was in its status as "a primary group in the true sense of the term. . . . The homogeneity of the people, the high moral standards, the religious idealism, and the firmly rooted mores and traditions are largely responsible for the community's solidarity and comparative absence of social maladjustment."[26] Community contacts are face-to-face, and its residents demonstrate a strong sense of place-based identity, warmly affirming both stable rural life and a small-town main street existence. Mayberry epitomizes these elements, and its four central sets—courthouse, the Taylor home, Floyd's barber shop, and Myer's Lake—become "homelike" for both characters and viewers.[27] The lessons taught and learned by *The Andy Griffith Show*'s cast of characters were informed by a down-home naïveté that resulted in small steps forward for life in Mayberry but giant leaps toward a more neighborly, sensible, grounded outlook for viewers caught up in rapid social change and its attendant ills and confusion.[28]

CERTAINTY IN A TIME OF RAPID SOCIAL CHANGE

In his discussion of images of the South on television, Eric Peter Verschuure contends that *The Andy Griffith Show* "simply chose to ignore the plethora of socially relevant issues that every day confronted the real towns of the South in the uneasy sixties" and remained "ignorant" of the trauma of the era.[29] Other critics such as Anthony Harkins argue that *The Andy Griffith Show, The Real McCoys, Petticoat Junction*, and others "depicted a bucolic and lily-white Southern landscape and celebrated the homespun goodness of Southern whites" as a restorative response to the racial and moral struggles of the day.[30] But the show, in fact, engaged with the zeitgeist of the 1960s in a different way. Rather than depicting unemployment, assassinations, burning cities, riots, or the controversy surrounding the Vietnam War, Mayberry was a respite—"the eye of the hurricane," as Don Vaughan observed[31]—offering an "avenue of escape," not just for Southerners but also for Americans from every geographic region through its gentle, comic depictions of "small, solvable problems."[32] Down-home reassurance, as it were.

In this, Mayberry followed a longstanding tradition of identifying the rural—the heartland—as the beating heart of the country. Almost 200 years earlier, Thomas Jefferson argued that the "yeoman farmer" and, by extension, the small rural town, were the embodiments of American civic virtue, the essence of democracy, and what made the country great.[33] That sentiment persisted into the 20th century on radio in programs like *Lum and Abner* as well as in a steady procession of literary narratives such as William Macartney's novel *Fifty Years a Country Doctor* (1938), Bellamy Partridge's *Country Lawyer* (1939), and Henry Beetle Hough's *Country Editor* (1940). The sentiment took the spotlight particularly during World War II, when rural America became, as Knepper and Lawrence suggest, "Hollywood's Pastoral Myth for the Nation," assuming the role of "the steady heart of a nation at war."[34] Periodicals such as *Life* magazine and the *Saturday Evening Post* valorized rural communities in stories such as MacKinlay Kantor's "Happy Land,"[35] as well as through cover images like the one on the *Saturday Evening Post* on April 28, 1942, which featured an idealized small town in which modest homes surrounded the local church and seemed to answer the periodical's question, "For What Are We Fighting?" As Knepper and Lawrence describe:

> One man plants a garden. Another man mows a lawn. Two men repair a roof. A woman hangs a quilt on a clothesline. A child plays by a tree. These neighbors work hard, cooperate, and live simply.[36]

Even as farmland was being turned into postwar suburbs, the fascination with small rural towns continued in publications such as *Life* magazine, which featured W. Eugene Smith's 1948 photo essay "Country Doctor,"[37] as well as in Walt Disney's iconic Main Street USA, which was featured prominently in Disneyland's opening in 1955. As written just a few years later, Mayberry and its quirky residents were direct descendants of this tradition, but in the context of 1960s unrest they had a distinctly different cultural function to fulfill.

As Tim Hollis notes, no other rural television sitcom ever became the cultural touchstone that *The Andy Griffith Show* did.[38] In large part, this may be because no other rural sitcom was as successful in conveying the good-natured moral messages delivered by Griffith and his friends. Eliciting laughs from the demeanors and idiosyncrasies of the characters themselves rather than carefully crafted jokes meant that the humor of the series (and the lessons around which it was carefully wrapped) was at once personal and universal. The show's comedy emphasized not only the humanity of the characters but also the shared sense of humanity between the inhabitants of Mayberry and series viewers. This led audiences, as Vaughan suggests, to identify with Mayberrians,[39] vicariously embracing their slow, simple lifestyle as not only the norm in the universe of the show but also as an "ideal" in their own, increasingly complex, turbulent worlds full of racial conflict and tension regarding shifting gender roles. For many viewers, Mayberry and its characters were an escape from the discomfort of rapid social change to halcyon days of tranquility—days that actually never were.

As Joey Fann observes, the series was brimming over with "lessons from a simpler time."[40] And those lessons—about neighborliness, honesty, fidelity, commitment, hard work, and other basic "American" values—are readily apparent in every episode, delivered by any one or more of the characters, regardless of age, experience, or social standing. Bringing up Opie, the youngest member of the Mayberry community is often the vehicle for such messages as he learns from his elders. In "Opie and His Merry Men," the young boy not only learns an instrumental lesson about not stealing (even, as Robin Hood did, to give to the poor) but also a more complex lesson that true richness is not material wealth, but family and friends. He, in turn, reminds Andy and Aunt Bee of that very lesson in "Mayberry Goes Bankrupt," when family friend Frank Myers loses his home and needs a place to stay. As George Lindsey, who played the backward but good-hearted filling station attendant Goober Pyle, related,

> Mayberry is a wholesome place where a keen respect for others is depicted in many ways. . . . The appeal of good storytelling usually is built upon having the audience become aware of the consequences caused by the characters' actions. . . . Thoughtful viewers are able to find meaningful lessons about morality, relationships, and responsibility from watching.[41]

Although Mayberry's residents share their innocent down-home humor with characters from other rural sitcoms of the era such as *The Beverly Hillbillies* and *Petticoat Junction*, there is a key difference in the intentionality: here rural characters do not generally function as tricksters, mocking or taking advantage of outsiders or those with less practical knowledge, nor do they revel in portrayals of ignorance. *The Beverly Hillbillies'* Clampett family, for example, offers a comical reflection of the "relatively rapid prosperity"[42]—from Depression-era hardships to suburban comfort— experienced by many Americans during the 1960s, and this sharp commentary about class and mobility creates opposition and antagonism between the rural "folk" and their Beverly Hills counterparts that is often framed as ironic hostility. Mayberry, however, ultimately maintains the high moral tenor of Jefferson's iconic rural community: characterized by members who display humility and the ability to laugh in the face of adversity and are bound by intimate, trusting relationships; a shared deep local knowledge; and a striving for success in ways not defined by material possessions. The series deliberately makes no direct commentary on the rapid social change and upheaval in the everyday world of its viewers, where civil rights, Vietnam, and the women's movement are blurring the boundaries between right and wrong, self and other, and the ills and benefits of "the way things have always been." The simplicity of Mayberry certainly both highlights and offers a temporary respite from the tension and confusion of change.

CONCLUSION: CAN YOU EVER REALLY GO HOME AGAIN?

Change eventually did come to Mayberry. In May 1964, the fourth season finale was the pilot of a new spin-off show starring Jim Nabors: *Gomer Pyle, U.S.M.C.* Just about a year later, a *TV Guide* story warned of "Trouble in Mayberry," suggesting that too much success was leading the show to its downfall, "unravel[ing] the close-knit world of Mayberry,"[43] in response to rumors that Don Knotts was also leaving the show; a real blow to the series because "the real humor derived to a large extent from the relationship between solid, twinkly-eyed old Andy and his overly efficient, slightly paranoid deputy. . . ."[44] Sure enough, on April 19, 1965, Deputy Barney Fife departed from the town.

Two troubled seasons followed as writers and producers tried a range of strategies for regaining the magical insanity that had been lost with Knotts's departure. Sam Bobrick, one of the show's writers, reflected: "I think *The Andy Griffith Show*, for me, jumped the shark when Don left. It became a [formulaic] situation comedy and not at its best."[45] Surprisingly, the show remained in the top 10, baffling all involved. In response, director Peter Baldwin speculated that the reason for this was that the show was *always* more than mere comedy, that "there was also a very sweet part" that transcended viewers' expectations for a laugh.[46]

For Andy Griffith, however, the show's magic had vanished. His counterpart, Sheriff Andy, was finding it difficult to keep his community insulated from the changing world outside its boundaries. So, in the 1967–68 season, when *The Andy Griffith Show* was the top program in the country according to the Nielsen ratings, Andy Griffith finally decided to leave the series. The show continued on in a new format as *Mayberry, R.F.D.*, with actor Ken Berry playing the central figure: farmer and city councilman Sam Jones. The show's pilot reunited much of *The Andy Griffith Show*'s cast—including Andy and Barney—for Andy's long-awaited wedding to his girlfriend, Helen. The reunion revealed not only that the comedy but also that the characters' deep, small town bond had not—and would not—diminish. In the final scene, Andy serenades Helen on his guitar. Then, a second voice chimes in, and the camera pulls back to reveal Barney, who has joined the newlyweds in their honeymoon suite.[47]

For viewers, Mayberry's magic had, at least for the moment, returned.

NOTES

1. Gustavo Pérez Firmat, *A Cuban in Mayberry* (Austin: University of Texas Press, 2014), 27–28.

2. Geoffrey Campbell, "Mayberry Is a Fictional Place, but a Very Real State of Mind," *Star-Telegram*, October 2, 2010.

3. "Some New Shows Getting Good Ratings," *Broadcasting*, October 10, 1960, 60.

4. "Andy Griffith Interview," *The Archive of American Television*, http://www.emmytvlegends.org/interviews/shows/andy-griffith.

5. Played by actor Frank Cady in the pilot.

6. Richard Michael Kelly, *The Andy Griffith Show* (Winston-Salem, NC: John F. Blair Publisher, 1985), 16.

7. "Barney's First Car," episode 90.

8. Daniel de Visé, *Andy and Don: The Making of a Friendship and a Classic American TV Show* (New York: Simon & Schuster, 2015), 153.

9. "Andy Griffith Interview," *The Archive of American Television*, http://www.emmytvlegends.org /interviews/shows/andy-griffith.

10. Ibid.

11. Ibid.

12. "Opie and The Spoiled Kid," episode 84.

13. *TV Guide*, June 20, 2004.

14. Ibid.

15. Kelly, op. cit., 5.

16. See, for example, Ferdinand Tönnies, *Gemeinshaft and Gesellschaft* (Leipzig: Fues's Verlag, 1887), and Weber, *Economy and Society* (Berkeley: University of California Press, 1978).

17. The Fun Girls appeared in three episodes between 1962 and 1965: "Barney Mends a Broken Heart," "Fun Girls," and "The Arrest of the Fun Girls."

18. The Darlings appear six times between 1963 and 1966.

19. Weber, op. cit.

20. "The Bookie Barber," episode 60.

21. "The New Housekeeper," episode one.

22. "The Pickle Story," episode 43.

23. Neil Brower, *Mayberry 101: Behind the Scenes of a TV Classic* (Winston-Salem, NC: John F. Blair Publisher, 1998), 140.

24. Fred Stone, "Chatting with the Editor" no. 3. Scrapbook, Will Rogers Memorial and Museum, Claremore, OK.

25. Ibid.

26. Loran David Osborn and Martin Henry Neumeyer, *The Community and Society* (New York: American Book Company, 1933), 23–24.

27. John O'Leary and Rick Warland, "Against the Organization Man." Pp. 73–86 in Mary M. Dalton and Laura R. Linder, *The Sitcom Reader: America Viewed and Skewed* (Albany: State University of New York Press, 2005).

28. Ibid.

29. Eric Peter Verschuure, "Stumble, Bumble, Mumble: TV's Image of the South," *Journal of Popular Culture* 16(3) (1982), 92.

30. Anthony Harkins, *Hillbilly: A Cultural History of an American Icon* (New York: Oxford University Press, 2004), 174.

31. Don Rodney Vaughan, "Why *The Andy Griffith Show* Is Important to Popular Culture Studies," *Journal of Popular Culture* 38(2) (2004), 397.

32. Ibid., 398.

33. Thomas Jefferson, "Notes on the State of Virginia." In *The Portable Thomas Jefferson*, edited by Merrill D. Peterson (New York: Viking Penguin, 1975), 217.

34. Martin Knepper and John Shelton Lawrence, "World War II and Iowa: Hollywood's Pastoral Myth for the Nation." In *Representing the Rural*, edited by Catherine Fowler and Gillian Helfield (Detroit: Wayne State University Press, 2006), 323.

35. *Saturday Evening Post*, November 28, 1942. The novel was adapted for the screen in 1943.

36. Knepper and Lawrence, op. cit.

37. October 11, 1948, http://time.com/3456085/w-eugene-smiths-landmark-photo-essay-country-doctor/.

38. Tim Hollis, *Ain't That a Knee-Slapper: Rural Comedy in the Twentieth Century* (Oxford: University Press of Mississippi, 2008), 178.

39. Vaughan, op. cit., 408–413.

40. Joey Fann, *The Way Back to Mayberry: Lessons from a Simpler Time* (Nashville: B & H Books, 2010).

41. George ["Goober"] Lindsey, "Foreword." In Fann, op. cit., xviii.

42. Harkins, op. cit., 194.

43. Cited in de Visé, *Andy and Don*, 155.

44. Ibid.

45. Ibid., 164.

46. Ibid.

47. Ibid., 189.

BIBLIOGRAPHY

Alderman, Derek H., Terri Moreau, and Stefanie Benjamin. "*The Andy Griffith Show*: Mayberry as Working Class Utopia." Pp. 51–69 in *Blue-Collar Pop Culture: From NASCAR to Jersey Shore, Volume 2: Television and the Culture of Everyday Life*, edited by Keith M. Booker. Santa Barbara, CA: ABC-Clio, 2012.

"Andy Griffith Interview." *The Archive of American Television*. http://www.emmyt vlegends.org /interviews/shows/andy-griffith.

Brower, Neil. *Mayberry 101: Behind the Scenes of a TV Classic*. Winston-Salem, NC: John F. Blair Publisher, 1998.

Campbell, Geoffrey. "Mayberry Is a Fictional Place, but a Very Real State of Mind," *Star-Telegram* (Ft. Worth, TX), October 2, 2010.

de Visé, Daniel. *Andy and Don: The Making of a Friendship and a Classic American TV Show*. New York: Simon & Schuster, 2015.

Fann, Joey. *The Way Back to Mayberry: Lessons from a Simpler Time*. Nashville: B & H Books, 2010.

"50 Greatest TV Dads of All Time," *TV Guide*, June 20, 2004.

Firmat, Gustavo Pérez. *A Cuban in Mayberry: Looking Back at America's Hometown*. Austin: University of Texas Press, 2014.

Harkins, Anthony. *Hillbilly: A Cultural History of an American Icon*. New York: Oxford University Press, 2004.

Hollis, Tim. *Ain't That a Knee Slapper: Rural Comedy in the Twentieth Century*. Oxford: University Press of Mississippi, 2008.

Jefferson, Thomas. "Notes on the State of Virginia." In *The Portable Thomas Jefferson*, edited by Merrill D. Peterson. New York: Viking Penguin, 1975.

Kantor, MacKinlay. "Happy Land," *Saturday Evening Post*, November 28, 1942, 9.

Kelly, Richard Michael. *The Andy Griffith Show*. Winston-Salem, NC: John F. Blair Publisher, 1985.

Knepper, Martin, and John Shelton Lawrence. "World War II and Iowa: Hollywood's Pastoral Myth for the Nation." In *Representing the Rural*, edited by Catherine Fowler and Gillian Helfield, 323–339. Detroit: Wayne State University Press, 2006.

Knotts, Don. *Barney Fife and Other Characters I Have Known*. New York: Berkley Boulevard Books, 1999.

Lindsey, George ["Goober"]. "Introduction." In Joey Fann, *The Way Back to Mayberry: Lessons from a Simpler Time*. Nashville: B & H Books, 2010.

O'Leary, John, and Rick Warland. "Against the Organization Man." In Mary M. Dalton and Laura R. Linder, *The Sitcom Reader: America Viewed and Skewed*, 73–86. Albany: State University of New York Press, 2005.

Osborn, Loran David, and Martin Henry Neumeyer. *The Community and Society*. New York: American Book Company, 1933.

Smith, Eugene. "Country Doctor," *Life Magazine*, October 11, 1948, http://time .com/3456085 /w-eugene-smiths-landmark-photo-essay-country-doctor/.

"Some New Shows Getting Good Ratings." *Broadcasting*, October 10, 1960, 60.

Stone, Fred. "Chatting with the Editor" No. 3, Scrapbook. Will Rogers Memorial and Museum. Claremore, OK.

Tönnies, Ferdinand. *Gemeinshaft and Gesellschaft*. Leipzig: Fues's Verlag, 1887.

Vaughan, Don Rodney. "Why The Andy Griffith Show Is Important to Popular Culture Studies." *Journal of Popular Culture* 38(2) (2004), 397–423.

Verschuure, Eric Peter. "Stumble, Bumble, Mumble: TV's Image of the South," *Journal of Popular Culture* 16(3) (1982), 92–96.

Weber, Max. *Economy and Society*. Berkeley: University of California Press, 1978.

5

Spy Versus Reality: *Get Smart,* Satire, and Absurdity

A. Bowdoin Van Riper

To "86" something means to reject it. Agent 86, however—Maxwell Smart—was enthusiastically embraced by American sitcom audiences of the mid- to late 1960s and can still bring chuckles to the millions of baby boomers who remember Get Smart's *first run (1965–1970). Created by masters of spoof Mel Brooks and Buck Henry, the show lifted spy-drama conventions and then dropped them into a universe not unlike Blake Edwards's* The Pink Panther. *In this chapter, A. Bowdoin Van Riper explores the sweep of* Get Smart *as one of the first and . . . smartest . . . satires to endure in sitcom form. Without it, television satires as distinct as* M*A*S*H *and* The Big Bang Theory *would look quite different from the forms we know, because they draw in their own unique ways on conventions established in* Get Smart.

A man in a tuxedo is seated in the audience at an orchestra concert when he is startled (along with those around him) by the loud ringing of a telephone. He excuses himself, leaves the auditorium, and repairs to a janitor's closet where he removes his right shoe and peels off its sole and heel to reveal a hidden phone, which he answers. Responding to the Chief's summons, he prepares to leave the closet only to find that he has inadvertently locked himself in. Annoyed but undaunted, he solves the problem by drawing a revolver and blasting the lock open. Climbing into a jaunty two-seater convertible parked outside the theater, he executes a flawless U-turn and confidently pulls up to the curb at his destination . . . located directly across the street. The opening credits roll as he double-times down a stairway to the basement and begins the first of 138 trips through the most famous series of security doors in television history.

Thus was Maxwell Smart, Agent 86 of the top-secret spy agency CON-TROL, introduced to the world in 1965.

The sequence of *Get Smart*'s black-and-white pilot episode before the credits conveys the essence of the character at the heart of the series in less than three minutes: quick thinking, fast acting, devoted to his work, comfortable with the tools of his trade, and yet prone to operate in a mental universe that intersects, at a slightly oblique angle, the one shared by the rest of the world. Smart was conceived by the show's creators, Mel Brooks and Buck Henry, as a cross between James Bond and Jacques Clouseau—the epically oblivious police inspector played by Peter Sellers in *The Pink Panther* (1963) and *A Shot in the Dark* (1964)—and both sides of the character are fully visible even in the opening moments of the pilot. The outré gadget is pure Bond, and the bizarre logic of the U-turn is pure Clouseau, but the closet scene is both at once and thus pure Smart. He is Clouseau the oblivious bumbler when he locks himself in but Bond the cool-headed man of action when he casually shoots his way out.

Get Smart (1965–1970) appeared at the height American popular culture's decade-long fascination with spies; it played the conventions of the spy-story genre remarkably straight. The 22-minute episodes were driven by missions that pitted CONTROL against its archnemesis KAOS and Max (Don Adams) and his beautiful, level-headed partner, Agent 99 (Barbara Feldon), in real danger. The comic core of *Get Smart* lay in the ongoing spectacle of Max, with his unshakable self-confidence and bizarre logic, colliding again and again with these grim realities and inexplicably not only surviving but also triumphing. *Get Smart*'s straight-faced portrayal of Max—the archetypal secret-agent character nudged over the line into absurdity—makes it a brilliantly effective parody of Cold War spy stories. At the same time, however, its portrayal of CONTROL—the archetypal white-collar workplace nudged over the same satirical line—makes it equally effective as a satire of bureaucracy. It achieved sitcom immortality not by mocking its clueless hero, but by mocking the pretensions and the absurdities of authority—particularly bureaucratic authority—in general.

A DIVERSITY OF SPIES

Like the drawing-room whodunit, the spy story was a British invention and remained largely a British specialty for decades after the first examples appeared in print. Magazines there devoted to spy stories existed during pulp fiction's golden age of the 1930s and 1940s but failed to produce their own equivalent of Dashiell Hammett, Robert Heinlein, or Max Brand. The American spy-fiction writers who penned paperback originals in the 1950s and early 1960s achieved (modest) commercial success but not critical acclaim. Edward S. Aarons's tales of CIA operative Sam Durrell (begun in 1955 with *Assignment to Disaster*) and Donald Hamilton's of black-ops agent Matt Helm (begun in 1960 with *Death of a Citizen*) were regarded as formulaic, escapism—a step up from the penny-a-word ghetto of the pulps perhaps but far short of British masters such as John Buchan, Eric Ambler, and Graham Greene. Cinematic spies of the 1940s and 1950s were likewise confined to weekly serials, series pictures, and low-budget B features designed to fill the bottom halves of double bills. On television, they appeared in a handful of short-run series but were overshadowed by Westerns and science-fiction adventures.

The rise of the spy story from the literary and cinematic ghettoes began with the 1960s and the Cuban Revolution, the erection of the Berlin Wall, the Bay of Pigs fiasco, and the stabilization of the nuclear standoff between the superpowers after the Cuban Missile Crisis.

Whether those larger events (and the valorization of counterinsurgency forces such as the Green Berets) contributed to the "spy boom" in American popular culture is beyond the scope of this essay. What *is* clear, however, is that President John F. Kennedy's enthusiasm for the James Bond novels catalyzed the process. Kennedy's identification of *From Russia with Love* as one his 10 favorite books in a 1961 *Life* magazine interview turned Ian Fleming's novels from minor midlist properties into best-sellers.[1] The newfound success of the novels translated in turn into success for the film adaptations, the first four of which appeared over the next four years, beginning with *Dr. No* in 1962. The film adaptation of Richard Condon's *The Manchurian Candidate*, arguably the first American espionage novel that could stand alongside the work of Ambler and Greene, appeared in the same year. Its dark themes—brainwashing, political treachery, and intimations of mother–son incest—offered audiences a counterpoint to the Bond films' emerging formula of "girls, guns, and gadgets," which crystallized in *Goldfinger* (1964).[2]

The box-office success *Goldfinger* opened the spy-story floodgates on screens both large and small. Harry Saltzman and Albert R. Broccoli, producers of the James Bond adventures, developed a second, grittier series of spy films—*The Ipcress File* (1965), *Funeral in Berlin* (1966), and *Billion-Dollar Brain* (1967)—that featured Michael Caine as Harry Palmer, a cynical, working-class British spy. Alfred Hitchcock, who helped to define the British spy film with *The Thirty-Nine Steps* (1935) and *The Lady Vanishes* (1938), among others, returned to it in *Torn Curtain* (1966). Other filmmakers rang their own changes on the now-flourishing genre. Stanley

Donen—better known for sleek, stylish musical comedies such as *Singin' in the Rain* (1952)—cast Gregory Peck and Sophia Loren in the sleek, stylish foreign-intrigue thriller *Arabesque* (1964). Norman Taurog cast Vincent Price as an archvillain bent on world domination in the cheerfully silly *Dr. Goldfoot and the Bikini Machine* (1965), and Michael Anderson brought the most influential British spy since Bond to the screen in *The Quiller Memorandum* (1966).

Napoleon Solo and Ilya Kuryakin, the first spy heroes to make a significant impact on American television, debuted in the fall of 1964 on *The Man from U.N.C.L.E.* Originally conceived as a (comparatively) realistic black-and-white adventure series, its second season (1965–66) featured color and—in imitation of the direction taken by the Bond films—more outlandish plots and more overt humor.[3] The series descended into outright spoof in its third (1966–67), but by then viewers interested in more realistic tales could find them in hour-long installments of *I Spy* (1965–68), *Mission: Impossible* (1966–73), and the British import *Danger Man*, broadcast by CBS under the accurate if unimaginative title *Secret Agent* (1964–66).[4] Another British import, *The Avengers* (1961–69)—in the midst of its own *U.N.C.L.E.*-like shift from realism toward fantasy—also reached American airwaves in 1965, bringing with it stylized visuals, wildly imaginative plots, and a star-making performance by Diana Rigg as heroine Emma Peel.[5] *The Wild, Wild West* (1965–69), which rounded out the lineup of mid-decade spy dramas, followed the adventures of two U. S. Secret Service agents on the post–Civil War western frontier. Its creator, Michael Garrison, described it in a moment of candor as "James Bond on horseback."[6]

From the very beginning, the spy stories that proliferated in American popular culture during the 1960s were wildly diverse in concept and tone. There was never a moment when the genre was pure, nor a moment when the stories that made it up were all played straight. The endorsement of *From Russia with Love* by JFK, the arch Cold Warrior, coexisted with the premiere of *Spy vs. Spy*—Antonio Prohias's wordless comic-strip satire of Cold War espionage—in *Mad* magazine.

In 1965, the dour realism of *The Spy Who Came in from the Cold*, the extravagant heroics of *Thunderball*, and the brightly colored silliness of *Dr. Goldfoot and the Bikini Machine* reached movie screens within six months of one another. The half-hour sitcom *Hogan's Heroes* (1965–1971)— about a World War II special operations team based inside an "escape-proof" German POW camp—could, with its team of specialist heroes whose plans rely on elaborate deception and the enemy's arrogance, be mistaken for an affectionate spoof of *Mission: Impossible*, had it not premiered a year earlier. Even within individual series, tone could vary substantially: the heroes of *I Spy* and *The Avengers* underscore their cool competence with Howard Hawks–style banter, even when the fate of nations hangs in the balance.

The first season of *Get Smart* (1965–1966) coincided, in retrospect, with the high-water mark of the 1960s spy-story boom. Its 30 episodes aired at a time when the spy story was being presented in forms ranging from grim adult drama to swashbuckling adventure story to teen comedy. Mel Brooks would go on to spoof the Western and the gothic horror film in *Blazing Saddles* and *Young Frankenstein* (both 1974), respectively, and Buck Henry would revive the spirit of the screwball comedy in his script for Peter Bogdanovich's *What's Up, Doc?* (1972), but in *Get Smart* they were playing not with a moribund genre—or even a tired one—but with a genre at the height of its popularity.

GET SMART AS GENRE PARODY

Get Smart's five-year network run was over by the time the spy-fiction boom ran its course in the first years of the 1970s. The series' creators, writers, and directors could thus assume that viewers were—by cultural osmosis, if not direct experience—familiar with the visual and verbal motifs of the spy story. This assumed familiarity is apparent from the first scenes of the pilot episode. It drops the viewer into the middle of Max's world—explaining nothing—confident that viewers will, without prompting, read a sharp-dressed man with a phone in his shoe and a gun in his pocket as a spy. The use of agents' code numbers in place of names, along with dozens of other details that establish the contours of Max's professional world, slip by the same way. No explanation is offered, nor is one needed. Max is "86," and his coworker is "99" in the same sense that James Bond is "007"; the trick phone booth into which he disappears at the end of the opening credits evokes the trick door that led from Del Floria's tailor shop to U.N.C.L.E. headquarters, or the hollowed-out tree stump (with periscope) that gave Hogan and his men access to the world beyond their camp. "The Chief" (known only by his title) is Bond's "M" or Quiller's faceless "Control."

Assuming a genre-savvy audience allowed *Get Smart* to fulfill, from the outset, cocreator Mel Brooks' dictum "Do what they do except just stretch it half an inch."[7] Max's shoe phone, the pilot episode's first visible sign that he *is* a spy, is a case in point. Miniaturized electronic devices had been available to the fictional forces of law and order since Dick Tracy strapped on his two-way wrist radio in 1946. The spy stories teemed with tiny electronic gadgets: miniaturized tracking beacons, portable Geiger counters, and—in *The Man from U.N.C.L.E.*—radios hidden in pens, cigarette cases, and lighters. Objects secreted in a spy's clothes—a garrote in a wristwatch, a spring-loaded knife in a shoe, or a gun in a hollow boot heel—were also standard genre fare. The humor in Max's shoe phone lies not in its existence or its concealment but in its absurdly clumsy, user-hostile implementation: the jangling ring that instantly breaks the agent's cover, the need to not simply remove but disassemble the shoe, and the fact that it uses a then-standard Bell System dial (introducing, as Max discovers at a critical moment in "Bronzefinger," the possibility of reaching a wrong number). The phone is a marvel of cutting-edge high technology gone ever-so-slightly wrong to lasting comic effect.

The "pushing" continues throughout the show's five seasons and in every visible corner of the series' fictional world. The suicide pills that CONTROL issues to its agents come in tasty fruit flavors that change from month to month. The fellow agent from whom Max receives information in the field appears not in unobtrusive public spaces like coffee shops and park benches but crammed into bus station lockers, street-corner trash cans, and—in one memorable episode—a front-loading industrial washing machine. The Chief's office is defended against eavesdropping not by electronic countermeasures or technicians sweeping for bugs, but by a rigid, clear plastic hood called the "Cone of Silence" that descends from the ceiling and covers both the Chief and whoever is seated opposite him. The Cone of Silence—like the hideously uncomfortable and increasingly bizarre hiding places into which Max's contact is stuffed—is one of the series' handful of running visual gags. It fails each time it is used—at Max's insistence and over the Chief's weary but ultimately futile objections—seemingly in a different way each time, like the giant catapult in Chuck Jones's classic Roadrunner cartoon "To Beep or Not To Beep" (1963).[8]

The characters' names—or, rather, lack of names—are a constant reminder of the fact that *Get Smart* takes place in a slightly surreal world one step beyond that of conventional spy stories. Adventure heroes with *nommes de guerre* are as old as Homer, and fictional spies have been using numbers in place of names at least since the 1920s, when the titular hero of the aviation pulp journal *G-8 and His Battle Aces* took to the skies over the Western Front. James Bond's iconic 007 designation solidified the convention, and the chorus of the theme song for *Secret Agent* famously declares "they've given you a number, and taken away your name." *Get Smart* pushes the convention into the realm of absurdity by not only giving every CONTROL agent a number but also having them use their numbers as a form of address even in public (where doing so would break cover) or in casual social settings (where doing so is harmless but bizarre). Max is the only field agent referred to by name; the rest remain numbers, setting up lines such as, "Do you realize, 99, that Agent 54 will be 36 today? My gosh, it seems like only yesterday that 54 was 35!" The joke reaches its apex with Agent 99, who is never called anything *but* "99"—even by Max, even when they are dating or (from midseason four) married.[9]

As a character, Max is a monument to Brooks's philosophy of that "extra-half inch." Every spy lies—deception and misdirection are part of the job—but Max's lies are so extravagant and improbable that the person being lied to immediately dismisses them, causing him to backpedal and render the lie even less credible. His attempts to negotiate a believable lie with the person he was trying to deceive were another of *Get Smart*'s running verbal gags, punctuated by the catchphrase "Would you believe . . . ?" and structured as formally as a knock-knock joke.

Max: I happen to know that at this very minute, seven Coast Guard cutters are converging on this boat. Would you believe it? Seven!

Villain: I find that pretty hard to believe, Mr. Smart.

Max: Would you believe six?

Villain: I don't think so.

Max: Would you believe two cops in a rowboat?[10]

The same principle extends to every aspect of his personality. Fictional spies—particularly James Bond and Napoleon Solo—are routinely depicted as suave ladies' men, but Max is completely unaware (for most of the first three seasons) that his beautiful female partner is smitten with him. Fictional spies are unflappably cool in the face of danger, but Smart veers between brazen heroism and equally brazen cowardice. Told by the Chief that he will be facing mortal danger on an upcoming assignment, Max is as likely to attempt to pass the mission off to another agent—even 99—as to respond with his famous catchphrase "and *loving* it!"

GET SMART AS BUREAUCRATIC SATIRE

Had *Get Smart* simply been a brightly colored, anything-goes farce about spies, it would likely have been eclipsed by feature films such as *Our Man Flint* (1966), *What's Up Tiger Lily?* (1966) and *Casino Royale* (1967), which explored similar territory and—with larger budgets and fewer censorship restrictions—had the freedom to push the boundaries of "anything" beyond what was possible on network television. Had it been simply been a spoof of genre conventions, it would likely have run its course in a season or two, as ostensibly "serious" spy stories such as *The Man from U.N.C.L.E.* and the James Bond films (which began a trial separation from reality with *You Only Live Twice* in 1967) edged ever closer to being spoofs themselves.[11] Creators Mel Brooks and Buck Henry chose, however, to make *Get Smart* not just a spy comedy but also an *office* comedy—a sharply observed satire of bureaucratic organizations.

The agent at odds with his own team was already a familiar trope in spy fiction by the 1960s. The protagonists of John Le Carré, Len Deighton, and Anthony Price novels struggled not only with enemy spies but also with empire-building middle managers, reputation-conscious elected officials, and representatives of "friendly" intelligence agencies both foreign and domestic. James Bond, and other conventionally heroic spies, repeatedly ignore, subvert, or openly defy their superiors in pursuit of their own agendas. Workplace-centered sitcoms of the 1950s and 1960s offered broadly similar situations in which likable main characters bamboozled or circumvented the authority of buffoonish bosses.

In both spy stories and sitcoms, the conflict was nearly always personalized: James Bond defied M, not the Secret Service; Dick Van Dyke and his fellow writers aimed their barbs at producer Mel Cooley, not the network; the likable rogues of *Sergeant Bilko* were at war with their commanding officer, Colonel Hall, and not the army itself. *Get Smart* moved the joke in a different direction, giving Max and 99 no antagonist within the CONTROL hierarchy to react against. However often he might express weary exasperation with Max, the Chief never slipped into the traditional roles of stern father (M), pompous fool (Mel), or rule-bound martinet (Col. Hall). He is, instead, a victim of the same faceless enemy that bedevils his agents: bureaucracy.

The fact that CONTROL exists to guard the safety of the free world does not keep it from behaving like any other large, hierarchical organization. Equipment malfunctions, critical jobs filled by employees incapable of doing them, and the ceaseless demands of day-to-day administrative tasks steal time from the actual important work of the organization. "Anatomy of a Lover" begins with a scene of the chief in his office, dictating an all-hands memo about agents' abuse of their coffee breaks. "CONTROL coffee mugs are *not* to be used for target practice," he declares sternly, doubtless in response to complaints from someone in the accounting division.[12] Other episodes reveal that CONTROL has a suggestion box, a banquet hall (where the Chief, much to Max's displeasure, insists that he hold his bachelor party), a bowling team, and an amateur dance band. The agency insists that its employees—even field agents—punch a time clock, and the agents respond in kind. "I'm on my lunch break," Agent 13 tells Max, explaining why he can't help identify the murderer of a scientist Max was assigned to protect. "A man has been murdered!" Max splutters. "Doesn't that mean anything to you?" But 13 is unmoved: "Not between 12:00 and 1:00."[13] Ironically, Max himself displays a similar clock-watching attitude a few episodes later: "Well, Chief," he declares, "it seems like we've got everything here wrapped up and we can go home for the weekend!"[14] Even for agents who face death in the line of duty and hold the fate of the Free World in their hands, the petty inanities of bureaucracy—and the petty rebellions they foster—are inescapable.

The intersection of rigid, complex procedures with the fluid nature of the spy business is fraught with possibilities for disaster, and the addition of Smart—slavishly devoted to the rules and utterly literal in his interpretation of them—makes comic disaster virtually inevitable. Unable to break the seal on his orders in "Rub a Dub Dub, Three Spies in a Sub," he rejects 99's suggestion that he tear open the opposite end of the envelope on the grounds that it specifically says "break the seal." Trapped under a malfunctioning Cone of Silence with the Chief in "The Whole Tooth," Max manages to free himself, but when an alarm sounds he immediately runs from the room to investigate, leaving his boss trapped. Telltale signs throughout the series suggest, however, that mindless compliance with inane rules and procedures is woven into the fabric of the agency itself. Access to the secret CONTROL training facility requires following an elaborate set of security procedures—that lead to the wrong house. No one, including the Chief, objects when the office computer orders Agent 99 laid off for budgetary reasons on the eve of a major operation. CONTROL's rulebook on when to burn secret documents is unavailable, having been declared secret and therefore burned.

ABSURDITY GOES MAINSTREAM

Television comedy had experimented with both satire and absurdity before but typically in programs with fluid, malleable formats: *Your Show of Shows* (1950–1954), *You Bet Your Life* (1950–1961), *The Ernie Kovacs Show* (1960–1961), and *That Was the Week That Was* (1964–1965). Through the 1950s and the first half of the 1960s, sitcoms left the fabric of everyday reality more or less intact. Exceptions were typically limited in duration or in scope. *The Dick Van Dyke Show*'s brilliant science-fiction parody "It May Look Like a Walnut" (1962) was a single episode, and *The Addams Family* (1964–1966) aimed its satire at a single target: middle-class suburban mores. *Get Smart* obliterated those limits. The conventions of the spy story and the absurdities of large, bureaucratic organizations were its ongoing, evergreen targets, but it found time, over the course of five seasons, to take swipes at a host of others.

Many sitcoms indulged in occasional parody episodes—sending up a specific film, as "It May Look Like a Walnut" did with *Invasion of the Body Snatchers,* or an entire genre like the Western or the detective story—but *Get Smart* made a cottage industry of them. Over the course of five seasons, it lampooned obvious targets such as *I Spy* (in "Die, Spy"), *Mission: Impossible* (in "The Impossible Mission"), *The Avengers* (in "Run, Robot, Run"), and the first three James Bond films, but its comic reach extended far beyond the spy genre. "Island of the Darned," for example, substitutes Smart for the big-game-hunter hero of "The Most Dangerous Game," while "That Old Gang of Mine" has him infiltrate a criminal gang reminiscent of those in *The Asphalt Jungle* (1950) or *Topkapi* (1964), and "Hoo Done It" pairs him with white-suited, aphorism-spouting detective Harry Hoo, a thinly veiled stand-in for 1930s cinematic sleuth Charlie Chan.[15]

Exacting in their attention to detail, the parody episodes were studded with small visual gags designed to reward viewers familiar with the source material or even with stories tangential—or entirely unrelated—to the one ostensibly being parodied. "Casablanca," for example, places a white-jacketed Max in a Moroccan café clearly modeled after Rick's, but shows 99—only a few tables away—inhabiting an entirely different Bogart movie: doing a credible impression of Lauren Bacall in *To Have and Have Not*, opposite a piano player evidently cast for his resemblance to Hoagy Carmichael rather than Dooley Wilson.

Even more atypically for a sitcom of its era, *Get Smart's* satirical reach extended beyond the boundary separating fictional worlds (its own or others) from the audience's real one. Shown a particularly diabolical-looking instrument of torture at CONTROL headquarters, Max remarks that it must have come from "a real terrorist organization." Without missing a beat, the CONTROL scientist in charge of the chair confirms his suspicions: it belonged to the IRS. In another episode, a mission briefing conducted by a pair of U.S. Navy admirals escalates into a competition to see who can commit more ships to the effort. "I'll just call those four destroyers and raise you four submarines," one admiral declares, pushing model ships across a map table like poker chips. The other exclaims, "You're bluffing!"[16] The show's most common satirical tool, however, was to have Max make an earnestly patriotic declaration that slowly twisted its way into absurdity, as in this exchange from "Island of the Darned":

99: [after their would-be assassin falls to his death] How terrible!

Max: He deserved it, 99—he was a KAOS killer.

99: Sometimes I wonder if we're any better, Max.

Max: What are you talking about, 99? We *have to* shoot and kill and destroy; we represent everything that's wholesome and good in the world![17]

A similar exchange ends "The Mild Ones" when Max, having rescued the prime minister of Blouvia from a motorcycle gang, asks what the Blouvian's mission was:

Chief: He was here to borrow 20 billion dollars from our government. After what happened we're lucky his country still wants to take our money.

Doll Baby [a reformed member of the gang]: What would be so terrible if they didn't?

Max: I'm surprised at you, Doll Baby! If they didn't take our money, they'd have no reason to resent us. And if they didn't resent us, we could never really be sure they were our friends![18]

Tame stuff, perhaps, in a world where *The Mouse That Roared* (1959) and *Dr. Strangelove* (1964) had appeared on movie screens, but still new to the staid world of 1960s sitcoms.

The sitcoms of the 1960s were utterly, almost defiantly, isolated from the social, cultural, and political tumult underway in the wider world. The network run of *Gomer Pyle, USMC* stretched from 1964 to 1969—beginning the month after the Tonkin Gulf Resolution and ending as the number of American troops in Vietnam peaked at 543,000—but the series, despite taking place at a U.S. Marine Corps training camp in California, never mentioned the ongoing and increasingly divisive war.[19] *Hogan's Heroes*, set during World War II, presented its German characters, even members the Gestapo, as utterly apolitical.[20] Even these series, however, were atypical of the era in even acknowledging the world outside the homes or offices in which they were set. The highest-rated sitcoms of the decade told family-centered stories with small problems and simple solutions.[21] Seen against that backdrop, *Get Smart*'s habit of not just acknowledging but also satirizing the real, politically fraught world made it daring and unusual.

Likewise, *Get Smart*'s forays into self-conscious absurdity were modest and infrequent by the standards of programs such as *The Monkees* (1966–68) and *Laugh In* (1968–73) that would turn them into a centerpiece only a few years later. They are, for he most part, tucked in around the edges of scenes and unremarked on by the characters witnessing them. A particularly sublime example occurs in "Bronzefinger" when Max opens the wall safe in the Chief's office and finds Agent 13 looking back at him. Left there, the scene would be one more iteration of a running gag, but it keeps escalating—sailing over the line into surrealism. "The Chief said I'd been out on field trips too long," explains 13, visibly pleased as he stares out from one of the smallest spaces he has ever inhabited, "so he gave me this nice soft office job." Max subtly acknowledges the absurdity of the Agent 13 gag for the first and only time in the series: "It's awfully small. Tell me, 13, how'd you get in there?" Matter of factly, 13 replies, "The Chief gave me the combination."[22] The world of CONTROL and KAOS is, such scenes hint, not only stranger than we realize but also perhaps stranger than we can imagine.

In this respect, *Get Smart* benefited from the fact that the work culture it set out to satirize—Cold War espionage and superpower gamesmanship—was, even in the real world, so bizarre that it perpetually teetered on the verge of satirizing itself. Max's gadgets, even after Brooks and Henry pushed them the famous "extra half-inch," often seemed to have come from the same research-and-development lab as the exploding cigars that the CIA was said to have sent to Fidel Castro. CONTROL's self-defeating efforts at internal security mirrored the increasingly byzantine efforts of real government agencies to protect "atomic secrets" and other sensitive information. "Political satire became obsolete," Tom Lehrer famously quipped, when Henry Kissinger was awarded the Nobel Peace Prize in 1973.[23] Stretching to be *more* ridiculous than the headlines was far from a new challenge for Lehrer; satirizing nuclear strategy (as he did brilliantly in songs such as "So Long, Mom" and "Who's Next?") grows difficult when the motto of the nation's nuclear strike force is "Peace Is Our Profession." Brooks and Henry spent five years in a similar dance: mining the absurdities of the Cold War for material while trying to avoid being outrun by them.

CONCLUSION

Get Smart is remembered today for the visual elements to which it repeatedly returned for comic effect—the Cone of Silence, phones hidden in everyday objects from shoes to sandwiches, the hallways full of doors, Max's oblivious bumbling, 99's long-unrequited adoration, and the impressive list of catchphrases added to the lexicon of American popular culture. "Sorry about that, Chief!" and "Missed it by *that* much!" can—particularly if delivered in an imitation of Don Adams' distinctive voice—still bring smiles of recognition from viewers who encountered the series in first run or in 1970s syndication. Lost along the way, however, is the quality that set the series conspicuously apart from other sitcoms of the era: its ceaseless and ceaselessly inventive mockery not only of spy-story conventions but also of government, mindless patriotism, the Cold War cult of secrecy, and the inanities of bureaucracy.

Embracing such mockery as its comic voice and spiking it with moments of surreal absurdity, *Get Smart* carried the irreverent spirit of sketch-based programs such as *Your Show of Shows*, *The Ernie Kovacs Show*, and *That Was The Week That Was* into the once-tame world of the situation comedy. It faded in its final season and a half as détente warmed the Cold War, the decade-long spy boom ran its course, and the marriage of Max and 99 opened the door to more conventional sitcom plots, but its mark was already made. Showing that sitcoms could be sharp-edged, satirical, and engaged with the world beyond the walls of their sets, it blazed a trail that *M*A*S*H*, *WKRP in Cincinnati*, and other series would follow in the 1970s and beyond.

NOTES

1. Michael O'Brien, *John F. Kennedy: A Life* (New York: Thomas Dunne, 2005), 793–794.

2. The *Saturday Evening Post* used the phrase on the cover of its July 17, 1965, issue, teasing a story on "The James Bond Cult."

3. On the evolution of the series see Jon Heitland, *The Man from U.N.C.L.E. Book* (New York: St. Martins, 1987), 37–64; and Wesley Britton, *Spy Television* (Westport, CT: Praeger, 2004), 35–56.

4. Britton, op. cit., 81–92, 93–98, 125–146.

5. Ibid., 64–70.

6. Susan E. Kesler, *The Wild Wild West: The Series* (Downey, CA: Arnett Press, 1988).

7. Quoted in Kyle Smith, "How Maxwell Smart and His Shoe Phone Changed TV," *Wall Street Journal*, March 21, 2008.

8. For a recap of the failures, see Carl Birkmeyer, "The Cone of Silence," *Would You Believe*, http://www.wouldyoubelieve.com/cone.html.

9. By season four, the fact that Max doesn't *know* 99's real name had become sufficiently canonical to serve as the basis for jokes. Her answering machine message says, "Hello, this is 99," her mother always calls her "Sweetie" or "Darling," and when she and Max are married, ill-timed noises blot out the sound of the minister repeating her name during the ceremony.

10. "Mister Big," *Get Smart*, pilot.

11. For the process in *The Man from U.N.C.L.E.*, see Heitland, op. cit., 175–193.

12. "Anatomy of a Lover," *Get Smart*, season two, episode one, first broadcast September 17, 1966.

13. "Casablanca," *Get Smart*, season two, episode six, first broadcast October 22, 1966.

14. "The Tooth, the Whole Tooth . . . ," *Get Smart*, season two, episode 14, first broadcast December 24, 1966.

15. Other targeted films include *The Wild One*, *Bonnie and Clyde*, *The Maltese Falcon*, and *The Prisoner of Zenda* (twice).

16. "Rub-a-Dub-Dub, Three Spies in a Sub," *Get Smart*, season two, episode nine, first broadcast November 12, 1966.

17. "Island of the Darned," *Get Smart*, season two, episode 11, first broadcast November 26, 1966.

18. "The Mild Ones," *Get Smart*, season two, episode 11, first broadcast December 9, 1967.

19. David Marc, *Comic Visions: Television Comedy and American Culture*, 2nd ed. (Hoboken, NJ: Wiley-Blackwell, 1997), 104–107.

20. Robert Shandley, *Hogan's Heroes* (Detroit: Wayne State University Press, 2011), xx. Though widely criticized for presenting the Third Reich as a troupe of comic-opera buffoons, *Hogan* was following a pattern common in serious World War II films of the era such as *The Enemy Below* (1957) and *The Great Escape* (1963) in focusing on "good Germans"—honorable, patriotic, and privately disdainful of Hitler—rather than hardcore Nazis.

21. Mary M. Dalton and Laura R. Linder, eds., *The Sitcom Reader: America Re-Viewed, Still Skewed*, 2nd ed. (Albany: State University of New York Press, 2016), 57–58.

22. "Bronzefinger," *Get Smart*, season two, episode 12, first broadcast December 3, 1966.

23. Stephen Thompson, "Interview: Tom Lehrer," *The A.V. Club*, May 24, 2000, http://www.avclub.com/article/tom-lehrer-13660.

BIBLIOGRAPHY

Britton, Wesley. *Spy Television*. Westport, CT: Praeger, 2004.

Dalton, Mary M. and Laura R. Linder, eds. *The Sitcom Reader: America Re-Viewed, Still Skewed*, 2nd ed. Albany: State University of New York Press, 2016.

Heitland, Jon. *The Man from U.N.C.L.E. Book*. New York: St. Martins, 1987.

Kesler, Susan E. *The Wild Wild West: The Series*. Downey, CA: Arnett Press, 1988.

Marc, David. *Comic Visions: Television Comedy and American Culture*, 2nd ed. Hoboken, NJ: Wiley-Blackwell, 1997.

O'Brien, Michael. *John F. Kennedy: A Life*. New York: Thomas Dunne, 2005.

Shandley, Robert. *Hogan's Heroes*. Detroit: Wayne State University Press, 2011.

Smith, Kyle. "How Maxwell Smart and His Shoe Phone Changed TV." *Wall Street Journal*, March 21, 2008.

Thompson, Stephen. "Interview: Tom Lehrer." *The A.V. Club*. May 24, 2000, http://www.avclub.com/article/tom-lehrer-13660.

PART 2

The Seventies

6

The Brady Bunch: A Thoroughly Modern Family?

Laura Westengard

"Mom always says don't play ball in the house." "Ooh! My nose!" "Marcia, Marcia, Marcia!" Somehow these mundane lines responding to everyday situations became catchphrases for a generation. The Brady Bunch (1969–1974) introduced Americans to something they had never seen on television before but was becoming increasingly common in society—the blended family. In "The Brady Bunch: A Thoroughly Modern Family?" Laura Westengard argues that the blended Brady household offered America something it needed during the tumultuous years of the late 1960s and early 1970s. It provided a reflection of some of the social change going on while never pushing viewers too far outside of their comfort zones. Its hipness factor was only overshadowed by its ultimate traditionalism.

In *Our Vampires, Ourselves*, scholar Nina Auerbach explains that every age embraces the vampires it needs.[1] In other words, vampires as metaphors appear and reappear throughout the centuries in various forms and with shifting meanings in response to the cultural fantasies, anxieties, and desires circulating in the public consciousness at the time. This makes the vampire metaphor simultaneously conservative and thoroughly modern as the metaphor plays with both the fear and the excitement generated by change. Bram Stoker's *Dracula*, for example, features the possibilities of technological innovation—from scientific vampire hunting to the recording devices used to track and transcribe the action throughout—and the threats of social change, including Eastern European immigration into cosmopolitan centers such as London. I would like to extend Auerbach's assertion to reflect on the world of sitcoms. In situation comedies, there is also an ever-present figure, a recurring trope. It is often cast simultaneously as the epitome of tradition and at the cutting edge of the social and political issues of the day, and its treatment reflects the public's conflicted reaction to change. I am talking about the family. In sitcoms, every decade embraces the family it needs.

The 1950s saw the peak of Cold War "containment culture" in which U.S. foreign policy aimed at containing the spread of communism filtered into the streets of suburban America via the "cult of domesticity," which resulted in "strictly censored television programming, the drop in average marriage age, the suburban housing development, the public elaboration of dating etiquette, and the rigidly constrictive and restrictive structure of female undergarments."[2] The 1950s had the Cleaver family from *Leave It to Beaver*, a vision of perfectly contained domesticity as a reflection of Western democratic values—the white picket fence in the suburbs, two kids, a working dad and stay-at-home mom, and the home featuring all the latest postwar domestic technologies.

Skipping the 1960s for a moment, the 1970s saw the increasing visibility of rights-based and environmental movements, and anti–Vietnam War protests were raging at the beginning of the decade. The 1970s had the Bunkers from *All in the Family*, their living room serving as a microcosm of shifting ideas and generational divide. Archie Bunker's old-fashioned ideas simultaneously gave voice to a kind of throwback sexism and racism while creating a platform for highlighting the most cutting-edge and controversial issues of the day even in the family itself, which includes his liberal, "with it" daughter and son-in-law, Gloria and Michael Stivic.

The 1980s was a decade of yuppies and Reagan-era economics. The yuppie narrative imagines that the hippies and protesters of the 1970s have settled down to become the upwardly mobile beneficiaries of the American Dream, working hard at corporate jobs to become successful no matter their race, class origins, or previous involvement in radical movements. They bought houses and Audis. The 1980s had the Cosbys from *The Cosby Show*, a wealthy African American family living in an upscale Brooklyn home with a physician father and lawyer mother. This family signaled racial progress in the new "color-blind" era while reflecting normative, bourgeois ideals.

The 1990s brought in the era of increasing popular awareness of gay and lesbian lifestyles and, with the advent of the Internet and e-mail, increasing access to networked community outside of the nuclear family. An alienated teen, once confined to the isolation of the suburban bedroom, could now log on to find others like them in chat rooms, expanding ideas around the possibilities of connection beyond the family and town one was born into. The 1990s brought us a relatively new phenomenon, the chosen families from *Friends* and *Seinfeld*. Both shows offered a core community of friends who serve as family, the living room replaced by the urban coffee shop. The intimacy of the two-parent household is replaced by a central pool of intimate friends and lovers who listen to your woes at the end of a workday, drive you to the doctor, discuss your love life, and sometimes participate in it. These chosen families work to redefine the understanding of family while often also erasing the race and class complexities of urban existence. The irony of this is that the shows can usher unsuspecting viewers into an unremarked-upon world of segregation and financial freedom that actually mirrors the *Beaver* suburbs more than the progressive urban values they outwardly proclaim. The family may have changed in terms of DNA, but it remains remarkably consistent, conservative, and bourgeois.

The 2000s extended the advent of the Internet into the age of social media and the infiltration of product placement into our most intimate spaces via smartphones, laptops, and tablets. Marketers have always been part of the sitcom experience, but the 2000s brought a level of data tracking and targeted commercial content to a height never before seen. The last part of the first decade brought us the Delgado-Prichett, Tucker-Prichett, and Dunphy families from *Modern Family*. The Dunphys interact explicitly with social media technologies (mom joins Facebook and embarrasses children) and product placement (dad wants nothing more than the new iPad for his birthday). These families, still creatures of the *Beaver* suburbs, approached the intrusive new world of data collection and commercial surveillance with comfort and even excitement.

Now for the 1960s. I would like to position the Bradys from *The Brady Bunch* as the family that television needed during that decade, though it actually ran from the tumultuous turn of the late 1960s into the early 1970s. *The Brady Bunch*, created by Sherwood Schwartz, first aired on September 26th, 1969, with an episode titled "The Honeymoon."[3] In the summer that preceded the first episode, Nixon withdrew 25,000 troops from Vietnam, a group of mostly transgender women of color fought back against police persecution in the Stonewall riots to spark the gay liberation movement, Apollo 11 landed on the moon, Muhammad Ali was convicted of dodging the draft, thousands gathered for a music festival in Woodstock, and the most famous "family" on the television was the one headed by murderous mastermind Charles Manson.[4] In that summer alone, the world seemed to have shifted. With the countercultural revolution, antiwar movement, and civil rights struggles, the late 1960s and early 1970s saw huge changes to values around family and domesticity.

The Brady Bunch entered into a cultural moment of social upheaval and purported to offer a thoroughly "modern" family, the blended one, but still occupying the older *Beaver* suburban backdrop that haunts sitcoms to this day. It was just modern enough to represent the changes to domestic life in an era when divorce rates were on the rise and new family structures were becoming unavoidable.[5] However, in the classic sitcom tradition that we see again and again, *The Brady Bunch* only pushed so far. "The Honeymoon" features the marriage of Mike Brady (Robert Reed) and Carol Martin (Florence Henderson). They each come to the altar with three children. Since his wife's death, Mike has been caring for his three sons Greg (Barry Williams), Peter (Christopher Knight), and Bobby (Mike Lookinland) with the help of live-in housekeeper Alice Nelson (Ann B. Davis). Carol, it seems, has been living at her parents' home with daughters Marsha (Maureen McCormick), Jan (Eve Plumb), and Cindy (Susan Olsen).

The series strongly implies that both Mike and Carol are single by virtue of being widowed, but only Mike's status as widower is confirmed. Carol's marital history is left a bit more ambiguous. In developing the concept, Schwartz considered the possibility that either of them might have been divorced rather than widowed, but "at the time the 'D' word wasn't an option on television," so he left the interpretation of Carol's past "open" (however, viewers have overwhelmingly assumed that both Carol and Mike were widowed).[6]

Propriety was central in the minds of sitcom writers and creators as censorship standards were stringent for what exactly could be depicted on television. The studios employed teams (at Paramount Studios they were called "program practices") to counsel writers on any "suggestive themes and words" that writers should avoid to bypass inspection by the censors, especially during the 1950s and 1960s.[7] For example, during Lucy's pregnancy on *I Love Lucy*, the show was not allowed to say the word "pregnant," *Gilligan's Island* and *I Dream of Jeannie* were barred from featuring the actresses' navels, married couples always slept in separate twin beds, and the toilet was a constant concern. CBS actually pulled the first episode of *Leave It to Beaver* in 1957 because it featured a toilet, eventually allowing the episode to air only if it showed the toilet tank only.[8] This stricture plays out in *The Brady Bunch* as well. Mike Brady, an architect, designs the house for his new family with one room for the three boys to share, one room for the three girls to share, and a single shared bathroom—notably, with no toilet to be seen.[9]

The concept for the show was ripped from the headlines of the 1960s and intentionally designed to be a cutting-edge piece of social commentary. Schwartz explains that he was struck with the idea for a show about a blended family after reading a 1966 headline in the *Los Angeles Times*: "In the year 1965, more than 29 percent of all marriages included a child or children from a previous marriage."[10] He nearly ran to the Writers Guild to register his idea, sensing that he was tapping into something relevant and resonant for viewers. Throughout its run, the show engaged with the language and issues of its time but never in ways that pushed viewers (or networks) beyond their comfort zones. In fact, it was difficult for Schwartz to sell the pilot for the series, originally called *Yours and Mine*. After shopping his script to CBS, ABC, and NBC, Schwartz sat on the concept for several years, and only when a movie with a similar premise and title (*Yours, Mine and Ours* with Lucille Ball and Henry Fonda, 1968) demonstrated the public's readiness for the blended family concept and its potential for financial success that Schwartz finally landed a contract with ABC. A second similar film success also in 1968, *With Six You Get Eggroll* starring Doris Day and Brian Keith had cemented the decision. Significantly, both movies focused as much on the romance as on the subsequent family building that would be at the center of the television show.

The financial conservatism at the heart of the network hesitation to produce the show is reflected in the ultimate conservatism of the show itself, even though it features a cutting-edge concept at its core. "The Honeymoon" doesn't dare mention the "'D' word," and though its title foregrounds the postmarriage consummation, the episode works to prioritize family over sexuality. As Mike and Carol check into their honeymoon suite at the hotel following a chaotic wedding scene, they have their first encounter with someone judging their familial structure and, by extension, policing their sexuality. After giving Mr. Brady an insinuating look regarding the honeymoon suite and asking him to sign the guestbook, the front desk clerk, Mr. Pringle, exclaims in confusion, "Uh uh uh uh oh, Mr. Brady. You have signed this Mr. and Mrs. Brady *and family*!"

> **Mike:** I forgot. It's force of habit. The kids aren't with us.
>
> **Mr. Pringle:** Well, you *did* ask for the honeymoon suite?
>
> **Carol:** Oh, it's quite alright Mr. Pringle. You see . . .
>
> **Mike:** It's alright darling. There is no need to explain. It's obvious this gentleman doesn't dig the modern generation.

In a marked shift from his earlier google-eyed insinuations, Mr. Pringle now averts his eyes from the unconventional couple for the remainder of the scene. This interaction is tinged with implied non-normative sexuality (or at least non-normative sexual *temporality*) and is designed to make Mr. Pringle look like a fool for misunderstanding the Bradys' "modern" arrangement. However, following the television practices of the time, the show does not allow sex to take center stage for long. As Mike and Carol enjoy their suite and a romantic room service dinner for two, their intimate time is overshadowed with concern for the children until they finally give in to their parental instincts:

Carol: You know the answer as well as I do.

Mike: Let's go.

Carol: Like this?

Mike: It's an emergency!

They proceed to rush out of the hotel in their nightclothes, gather the children, pets, and housekeeper, and usher them all back to the honeymoon suite.

In its comedic climax, the show shifts focus from sexual consummation to family communion and thereby places itself on the forefront of late-1960s family dynamics while consciously averting its eyes from the unsavory causes (divorce) and results (nontraditional sexual practices) of the blended family. In this way, it successfully walks the fine line between cultural evolution and suburban conservatism.

Similarly, *The Brady Bunch* integrates other issues of its time in ways that perform progressiveness while ultimately remaining traditional. In "The Liberation of Marsha Brady," (season two, episode 19), a television crew visits Marsha's middle school to ask young women their opinion on the women's liberation movement. Marsha, when asked if she is "for" women's liberation, appears to have never considered the question before.[11] She tentatively says "I guess I am" but ends the interview with a much stronger statement about how girls "certainly should" do something about being put down simply for being girls, a statement that she immediately regrets once she realizes the repercussions she will face from her brothers when she gets home.

Her interview sparks conversations and conflicts about gender equality throughout the household and eventually prompts Marsha to apply to join the Frontier Scouts, a troupe similar to the Boy Scouts in which Greg is a member and Mike is a leader. After determining there is nothing in the manual that explicitly forbids girls from joining the group, the leaders allow Marsha to attempt a series of initiation field tests. Greg, of course, as a stereotypical boy of the time, has determined to sabotage her each step of the way. Despite the uphill battle, she passes the field tests, leaving viewers not only with the language of "women's liberation" and some simplified statements about its causes but also with a lesson about how women are capable of overcoming challenges via sheer tenacity and determination, a lesson whose importance has never diminished.

As with "The Honeymoon," however, the end of the episode drastically undermines any progressive politics then at work. Just before the initiation ceremony, Marsha announces that she will not be attending. She explains,

"Chopping and tracking is nice, I guess. If you're a boy. It really is! I just wanted to prove to myself that I could do it even though I'm a girl." Now that she had done that, she admitted that she had no interest in actually joining the Scouts. Instead, she turns to Carol and asks if the "new fashion magazine" had arrived yet, and the two run upstairs together to enjoy some feminine bonding time while Greg and Mike leave the house together to attend their Scouts meeting, musing about the fickleness of women.

The subversion of norms sparked by the episode's opening scene allows the show to position itself as cutting edge and address the issues raised by "women's lib." Ultimately, however, its conservative values around gender are reestablished with a comforting return to normative gender stereotypes, including a spatial punctuation in which the women retreat deeper into the domestic space and the men make their way out into the larger world.

Indeed, gender conflict drives many of the episode plotlines, resulting in a pervasive "sexist subtext" that was "often hidden beneath an egalitarian façade."[12] Notably, however, the show generally avoids integrating issues of race or the language of civil rights or other race-based movements. Schwartz deliberately cast a white housekeeper, not because he wanted to maintain an all-white cast, but because he "thought minorities had been typecast long enough" and "wanted to cast someone away from those usual stereotypes."[13] This reasoning did not extend, of course, to the casting of a minority in any other major role in the show, which remained exclusively white until its final season. With "Kelly's Kids" (season five, episode 14), the show begins to incorporate a storyline in which friends and neighbors, Ken and Kathy Kelly, decide to adopt Matt, a blonde-haired, blue-eyed eight-year-old boy.[14] By the end of the episode, they decide to also adopt his two friends from the Terrace Adoption Home, Dwayne and Steve. When the Kellys visit the home to begin the new adoptions, they give each other brief, surprised glances when they first meet the boys on the playground and discover that they are African American and Asian American. Rather than discuss the realities of establishing a racially mixed family and its potential impact on the boys, they demonstrate their progressiveness by foregrounding gender commonality over racial difference. They rush to Mike and Carol Brady for advice on their situation:

> **Ken:** The fact that Dwayne is black and Steve is Oriental surprised us a little bit at first but what difference does that really make?
>
> **Kathy:** After all, a boy is a boy is a boy whether he is white or black or yellow or blue!

Like "The Honeymoon," the episode features a minor character who represents those who "don't dig the modern generation." Neighbor, Mrs. Payne, attempts to play the "I'm not racist but . . ." card, but it is obvious that she is offended by her new racially diverse neighbors:

Mrs. Payne: Mr. Kelly, I see you now have several children.

Ken: Three, all together.

Mrs. Payne: Of various colors, one might say.

Ken: You just did.

Mrs. Payne: Mind you, I'm not a bigot. I believe that black and yellows, everybody has a place in our society. Why, Mr. Payne and I even manage to be cordial to the Shapiros on the next block.

Ken: That's very generous of you.

Mrs. Payne: We try. Nevertheless, three small boys are apt to be destructive, especially the minorities.

The inclusion of the racist neighbor serves as a foil to the Kellys and the Bradys to position them as progressive in their views on family and race. However, the show reverts to gender stereotypes ("a boy is a boy is a boy") in deflecting any racist impulses on the part of the Kellys (remember, out of all the children at the racially diverse adoption home, Ken and Kathy's *first* choice was the blonde-haired, blue-eyed white boy).

Viewers may have picked up on the insidious racist and sexist messages of the show to varying degrees, but that didn't necessarily stop them from tuning in. Filmmaker Spike Lee, himself a child of the 1960s, makes this point in his 1994 movie *Crooklyn* about growing up in Brooklyn, New York, in the 1970s. The African American children in the movie can sing along to the theme of *The Brady Bunch* as well as any white kids. In an interview with Roger Ebert, Lee recalls his own childhood:

> In our house when we were growing up, we only had one television. We weren't allowed to watch television on school nights. So Friday nights came around, and the Knicks were usually on Channel 9. They were on against the Partridge Family and the Brady Bunch and what was on the TV was decided by a vote. So I tried to lobby with my brothers and sister: 'I'll give you a piece of candy. I'll give you a dollar. Just let me watch the game!' I always got outvoted and we had to watch those shows.[15]

Lee's reluctance to watch the Brady and Partridge families lost out to the desires of his family members, implying that however white the show may have been, some of its viewers of color were willing to accept a lack of racial representation and others were more critical of the show's de facto segregation.

Eventually, the show's creators realized that they could tap into a previously ignored demographic if they incorporated storylines that explicitly addressed race in the way their past storylines had addressed gender. It seemed that racial narratives and characters of color had the potential to extend the show's relevance. By 1974, the show's original blended family had been normalized in American culture and was no longer breaking boundaries in the same way as when the show premiered in 1969, and the inclusion of a *racially* blended family was what the show's creators felt they needed to get back to the forefront. However, neither the Kelly kids, nor any other major character of color, are ever meaningfully integrated into the series (they never appear again after the "Kelly's Kids" episode). Schwartz mentions that they featured this new kind of blended family on the show in an attempt to create a spinoff called *The Kelly Kids*, but he doesn't reflect on why that spinoff was never picked up.[16] Perhaps advertisers still saw people of color as simply adjuncts to their primary, and white, audiences.

Culturally, why weren't the Kellys the family America needed in the mid-1970s? After the Bradys appeared as the first blended family on television, the 1970s featured other nontraditional family structures, including the divorced single-parent household of *One Day at a Time* (1975) and, finally, the interracial adoption of *Diff'rent Strokes* (1978). Presumably, *The Brady Bunch* opened the door for these shows to appear as television continued to push the definition of "family" throughout the 1970s, but there was no real proliferation of imaginative family structures even though they existed. Perhaps *The Kelly Kids* pushed a little too hard or didn't simultaneously return to tradition firmly enough. The country may not have been quite ready to accept an adorable racially blended family in 1974; even when *Diff'rent Strokes* made it to the air in 1978, it relied on a narrative of class-based charity to smooth out the discomfort of the interracial household (millionaire Philip Drummond adopts his housekeeper's children when she dies and moves them from their home in Harlem to his to give them a better life). It seems that *The Brady Bunch's* particular blend of gentle hipness and ultimate conservatism was what the viewers needed to see in those years of historical upheaval—and even through its syndication in the 1980s and 1990s.

The Bradys have continued to occupy a prominent place in the popular imagination since their original run from 1969 to 1974, even gaining popularity in the 1980s. The 1990s and 2000s saw a new relationship with the Brady family. Although they were certainly popular (feature films *The Brady Bunch Movie* and *A Very Brady Sequel* were released in 1995 and 1996, respectively), as Mimi Marinucci points out, its continuing cultural presence was primarily sustained via the ironic lens of Generation X. In other words, by the 1990s the Bradys had become satire, now representing the laughably saccharine innocence of a past generation rather than the new frontier of family.

With each decade, fresh modern families are taking the Bradys' place, almost always offering viewers a similar blend of cutting-edge content and comforting traditionalism and, of course, giving viewers the families they need to help navigate the fears and fantasies of their own time and place.

NOTES

1. Nina Auerbach, *Our Vampires, Ourselves* (Chicago: University of Chicago Press, 1995).

2. Alan Nadel, *Containment Culture: American Narratives, Postmodernism, and the Atomic Age* (Durham, NC: Duke University Press, 1995), 117.

3. Sherwood Schwartz, "The Honeymoon," season one, episode one, directed by John Rich.

4. "1969: An Eventful Summer." CNN.com, http://www.cnn.com/2009/US/08/09/summer.1969.timeline/index.html?_s=PM:US.

5. Ana Swanson, "144 Years of Marriage and Divorce in the United States, in One Chart." *Washington Post*, June 23, 2015, https://www.washingtonpost.com/news/wonk/wp/2015/06/23/144-years-of-marriage-and-divorce-in-the-united-states-in-one-chart/?utm_term=.eaf570e52d31. Accessed April 19, 2017.

6. Sherwood Schwartz and Lloyd J. Schwartz, *Brady, Brady, Brady: The Complete Story of* The Brady Bunch *as Told by the Father/Son Team Who Really Know* (Philadelphia: Running Press, 2010), 24–25.

7. Ibid., 125–126.

8. Ian Lendler, "A Timeline of TV Censorship." CNN.com, http://www.cnn.com/2007/LIVING/wayoflife/07/31/censorship/.

9. Schwartz and Schwartz, op. cit., 107.

10. Ibid., 16.

11. Sherwood Schwartz and Charles Hoffman, "The Liberation of Marsha Brady," season two, episode 19, directed by Russ Mayberry; aired February 12, 1971.

12. Mimi Marinucci, "Television, Generation X, and Third Wave Feminism: A Contextual Analysis of *The Brady Bunch*," *Journal of Popular Culture* 38 (2005), 505–524. doi:10.1111/j.0022-3840.2005.00126.x

13. Schwartz and Schwartz, op. cit., 61.

14. Sherwood Schwartz, "Kelly's Kids," season five, episode 14, directed by Richard Michaels; aired January 4, 1974.

15. Roger Ebert, "A Family Tree Grows in Spike Lee's 'Crooklyn,'" *Interviews*, August 5, 1994, http://www.rogerebert.com/interviews/a-family-tree-grows-in-spike-lees-crooklyn.

16. Schwartz and Schwartz, op. cit., 159.

BIBLIOGRAPHY

Auerbach, Nina. *Our Vampires, Ourselves.* Chicago: University of Chicago Press, 1995.

Ebert, Roger. "A Family Tree Grows in Spike Lee's 'Crooklyn.'" *Interviews*, August 5, 1994.

Lendler, Ian. "A Timeline of TV Censorship." CNN.com, http://www.cnn.com/2007/LIVING/wayoflife/07/31/censorship/. Accessed April 23, 2017.

Marinucci, Mimi. "Television, Generation X, and Third Wave Feminism: A Contextual Analysis of *The Brady Bunch.*" *Journal of Popular Culture* 38 (2005), 505–524.

Nadel, Alan. *Containment Culture: American Narratives, Postmodernism, and the Atomic Age.* Durham: Duke University Press, 1995.

"1969: An Eventful Summer" CNN.com, http://www.cnn.com/2007/LIVING /wayoflife/07/31/censorship/. Accessed April 19, 2017.

Schwartz, Sherwood, and Lloyd J. Schwartz. *Brady, Brady, Brady: The Complete Story of* The Brady Bunch *as Told by the Father/Son Team Who Really Know.* Philadelphia: Running Press, 2010.

Swanson, Ana. "144 Years of Marriage and Divorce in the United States, in One Chart." *Washington Post.* June 23, 2015, https://www.washingtonpost.com /news/wonk/wp/2015/06/23/144-years-of-marriage-and-divorce-in-the -united-states-in-one-chart/?utm_term=.ca36e5c04b27.

7

All in the Family: A Sitcom about a Changing America That Changed America

Martin Kich

When All in the Family (1971–1979) *first appeared, American sitcom audiences had seen nothing like it. Perhaps only Ralph Kramden of* The Honeymooners *had presented the combination of likability and distaste that Archie Bunker brought to television. Since then, of course, we've watched many such characters, including Al Bundy in* Married . . . with Children, Homer Simpson *in* The Simpson's, *and Frank Underwood in the more serious recent drama of* House of Cards. *Bunker took Kramden into the political realm (something reversed in Bundy's and Simpson's case), helping set the stage for Underwood—and, as Martin Kich alludes in the following chapter, even for the success of Donald Trump.* All in the Family *burst a sitcom dam of pent-up frustration against network constraints; the flood that followed became stronger every year to the point that now almost anything goes—even on the networks, which remain the most timid venues of American television.*

All in the Family is not simply one of the most influential situation comedies in the history of American television. It remains one of the most influential shows of any type ever broadcast on American mass media. It is not an exaggeration to say that the programming that followed was considerably different from the programming that preceded. After *All in the Family*,

American television became less predictably a medium that reinforced mainstream American values and celebrated cultural continuity and became a medium that more often questioned ingrained, reflexive cultural assumptions and accommodated divergent cultural perspectives. On the most obvious level, *All in the Family* made the treatment of divisive political, socioeconomic, and cultural issues not just an element but the central and driving element of the entertainment that it provided. Moreover, the characters talked about those issues as "real people in the real world" often talked about them. Although current cable programming that shows no concern with censoring obscenities owes its existence to the success of *All in the Family*, that programming highlights, in retrospect, the considerable constraints on the Bunkers' "real talk" and the overstatement in critical assertions about the degree to which the show represented a coarsening of American popular culture that has proved extremely damaging.

In an article written for the *Journal of Popular Culture*, Dennis E. Showalter assesses the continuing significance of *All in the Family* that is neither exhaustive nor current but remains highly suggestive:

> Whether originally developed as spinoffs, counterattacks, or imitations, programs such as *Maude* and *The Jeffersons*, *Sanford and Son* and *Lotsa Luck*, *Hot L Baltimore* and *Chico and The Man*, are all part of Archie's extended family. And if discussion of the series' message and meaning no longer occupies a prominent place in the media's entertainment columns, *All in the Family* continues to attract attention from other sources. It is presented as a source of pop theology, with Edith as a "little Christ." It has been linked with classical drama, with Mike described as "descending from the glutton figure of the Greco-Roman stage." It is even the subject of at least two doctoral dissertations.[1]

Although *All in the Family* has long been regarded as a landmark series in the history of American television, it was not an immediate favorite of either critics or television audiences. In an article for *The New York Times* in which he reported that the series had risen to the top of the Nielsen rankings, George Gent includes the following description of its initial reception:

> [*All in the Family* has] outranked such longtime favorites as *Marcus Welby, M.D.*, *Laugh-In*, *Bonanza*, *Gunsmoke*, and Lucille Ball. After its strong showing in the Emmys, its high ratings might seem inevitable, but it did not look that way when the series was introduced to viewers last January.
>
> [It] opened to a mixed critical reception, with some East Coast reviewers dismissing the program as unfunny and as a potential contributor to the bigotry it was supposedly spoofing. Many of these same critics later had second thoughts.
>
> Nevertheless, the series got off to a slow start, ranking 55th in the Nielsens after its first week and not moving higher than 46th until mid-March, when it fell back into the 50s again. It was not until mid-April that

the program—spurred by word-of-mouth recommendations by viewers—began to climb, with a sudden spurt into the 14th position.[2]

Less than four months later, Laura Hobson cited the outpouring of praise being directed toward the show by television critics such as Cleveland Amory, Tom Mackin, Norman Dresser, and Jack Gould. Writing for *TV Guide*, Amory had proclaimed that *All in the Family* was "'not just the best-written, best-directed, and best-acted show on television'" but absolutely "'the best show on television.'"[3] Then Hobson cited critics such as John Leonard, Fred Ferretti, Stephanie Harrington, and Whitney Young Jr. who had previewed or provided early reviews of the show and dismissed it as a gratuitous exercise in showcasing bigotry that was as unsavory as it was unfunny.

Clearly, the elements of *All in the Family* that provided its "shock value" were a significant cause of the network's reluctance to promote the show as enthusiastically as it might have and an equally significant reason for the almost unprecedented word-of-mouth increase in viewership. Many viewers sought out the show simply to hear Archie freely use ethnic slurs such as "Mick," "Dago," and "Hebe." Lenny Bruce's provocative use of obscenities in his stand-up routines as a First Amendment test, recounted in part in his autobiography *How to Talk Dirty and Influence People*, and George Carlin's stand-up routine "Seven Words That You Can Never Say on Television" provide a sort of cultural bracket around *All in the Family*'s introduction of "offensive" language to network programming. Bruce and Carlin both faced criminal prosecution for their on-stage use of sexual obscenities, but Bruce also included ethnic and racial slurs in his stand-up routines, and Richard Pryor then began to "appropriate" racial slurs in his stand-up routines and recordings. So, *All in the Family* can be seen as a salient event in a broader cultural and political effort to challenge the concept of "bad language" and to shift the focus to the objectionable assumptions, viewpoints, and actions that were permitted to flourish behind the social façade of maintaining decorum and civility.

Nonetheless, just as *All in the Family* would never have gotten on the air if it were as bluntly "offensive" as the stand-up routines of Bruce, Carlin, or Pryor, it would not have remained popular if the only level, or the primary level, on which it engaged its audience was its shock value. The series has earned its place as a landmark in American television history because of its historical timing and its ensemble cast. It is more than a little ironic that a series that seemed so completely American actually had its model in the British series *Till Death Do Us Part*. Moreover, *All in the Family* almost certainly would not have resonated had it aired five years earlier or five to 10 years later. In the late 1960s, the dreamy disengagement of the hippies, the "Flower Children," had given way to political radicalism, embodied by groups such as the Yippies. The disillusionment that drove the growing radicalism had, of course, several converging causes: the escalation of the Vietnam War and the resulting political unrest, particularly on college campuses; the assassinations of political leaders with a special significance for the young; the shift from the nonviolent resistance that had characterized the civil rights movement to the assertion of black nationalism by groups such as the Black Panthers; and the emergence of the feminist and gay rights movements. By the late 1970s, this political radicalism would dissipate, dissolving into the materialism associated with the upwardly mobile, young, urban professionals—the "yuppies" of the early 1980s. So when Michael Stivic begins dating and then marries Gloria Bunker, the result is not just a generational conflict—a representation of the so-called generation gap that defined largely generational disagreements over political, socioeconomic, and cultural issues in the 1960s and 1970s. Nor is it just a confrontation between increasingly anachronistic "conventional" or "traditional" American values and the mainstreaming of the values associated with the "counterculture"—such as opposition to the Vietnam War and the assertion of civil rights, women's rights, and gay rights. Nor is it just a confrontation between working-class parochialism and a college-educated worldview. It is all of those things at once at the historical moment when all of these tensions converged to create a sense of national crisis that was increasingly framed as a cultural cataclysm.

In itself, the setting of *All in the Family* provides a highly ironic but banal counterpoint to the broader convulsive events that are frequently referred to in the conversations that occur there. As in *The Honeymooners*, most of the action in *All in the Family*, especially in the first four or five seasons, occurs in the room just inside the Bunkers' front door. In this case, however, the room is not the kitchen but a combination living room and dining room, with the door to the kitchen at the opposite end of the room from the front door. Compared to the Kramdens' small apartment in Brooklyn, the Bunkers' house is spacious but still quite modest by broader standards. At the center of the room is Archie's chair. This chair is not only the cause of recurring comic moments as various individuals sit in the chair—either because they don't know what a major faux pas doing so is in Archie's eyes or, in a distracted moment, they simply forget—but also and more important the chair is the focal point for most of the action that occurs. In addition, although the camera only rarely ascends the stairs to the second story of the Bunkers' house, another recurring comic motif is Archie's ascension of the stairs to the bathroom, with the sound of the flushing toilet, in effect, announcing his imminent descent of the stairs and return from one "throne" to another.

Because of Archie's name-calling—most notably, his recurring references to Edith as "Dingbat" and to Michael as "Meathead"—it might be easy to overlook the carefully calibrated characteristics of the four main characters and the dramatic balance achieved through the complex ways they play off each other.

The relationship between Archie and Edith is certainly much more nuanced than it might seem. Archie's reflexive expressions of his bigotry have a parallel in his sometimes merciless derision of his wife, but most of it goes right past Edith. One might think that she is simply too slow-witted to recognize the insults, but that would mean accepting Archie's caricaturing of her, which Archie himself does not really believe. Edith has long accommodated Archie's less attractive traits, having decided that he is a good husband and a good man at heart, and has focused on being as devoted a wife and a mother as she can be. By those measures, however anachronistic they now seem and may have seemed even in the 1970s, especially to younger viewers, Edith is actually a better wife than Archie is a husband, something that he himself recognizes and admits in less guarded moments. Moreover, as the series develops, Edith emerges as someone capable of transcending her husband's bigotry, of accepting a variety of neighbors and other acquaintances for who rather than what they are. In a few instances, she even directly confronts Archie about his behavior and attitudes and forces him to back down. Some of this reflects her gradual evolution as a person and her response to changing times, but she never really changes as much as the world is changing around her and her family, and she never ultimately rejects her husband or the roles that she has assumed to sustain their family.

Although Michael and Gloria have fewer pointed conflicts and relatively fewer recurring surface tensions in their marriage, their relationship is actually more fragile than Archie and Edith's relationship, and not simply because they are much younger and have less shared history. Despite her attraction to Michael and her embrace of his progressive outlook, Gloria remains true to her roots—that is, she remains at heart quite attached to her blue-collar cultural background. In effect, she adopts many facets of Michael's political outlook but does not have the benefit of the experience that has informed his outlook. For awhile, she and Michael can navigate the differences in their perspectives, but those differences become more pronounced as he finishes his PhD and then succeeds in finding an academic position. With their new baby, Michael and Gloria leave Archie and Edith behind. Even before they leave, however, Michael and Gloria have been trying to address the strains in their relationship, and it is not surprising that they decide to divorce not all that long after they relocate.

Although the two marriages are critical to the dynamic in the Bunker household, at the core of that dynamic is the relationship between Archie and Michael. That Gloria and especially Edith remain genuinely interesting characters is a tribute to the show's writers. Despite enduringly powerful episodes such as the one treating Edith being attacked by a serial rapist, the show reflects Archie's blatant sexual chauvinism and Michael's more subtle manifestations of it. Although the female characters are certainly more than background figures, for the most part, they do not dominate the foreground. So, in this sense, the show is itself a representation of the sexual chauvinism that it was in other ways vigorously critiquing. In any case, it is significant that although Michael is more educated than everyone else in the household, he also comes from a blue-collar background. He does not come across as a bookworm and doesn't even look particularly studious. In fact, despite his beard, his somewhat longer hair, and his tie-dye T-shirts, he seems much more physically imposing than any stereotype of a hippie. Even more important, as he attends graduate school, he and Gloria are dependent on Archie financially, and although Michael bristles at Archie's continual snide references to that dependence, Michael's resentment is mitigated to a considerable extent by his self-consciousness about being so dependent and, underlying everything else, his genuine gratitude to Archie. On the other hand, Archie ultimately exhibits some pride in Michael's accomplishments, though it is subsumed under the realization that Michael, Gloria, and the baby will not only be moving out but also moving away.

Unlike many other situational comedies, *All in the Family* had a built-in limit on its longevity. Michael could not remain in graduate school forever (though seven years may actually be on the short side of the average time it takes for most graduate students to complete both a master's and a doctoral degree), and as soon as he found a job, he and Gloria would not only be moving out but also, and more important, no longer be financially dependent on Archie. And because of the historical moment to which the series was such a provocative response, the dilution of the tension in the relationship between Archie and Michael could not really be made up by simply introducing other characters and new conflicts. The generational tensions that marked the historical period were layered onto the hostility between father-in-law and son-in-law, and the family unit was too small to make additions and shift the points of tension in a manner that would not seem contrived. This absence of the core tension became apparent after Rob Reiner and Sally Struthers left the show. By the time Jean Stapleton left several seasons later, the show was clearly a shell of its former self. Because so little of the "family" remained, the series was renamed *Archie Bunker's Place*, and Archie was transformed from a loudmouthed bigot into a more subdued if crotchety widower raising his grandniece, Stephanie. Notably, at this point in the history of the series, the bar competes with and then arguably replaces the living room as the focal setting.

The dilemma confronting the creators of *All in the Family* also confronted the creators of other situation comedies of the period, all of which suffered as some characters left and alternate characters were introduced. Consider how the impact of *M.A.S.H.* was diluted by the substitution of Sherman Potter for Henry Blake, Charles Emerson Winchester for Frank

Burns, and B. J. Hunnicutt for Trapper John McIntyre. In each case, subversive eccentricity was replaced by idiosyncratic normality. The series effectively reverted in many ways to the "safety" of the genre's formulas established in the 1950s and 1960s. Max Klinger even stopped wearing dresses and, in replacing Radar O'Reilly as the company clerk, became a fairly ordinary GI from an ethnic background. Likewise, the shift from the living room of *All in the Family* to the bar of *Archie's Place* may simply have reflected the recognition that once everyone but Archie had left the Bunker home, it was hard to repopulate it. But it may have also reflected the shift toward entrepreneurship that would mark the Reagan era. (There is a parallel shift in John Updike's Rabbit Angstrom novels between *Rabbit Redux* and *Rabbit Is Rich*.)

What happens to the Bunker household and even what happens to Archie himself may be natural and even predictable, but it does not make for compelling comedy. In a recent interview, Norman Lear acknowledged again that Carroll O'Connor could not have been less like Archie Bunker.[4] Perhaps as Carroll O'Connor became increasingly the series' sole focal point, he had the writers move the personality of the character that he was playing gradually closer to his own personality. Indeed, in the subsequent long-running series in which he starred, *In the Heat of the Night*, O'Connor refashioned the volatile, bigoted white sheriff played by Rod Steiger in the film into a model of self-control, fairness, and open-mindedness. So, in some ways, the later character can be seen as an extension of the Archie Bunker that O'Connor ultimately ended up portraying.

I would like to come full circle back to Laura Hobson's article, which I discussed at the beginning of this article. Recall that Hobson cited a significant number of prominent critics who had initially dismissed the show as a gratuitous exercise in highlighting offensive language and attitudes before many of them reappraised the show and reversed those opinions— as well as a few critics who proved to be ahead of the curve and praised the show from the start. Hobson cited those opinions not to take one side or the other or to find some middle ground between them. Rather, she was framing a distinctly different argument about the show—namely, that its treatment of bigotry was too restrained: "Hebe, spade, spic, coon, Polack— these are the words that it's central character, Archie Bunker, is forever using, plus endless variations, like jungle bunnies, black beauties, the chosen people, yenta, gook, chink, spook, and so on. Quite a splashing display of bigotry, ... but nowhere near enough of it."[5] Indeed, although Archie Bunker relentlessly and thoughtlessly tosses off ethnic and racial slurs, Hobson is acutely perceptive in emphasizing that however shocking that language might have been to a network television audience—because they were hearing it on network television—it was mild in comparison to that likely heard by people in their own workplaces, neighborhoods, and homes.

In essence, Hobson is arguing that the ugliness of racism and other igno-ble "isms" cannot be fully understood and effectively opposed if sanitized and made seemingly benign by caricature. Indeed, in most contexts, the ethnic and racial slur words are themselves not the ugliest expressions of ethnic and racial prejudice. More often than not, that prejudice is expressed with profuse obscenities and through the articulation of sentiments so ugly that they make the slur words themselves seem almost euphemistic by com-parison. If one ran an unedited video of a Ku Klux Klan meeting side by side with an episode of *All in the Family*, the video of the Klan meeting would be more profoundly disturbing. But it is probably also true that if one substituted a video shot in many "ordinary" neighborhood bars or even many living rooms for the Klan video, the episode—*any episode*—of *All in the Family* would seem tame in comparison. It has become a truism about the period that television brought the Vietnam War into America's living rooms and profoundly changed our attitudes toward war and our appreci-ation of the terrible costs of war. But this truism masks the extensive cen-sorship of what was actually reported from the battlefields. What Americans were seeing was, in fact, a selective exposure to the war's horrors. There is a parallel, I think, in how *All in the Family* selectively exposed the cultural biases underlying some of the uglier realities of American life. Just as GIs who served in Vietnam were aware that the television coverage of the war in Vietnam provided just glimpses of what they saw there, so those who were most directly engaged in the domestic political and cultural conflicts that *All in the Family* was treating knew firsthand that the Archie Bun-kers of the period were apologists for and enablers of far more malignant figures and ideologies.

With the advantage of more than four decades of hindsight, I would like to take Hobson's point two steps further. First, beyond not exposing the true ugliness of prejudice, the popularity of *All in the Family* to some extent may have had the unintended consequence of "mainstreaming" and even legiti-mizing that prejudice. At about the same time as *All in the Family* debuted on network television, Francis Ford Coppola's film adaptation of *The God-father* was released. Like Mario Puzo's novel, which had been the best-selling work of fiction for several years running, the film was not just an immediate critical success but also a commercial blockbuster, with long lines of theatergoers literally stretching around city blocks in cities and towns across the country for tickets. Given that level of critical and com-mercial success, it may be difficult to remember that Italian American groups loudly and visibly protested against the making and release of the film, charging that it reinforced all-too-common stereotypes of Italian Americans as nefarious criminals. But it may be even less remembered that Italian American mobsters themselves initially, and in some cases sinisterly, expressed their own concerns about how they would be portrayed.

Ironically, however, soon after its release, many mobsters began to embrace the film, seeing in Marlon Brando's portrayal of Vito Corleone a somewhat idealized version of their own self-perceptions or ambitions. I would like to suggest that the popularity of *All in the Family* and the three-dimensional portrayal of Archie Bunker as a fundamentally decent man whose behavior has been warped by deeply ingrained prejudice may have had the unintended consequence of allowing some bigots to feel at least somewhat legitimized. Conversely, some Americans who were less directly affected by bigotry felt that the problems associated with bigotry might be somewhat exaggerated.

My second addendum to Hobson's argument requires giving a further turn to the first one. Earlier in this essay, I emphasized the importance of the generational conflict being set against the particular historical moment in accounting for the impact of the show. Especially for many of the younger members of the original audience for the show, who would be the most likely to be troubled by the continued existence of ethnic and racial prejudice (as opposed to the simple expression of such prejudice on a public medium), the rejection of Archie's point of view would have been at least somewhat mitigated by their affection for their grandparents and parents, among whom such prejudice would have been more commonplace, even if it was left largely unexpressed. There is an episode of *All in the Family* in which Archie Bunker and Michael Stivic get accidentally locked in the cooler at the bar that Archie has bought. As the night wears on and they become less guarded, in part because they have been drinking, the two characters start to open up to each other. Michael is particularly affected by Archie's account of how he got the childhood nickname of "Shoebooty." One of his shoes had become worn out beyond repair, and because his parents were too poor to afford to buy him a new pair of shoes, Archie had to wear a boot on one foot and the remaining shoe on the other foot. Michael is reminded that he has relatively little genuine and immediate sense of the hardships endured by his parents' generation, who lived through the Great Depression and the world war, and he recognizes that he should be less quick to judge the effects that those formative experiences had on the psyches and the values of that generation—on the ways in which they not only view the world but also have managed to navigate the world in trying to provide an idealized better life for their children. Understanding the sources of bigotry does not justify it and should not mitigate opposition to it. On the other hand, the failure to understand the sources of bigotry runs the risk of reducing the opposition to it to a sort of parallel simplemindedness. Arguments that account for complexities are much harder to make than slogans are to contrive, but arguments that account for complexities are ultimately the only ones worth making, the only ones that have a sustained impact.

Although for a decade or two after *Archie's Place* went off the air, *All in the Family* was widely seen in syndication, it seems to have become a less popular syndicated show. The generation that came of age during the Great Depression and the Second World War has now largely passed on, and Michael and Gloria Stivic's generation are now grandparents and either retired or approaching retirement age. Many of the issues related to ethnic and racial prejudice that shows such as *All in the Family* attempted to confront in the 1970s are still with us today—though the European ethnic slurs and the slurs against Jews and Roman Catholics have largely given way to anti-immigrant—that is, anti-Latino and anti-Islamic—slurs. But the protests against such prejudice are now fueled not just by outrage at the prejudice itself but also by outrage at the fact that such prejudice has been allowed to persist for the half-century since the salient legislative achievements of the civil rights era.

In my essay on *The Honeymooners*, I closed by addressing the criticism directed at that situation comedy because it makes light of Ralph Kramden's recurring threats of spousal abuse, and I noted that we have now become acutely aware of the many ways in which such abuse has been legally and culturally minimized to protect abusers. I think that an analogous point can be made about Archie Bunker's bigotry. It is now less shocking than simply appalling to see a middle-aged white man thoughtlessly mouthing ethnic and racial slurs. In many respects, Donald Trump's candidacy and now presidency has not only attempted to legitimize open expressions of demonstrations of bigotry but also created a dividing line between those who are willing to accept that idea that "some" bigotry may be acceptable and those who are committed to the idea that all bigotry is simply unacceptable.

I had just finished this article, when I coincidentally came across the article "Norman Lear Sits Down with *Salon*: Trump Is the Middle Finger of the American Right Hand,'" written by Andrew O'Herir for *Salon*. Although the article was actually published in July 2016, I found it through an item in the September 28, 2016, *PM* digest newsletter distributed by the *Daily Beast*. The subtitle comes from one of Lear's remarks late in the interview. When O'Herir asks, "Would Archie vote for Donald Trump?," Lear responds:

> I don't think so at all. I think it could be a really good episode. Oh my God, it would make a really great episode. Him arguing with Mike and defending Donald Trump—I would love to do that.
>
> Because there isn't much by way of leadership across the nation that Trump *doesn't* represent as the asshole he is. They're not all a bunch of assholes. But everything he reflects is what corporate America reflects.
>
> And then, you'd actually see Archie go to vote. And in the end, he wouldn't be able to do it. I really don't think he would.

> I think of Donald Trump as the middle finger of the American right hand, and they are saying, "This is the kind of leadership you give us everywhere? Corporate America, political America, fuck you." And he represents that middle finger.[6]

I would like to believe that Lear is right, but among all of those in the Republican party who have denounced Trump for his own bigotry and for attracting the political support of bigots, I have not seen a large number of figures who have themselves been called out previously for being bigots or even for being pointedly insensitive on matters of race and religion.

Okay, maybe Glenn Beck.

In any case, this recent interview provides a fairly seamless segue into an article written by Michael K. Chapko and Mark H. Lewis for the *Journal of Psychology* in the mid-1970s. In "Authoritarianism and *All in the Family*," they report on a survey that they conducted to determine if viewers with ethnocentric viewpoints and those who are responsive to authoritarianism responded differently to the show in general and to Archie Bunker more specifically than other viewers. On the question of the relationship between ethnocentrism and viewing, they conclude:

> The data give no support to the notion that either high or low ethnocentric individuals differ in the frequency with which they watch *All in the Family*. The show does not cater only to one group but seems to have appeal to both high and low ethnocentrics. It is therefore likely that the two groups assimilate the content of the show toward their own positions.[7]

On how viewers judge Archie Bunker, they report:

> Archie Bunker is viewed as a likable loser. People neither agree with him nor see him as being similar to themselves, possibly because they see him as a loser. These perceptions are somewhat modified by the authoritarianism of the viewer so that, in general, high authoritarians see him in a somewhat more positive light on all dimensions.
>
> Extrapolating from the research questions discussed above to the more general question of the popularity of the show and its effects on the public can be only tentative at this point. Even though high compared to low authoritarians view Bunker as being more similar to themselves, they still see themselves as being dissimilar to him. This makes it unlikely that they are receiving the message of the show . . . that "it does you no good to be a bigot" or by O'Connor that it helps ethnocentrics understand "their own feelings and their own prejudices."[8]

Their concluding sentence, however, seems especially prescient about the seemingly evolving responses to the show and the relation of those responses to the reactions to Donald Trump's presidency:

> Even though Bunker is clearly bested in most of his battles, the show may be one of the few places in the mass media where their own [i.e., the authoritarians'] attitudes are consistently and openly expressed.[9]

NOTES

1. Dennis E. Showalter, "Archie Bunker, Lenny Bruce, and Ben Cartwright: Taboo-Breaking and Character Identification in All in the Family," *Journal of Popular Culture* 9(3) (Winter 1975), 618.

2. George Gent, *"All in the Family* Takes First Place in the Nielsen Ratings," *The New York Times*, May 25, 1971, 79.

3. Laura Hobson, "As I Listened to Archie Say 'Hebe,'" *The New York Times*, September 12, 1971, D1.

4. Andrew O'Herir, "Norman Lear Sits Down with Salon: Trump Is the Middle Finger of the American Right Hand,'" *Salon*, July 14, 2016, http://www.salon.com /2016/07/14/norman_lear_sits_down_with_salon_trump_is_the_middle_finger _of_the_american_right_hand/.

5. Hobson, op. cit.

6. Ibid.

7. Michael K. Chapko and Mark H. Lewis, "Authoritarianism and *All in the* Family," *Journal of Psychology* 90 (1975), 247.

8. Ibid.

9. Ibid.

BIBLIOGRAPHY

Chapko, Michael K., and Mark H. Lewis. "Authoritarianism and *All in the* Family." *Journal of Psychology* 90 (1975), 245–248.

Gent, George. *"All in the Family* Takes First Place in the Nielsen Ratings." *The New York Times*, May 25, 1971, 79.

Hobson, Laura. "As I Listened to Archie Say 'Hebe.'" *The New York Times*, September 12, 1971, D1.

O'Herir, Andrew. "Norman Lear Sits Down with Salon: Trump Is the Middle Finger of the American Right Hand.'" *Salon*, July 14, 2016, http://www.salon .com/2016/07/14/norman_lear_sits_down_with_salon_trump_is_the _middle_finger_of_the_american_right_hand.

Showalter, Dennis E. "Archie Bunker, Lenny Bruce, and Ben Cartwright: Taboo-Breaking and Character Identification in *All in the Family.*" *Journal of Popular Culture* 9(3) (Winter 1975), 618–621.

8

"I'm Every Woman": The Cultural Influence and Afterlife of Florence Johnston of *The Jeffersons*

Stacie McCormick

The Jeffersons *(1975–1985) offered viewers a vision of upward mobility in a moment of social and political upheaval as George and Louise Jefferson finally "got a piece of the pie" promised them by the American Dream. In " 'I'm Every Woman': The Cultural Influence and Afterlife of Florence Johnston of* The Jeffersons*," Stacie McCormick explores the role of Florence Johnson, the Jeffersons' "self-assured and witty maid." Arguing that Florence's character allowed the show to explore a number of controversial issues of the day, including labor, race, and gender, McCormick points to Florence as an important signifier of the shifting treatment of race on television in the 1970s and 1980s, specifically in the reimagined depiction of the black maid figure.*

> Let's face it. I am a marked woman, but not everybody knows my name. "Peaches" and "Brown Sugar," "Sapphire" and "Earth Mother," "Granny," God's "Holy Fool," a "Miss Ebony First," or "Black Woman at the Podium": I describe a locus of confounded identities, a meeting ground of investments and privations in the national security of rhetorical wealth. My country needs me, and if I were not here, I would have to be invented.
>
> —Hortense Spillers's "Mama's Baby, Papa's Maybe: An American Grammar Book"

Debuting in January 1975, *The Jeffersons* appeared at the culmination of three major American protest movements: the labor movement, the civil rights movement, and the women's movement. By the time the show appeared on Saturday nights, the American viewing public had already become familiar with seeing protests play out on their television screens.[1] This kind of specular engagement with various social movements left an indelible mark on the psyches of most Americans. These movements would come to be embodied in the figure of one self-assured and witty maid: Florence Johnston of *The Jeffersons* (played by Marla Gibbs).

Like the speaker in Hortense Spillers's quote, Florence came to represent a multitude of identities and personas that allowed the show to tackle controversial issues of labor, race, and gender in ways that other shows had not. Although a great number of critical readings exist of African Americans and their representations on television, the figure of Florence of *The Jeffersons* remains undertheorized. However, looking closely at Florence reveals television at a crossroads in its depiction of African Americans. The show and the character of Florence signified a merger between quality television and relevance programming while at the same time pushing against traditional representations of African American maids within the entertainment industry. With this in mind, the show's signature tune "Movin' on Up" (one of the most memorable of all television theme songs) wasn't just a narrative of arrival but also one of aspiration. The presence of the working-class Florence kept issues of racial, gender, and labor progress front and center even as George (Sherman Helmsley) and Louise (Isabel Sanford) signified the gains of long-fought struggles of the civil rights movement. Because of this, Florence remains one of the most transformational characters of 20th-century television.

In my analysis of Florence Johnston's cultural impact and enduring legacy, I will first consider her intervention in reshaping the role of the black maid on television. Using this as a launching point, I will chart her development on *The Jeffersons* and how it resulted in her being a flexible figure who articulated issues of race, gender, and labor. Finally, I will highlight Marla Gibbs's labor activism and the establishment of the Florence Johnston Collective as a reflection of the long-standing influence of the character of Florence Johnston.

One way to contextualize Florence's unconventional role is by understanding how she complicated the boundary line between "quality television" and "relevance programming." According to Kirsten Marthe Lentz:

> During the 1970s, the television industry adopted two kinds of terminology for describing these newly renovated shows [new programming produced by MTM and TAT/Tandem Production companies]: *quality television* and *relevance programming.* [Sic] Appeals to "quality television" largely promised to improve the television text aesthetically, while appeals to "relevance"

promised that television shows would become more responsive to the social and political milieu of the 1970s.[2]

Lentz also notes that quality television was largely associated with feminism, whereas relevance programming was most closely connected with racial representation—both of which produced epistemologies about gender, race, and representation that affected intellectual understanding of these issues even into the 21st century.[3]

Citing *Maude* (another spinoff of *All in the Family*) as a show that begins to blur the line between quality television and relevance programming, Lentz argues that *Maude* attempted to "represent the project of feminism and a critique of white, liberal racism in tandem."[4] What *Maude* exposed was the artificial boundary between the categories of quality television and relevance programming, which assumed that the concerns of feminism and antiracist ideals were separate. In many ways, *Maude* made a path for the figure of Florence Johnston to emerge. In her role as a black female maid, Florence forced audiences to think in deeper ways about the dynamics of intersectional oppression by showing how racial oppression is often compounded by gender and class oppression.

Florence openly embodied Kimberlé Crenshaw's concept of "intersectionality," a term signifying the multiple and intersecting struggles that often get overlooked in discussions of identity politics. Crenshaw says, "the problem with identity politics is not that it fails to transcend difference as some critics charge, but rather the opposite—that it frequently conflates or ignores intragroup differences."[5] The character of Florence Johnston does not allow for this disregard of intragroup differences. We can also see Florence as an early black feminist voice.

TELEVISION'S BLACK MAIDS AT THE CROSSROADS

Because Florence was a character that revised the historical role of the African American maid, her depiction is more experimental and less easily reconciled into the narrative of the show. Although Florence appears on the debut episode of *The Jeffersons* in 1975, she doesn't become a regular part of the cast until season two. In her first episode, however, she instantly troubles the narrative of success wrought by the civil rights movement that the show initially seemed to be promoting. Critic Gary Deeb leads in his review of the show's first episode with two questions: "Can a nouveau riche black family find happiness in a Manhattan high rise? Will George Jefferson force his wife to hire a maid?"[6] At the time of its premiere, a central perception of the show was that it was largely going to trace the sometimes tumultuous road away from near poverty to high society for George and Louise. When Florence appeared, however, it was clear that the show would explore more than that.

The early episodes of the show suggest a public debate amongst the producers and writers on just how to depict Florence Johnston. This is represented in the first episode where the central conflict was Louise's resistance to even hiring a maid. The Jeffersons ultimately interview and hire Florence. However, when she learns that the Jeffersons own the apartment and that black women like Helen Willis (Roxie Roker) also live in the same building, she asks the iconic question, "Well, how come we overcame and nobody told me?" The line elicited raucous laughter from the live studio audience, yet underneath the laughter was an incisive commentary that even though African Americans have made gains, the project of civil rights was ongoing rather than complete. Florence's presence also added an element of authenticity to the show for viewers who might have been resistant to invest in narrative about a successful black businessman who ascended from poverty to wealth. Kirsten Lentz explains that many of Norman Lear's shows were held to expectations of racial authenticity. She argues that television "ensconced itself in racial realism," promoting stereotypes of race that broad audiences were comfortable with.[7] The kind of realism that Florence offered paralleled shows such as *Good Times* (1974–1979), which depicted low-income African American households.

Although she served as a conscience keeper for George and an "authentic" representation of African Americans, it was unclear how Florence would be used once she became more embedded into the show. This is evidenced by the limited episodes focusing on her character early in the show's development. The episode "Florence's Problem" (the last episode of season two) illustrates this struggle. In the episode, Florence is contemplating suicide. Not having much to live for (as she thinks), she makes plans to enjoy her last days in New York City acting as a tourist and then dying quietly by overdosing on pills. Once they learn of her plans, the Jeffersons actively dissuade her from carrying out such an act, thereby producing a greater intimate connection between them and their "help." It is then that Florence becomes more intricately bound into the show and the lives of the Jeffersons. By season three, she moves in as a live-in maid. During this time, the show not only experimented with Florence from a mental health perspective but also depicted her early on as a devout Christian woman. It was clear that this character was a departure from the traditional template of the maid, and the show was willing to pursue this line to see where this narrative thread went.

By the time Florence appeared on television in the 1970s, the role of the black maid had undergone various iterations. Most famously, the first black maid to be featured on television was Beulah (played by Ethel Waters and later by Louise Beavers) who starred in *The Beulah Show* (1950). In *Shaded Lives: African American Women and Television*, Beretta E. Smith-Shomade describes her position: "Beulah's centrality came through her guidance of the white family through crisis."[8] Ultimately, the show (along with its con-temporary *Amos 'n' Andy*) was condemned by the NAACP, which cited den-igrating portrayals harkening back to the minstrel era. The organization subsequently joined forces with other entities to have the shows taken off the air.[9]

When another African American maid was featured on television with the appearance of Esther Rolle on *Maude* and later in her own spin-off on *Good Times*, there was a clear intention to rehabilitate the image of the maid. In the documentary *Color Adjustment* (1991), Esther Rolle explains that her goal was to redeem the role of the black domestic worker. Notably, she also demanded a husband. This request brought to light television's his-toric erasure of black fathers from their households.[10] Marla Gibbs was also sensitive to the need to restore dignity to the role of maid. In a 1980 interview "Marla Has Got It 'Maid' with The Jeffersons," she makes the point that "Folks look down on household jobs. . . . It's gotten to be a stigma. Yet I can remember when it was the only job around for a black woman. I'm doing my best as Florence to say 'Hey, it's alright.' After all it's a matter of geography. In France, being a maid or waiter is called a profession." Con-sidering Esther Rolle's and Marla Gibbs's ownership of the figure of the maid, they clearly aimed for and achieved greater depth in depictions of the African American maid on television. Florence Johnston's role in par-ticular changed the stereotypical temperament and even the appearance of the black maid. Most black maids in entertainment were heavier in stat-ure. The decision to present them in this way was borne of an effort to more closely align them to the mammy figure.[11] Marla Gibbs, however, was not a heavy woman, which made it difficult to easily reconcile her into the image of the mammy.

Although Florence Johnston did not comport with the mammy icon, many critics argued that she intersected with the figure of Sapphire. This role was introduced to television with the character Sapphire (played by Ernestine Ward) on the *Amos 'n' Andy* show. This was the location where viewers often critiqued Florence's character as staying too close to stereotype—and conforming to the role of the sassy, emasculating black woman. According to K. Sue Jewell,

> The Sapphire image of African American womanhood, unlike other images that symbolize African American women, necessitates the presence of an African American male. When the Sapphire image is portrayed it is the African American male who represents the point of contention, in an ongo-ing verbal dual between Sapphire and the African American male. Her sheer existence is predicated upon the presence of the corrupt African American male whose lack of integrity, and use of cunning trickery pro-vides her with an opportunity to emasculate him through her use of verbal put-downs.[12]

In these terms, the interaction between Florence and George Jefferson would certainly fit this framework. The verbal sparring between Florence and George became a staple of the show early on with the running joke of the show being that George could never beat Florence in a bet or at any game requiring skill.[13]

K. Sue Jewell argues that Florence was the synthesis between the mammy and Sapphire.[14] However, when tracing Florence's development over the course of the show, her relationship with George Jefferson is clearly more complicated than it appears. At points, she functions as an ally in protecting him from shady businessmen or supporting him when he suffers a defeat; therefore, she is not singularly an antagonist. The episode that notably marks the turning point in their relationship is "Louise Gets Her Way" (season three). In this episode, George is resistant to hiring Florence as a live-in maid, but when she saves him from being tricked into buying damaged vans for his cleaning business, the "nosy-ness" that George condemns early in the episode becomes a trait by which he praises her—it has saved him from financial exploitation. Notably, Florence seizes this opportunity to advocate for better wages for herself. When she explains her circumstances to articulate what she needs, she makes clear her intersectional identities that have historically limited individuals like her from financial and social ascendance. She states, "I ain't a man. I ain't white. And I ain't rich" to uproarious applause. This moment echoes Sojourner Truth's iconic words in her speech "Ain't I a Woman?" where she argues for recognition of black women as subjects equally deserving of rights. For me, this moment transforms Florence from the stereotype of single, black, mammy or maid, Sapphire into labor heroine. Ultimately, the show coalesces around this depiction of her, continuing throughout the remainder of its 11-season run.

FLORENCE AS "EVERY WOMAN"

Florence's flexibility as a black feminist labor icon was supported by a convergence of cultural and political transformations in late 1960s and early 1970s America. Aretha Franklin's 1967 "Respect" had set forth a narrative of power that emboldened black women in particular to demand to be treated with dignity. Concomitantly, in 1968 Shirley Chisholm became the first black woman elected to the U.S. Congress. She then went on to be the first major party black candidate to run for president of the United States in 1972. Her book *Unbought and Unbossed* (1970) elevated black women's voices at a key time in American history. In this same year that *Unbought and Unbossed* was published, Angela Davis was arrested and tried for murder conspiracy in a fatal courtroom takeover in Marin County, California. Building on all of this, Chaka Khan's chart topper, "I'm Every Woman," which espoused a message of female empowerment and versatility, was released in 1978 just as Florence had become a staple of *The Jeffersons*. While the confluence between Chaka Khan's hit and Florence's new success was coincidental, there is no doubt that the producers of the show had found its "every woman" figure in Florence Johnston.

Before Florence became the Jeffersons live-in maid and an official recurring character in the cast, the show had been attempting to draw out the complex dynamics of identity politics that were part of the national conversation in the wake of the gains of the civil rights movement. The show also extended some of the plot lines begun in *Maude* with its critique of racism and sexism. "George and the Manager" (season two) illustrates the shows early reckoning with gender and racial politics as intertwined subjects. In this episode, George must hire a new manager for one of his cleaning stores after his male manager abruptly quits. Louise suggests that George hire Emily (Rhoda Gemignani), his five-year employee who also happens to be a white female. To mask his resistance to hiring a woman, George explains that he wants to hire a black person to manage the store as a show of solidarity with his community. He then tasks his son, Lionel (Damon Evans), to find a suitable replacement via an employment agency. Lionel's candidate, although having the gender-ambiguous name of Dale Parker (Norma Donaldson), is a black woman, which places George at odds with his initial excuse that he only wanted to hire an African American. After much back and forth, George reveals that he doesn't want a woman running one of his stores because a "woman is not happy being a boss; she's got to be bossy."

Ultimately, the black female candidate explains to George (after being thoroughly offended by his blatant chauvinism), "If you want to help blacks, remember that some of your brothers are sisters." The episode ends with George being chastened by a multigenerational collection of women from his mother (Zara Cully) to Lionel's then-girlfriend Jenny (Belinda Tolbert). This episode establishes a character trait within George that had yet to be explored in detail. Having succeeded at becoming an employer, he must now reckon with issues of discrimination and equity.

After this episode, it becomes clear that George is an employer in clear need of reform. Once this aspect of George's character was established, Florence's key role expanded to encompass her role as comedic foil to George, delivering verbal jabs and keeping him honest to disenfranchised laborers who represent the cultural and economic backgrounds from which he came. I want to focus now on episodes that provide examples of Florence's progressive transformation into a labor heroine and "every woman" figure for the working class. The show moves her from articulating her personal struggles to representing the voices of those most invisible in the labor system.

As a way of framing the specific labor issues Florence faces as a black woman, the show uses slavery as an urtext that echoes throughout subsequent experiences of African Americans in labor. The inclusion of slavery on the show functions at times contradictorily as both a critique of the labor dynamics on the show and as marker of progress. As evidence of the varied inclusions of the subject of slavery on the show, *The Jeffersons* often dealt with this history in irreverent and satirical ways. For instance, in an attempt to garner attention for his cleaning business, George pretended to be the great-grandson of President Thomas Jefferson, going as far as dressing like Jefferson for pictures in the episode "George and the President" (season three).

This episode also illustrates the writers' and producers' awareness of the zeitgeist and the increasing dissemination of accounts that Thomas Jefferson had fathered children with his slave Sally Hemmings. Fawn McKay Brodie's best-selling book *Thomas Jefferson: An Intimate History* (1974) was the first major study of Jefferson and his use of Hemmings as a concubine. Some years later in 1979, Barbara Chase-Riboud produced the novel *Sally Hemmings*, a fictional reimagining of Hemmings's life. Without question this era marked an increased attention to the possibility of Jefferson having nonwhite or mixed race descendants to which the show responds. It also highlights the entangled legacies of slavery that challenge notions of racial purity.

Beyond satire, we see slavery used to critique the labor dynamics of the show with two episodes featuring Florence: "Florence in Love" and "George Needs Help." Both episodes suggest that George risks losing his way as an employer by mirroring a slave master. Although this analogy is a great stretch, the situation-comedy genre allows for these kinds of leaps when done under the guise of humor. The use here, however, is also a nod to the significance of George's accomplishment and the journey of African Americans in the country when, just over 100 years earlier, slavery was still an American institution. These references to slavery serve as both a reminder to the audience and a calling card for George when he overreaches.

"Florence in Love" (season three) most forcefully uses the narrative of slavery to highlight George's transgressions as a boss. In this episode, Florence has an overnight guest, T. J. Davis (Robert DoQui), who Louise and George discover in their home while Florence is away. In a confrontation with Louise and George, Florence stands between them in the living room as George reminds her, "We're the boss and you're the maid." The argument escalates into George attempting to police Florence's intimate life and Louise not being supportive of her either. Feeling alienated, Florence quits.

However, after realizing that she has nowhere to go, she returns to the Jefferson household on George's condition that she start acting like a "real maid." To this Florence springs into action, transforming herself into a mammy or Aunt Jemima figure and referring to George as "Massa Jefferson." She even goes as far to buy a maid's outfit reminiscent of Butterfly McQueen's character, Prissy, in *Gone with the Wind.*

Neighbor Harry Bently (Paul Benedict) notices this and expresses that he feels as though he has stepped into a scene from the movie. Florence's gestures and Southern affectations begin to annoy George to such an extent that he asks her to cease with the act. She immediately drops character and instructs him to "Say please." He does so, thereby overturning the power dynamics and restoring the balance to the show. She also states that she's ready "to take off this dumb dress, so I can stop acting like a dumb maid for a dumb master." In this line, it is clear that Florence represents a strong departure from traditional depictions of black maids in television. It also serves as a reminder to George of the kind of boss that he should not become.

In the season four episode "George Needs Help," we see the show referencing slavery again—this time in the form of folktales, which represented many slaves' subversive attempts to gain power over their masters. These tales often contained a trickster figure. Trudier Harris explains, "By definition, tricksters are animals or characters who, while ostensibly disadvantaged and weak in a contest of wills, power, and/or resources, succeed in getting the best of their larger, more powerful adversaries."[15] This episode shows Florence and another employee of George's dry-cleaning business conspiring to outwit George. The episode features a conflict in which George is overworked and Louise asks him to hire a general manager so that they can spend more time together. George is resistant to giving over that much power in his business; however, his Brooklyn store manager, Clarence (Teddy Wilson), is a perfect fit for the job.

Because George is so resistant to the idea, he insults Clarence and all but calls off the effort. While George and Louise confer in the kitchen, Florence sits Clarence down to tell him a folktale about the alligator and the two bunnies. (The presence of the bunnies signals a reference to the Brer Rabbit tales that feature in African American folklore.) Florence explains that the two bunnies wanted to cross a river but needed the alligator's help. The first bunny approached the alligator by insulting him while the second tried the tactic of being nice and complimentary to the alligator as a way to bolster his ego. Ultimately, the alligator takes the second bunny across the river. When Florence is done telling the story, Clarence declares to Florence, "I gotta learn to be a smart bunny rabbit." Ultimately, Florence's advice works and Clarence gets the job. Florence as a communicator of folk wisdom in solidarity with George's other employees makes her a labor ally outsmarting the power structure to achieve gains for herself and those like her.

Season four shows Florence hitting her stride as a labor advocate; the episode "Florence's Union" most powerfully illustrates this. Florence has been approached to be president of the maid's union in their building, a job she strongly desires. However, the group has nowhere to meet, so Florence aligns with Louise (who references her own work as a maid before her family's success), and Louise offers their home as a space to hold the meeting. George learns of this plan and assumes that H. L. Whittendale (a business icon to George and an elusive figure who George can never seem to meet) is on board because his maid, Milly (Barbara Mealy), is present during the planning for the meeting. However, Whittendale (Jack Fletcher) is not a supporter and threatens Milly's job, which she depends on to pay her children's college tuition. When George and Whittendale finally meet, Whittendale insults Louise and Florence. He also refers to George and the other individuals in the room as "you people." George summarily throws Whittendale out and stands in support of the maids, whom Florence has renamed "The United Sisterhood of Household Technicians."

The renaming of the maid's union also calls attention to the ideas of sisterhood that the episode was promoting in the form of the multiracial coalition of women gathered with Florence. The group features whites, African Americans, and Latinas, among others. This meeting also calls attention to the many struggles maids face. Many of them live in poverty and don't have resources to buy food. They have no paid vacation time, health insurance, or pension plans. In highlighting these issues, the show, through Florence, brings awareness to poor working conditions of domestic laborers.

The show explores labor injustice in greater detail as Florence gets further intertwined with her employers, who come to think of her as family. This relationship is fraught with tension, however, because it is clear that Florence is not of the economic status of her employers and their friends. The show exploits this tension in the episode "Social Insecurity" (season nine) in which the disparities within the Jefferson household are most starkly represented.

The show opens with Helen and Louise entering with bags from a shopping spree at Bloomingdale's. Florence enters after them declaring that she only bought a pack of gum. This conversation reminds Tom (Franklin Cover) that he recently saw a bag lady who reminded him of Florence. Of course, this offends Florence, who registers that although she accompanies them on shopping trips, she occupies a starkly different economic position than the Willises and the Jeffersons. The group (Helen, Tom, and Louise) begin to discuss the importance of having economic security and discuss their pension savings plans. Florence realizes in that moment that she has no such plan and that her employers have not supplied it. Louise sees a quick fix and reassures Florence that she will support her in requesting a pension plan from George. To both of their surprise, George emphatically declares "No." In response, Louise and Florence (joined by several other friends in the building) conduct a strike in support of Florence. They construct picket signs and chant "George Jefferson is unfair!" Again, Florence espouses a familiar concern of many working-class individuals without pensions whose employers have no plans to rectify their situations.

George later reveals by a videotaped will and testament that he has established a trust fund for Florence that functions as a pension. His reasoning for not telling her this earlier, he explains, is that he did not wish for her to be nice to him, preferring an antagonistic relationship to a peaceful one. Here, George speaks to one of the issues the show faced nearing the end of its 11-season run. For years, viewers enjoyed Florence and George's jocular exchanges, but Florence had become a central character in her own right. Thus, they created *Checking In* a spin-off written for Florence's character.

Produced in 1981 by Norman Lear and TAT Communications, *Checking In* featured Marla Gibbs in her signature role as Florence. Florence had taken a job offer to be executive housekeeper of the fictional St. Frederick Hotel in Manhattan. Because of low ratings and a writer's strike, the show only lasted four episodes.[16] The show explored Florence's experiences of life on the other side of the table as a manager of hotel maids and working alongside those in power to ensure the successful operation of the hotel. This turn of fortune, however, might have been alienating to audiences who had come to know Florence as a working-class hero. Speaking about the show in the interview "The Jeffersons—Marla's not as Bleeping Fast as Glib Florence," Marla Gibbs remarks, "Florence's main appeal is that she's one of the masses, and one the masses can identify with. Having her join the power lost her that appeal."[17] Gibbs's assessment of Florence as "one of the masses" was an accurate capture of her enduring appeal.

THE AFTERLIFE OF FLORENCE JOHNSTON

For Marla Gibbs, Florence was not just a role but an opportunity to depict the invisible struggles of the American working-class and low-wage laborers. Gibbs used that activist spirit and applied it to her own philanthropy and public appearances. The article "Gibbs Urges Blacks to Rebuild Communities" (1990) highlights Gibbs advocacy for the rebuilding of black communities in Los Angeles, citing children as the most important beneficiaries of such an effort. The article also references her creation of Crossroads Arts Academy, a performing arts school, in 1982 (during her time with *The Jeffersons*). The school was designed to nurture talent—young and old— in inner-city Los Angeles. Most interestingly, the school also instructed learners on making a living in urban growth areas—working as waiters and waitresses. Both on stage and off, Florence's "authenticity" as a labor hero resonated with many viewers, particularly those who were passionate about labor issues and used Florence as a potent representation of their concerns.

In addition to Tumblr accounts dedicated to Florence's character, the Florence Johnston Collective offers support to laborers. The group articulates its connection in these terms: "Our struggle is a continuation of the militants of the past. Florence Johnston is a cultural figure who represents our contradictory history as childcare, aides, respite, education, and service workers, and as working class women and people of color."[18] They follow this statement with a clip from the episode "Florence's Union" referenced earlier in this essay. The list detailing the collective's "contradictory history" as aides, service workers, caregivers, etc. reflects the flexibility of Florence's role on the show. Her dynamic presence allows for groups composed of wide-ranging experience to gather around her persona as an articulation of their varied but intersecting investments.

As we think about the enduring legacy of someone like Florence Johnston, we are forced to conclude that her influence transcends one single area of impact. Her progressive "move on up" in the show's hierarchy from comedic foil to George to black feminist voice and enduring labor icon signals the power of a role and coextensively a television show.

NOTES

1. See Sasha Torres's *Black White and in Color: Television and Black Civil Rights* (Princeton, NJ: Princeton University Press, 2003) and Bonnie Dow's *Watching Women's Liberation, 1970: Feminism's Pivotal Year on Network News* (Chicago: University of Illinois Press, 2014).

2. Kirsten Marthe Lentz, "Quality vs. Relevance: Feminism, Race, and the Politics of the Sign in 1970s Television." *Camera Obscura*, 15(1) (2000), 46–47.

3. Ibid., 47.

4. Ibid., 69.

5. Kimberlé Crenshaw, "Mapping the Margins: Intersectionality, Identity Politics, and Violence Against Women of Color." *Stanford Law Review*, 43 (1991), 1242.

6. Gary Deeb, "Now the Jeffersons Battle the Nielsens, Not the Bunkers." *Chicago Tribune*, January 17, 1975.

7. Lentz, op. cit., 58.

8. Beretta E. Smith-Shomade, *Shaded Lives: African American Women and Television* (New Brunswick, NJ: Rutgers University Press, 2002), 11.

9. Ibid.

10. Until this point, most black women appeared on television as single mothers. Although Florence, too, is single, *The Jeffersons* offers comprehensive depictions of black men as fathers and mates in ways that few shows had done before.

11. K. Sue Jewell, *From Mammy to Miss America and Beyond: Cultural Images and the Shaping of US Social Policy* (New York: Routledge, 1993), 49.

12. Ibid., 45.

13. bell hooks in *Black Looks: Race and Representation* (1992) describes black women's vexed relationship to Sapphire. Although hooks describes how young women like her found Sapphire of the Amos 'n' Andy show unappealing ("She was not us," hooks proclaims), she notes that "grown" black women embraced her as misunderstood and resented the way she was mocked as a bitch and a nag (hooks 1992, 120).

14. Ibid., 48.

15. Trudier Harris, "The Trickster in African American Literature," *Freedom's Story: Teaching African American Literature and History*. National Humanities Center, http://nationalhumanitiescenter.org/tserve/freedom/1865-1917/essays/trickster.htm.

16. See the Archive of American Television interview with Marla Gibbs on *Checking In* at http://www.emmytvlegends.org/interviews/shows/checking-in.

17. John Stanley, "'The Jeffersons'—Marla's Not as Bleeping Fast as Glib Florence," *San Francisco Chronicle*, March 24, 1985.

18. See Florence Johnston Collective. "Who Is Florence Johnston?" https://florencejohnstoncollective.wordpress.com/2013/07/24/why-florence-johnston.

BIBLIOGRAPHY

"Checking In (Interview with Marla Gibbs)." Archive of American Television, http://www.emmytvlegends.org/interviews/shows/checking-in.

Crenshaw, Kimberlé. "Mapping the Margins: Intersectionality, Identity Politics, and Violence Against Women of Color." *Stanford Law Review* 43 (1991), 1241–1299.

Deeb, Gary. "Now the Jeffersons Battle the Nielsens, Not the Bunkers." *Chicago Tribune*, January 17, 1975.

Dow, Bonnie. *Watching Women's Liberation, 1970: Feminism's Pivotal Year on Network News*. Chicago: University of Illinois Press, 2014.

"Gibbs Urges Blacks to Rebuild Communities." *New Pittsburgh* (PA) *Courier*, November 10, 1990.

Harris, Trudier. "The Trickster in African American Literature." *Freedom's Story: Teaching African American Literature and History*. National Humanities Center, http://nationalhumanitiescenter.org/tserve/freedom/1865-1917/essays/trickster.htm.

hooks, bell. *Black Looks: Race and Representation*. Boston: South End Press, 1992.

The Jeffersons: The Complete Series. DVD. Directed by Jack Shea. Produced by Norman Lear. Shout! Factory. Producer Brian Blum. 2014.

Jewell, K. Sue. *From Mammy to Miss America and Beyond: Cultural Images and the Shaping of US Social Policy*. New York: Routledge, 1993.

Lentz, Kirsten Marthe. "Quality vs. Relevance: Feminism, Race, and the Politics of the Sign in 1970s Television." *Camera Obscura*, 15(1) (2000), 44–93.

Riggs, Marlon. *Color Adjustment*. Produced by California Newsreel. 1991. Kanopy Streaming. 2015. Online via Texas Christian University.

Smith-Shomade, Beretta E. *Shaded Lives: African American Women and Television*. New Brunswick, NJ: Rutgers University Press, 2002.

Spillers, Hortense J. "Mama's Baby, Papa's Maybe: An American Grammar Book." *Diacritics*, 17(2) (1987), 65–81.

Stanley, John. "'The Jeffersons'—Marla's Not as Bleeping Fast as Glib Florence." *San Francisco Chronicle*, March 24, 1985.

Torres, Sasha. *Black White and in Color: Television and Black Civil Rights*. Princeton, NJ: Princeton University Press, 2003.

Witbeck, Charles. "Marla Has Got It Maid with 'The Jeffersons'[sic]." *Chicago Tribune*, August 12, 1980.

9

Writing *One Day at a Time*: Reflections on a Life Inside the Tube

Christine Tibbles McBurney

Sometimes the import of a show can more effectively come into focus when a light is turned inward by an insider. In this autobiographical piece, Christine Tibbles McBurney reflects on her experiences as a screenplay writer for One Day at a Time *(1975–1984) and as part of a family of television sitcom writers. By taking us into the pitch room and connecting that experience to the show's historical and social context, Tibbles McBurney offers new insights into the show that broke ground with its depiction of a divorced single mom trying to make it with her children in the city. In contrast with earlier sitcoms that presented idealized suburban families such as* Leave It to Beaver, One Day at a Time *pushed the envelope on issues of its day and gave viewers a more realistic representation of struggles that they could relate to, something that continues to resonate today as* One Day at a Time *has been rebooted in 2017 by Netflix and now features a Cuban-American family headed by a newly divorced single mom.*

Nineteen eighty-one. The streets of Hollywood were gritty and neglected. Homeless people shuffled past shops selling cheap trinkets about movie stars and glamor. There was no glamor apparent on the world-famous corner of Hollywood and Vine, where my yellow 1954 Chevy pickup idled at a signal. As I was waiting for the light to turn green, I saw, in my rear-view mirror, two men on foot, catapulting through traffic. Before the line of cars could move on, I realized both of these men were brandishing guns, running like crazy, one in hot pursuit of the other, their faces masks of terror, their bodies lurching forward. Weaving through our cars, guns aloft, the men disappeared down Vine as the light turned green.

I had worked in the Screen Extras Guild and the American Federation of Television and Radio Artists all through college as an "extra," so my first thought was, "They're filming." I looked for the cameras, the honey wagons, the grips, as the two men flailed their guns next to my truck window. A typical scene in my strange city. Hollywood and Vine seemed a likely place to shoot a chase scene. But this chase was real, and these men were desperate. This literally happened as I was on my way to a pitch meeting at Metromedia, the studio on Sunset Boulevard where Norman Lear's Tandem Productions shot *All In the Family, Maude, Diff'rent Strokes, The Facts of Life, Hello Larry,* and *One Day at a Time.*

My meeting was in in a room of six men, writers and show runners for *One Day at a Time.* I had just seen two handguns in sweaty hands waving outside my truck window, so the nerves that a pitch meeting could engender were gone. When I told the men "You're not going to believe what just happened!" it definitely broke the ice.

One Day at a Time ran from 1975 to 1984 on CBS. Bonnie Franklin played Ann Romano, a divorced mother of two. Mackenzie Phillips played older sister Julie, and Valerie Bertinelli was younger sister Barbara. Pat Harrington played a superintendent in their building, Dwayne Schneider, who showed up to dispense street wisdom and a hypermasculine yet benign presence. As I took notes in that pitch meeting, I reflected on how truly strange this Los Angeles reality was. That brief encounter with handguns was a reflection of the world outside, a world that was heady and dangerous all at once.

In the mad, swiftly morphing American landscape of the 1970s, when *One Day at a Time* was developed, it was one of the first sitcoms to portray a young, divorced woman alone in a move to a big city (Indianapolis). Married at 17, Ann was discovering the hardships of looking for her first real job, raising her teenage daughters alone, trying to wrest child-support payments from an absent, deadbeat dad in the aftermath of her divorce. The wisdom that emerged from Ann Romano was a woman's wisdom, a woman's wit. Norman Lear was plugged into the zeitgeist; the shows he developed in this era about women emerging from their roles as housewives and mothers to become dynamic people with their own minds who were ready to conquer the world or at least take their place in it. The series was based on the experiences of Whitney Blake, a writer and actress who had raised three children after her divorce. She and her husband, Allan Manning, created the concept that Lear developed. Earlier sitcoms such as *Father Knows Best, Ozzie and Harriet, Leave It to Beaver,* and *The Donna Reed Show* reflected and celebrated the nuclear family, mother and father happily intact, dispensing wisdom to wisecracking or adorable children. In contrast, Norman Lear and others were displaying the women's movement, divorce, a crisis of faith, civil rights—all the "new" changes in our society.

By the time the 1970s rolled around, the Beatles and Rolling Stones had replaced Elvis and Timothy Leary had admonished us to "Turn on, tune in, drop out." The innocence of the earlier era was our changing society and being reflected in television, albeit often with a somewhat bland translation.

When I pitched my idea at Metromedia, *One Day* had been on the air six years. At that time, Mackenzie Phillips had substance abuse issues that were well known. She had been fired from the show to enter rehab in 1980, returned in 1981, had a relapse, collapsed on the set, and was finally written out. The subsequent story lines had Ann meeting an artist, Nick (Ron Rifkin), with whom she spars and then becomes attracted to. Nick and Ann are getting closer when Nick is killed by a drunk driver. Nick's son Alex (Glenn Scarpelli) is bereft, lost and alone. Alex is adopted by Ann and lives with her and Barbara, replacing Mackenzie Phillips as a member of the family. Alex had been on the series long enough to be getting used to his new home and needed a story line of his own when I had my meeting.

In the *One Day* pitch meetings, I was the sole female, in my 20s, and in a room of middle-aged men at the top of their game in the industry. They were quick, smart, and funny and had little patience with small talk. Time is always of the essence in TV, and getting the story line across quickly and cleanly was the goal. I was aware that they wanted a female take on the story lines, but it wasn't really necessary in their eyes. Of course, women were and have always been part of the industry but were still a distinct minority. Navigating that (mainly) white, male world was an education in itself. I was a different generation than these men. They were, no doubt, looking at and exploring the world of feminism; it was written into the concept of the show, by a woman, but in these meetings, I did not feel Whitney Blake's presence. To me, Ann's character insisting on being called "Ms. Romano" wasn't exactly revolutionary. To the networks, of course, it was.

The premise of my pitch, "Alex's First Love" (season seven, episode nine) was based on a childhood memory.[1] Since kindergarten I had a best friend, Joanne. We grew up together, two gangly kids running all over the streets and empty lots of our neighborhood. Suddenly, when we turned 13, Joanne morphed into a curvy, gorgeous creature. I was still a skinny, shy little girl, and this metamorphosis taking place in Joanne was stunning to me, especially when we walked into west Los Angeles and 18-year-old guys were hitting on her and ignoring me. This had stuck in my head, and I pitched the flavor of that experience to the guys in the room.

In "Alex's First Love," 13-year-old Alex is called up by a classmate, Joanne (Kelly Gallagher), who asks if she can come over. Ann is charmed that Alex's little pal is dropping by. Schneider can't wait to get a load of the sweet young kid and sees a sexy girl in skintight clothing approach in the hall. He preens and flirts until he discovers this is Alex's "little friend." Ann and Barbara are flummoxed by this siren, who looks at least 18, when Joanne tells them she's three weeks younger than Alex. The kids go to a movie and are many hours past their curfew. Joanne's father, Mr. Boyer (Terence McGovern), slams into Ann's apartment after a heated phone call, blaming "the boy" for any and all nefarious deeds that might have happened. Ann is incensed at this blanket prejudice until she discovers Joanne's dad is also divorced and raising her alone. Joanne has talked him into buying her outfits—"Everybody wears this, dad"—and he's clueless about fashion and girls' tastes. Ann and Joanne's dad feel compassion for each other's roles, the kids finally return, and nothing untoward has happened except kissing. The parents are stern but relieved, and Schneider takes Alex aside for a "birds and bees" talk. Alex says not to worry; in biology, they're already up to social diseases.

The men in the meeting liked the role reversal of the parents and dealing with the oft-cited cliché that boys are always predatory and that girls, who are in reality without experience, can telegraph sexuality though they have little true knowledge of what they're presenting. The assumption that girls who dress provocatively "deserve what they get" was and remains a common prejudice. The writers resonated to my female point of view, a take on budding sexuality, all its complicated issues, and a look at the prejudices women and men, boys and girls, are subject to from a very young age. Though a sitcom is always going for the laughs and lighthearted can also be lightweight, at least *One Day* was looking for stories that were more of its time, which was radically different from the TV eras that preceded it.

The 1970s was a volatile time, a strange and fascinating era to come of age. The Vietnam War had been raging for two decades, and the second wave of the feminist movement was flowering. Starting in the early 1960s, John F. Kennedy's "Camelot" had been cruelly destroyed, Martin Luther King Jr., Malcolm X, and Bobby Kennedy were assassinated one by one. Their deaths created a melancholy that deeply colored the generation that had fought in World War II and the generation that was coming of age. The 1950s are often portrayed as an innocent era, but we as kids heard shrill sirens in the schoolyard and had to jump under our desks daily to prepare for nuclear war. It affected the psyches of a huge swath of people. By the time the 1970s were unfolding, the 1960s counterculture was being appropriated by ad men, movies, and TV. Television itself had been entering our homes for just over 20 years, and it was here to stay. Smog in my hometown, Los Angeles, was wickedly toxic. Breathing was not on the menu. I was in college when Neil Young's song "After the Gold Rush" had a line about

"Look at Mother Nature on the run in the 1970s"—that line was poignant and literal. I saw the movie *Network*, and the brilliant Paddy Chayefsvky caught that moment in all its soul-ravaging glory. He was frighteningly prescient about the future wave of reality TV, and one of the main characters, a woman, was even more bloodthirsty, cutthroat, and soulless than the "suits" who ran the network. The older males were the ones who had enough conscience left to wrestle with their very souls, but the new generation represented by cynical young Diana Christensen (Faye Dunaway) lived for ratings. Ratings at any cost. When I saw this movie, I was deeply stricken by the truth of Chayefsky's worldview; it struck home at a time when I was venturing into the world of television writing. I knew it was written as comedy, but it was incredibly dark.

This was the world into which I walked when I sold a script for *Love, American Style* (Paramount Television, 1969–1974). This sitcom featured romantic vignettes in an anthology format that reflected, or so its creators hoped, "Dating and mating in the swinging 1970s."[2] The series drew a huge roster of talent, including Milton Berle, Sid Caesar, Sonny and Cher, Tiny Tim, and lots of up and coming actors such as Harrison Ford, Diane Keaton, Kurt Russell, and Meg Ryan ad infinitum. *Happy Days* (1974–1984) was a spinoff of *Love American Style*.

My episode was called "Love and the Golden Worm" (season five, episode 14).[3] The story was about an arranged marriage by an extremely traditional Chinese father (Keye Luke) and his son (Ernest Harada), who represented the younger generation. The son was absolutely against arranged marriages; the idea seemed to strike a chord in this era that was throwing aside tradition for good or ill. Of course, the "arranged" couple fall in love despite their objections. Despite shows like this, which celebrated a certain American innocence, the world of television felt simultaneously dangerous, exciting, and antiseptic, at least in my eyes.

The Mary Tyler Moore Show (1970–1977) was one of the first sitcoms whose protagonist was a single woman trying to make it in the city. *That Girl* (1966–1971) starring Marlo Thomas paved the way for *Mary Tyler Moore*, portraying a single girl who wanted a career, not marriage. This content looks tame now, but these shows were definitely empowering a huge group of women who for generations had never really considered anything but marriage and family. These shows were reflecting the pivot from the America of the 1950s and early 1960s to the societal changes that were occurring in the late 1960s and early 1970s.

One Day at a Time tackled issues such as drugs, sex, and rape, subjects that were avoided in earlier sitcoms. For example, in the two-part episode "Barbara's Friend" (season three, episodes 9–10), Melanie Walsh (Lindsay V. Jones) has decided Barbara is her best friend.[4] She is clingy and demanding and wants Barbara to help her get a date with a boy from school. The boy is

Cliff Randall (Scott Colomby). He has a crush on Barbara and asks her in front of Melanie to a Grateful Dead concert. Melanie believes Barbara has betrayed her. They argue, and later Barbara gets a phone call from a cheap motel; Melanie has swallowed a bottle of pills in a suicide attempt. Melanie is found and taken to a hospital, where she is in grave condition. Barbara is wracked with guilt. Melanie's parents arrive, full of themselves and not sympathetic to their daughter's "attention-seeking" plight. Ann convinces Barbara that it is not her fault, and the parents are told by the doctor to get psychiatric help for their daughter and themselves. This was not your *Leave It to Beaver* story line. It was a changing world, and television was revealing it, even in the light of commercialism and a tendency for the networks to "soften" these gnarly subjects.

I was born into a television family. My father, George Tibbles, was a jazz pianist who played on one of the first variety shows, *The Al Jarvis Show*, in 1949. On that show, my dad accompanied, among many other performers, a young singer and actress, Betty White. The family lore was that dad watched the sketches as he played, and thought "I can do this." TV in the early days was an open world with infinite possibilities, as are the Internet and new technologies now. Dad studied comedy and jokes, making the gradual change from pianist to television writer. Al Jarvis was a launching pad for both my dad and Betty, and in 1950 they developed her sitcom, *Life with Elizabeth*. My birth was announced on that show by Betty, so for me, being a part of TV is deep!

I was literally part of the "old wave" of nuclear family sitcoms when I was a young child. My dad went on to do *Leave It to Beaver*, *The Munsters*, and *The Addams Family*, and he created *My Three Sons* with producer Don Fedderson in 1960. When *My Three Sons* debuted, the story line was a departure from the family-centric sitcoms that had been the mainstay; an all-male household in which Fred MacMurray's character, Steve Douglas, was inhabiting the role of both mother and father, dispensing wisdom as he best he could without a woman's voice in the story. This was unusual at the time and obviously hit a chord with the nation; *Sons* was on the air for 12 seasons. Of course, women would enter the picture as the boys grew up, got married, and had children. But that original testosterone-driven idea was what sold the show. *One Day* was a gender reversal from *My Three Sons*, a world in which the woman's voice was paramount. Ann had a job in advertising, raised the girls alone, and dispensed wisdom best she could—as Steve Douglas did in his all-male household. In the new reboot of *One Day at a Time* on Netflix, a Cuban family is watched over by a strong matriarch (Rita Moreno), and the voice of women handling life without an obvious male presence is underscored as in the original show.

TV was part of the landscape growing up in my own home and in the world (especially in the United States). Despite children jumping under those desks while sirens screamed, memories of that era when my father was writing these shows was idyllic. My dad had a musician's irreverent sense of humor, which he passed on to all of his kids. Our parents took us all over the world, and when we traveled my dad took his upright Royal typewriter (which he preferred because it had hard action like a piano). He mailed scripts to the studios from exotic ports. Hearing the "clack" of his typewriter on ships and in hotels is a deep memory. So many of his ideas came from these travels: an episode of *My Three Sons* in which the Douglas family travels to Scotland to visit a family home and the movie *Munster, Go Home* in which the Munsters inherit a haunted manor, were all taken from my dad's English background and travels.

Speaking of *The Munsters*, it's interesting to reflect on the "supernatural" bent of television in the 1960s that dotted the American landscape. *Bewitched, The Munsters,* and *The Addams Family* were all launched in 1964. Dad took my sister and me to set of *The Munsters*, and I was amazed to see that in person, Herman, Lily, and others had blue-green faces! Since TV was still in black and white, I had no idea that they painted every character this strange, pallid color, which really translated as a deathly glow. Very cool. Perhaps the deep changes that were part of America (and the world) were reflected in these stories of "monstrous" families who just wanted to be loved and were loving and real inside their weird worlds. Perhaps this was trying to capture the racism and sense of "other" that was part of our culture from the beginning. It certainly hit a chord in the country. Though all of those shows were only on the air a few years, they remain wildly popular even today.

The world I grew up in was literally inside the tube. We watched TV the way other families did not. My dad was always talking shop, dissecting plot lines, story arcs, endings. Like being in the family of a tailor, a professor, or a butcher, for us both music and writing were part of our family's fabric. We learned the ropes through all our connections to television. Watching TV wasn't for entertainment, it was for learning.

My brother, Doug, was the oldest of four, and the only son in our family. Doug was and remains brilliant with words and creative ideas, so it was natural my dad would pass him the writing baton. Doug had a highly successful career of his own, writing episodes of *My Three Sons, Bewitched, The Andy Griffith Show, The Munsters,* and many more. Doug wrote TV for many years until he became a drummer and moved to Massachusetts to pursue music. I was still in grammar school when these shows were being produced, but I wanted to emulate my dad and brother. My dad was from a musical heritage; his grandmother, who taught him piano, had been brought over from Italy to New York, handpicked by famed conductor Arturo Toscanini to play in the New York Metropolitan Opera. So I wasn't treated as "the girl" by my dad, as opposed to expecting my brother to take the reins.

My dad knew women were formidable, and he had no prejudices against women in the market place. He taught me script structure, and he was the absolute best and an amazing script doctor until his death in 1987. He was working on *Throb* at that time, writing (and still playing piano) up to his death.

Writing for television, just getting in the door, is a heady experience. I had always longed to be a writer, but I was more the Bloomsbury school than the *Three's Company* (1976–1984) school, which was existential for me. I love the talented actors on the show, but the premise felt weak, flaccid, and incredibly sexist. When I saw Chrissy (Suzanne Somers) wearing panties that were fringed in lace like a sexy, scary child's diaper, I wanted to commit hara-kiri on the front lawn.

This was the rub. I adored Virginia Woolf, and in 1976 wrote a treatment with a writer friend, Lucinda Smith, on the life of Virginia Woolf and the Bloomsbury Group. I took it to my agent at the time, and he told me in no uncertain terms, "If it isn't *Charlie's Angels*, throw it in the trash." Though I have had many scripts in development over the years, they haven't come to fruition (a writer's oft-told melancholy tale), and the sexism of the industry, especially when I was young, was rampant. Yes, *Charlie's Angels* was about empowering three women to be female James Bonds, but "jiggle" was the watchword of the day. They could wield a gun, but usually in a diaphanous gown or a bathing suit.

My friend and writing partner, Maurya Coleman, and I sold a series idea in the late 1970s to Al Burton, Norman Lear's director of development, who worked on such hits as *The Jeffersons*, *Square Pegs*, *Diff'rent Strokes*, and *Mary Hartman, Mary Hartman*, a surreal take on American life. Our premise, *Rootsie Too*, was about a catholic school in south-central Los Angeles, in which Irish nuns teach young women navigating that world in the 1970s, a place both hostile and creative. Maurya went to St. Michael's in south-central, and "Rootsie Too" was one of many of St. Michael's amazing, funny, rocking sports cheers. Al Burton bought it on the spot, but it languished. We discovered why when another producer later told us, "I don't want a show about the Queen of Watts." Reagan was running for election at the time, and his "welfare queens" remarks were on TV. So much for trying to shine a positive light with a female viewpoint on a Los Angeles neighborhood that has always been shunned.

My father had a philosophy about life: "The world moves in fits and starts toward fairness, towards democracy. We have stumbled along, from the cave until now, hoping to find love, joy, equality along the path." This is the way he felt, when breaking into television just after the second great war. He didn't expect the jokes of the day to create Utopia, he just hoped making someone laugh was enough. Television, especially network television in which censors and worrywarts rule the day, tends toward the not so subtle or the just plain bland. From *I Love Lucy* whose protagonist was a wacky but smart woman to the parents dispensing wisdom to their kids in the shows of the 1950s and 1960s, to the groundbreaking shows that took a look at feminism, racism, and ignorance, a little lurch toward equality, empowerment, and intelligence was made.

One Day at a Time was attempting, though softly, to reflect these changes. As Mary Tyler Moore and Marlo Thomas made being a single woman with a career a popular concept, so did Ann Romano show us the trials of divorce and single parenthood. When Norman Lear was asked if he changed society with his roster of shows, he said, "No, we reflected society. We didn't change it."[5]

Because my parents were young during the nihilistic days of World War II, they found a way to find joy despite the pain. I believe that the TV shows of the early era reflected this need: it was vanilla, but vanilla with hope. It was putting a toe into antinihilism. When we were growing up, our parents gave us a platform to accept or reject these precepts. The world of early sitcoms, at their best, were charming and lighthearted, with characters who embodied a thoughtful, grounded ideal.

Growing up, I had the luxury of both watching the tube and studying great literature. In my youthful (and somewhat naive) idealism, I hoped to convey a more literate view in the TV world of the 1970s and 1980s and through to the present. TV wasn't really having it, but it does attempt a sporadic evolution. My childhood worldview and sense of place shaped by television, appeared sometimes sublime, sometimes devastatingly tone deaf about the state of our world. Trying to break through the deep barriers that were put up in those days felt schizophrenic. In *One Day*, as in so many shows, they were exploring the "gritty," the difficult, but with a laugh track.

To Diana Christensen in *Network*, ratings were God. Sponsors rule the roost, true art can slip in, but more often it is rejected in favor of pablum. My association with TV is layered: A true love of the silly, fun, shows that celebrated midcentury America; a deep appreciation of the groundbreaking art in shows like *All In the Family*; and a simultaneous repulsion with the selling of greed, violence, gratuitous sex, and meanness used, especially today, to sell product.

This is why I paint.

NOTES

1. Christine Tibbles, "Alex's First Love," *One Day at a Time*, season seven, episode nine, directed by Alan Rafkin; aired December 27, 1981.

2. *Love American Style*, TVguide.com, http://www.tvguide.com/tvshows/love -american-style/cast/202795/.

3. Christine Tibbles, "Love and the Golden Worm," season five, episode 14, segment directed by Peter Baldwin; aired January 4, 1974.

4. Michael S. Baser and Kim Weiskopf, "Barbara's Friend," directed by Herbert Kenwith; aired November 29, 1977.

5. "Norman Lear Biography," *Internet Movie Database*, http://www.imdb.com /name/nm0005131/bio.

.

10

Lights Out in the Newsroom: *The Mary Tyler Moore Show*'s WJM and the Decline of Television News

Aaron Barlow

In one of the most famous openings in television, we see Mary Tyler Moore navigating her way through the big city as a single, working woman. In an iconic gesture of success, the final frame freezes on Mary tossing her beret up in the air. With that opening, "You're gonna make it after all" became the rallying cry for a generation of women. In "Lights Out in the Newsroom: The Mary Tyler Moore Show's *WJM and the Decline of Television News," Aaron Barlow reflects on what did not make it past the final season of* The Mary Tyler Moore Show *(1970–1977)—the television news industry as it once was. As he reflects on the shift from "real" to "fake" news in the contemporary moment, Barlow argues that* The Mary Tyler Moore Show *marked the moment when television news "completed the trade of journalism for ratings."*

When Mary Tyler Moore's character Mary Richards turns out the light and closes the door on the WJM newsroom at the end of the last episode of her *The Mary Tyler Moore Show* (airdate March 19, 1977), she also symbolically shuts down the remaining significant attempts of the time to provide real news on television, particularly at local stations. The three "real" news professionals, Associate Producer Richards, Executive Producer Lou Grant (Ed

Asner) and Head Writer Murray Slaughter (Gavin MacLeod) of the station's small news staff have all been fired by the new station management. Only buffoon newsreader Ted Baxter (Ted Knight), a man with no actual experience with news gathering or writing, keeps his job.

Since that time, much of television news—from the smallest local station to the largest of the networks—has completed the trade of journalism for ratings. Ratings—the very rationale for the changes at WJM and once a constant irritant to television news everywhere—has triumphed. The struggle between ratings and reporting, nearly as old as television itself, is not only over but also nearly forgotten.

There had long been a tradition (mainly a network tradition, but it had trickled down to the image of the local anchor as well) of "earning" the anchor chair through a successful career of shoe-leather work by a real reporter. That tradition has disappeared, another victim of the turn away from real journalism. Only its image remains.

The Mary Tyler Moore Show heralds the death of real news, the birth of fake news, and the replacement of the news anchor (someone with genuine journalistic experience) with entertainers whose skill lies in looking and sounding the part.

Today's top news anchors succeed because they are entertainers adept at one particular role, though some of them do struggle mightily to maintain the pretense of journalistic experience and skills (and a few actually possess them) beyond their newscasts and shows. Sometimes, as in the cases of former Fox News star Bill O'Reilly and Brian Williams, former NBC Nightly News anchor, today's anchors can veer into falsehood to pad the reportorial resumes that, they believe, add real gravitas to their grave on-screen demeanors. O'Reilly, for example, was in Buenos Aires, Argentina, during the Falklands War, but the story he tells of his own encounter with violence there does not hold up under scrutiny. The CBS (O'Reilly's network at the time) report for the evening he likes to recount "said nothing about people being killed. It does not match O'Reilly's dramatic characterization of the event."[1] Williams lost his job for what NBC found to be "inaccurate statements"[2] about events he'd been involved in as a journalist. Both men conjure images of Ted Baxter for the millions of Americans old enough to remember the then 40-year-old *The Mary Tyler Moore Show.* Younger audiences had to make do with Ron Burgundy, Will Ferrell's bumbling, Baxteresque character in the 2004 film *Anchorman: The Legend of Ron Burgundy* and its 2013 sequel, *Anchorman 2: The Legend Continues* that take place in the 1970s and early 1980s, the era of Ted Baxter on television. In either case, it is Baxter, that "shallow, aging, needy newscaster,"[3] who is the model today's anchors want to avoid but often seem to emulate, making them laughingstocks, the one thing a "serious" anchor cannot abide.

Knowing the pitfalls of their profession, O'Reilly and Williams felt they had to try to match the real journalistic accomplishments of the earlier generation of television anchors, especially because failing to do so always brings up the specter of Baxter even many years later. They know they live and die on television by their ratings and their value as entertainers (they are both certainly skilled at creating effective screen personae), but they want to imagine their success is based on the older values of the newsroom—on real reporting. O'Reilly and Williams both started out in small-market television news, so they know full well the necessity of appearance over substance, but they wanted parity with reporters (primarily print) who actually went out into the field to find stories and even ventured into danger. They wanted to ensure that nobody saw them as simply pretty faces of the Baxter variety. Feeling like people see them as something akin to Chris Robinson, who acted in the role of a doctor on the soap opera *General Hospital* and says in a 1980s advertisement for Vicks cough syrup, "I'm not a doctor, but I play one on TV," anchors such as O'Reilly and Williams sometimes bend too far backward to prove they are the real journalists they imagine themselves to be.

There's a certain irony to the position of the anchor as entertainer, for he or she is *not* a performer of the ordinary sort. WJM's Sue Ann Nivens (Betty White) is much more the standard variety local TV star than Baxter. Cheerful (in a clearly fake way), she can banter and talk her way through any situation, much like contemporary talk-show hosts, especially of the daytime variety such as *The View*. The success of this type of show has had an impact on news programs, particularly (but not exclusively) at the local level. Even in the 1970s they had begun to emulate the emerging "happy talk" style of news presentation.

"The Good Time News," the opening episode of season three (airdate September 16, 1972), illustrates the problem this shift poses for a limited performer such as Baxter—as well as pointing out problems with television news that resonate in 2017 as much as they did 45 years earlier.

Baxter, whose entire *shtick* is the appearance of seriousness superimposed on nothingness, cannot adapt to a new format in which the hosts chitchat while sitting in easy chairs wearing colorful blazers and no ties: it is not what he knows. Nor can he handle a shift from sole anchor to cohost, especially not one in which he is expected to play straight man to someone else. He doesn't believe he is a comedian (though he is that in more ways than one) so, when he overhears Richards describing his new role that way, he overreacts, ruining the debut of the new format.

Prior to that debut broadcast, station executive Jack Stoneham (Robert Hogan) had held a meeting with Grant, Richards, and Baxter in which he insists that a new and more entertaining format for news be tried as a counter to sagging ratings. Grant responds to his suggestion:

Grant: We're talking about news here . . . news. Our job isn't to make people laugh; it's to let them know what's happening. I can live with ratings. When I was an editor, I used to live with circulation numbers, but when the circulation went down, we didn't put the comics on the front page. News is truth, Jack, and I'm not going to make it into something fake.

Stoneham: Why not?

Grant: Why not?

Stoneham: Well, after all, Lou, there's fake, and then there's fake.

This exchange epitomizes the battle that has gone on in television news almost since its inception, one that has directly led to the mistrust of the "mainstream media" in the second decade of the 21st century—especially when you add the Baxter image into the mix.

The cynicism of Stoneham's "there's fake, and then there's fake" has become the heart of criticism of television news media in particular, although it extends to criticism of Internet news and even such august news organizations as *The New York Times*—in the eyes of Donald Trump, at the very least. The debate became contentious at the end of the 2016 election and the start of the Trump presidency. All sides know that the pretense of seriousness, particularly on the part of anchors, is a sham. All sides know that they participate in fakery, while believing that their own falsehood is justified but the other is not.

This creates a mockery of the news business as Grant views it, moving it from the vaunted "news" (note the repetition in the scene) of his past, transforming it into something whose only goal is to amuse—and to do that for money by amusing as many people as possible.

The pull of ratings success has been so strong that news organizations, and particularly those who broadcast on television, have moved far from their mission as journalists, becoming organizations whose products simply look like journalism, much as Baxter is supposed to simply look like an experienced reporter rewarded with a news anchor chair. It is fear of being called out for this that leads anchors such as O'Reilly and Williams to enhance their experiences.

Fear of being seen as Baxters led them into lying. Neither O'Reilly nor Williams is particularly noteworthy in this; the cycle of change in television journalism from the serious reporting that had begun to be seen in the 1960s and 1970s to a ratings-driven set of entertainments of diminished news value had long been complete even as their careers were taking off. Only nostalgia for a more muscular view of the anchor's role remained.

The Mary Tyler Moore Show did not, of course, cause the decline of television news, but it certainly did document its start, and it influenced public perception of that decline and provided its emblem in Baxter. This needs no more proof than that both conservative radio host Rush Limbaugh[4] and liberal television pundit Keith Olbermann[5] have mocked O'Reilly as Baxter.

The Mary Tyler Moore Show confirmed the suspicion that much local coverage is show, not substance, and that ratings, not news coverage, drive the reporting. This suspicion has trickled up to the networks, where real news coverage once had a home. It has cemented the cynicism that had been growing since the 1960s over the vapid nature of the news arm of what Newton Minow, in an address to the National Association of Broadcasters on May 9, 1961, had already called "a vast wasteland."[6]

This, of course, is not the only reason *The Mary Tyler Moore Show* is one of the most influential sitcoms of American television broadcasting. In addition to three spin-offs (*Rhoda, Phyllis,* and *Lou Grant*), the show also created or enhanced the influential careers of major stars such as Ed Asner (whose *Lou Grant* ran from 1977 to 1982, winning 13 Emmy Awards and even a Peabody Award for MTM Productions), Betty White (*The Golden Girls*, 1985 to 1992, and so much more), Gavin MacLeod (*The Love Boat*, 1977 to 1986), Valerie Harper (*Rhoda*, 1974 to 1978), and others. It was also the most significant early "working woman sitcom,"[7] and it provided a new model of continuity through character and relationship growth beyond mere situation and situational change. In addition, as a show that did not attempt to include children in its target demographics, it was one of the shows of the early 1970s that introduced topics of a sexual nature into situation comedies for the first time. Any of these factors is significant enough to place *The Mary Tyler Moore Show* on any list of influential American sitcoms. But it is the image of the newsroom and especially the news anchor it creates that continue as enduring cultural icons.

When *The Mary Tyler Moore Show* first aired on September 19, 1970, television news was in its heyday. Legendary anchor Walter Cronkite was a robust 53, more than a decade away from retirement from the CBS news anchor chair he had occupied for eight years already. *The Huntley-Brinkley Report* on NBC had ended its nearly 14-year run the previous July, replaced by *NBC Nightly News* hosted by holdover David Brinkley along with John Chancellor and Frank McGee. Harry Reasoner and Howard K. Smith anchored the *ABC Evening News*. All of these anchors had been involved in the growth of television journalism—and not just as news readers. Most of them started either during World War II (in radio and print journalism) or shortly thereafter. They were seasoned reporters with serious reputations.

The reputations of the network news organizations that the anchors represented were cemented by reporting during the Vietnam War, which brought news into the home in a fashion, as the cliché goes, never before seen (quite literally). TV reporters such as Dan Rather soon made their reputations through astute questions posed at White House daily briefings and presidential press conferences as the Watergate scandal unfolded and the Vietnam War wound down, leading (as in Rather's case) to their own turns in the anchor chair. The prestige of the news divisions made it worthwhile for the networks to invest heavily in them, whether they showed a profit or not, especially since it was believed that people, after turning to watch their favorite news program, wouldn't touch the dial, staying to watch the following less costly and more profitable programming. For a time, it seemed as though the news departments of the networks (this never applied to local news) would one day rival *The New York Times*, the *Washington Post*, and the *Wall Street Journal*.

At the same time, there was already that growing rift in television news, one generated by the differing needs and resources of local versus network news as well as by the desire for profits that was beginning to influence decisions about news programming. In the early days of television, local stations were not as powerful as they would later become when production costs came down and income escalated. They had to make do with what they could find, often relying on cheaply produced children's programming that relied on readily available and inexpensive cartoons more than anything else and on programs like the one Nivens hosts on the fictional WJM, *The Happy Homemaker*, which requires little more than a counter and a wall oven for sets. Shoestring operations were par for the local station course, and WGM (last in its market when Mary Richards joins the staff) was no different. Throughout the run of the show, characters pine for the glamour and prestige of network status, either through jobs taking them there or through the reflected glory of friends at the networks.

Local news, even though done on the cheap, *was* a prime station income generator even by 1970. It's just that the money was not huge. Competition between stations, therefore, became fierce, as it generally is, when the pie is small—not so much in the coverage of news itself (they all featured much the same stories in any individual market) as in the personalities of those who presented it. This was a result of the limited and expensive technological resources available for news gathering and not from older news media traditions.

In the 1950s,

> [most] local stations offered little more than brief summaries of wire-service headlines, and the expense of film technology led most to emphasize live entertainment programs instead of news. Believing that viewers got their news from local papers and radio stations, television stations saw no need to duplicate their efforts. Not until the 1960s, when new, inexpensive video and microwave technology made local newsgathering economically feasible, did local stations, including network affiliates, expand their news programming.[8]

By the 1960s, however, the tradition of personality-driven local news was well established. The only restrictions on who could hold the anchor seat were popularity and looking like a network television anchor—looking like a "real" journalist—with an emphasis on "looking like." Baxter's character was created out of the local news personalities—shallow, ignorant, uncaring; he only looked the part of an experienced and competent anchor. Though he was allowed to grow as a personality over the run of *The Mary Tyler Moore Show*, his essential lack of substance as a newsman never changed.

In 1970, Americans were not as cynical about the news media as they have become in the decades since. They still believed in honest reporting and in the basic fairness of the media. Today, a show like *The Mary Tyler Moore Show* could never get on the air—unless it portrayed the newsroom as a backbiting, striving place. The ethics of journalism shown through Richards, Grant, and Slaughter is kept quite separate from the buffoonish Baxter and the smiling but dangerous Nivens who, it is made quite clear, is an entertainer and not a newswoman. The show was never meant to criticize the entire profession of journalism, only the on-air personalities and executives who relied on them for profits.

We see that confirmed by the final spin-off from *The Mary Tyler Moore Show*, *Lou Grant*, which started soon after *The Mary Tyler Moore Show* ended. By 1977, American journalism was beginning to change. In the wake of the Watergate scandal and the fame and fortune that seemed to have accrued to *Washington Post* reporters Bob Woodward and Carl Bernstein with the book (and subsequent movie) *All the President's Men*, young people (especially) were starting to see journalism as a means to their own fame and fortune—but they were eliding the work that goes into creating a successful journalistic endeavor (something of an irony, for that's what the book and film are about). They were beginning to think of Baxter and Nivens as the exemplars, not Woodward and Bernstein, even though neither of the former is really a journalist or even really plays one on TV. Being a journalist was no longer the goal; being perceived as one on television was—shades of Robinson and his Vicks ad!

The importance of this to the creators of *The Mary Tyler Moore Show* is illustrated by their move, in *Lou Grant*, from a television newsroom to a big-city newspaper newsroom.

When James L. Brooks and Allan Burns, creators of *The Mary Tyler Moore Show* and astute judges of American popular culture in the 1970s, were casting around for a show to fill a commitment they had made to CBS for a successor, they were quite aware of the new American reverence for print journalism on the heels of the Watergate scandal. Though network news on television had also reached its high-water mark (on the heels of its important Vietnam coverage) with Watergate, it was print journalists, particularly Woodward and Bernstein, who had become legendary. In Grant,

Richards' newsroom boss, the producers already had an established and popular character with a background in print journalism, someone also a part of the generation of reporters with actual military experience in World War II, either as reporters or, as in Grant's case, as a soldier. Grant, they correctly believed, could carry a serious hour-long drama set in a "real" newspaper.

Having milked the foibles of the faux journalist and anchor through Ted Baxter, Brooks and Burns decided to go the other direction, back into the print newsroom where real reporting still took place—at least in the imagination of the American population at large. Though it was absolutely a spin-off of *The Mary Tyler Moore Show*, they took their new show to a place where the people involved were actually the discoverers and writers of news, not simply its preparers, presenters, and readers.

It was veteran television political reporter Sander Vanocur who, among others, urged Brooks and Burns to bring Grant back into print journalism for the new series.[9] Unlike television journalism which, as Brooks and Burns had already proven, could be easily spoofed and passed on without much effort, print journalism would require a different approach. " 'We didn't feel we could do newspapers adequately in a half-hour. We wouldn't be able to do justice to it,' Burns recalled."[10] Even then, a generalized lack of respect for television journalism could not be hidden. For all of its recent successes, it still had failed to reach parity with its print brethren. To this day, it still has not—as the cases of O'Reilly and Williams (and others) illustrate.

As Brooks and Burns were discovering, it takes more than humor to explore real journalism. It takes words, in all of their aspects, and serious research. While they were exploring this as they developed *Lou Grant*, they were also finishing up the seventh and final season of episodes for *The Mary Tyler Moore show*, including more than one episode that addresses some of the issues that would become front and center on their new spin-off.

In one of the last of the season's episodes, "Murray Ghosts for Ted," broadcast on February 19, 1977, just one month before the finale, Baxter proves unable to write a 1,500-word article on freedom of the press for a newspaper that had commissioned it, having assumed that he was, in fact, a journalist and could write. He isn't and he can't, and he secretly asks Slaughter, the newswriter, to ghostwrite the article for him, agreeing to pay him the full amount commissioned. The article is a success, with even the state's governor quoting from it—and *Readers' Digest* offers to reprint the article for more than 12 times the initial commission. Grant and Richards, who realize that Baxter could never have written the article, force him to confess that Slaughter was the real author. Baxter, reconciled to admitting the truth, comments, "I tell you, this is a great country. You know what makes it great? Because you don't have to be witty or clever as long as you can hire someone who is."

A fitting epitaph for television news anchors.

The episode points out the difference between the face of the news and the substance, two things that television forces apart but that print mostly holds together. It is also a particularly appropriate foreshadowing of *Lou Grant*, which has returned the title character to print journalism within a dramatic context rather than a continuation of the comedy of *The Mary Tyler Moore Show*. There's even a reference to Woodward and Bernstein in the episode, with Baxter mentioning "Woodward Bernstein" as one of the "giants of journalism." Though they were famous because of their Watergate investigative reporting and their subsequent book (not to mention the movie), they were both in their 30s then—hardly yet qualifying as giants (though their legend was continuing to grow).

The quality that makes a television show last beyond its initial run is a mix of timeliness and timelessness—that is, it has to fit the needs of the audience of its first broadcast but it also must be able to speak to future times as well. Given the breadth of its topics, *The Mary Tyler Moore Show* manages to do both. In the specifics discussed here, its creators weren't imagining a news environment like that of the second decade of the 21st century, but they managed to present characters whose challenges resonate within the trauma of that environment.

Trust in news media had collapsed in the United States. The ideal of the time—Walter Cronkite as a rock of American confidence in times of great trial—is gone. No newscaster today at any level could master the gravitas Cronkite showed when announcing the assassination of President John Kennedy in 1963. When Cronkite spoke out against Lyndon Johnson (tacitly) and the Vietnam War in February 1968, the nation listened—as did the president, who announced that he would not run for reelection just a month later. There is no one in the U.S. news media today who retains that sort of respect from the American populace. Instead, there is suspicion from every side that each news anchor (at the very least) retains something else—a similarity to Ted Baxter—and that the newsroom is nothing more than a generator of entertainment.

NOTES

1. David Corn and Daniel Schulman, "Bill O'Reilly Has His Own Brian Williams Problem," *Mother Jones*, February 19, 2015, http://www.motherjones.com/politics/2015/02/bill-oreilly-brian-williams-falklands-war.

2. James Poniewozik, "Why Brian Williams Lost His Job, and Why He Has a New One," *Time*, June 18, 2015, http://time.com/3926988/brian-williams-nbc-fired-new-show.

3. Jennifer Armstrong, *Mary and Lou and Rhoda and Ted: And All the Brilliant Minds Who Made* The Mary Tyler Moore Show *a Classic* (New York: Simon & Schuster, 2013), 135.

4. Christina Wilkie, "Rush Limbaugh Mocks Bill O'Reilly in Book," *The Hill*, May 25, 2010, http://thehill.com/capital-living/in-the-know/99609-rush-limbaugh-mocks-bill-oreilly-in-new-book.

5. Peter Boyer, "One Angry Man: Is Keith Olbermann Changing TV News?" *The New Yorker*, June 23, 2008, http://www.newyorker.com/magazine/2008/06/23/one-angry-man.

6. Newton Minow, "Television and the Public Interest," National Association of Broadcasters, Washington, DC, May 9, 1961, http://www.americanrhetoric.com/speeches/newtonminow.htm.

7. Geoff Hammill, "The Mary Tyler Moore Show: U.S. Situation Comedy," Museum of Broadcast Communications, http://www.museum.tv/eotv/marytylermo.htm.

8. Charles Ponce de Leon, *That's the Way It Is: A History of Television News in America* (Chicago: University of Chicago Press, 2015), 12.

9. Douglass Daniel, *Lou Grant: The Making of TV's Top Newspaper Drama* (Syracuse, NY: Syracuse University Press, 1996), 22.

10. Ibid., 23.

BIBLIOGRAPHY

Armstrong, Jennifer. *Mary and Lou and Rhoda and Ted: And All the Brilliant Minds Who Made* The Mary Tyler Moore Show *a Classic*. New York: Simon & Schuster, 2013.

Boyer, Peter. "One Angry Man: Is Keith Olbermann Changing TV News?" *The New Yorker*, June 23, 2008.

Corn, David, and Daniel Schulman. "Bill O'Reilly Has His Own Brian Williams Problem." *Mother Jones*, February 19, 2015.

Daniel, Douglass. *Lou Grant: The Making of TV's Top Newspaper Drama*. Syracuse, NY: Syracuse University Press, 1996, 22.

Hammill, Geoff, "The Mary Tyler Moore Show: U.S. Situation Comedy," Museum of Broadcast Communications, http://www.museum.tv/eotv/marytylermo.htm.

Minow, Newton. "Television and the Public Interest," National Association of Broadcasters, Washington, DC, May 9, 1961.

Ponce de Leon, Charles. *That's the Way It Is: A History of Television News in America*. Chicago: University of Chicago Press, 2015.

Poniewozik, James. "Why Brian Williams Lost His Job, and Why He Has a New One." *Time*, June 18, 2015.

Wilkie, Christina. "Rush Limbaugh Mocks Bill O'Reilly in Book." *The Hill*, May 25, 2010.

11

Mary Hartman, Mary Hartman: The 1970s and the Birth of the Surreal Sitcom

Jerry G. Holt

Almost no one in television or advertising paid attention when Mary Hartman, Mary Hartman, *a sitcom spoof of the soap-opera genre, first appeared in 1976. A syndicated show, it could not compete with the heft of network publicity, and it appeared on local stations at irregular times, plopped into the schedule at whatever spot happened to be available, often late at night. Ratings sweeps were a month away; the almost immediate popularity of the show was only known by direct-response marketers who depended on immediate telephone and mail responses to their ads—who woke up quickly and scrambled to buy as many spots as possible before Nielsen and Arbitron results bumped the costs sky-high. In this chapter, Jerry G. Holt makes the case that the influence of the show, much like the show itself at first, can be vastly underestimated.*

Between the times that *Mary Hartman, Mary Hartman* premiered on January 5, 1976, and its finale on July 1, 1977, the United States changed presidents, endured a bicentennial celebration, and plunged headlong into the uncharted territory of disco music. Gerald Ford, most remembered now for bumping his head at inopportune times, would lose the 1976 election in large part because he carried the taint of the disgraced

Nixon administration—and he would lose to a figure that many considered a breath of innocent air: Jimmy Carter. The former Georgia governor indeed projected a sense of innocence: he had never served in Washington, and he had the physical appearance of a grown Huck Finn. Though he would shock the country in April 1976 by telling a *Playboy* magazine interviewer that he had "committed adultery many times" in his heart,[1] the nation gave him a pass. He was simply the purest person running.

January 1976 was indeed a kind of turning point for this nation. The wreckage of the U.S. war effort in Vietnam still stung, and the Watergate scandal with its presidential resignation still sowed seeds of disillusion. The entertainment industry in general was anxious to cheer us up: it would be during this time frame that George Lucas began the *Star Wars* franchise, calculated, by the director's own admission, to take us back to our collective childhood—back to an "innocent" time.[2] Lucas had searched for the zeitgeist and found it: our collective gasp was nearly audible as we cried out for something—more positive. It had only been four years since Noah Cross in *Chinatown*, that devastating analysis of the American character, told us that at the right time and in the right place a human being is capable of "anything."[3] Yes it's true; we came to reply, stifling thoughts of My Lai. But please. Let us forget it for awhile.

The waifish Mary Hartman arrived right in the middle of all this. The opening credits of that first episode, set to throbbing music, suggested that we were about to see a new soap opera, and a nighttime one at that. But then we were thrust into Mary's loopy kitchen, where everything shouted brand name, even as the tiny television on the kitchen counter hawked even more products. Here is Mary primly garbed in what appears to be a pinafore and speaking in that half-a-beat-off way that let us know that she was at once here—and also faraway. "Does that look like waxy yellow buildup?" she demands of her sister, pointing at a section of the kitchen floor. She stares. And then, just as Brandon Nowalk has pointed out, Mary intones, "It *is* a little waxy, isn't it?"—just as her gaze turns straight into the camera. She is looking at us.[4] And yes—we *were* a little waxy by this point in the 1970s. Maybe that is why it took us a bit to realize that what we initially took for a nightly soap was in fact something quite different—a dark, genre-exploding situation comedy that could turn downright tragic at any given moment.

Through two seasons and 308 episodes—five chapters a week—Mary Hartman would grow at once even stranger and even more accusatory, demanding that America find itself in this downtrodden bunch in Fernwood, Ohio. They weren't an easy bunch to love—as producer Norman Lear found out when he pitched the show to all three major networks of the time—only to be repeatedly rebuffed. At that point, Lear tried syndication—a new concept for him. Ninety stations agreed to a first season—and 50 signed up for a second. By this measure, the show became a flash-in-the-pan hit and developed a cult audience. And that cult clearly found much in the *Hartman* crew to love.

Here is Mary herself, married with a daughter and clearly suffering from something close to posttraumatic stress disorder. Though she's seen far too much, she's basically seen it on television along with plenty of commercial filler—but Mary has enough of a sense of the outside world to know that something is gravely wrong. And she is activist enough to be nagged by the thought that she should be doing something about it. Here is husband Tom, an assembly-line guy suddenly and irritatingly afflicted by sexual impotence. There's a grown, ditzy sister, an even ditzier mom, and a grand-father who has exposed himself enough times to get the *nom de plume* "The Fernwood Flasher." Then there is the Hargis couple next door: Loretta dreams of being a country singer (one of her original compositions is titled "It Feels So Good When You Feel Me"), and her much older husband, Char-lie, works double shifts to support her fledgling career. They're really not all that easy to like—in fact, they're much more likely to inspire shock than empathy in viewers—but we kept coming back night after night in parts *because* of the shocks: impotence was a milder one. Viewers would also wind up grappling with murder, voyeurism, adultery, homosexuality, all kinds of women's issues—and drugs. Safe to say, something was always happening in Ferndale.

Mary Hartman, Mary Hartman was the brainchild of Norman Lear, even then a veteran television producer. Famous for highly successful weekly shows such as *All in the Family, Chico and the Man,* and *The Jeffersons,* Lear was no stranger to issue-driven comedy, and he had a real knack with cul-tural casting. Amusingly, when Lear, who is Jewish, was asked why, with his several ethnic directions, he had never made a show about a Jewish family, he replied, "All my families are Jewish."[5]

In fact, all Lear's families have been just that—families beset by and cop-ing with problems that beset all families, no matter their ethnicity, in the last part of the 20th century. Many may not remember that the year after Mary Hartman premiered, Lear tried another nighty "soap" that concerned itself with family in a strikingly different way. *All That Glitters* ran from April 18, 1977, through July 15, 1977, for a total of 65 episodes. Although a flop, the show dealt with the surrogate family that worked for an interna-tional corporation named Globatron, a typical enough situation except that Globeratron existed in a parallel universe where the roles of men and women were reversed—and where women were completely in charge. The basic gimmick: men were treated as sex objects. It may well be that despite the women's rights breakthroughs of the 1970s, audiences were just not ready for that kind of role reversal, and that is sad because the show clearly had wit and insight. It even gave television its first transgender character in the person of fashion model Linda Murkland, who was played by Linda Gray. *All That Glitters* probably deserved better than the national brush-off it received.

No such problems with *Mary Hartman*. It found its audience in remarkably short order, and it came down to a basic premise: you're either on the bus or off the bus here—you get it or you don't. Those who took the show at surface value quickly lost interest; those who felt themselves consciously caught up in the social and political upheavals of the 1960s and 1970s found something deeply endearing about the Fernwood crew.

Some of those early viewers certainly had knowledge of a book that could well have been the show's initial inspiration: *The Feminine Mystique*, by Betty Friedan. This 1963 breakthrough work was based in interviews the author did with her own graduating class of Smith College 15 years earlier. Her classmates, Friedan found, seemed to be facing what she called "the problem that has no name," a condition brought on by the clear fact that the so-called American Dream had made them anything but happy.[6] They had husbands, children, and nice homes—but they were deeply discontented. Something was missing—and that "something," of course, turned out to be purpose: domesticity was simply not enough. And so these women took to pills, therapists, and anything else that might fill such a void.

Our first view of Mary Hartman is creepily like a page from Friedan's book. Something is clearly wrong here. Her husband, Tom, is a blue-collar worker, but he makes a nice living. Mary has the house, the daughter, and even the extended family, however problematic it can be. But she spends her days and nights in a kind of stupor that turns the condition of her kitchen floor into a major issue, even as she finds herself turning more and more to the television and its advertising as her primary form of both information and communication. Give her a college degree and she is textbook Betty Friedan.

Even so, for most of the first season, Mary is placed in the precarious position of being the sane anchor of a cast of loonies who spin off in all directions. From its beginning, the show was filled with brand-name "cultural dreck" references—but even these quickly became pretty esoteric; a reference to a "moist towelette" turns up in episode eight. And Mary does cling to her commercial culture: "Everything's going to be all right," she tells her squabbling clan as they try to bail Grandpa, who has exposed himself yet again, out of jail. "Afterwards we're all going to go to the House of Pancakes."

Throughout, the topicality remains intact. Husband Tom battles impotence in a pre-Viagra world. Sister Debbie is promiscuous. Despite herself, Mary is drawn to police officer Dennis Foley, and he to her—and adultery does ensue. With all these hot buttons being hammered, can it be long before a gay character appears? One soon does in the person of neighbor Howard McCullough.

And then there is that fact that the 1960s had, quite accidentally, pioneered an entire new way to watch television: stoned. Relaxed marijuana laws had taken effect in California literally on January 1, 1976, and Chevy Chase, John Belushi, and others were already pioneering cannabis comedy on *Saturday Night Live*. Just as the pot culture knew where to find its music, it soon found out where to find is television, and Mary Hartman was ideal for midnight tokers. By the time the real-life David Susskind invites Mary onto his show at the end of the first season, the inside references and reefer humor were the core of the show.

Mary: But the man had a *gun*! It was a *tiny gun*!

Officer Foley: Are you sure?

Mary: Well—maybe not. Maybe it was a *tiny man*!!

Quite early in the game—in episode 37 of the first season—the Hartmans would confront the marijuana issue directly as Mary and Tom find a joint in their daughter's room and then proceed to get stoned so they can lecture her about—what else?—getting stoned. Today's audiences are used to this strain of humor in our media; it came to some kind of apotheosis in *The Big Lebowski* in 1998. But in those days, episode 37 was a bit of a breakthrough: the show had now established its target audience, culturally savvy sixties survivors. After Mary breaks down on the Susskind show—a pure casualty of Friedan's "problem that has no name"—she is institutionalized only to be rescued by . . . Gore Vidal. By this point, the show had become deliriously self-referential: in the mental hospital, Mary is thrilled to be part of a Nielsen rating focus group.

Even as America passed its bicentennial year writhing in the gothic house of Vietnam and Watergate, television comedy like the Lear productions and, of course, *M*A*S*H* showed new directions by opening dialogues that we had been afraid to enter into before. Mary Hartman will remain an example of such a dialogue. In fact, it is quite remarkable to view the show today and marvel at how contemporary it seems. As Don McGregor points out, the pervasiveness of commercials has become only more omnipresent in our lives—even the Super Bowl now attracts viewers for its new commercials as much as the game itself.

And none of Mary's many travails has exactly gone away: gender and equality issues haunt us even more today—and that countertop television of Mary's, the one that brought only news of war, famine, and pestilence every time she turned it on is still the same set. Today, it just has a plasma screen.

NOTES

1. Robert Scheer, "Interview with Jimmy Carter," *Playboy*, November 1976, http://www.playboy.com/articles/playboy-interview-jimmy-carter.

2. Vinne Mancuso, "George Lucas: *Star Wars* Is a Film for 12-Year-Olds." *Observer*, April 13, 2017, http://observer.com/2017/04/george-lucas-says-star-wars-is-for-12-year-olds.

3. *Chinatown*, directed by Roman Polanski, Paramount Studios, 1973.

4. Brandon Nowalk, "*Mary Hartman, Mary Hartman* Combined Soap Opera, Satire, and Nightmare," *A.V.Club*. December 9, 2013. http://www.avclub.com/article/mary-hartman-mary-hartman-combined-soap-opera-sati-106307.

5. Cindy Sher, "Norman Lear on Making TV That Breaks Ground." *Jewish Telegraphic Agency*, December 5, 2015, 10.

6. Betty Friedan, *The Feminine Mystique* (New York: W.W. Norton, 1963), 4.

BIBLIOGRAPHY

Buening, Michael. "*Mary Hartman, Mary Hartman*: The Complete Series," www.popmatters.com. February 26, 2014.

Friedan, Betty. *The Feminine Mystique*. New York: W.W. Norton, 1963.

Lear, Norman. *Even THIS I Get to Experience*. London: Penguin Books, 2004.

Lockwood, Daniel. *The Mary Hartman Story*. New York: Bolder, 1976.

Mancuso, Vinne. "George Lucas: *Star Wars* Is a Film for 12-Year-Olds." *Observer*, April 13, 2017, http://observer.com/2017/04/george-lucas-says-star-wars-is-for-12-year-olds.

Nowalk, Brandon. "*Mary Hartman, Mary Hartman* Combined Soap Opera, Satire, and Nightmare." A.V. Club, December 9, 2013, http://www.avclub.com/article/mary-hartman-mary-hartman-combined-soap-opera-sati-106307.

Scheer, Robert. "Interview with Jimmy Carter." *Playboy*, November 1976, http://www.playboy.com/articles/playboy-interview-jimmy-carter.

Sher, Cindy. "Norman Lear on Making TV That Breaks Ground." *Jewish Telegraph Agency*, December 5, 2015.

PART 3

The Eighties and Nineties

12

More Than Friendship: *The Golden Girls* as Intentional Community

Jill Belli

Rose, Blanche, Dorothy, Sophia, and cheesecake. For many, these words conjure a vision of a peak-1980s tropical pastel kitchen, four women in their golden years, and a friendship that outlasts economic hardship, sickness, and even romantic attachments. The cultural impact of The Golden Girls *(1985–1992) is undeniable. In "More Than Friendship:* The Golden Girls *as Intentional Community," Jill Belli not only explores the nostalgic resonance of the show—inspiring everything from Golden Girls–themed coloring books to cafes—but also reads the series as a "radical experiment in alternative community-building" and as a "model for what possibilities might emerge from an effective reorganization of women as housemates, friends, family, and community." The* Golden Girls' *vision of female-centered community has inspired numerous shows since its run, including* Living Single, Sex and the City, *and* Grace and Frankie.*

Many senior citizens who face the prospect of living alone on fixed incomes or spending their final days in nursing homes are seeking peers to form community with so that they don't have to endure the burden of aging alone. This "shared housing" is "[t]ypically a women's arrangement" that "can provide financial, physical and emotional security."[1] One solution for older adults is a "golden girls" house,[2] which includes living arrangements and a service to match potential housemates together. This matching service, the "Golden Girls Network," has as its tagline, "Living Life Like It's Golden," and its homepage adopts the speculative vision, "Imagine a House Filled with Friends."[3] Advocates claim these houses offer aging women vibrant lives, camaraderie, and active social lives.

> Simply put, a Golden Girls house creates an intentional community for female friends around the age of 50 to live together under the same roof. . . . The benefits of creating a shared living situation are many: companionship, laughs, and the support of women at a similar point in life. Other advantages simply unfold as you live this lifestyle.[4]

These "golden girls" houses draw on the success of the original, fictional "golden girls," four older females living together in a private home in Miami, Florida. *The Golden Girls*, a beloved, hilarious television sitcom created by Susan Harris features Bea Arthur as the tall, wise, no-nonsense divorcée Dorothy Zbornak; Rue McClanahan as the sultry, sex-crazed, Southern belle Blanche Devereaux; Betty White as the naïve, kind, optimistic Rose Nylund; and Estelle Getty as the short, sassy, sarcastic mother figure (real mother to Dorothy, surrogate to Blanche and Rose). *The Golden Girls* premiered in 1985 and aired its last episode in 1992, enjoying enormous popularity for the entire duration of the show's run and remaining in syndication since 1989.[5] *Golden Palace*, a short-lived spin-off of *The Golden Girls* used the premise of three of the women (Blanche, Rose, and Sophia) purchasing and trying to run a hotel; it aired for just one season.[6]

Watching *The Golden Girls* now evokes nostalgia, and the show remains compelling and relevant even in reruns 30 years later.[7] Audiences and critics from the 1980s to today have labeled the show as progressive. The show was one of the first sitcoms to feature a core cast of mature women[8] and was popular with that viewing demographic as a result.[9] *The Golden Girls* also raised critical social issues on mainstream television, continuing a trend that Norman Lear started in the 1970s on shows such as *All in the Family* and its spin-off, *Maude*, in which Bea Arthur and Rue McClanahan also starred.[10] Over the seven-year run of *The Golden Girls*, the show's writers confronted serious issues: divorce, extramarital affairs, senior citizens' sex lives, homosexuality, menopause, unplanned and teenage pregnancy, prostitution, the AIDS epidemic, addiction, fears of living alone and aging, mental illness, suicide, sexual harassment, ageism, and sexism, to name just a few. In its treatment of mature women, feminist ideals, and key social issues of the day, *The Golden Girls* continually broke new ground for sitcoms.[11]

What has been discussed less, however, is the radical experiment at the core of the show: building an intentional community of older women. This was speculative for the networks because they weren't sure that this premise would resonate with their prime-time audiences. But it was also speculative in a more utopian sense, one focused on imagining alternative ways of being and living, creating the good life, building the good society, and fostering better people through designing better circumstances. Utopianism entails not only *how* we could live but also how we *ought* to live. In this light, *The Golden Girls* is alternative community building, and the series explores possibilities that might emerge from an effective reorganization of women as housemates, friends, family, and community.

"WE SHARE OUR LIVES TOGETHER": FRIENDSHIP, FAMILY, COMMUNITY

As the sitcom's catchy theme song "Thank You for Being a Friend" highlights ("you're a pal and a confidant"), the women's friendship, trust, and support form the show's core.[12] Their individual and collective relationships are a stable resource that allows the girls to flourish individually and collectively in this experiment in productive group living. The women's intimacy, a result of their shared lived experiences and feelings, runs so deeply that even when at a loss for words, the women can empathize and communicate effectively. For example, after Dorothy is emotionally distraught when Blanche becomes good friends with her ex-husband, she is unable to convey her feelings to Blanche, but nonetheless Blanche is able to articulate them back to her, with her description of feeling "magenta": "No way to really explain it, but fortunately between friends you don't really have to."[13] Although the women are best friends, they are also much more than four gal pals: they are a community of women, people who come together consensually and with the intention of building better lives.

The Golden Girls aired at a fortuitous time. Many baby boomers were approaching their golden years, contemplating life beyond retirement and who would take care of them. This sitcom offered a model for how older women could take care of themselves with the support of an alternative family and intentional community. In "The 'Golden Girls': A Sociological Analysis of One Model of Communal Living for the 21st Century," Josephine Ruggiero discusses "what makes this sitcom relevant to the theme of creating livable communities." She likens the four women to "the four musketeers of housemates," highlighting how "these women were 'in it' together. Despite their individual idiosyncrasies, different personalities, and the challenges of house sharing, they formed a group bound by financial need and by personal choice. Most importantly, these women cared about one another's well-being."[14] This final point about mutual care is crucial because research consistently affirms that robust social networks are key to a person's overall well-being. As people age, these social networks are harder to sustain as the traditional nuclear family weakens from family members moving away, dying, or simply changing their personal priorities.

Blanche, Dorothy, Rose, and Sophia rejuvenate their lagging social networks by forming a "chosen family," a unit not bound by blood or legal ties but by choice, love, respect, and circumstance. *The Golden Girls* embodies the shift from the traditional nuclear families of the early sitcoms to more nontraditional families and friends of the 1980s.[15] The four women live, love, and refer to one another as family from the pilot to the final moments of the series finale, when Dorothy professes, "You'll always be my sisters. Always."[16] Their charisma is so natural that outsiders also mistake them for a family. In "'Twas the Nightmare Before Christmas" (season two, episode 11), a series of unfortunate events means the women are unable to make it home to their respective families on Christmas Eve, so they end up cranky and down in the dumps at a roadside diner. Their spirits are lifted when their server, mistaking them for relatives, says, "The way you were teasing and talking to each other I thought you were family for sure."[17] In the 100th episode, family is called into question when Dorothy and Sophia face the prospect that they might not be biologically related because of a hospital mix-up at birth. Dorothy is distraught. Blanche serves as the voice of reason and reassurance, affirming that family means much more than biology: "What's the difference if she did or didn't give birth to you? You two really know each other, and you really love each other. A lot more than most mamas and their children ever do. Nothing that has happened, or will happen, can ever change that."[18]

Although nothing can change their treatment or views of one another, the women are still vulnerable, just like other marginalized communities and alternative families, when their "chosen family" is not recognized by those in power and when they are denied the rights that accompany this designation. Challenges to their legitimacy as family frustrate but ultimately fortify their mutual affection and solidarity. In "That's for Me to Know" (season seven, episode four), a city inspector comes to discuss a permit for a hot tub, finds out Blanche is renting to three people, and gives the devastating news that improvements costing $10,000 are needed to have the women all remain living there. Dorothy stands her ground with the inspector, "You see, we're a family here, well, not the conventional one, but, we love each other. . . . It's real love Mr. Benson. It's an honest love . . . but we're a family nonetheless and, you can't break us up." This moving tribute, unfortunately, is not enough to change the law, so Blanche must take the legal step to ensure their community continues: "I've decided to share the title with you. We'll sign the deed tomorrow. That way you'll have equity, and nobody can make you leave!" While at first hesitant to share her house and memories with the other women, she realizes, "we're family now, so now it's our home!"[19] Another barrier is faced after Rose has a heart attack and the other women are not allowed to visit her in the hospital because they are not blood relatives. Their relationship is devalued and misunderstood both by the nurse ("Look, I'm sure you're very close to Mrs. Nylund, and I'm sure you 'feel' like family, but . . .") and Kiersten, Rose's daughter. After Sophia tells Kiersten, "these two women love her like a sister, and I love your mother like she was my own," she is rebuffed by Kiersten: "Yeah, well you're forgetting one thing though. I'm her daughter, you're not her family." When Dorothy explodes with grief and anger, "Why does everyone keep saying that! We share our lives together." Kiersten minimizes their relationship, "You share a house together." Kiersten finally comes around and lets them see Rose after she realizes that the women will take care of Rose and share the financial burden of her recovery.[20]

How these women deal with these obstacles and prioritize their chosen family promotes their sisterhood as central to their beliefs about good, sustainable, happy living and contributes to the development of their "feminist utopian consciousness."[21] The series' pilot establishes this ethos, which recur through all seven seasons.[22] Blanche is in a fast-moving relationship with Harry, whose marriage proposal she accepts. As the wedding approaches, the women prepare for the aftermath of Blanche's marriage, an event threatening their living situation, economic security, and overall well-being. Rose is particularly distraught and sensitive to the devastation their community will suffer as a result. Rose addresses the dire economic reality (since this is Blanche's house, she worries that "we'll become bag ladies!") but also hints at the joy and companionship that her housemates provide. Reflecting on losing this social network, she laments, "We're alone" and there are "too many years left: I don't know what to do" (Dorothy sarcastically tells her to "get a poodle"). Rose views their home as community, labeling it a "miracle" that the three of them found one other when they were "all so lonely." Dorothy offers a reality check, reminds her that they "both answered an ad to share Blanche's house that we found in the supermarket! It was not the Resurrection. It is hardly a miracle." Rose replies, "to me it was a miracle, because we're happy." Indeed, as it progresses, the series builds on this happiness and models a community that moves beyond simply "shared housing" and a safety net to one that allows the women to flourish authentically.

The pilot also rejects undesirable models of community for older women through the introduction of Sophia, Dorothy's mother. Her despised retirement home, Shady Pines, has just burned down, so she moves in with Dorothy, Blanche, and Rose. Sophia transitions from an unhappy living situation with no freedom and agency to a happy one in which she is valued as a person rather than pitied or tolerated for her age. Sophia also completes the community of four women, becoming an integral and indispensable part of the family of friends.[23] The pilot ends as Harry is unmasked as a bigamist and flees with the police in pursuit, and Blanche mopes around the house for weeks. When Blanche finally comes out of her room, she affirms the other women as being central to her recovery: "then I realized I was good because of you. You're my family, and you make me happy to be alive."

This community was not always paradise, however: it required mutual, active work to create the interpersonal dynamics that viewers cherish. The season one finale, "The Way We Met," reveals that Blanche, Dorothy, and Rose did not always get along and were even to the point of moving out after a rough start together. Their differing personalities and preferences clashed, and the women couldn't stand each other until a serendipitous St. Olaf story and cheesecake purchase provided a glimmer of hope, establishing some common ground.[24] Throughout the series, late-night binging and gossip sessions remain a cornerstone of the community, solidifying their shared interests, desires, and needs and blending their four histories, traditions, and personalities. In "The Golden Girls Share Signature Stories: Narratives of Aging, Identity, and Communal Desire," Christine A. Berzsenyi analyzes the women's storytelling and its role in forging bonds among them and with their viewing audiences at home.[25] Although these women's bonds are strong, they don't fully immunize the household against problems. A few years into the series, the four women seek the help of a therapist because of their constant fighting. After a short session, he makes his professional ruling: "You are incompatible. You seem to bring out the worst traits in each other. I'm surprised that you were able to live together this long without killing each other." Surprised and saddened by his advice to part ways, the women try to come to grips with this reality when Sophia reminds them, through one of her classic stories, that all communities go through struggles. "Picture it, Miami, 1987, a house. . . . Four women, friends. They laugh, they cry, they eat. They love, they hate, they eat. They dream, they hope, they eat. . . . The point I'm trying to make is, what's going on here is living. Just because you have some rough times doesn't mean you throw in the towel. You go on living. And eating."[26] Even though they are hard on one another, there is a lot of patience, understanding, love, and tolerance.

"EVEN IF WE GET MARRIED, WE'LL STICK TOGETHER": THE SISTERHOOD COMES FIRST

The pilot concludes with a pledge of loyalty. Rose wants to celebrate "that we're together." Dorothy adds, "And no matter what, even if we get married, we'll stick together." This rewriting of the "bros before hos" mentality values sisterhood as enduring and valuable, something sacred to be prioritized over romantic relationships, which may come and go. Although there are recurring male characters in the show—most notably Stan Zbornak, Dorothy's ex-husband, and Miles Webber, Rose's steady boyfriend in the later seasons—it is the relationships among these four women that form the heart of their community and the show's success. Men remain peripheral to the women's overall well-being; in fact, it is the absence of men that allows their alternative female community to flourish. Dorothy's husband of 38 years, Stan, recently left her for a younger woman, while the husbands of the other three women passed away years earlier: Blanche's husband, George, was killed by a drunk driver; Rose's beloved husband, Charlie, died of a heart attack while making love to her; and Sophia's husband, Sal, succumbed to illness after a long marriage. In stark contrast and challenge to fairy tales, in which "happily ever after" is procured by marriage and ends the story, *The Golden Girls* explores how women reimagine what their lives are and should or could be like after marriage.

Men pass through the set playing second fiddle to the women, reversing a trend of women serving to accessorize men in sitcoms of the previous few decades. Starting with Harry's proposal in the pilot, men also present a constant threat of destroying the community. Although Dorothy actually breaks up the community by marrying Blanche's Uncle Lucas and moving out in the series' finale, *The Golden Girls* includes several other marriage proposals, weddings that almost happen, and other romantic obstacles. Men are destabilizing forces, too, when the women fight over them, allowing competitiveness and jealously to take hold, such as when actor Patrick Vaughn comes to town and secretly has relationships will all the ladies in the neighborhood, when Dr. Eliot Clayton is dating Dorothy but hits on Blanche, when Blanche and Sophia both date Fidel Santiago, and when Dorothy shows Blanche up at the Rusty Anchor with her singing skills and popularity with the men.[27] These temporary imbalances are useful for comic relief and to drive the plot, but more important is that they demonstrate how these conflicts and differences get negotiated, with each woman at times serving as mediator to restore the peace of the community.

This community becomes crucial when nonromantic trials and tribulations face the women. When their house is robbed, Rose becomes so fearful she can't function and articulates that she felt safer with a man in the house.[28] Dorothy suffers chronic fatigue disorder and suffers neglect and disregard from her doctor.[29] Blanche is sexually harassed by her professor.[30] The series continually confronts men trying to take advantage of women, situations that ultimately help the women's resiliency, resolve, and independence grow. For example, when a home-security system salesman aims to capitalize on the women's fear of being robbed, Dorothy throws him out of the house with promises to give their business to his competitor. And when a plumber condescendingly states that to install a toilet "you gotta be a man for god's sake!" Dorothy and Rose tackle redoing the bathroom on their own.[31] The women develop self-reliance rather than rely on men as they did when they were housewives. They learn to activate their individual strengths as well as capitalize on their friendship, feminist sisterhood, and communal power.

"ONE PERFECT LADY": COMMUNAL STRENGTH AND BEAUTY

Because each character has a strong personality and distinctive flair, there are countless quizzes to identify which "golden girl" someone is. In fact, the game of figuring out whether she (or even he) is a Blanche, Dorothy, Rose, or Sophia remains a perennial favorite of fans. However, the women often act in ways that defy these expectations, allowing for the growth and flexibility necessary for their living community to adapt and thrive. Moreover, regardless of the individual person, the women are always more powerful together than they are alone.[32] This synergy is showcased most beautifully in "The Artist" (season three, episode 13), an episode centered on a sculpture that combines all of the "best features" of Blanche, Rose, and Dorothy to represent "one perfect lady."[33]

On some levels, the episode can be interpreted as Blanche, Rose, and Dorothy pettily competing for the attentions of an unavailable man, gay Hungarian sculptor Lazlo, and desiring both his love and to be his naked muse for his next sculpture. Unbeknown to the others, each woman is secretly posing for him and believes herself to be the sole inspiration for the sculpture. The "Storyline" for this episode on *IMDb* highlights this negativity ("Blanche, Rose, and Dorothy find themselves vying for the attention of the same artist, while Sophia takes up practical joking"[34]) as does Hulu's description ("Dorothy, Blanche and Rose each secretly pose nude for a Hungarian sculptor") and the synopsis in Wikipedia episode guide: "Suave, sexy artist Lazlo chooses Blanche as his nude model for a sculpture. When Blanche sneaks a peek at Lazlo's sketches, she is indignant: the pictures resemble Rose. Dorothy soon reveals that Lazlo asked her to pose, too, and the three bicker over which of them will be immortalized in stone."[35] These blurbs call attention to antics, arguing, secrecy, and competitiveness as well as the brazenness of older women posing nude, characterizations that undermine this episode's positive message about the women's collective strength, beauty, and community.

Lazlo keeps the women (and the audience) in suspense about his choice of muse; finally, when the sheet is drawn at the museum, they are surprised to see a woman they do not recognize. Dorothy asks the question on everyone's minds: "Lazlo, let me be the first to tell you what a simply stunning piece of art this is. . . ."Now who the hell is it?" Lazlo explains:

> You see, in this statue, I wanted to convey strength and character, so I chose Dorothy. [Dorothy: "I knew it, I knew it!"] Then I dropped her. [Sophia: "Like so many before you!"] I decided I needed more sensuality and vitality, so I turned to my sketches of Blanche. [Blanche: "I knew it!"] And then I put them away. I wanted more softness, more sweetness. So I went to my sketches of Rose. [Rose: "You mean that's me up there?"] No. [Dorothy: "Well then who

is it?"] It is all of you! The answer finally came to me. Why not take the best features of each lady to create one perfect lady. That is what you see. You know, it is not hard to understand why you are such good friends. You complement each other very well indeed.

This sculpture, literally a physical melding of the three women, concretizes the symbolic "molding" that Anne K. Kaler describes in "'Golden Girls': Feminine Archetypal Patterns of the Complete Woman": "The mold is a familiar one because it is complete. The show is a success because of its essential recognition of the complex four-fold nature of human personality, typified by each of the characters—virgin, spouse, mother, and wise woman."[36] Many attribute the sitcom's magic to the four "types" of its leading women: critics have referred to this amalgam as the "quaternity" (Kaler)[37] and "female foursome" (Burns-Ardolino),[38] as well as the "power of four" (Colucci).[39] As this oft-overlooked episode beautifully and straightforwardly illustrates, the women complete one another, and their power is their communal power.

"AN EXPERIENCE THAT I'LL ALWAYS KEEP VERY CLOSE TO MY HEART": AN EVER-GROWING COMMUNITY

Generations of fans still lament that the series ended, expressing a desire for longevity echoed by the four women themselves. This impossible wish is made comically apparent when Rose wants the other women to freeze their heads if they die so they can reestablish their community in the distant future.[40] Though cryogenics and network ratings couldn't preserve the sitcom in its original incarnation, the show's popularity transcends time and demographics, and *The Golden Girls* "continues to circulate as residual media text with a cult fandom."[41] The community of the "girls" still endures, primarily through its robust, committed community of fans, even 25 years after new episodes stopped being produced. The final chapter of Jim Colucci's *Golden Girls Forever* is a tribute to the show and its lasting power, especially in its "Conclusion: The Girls Are Still Golden Today."

The legacy and impact of the sitcom manifests in diverse ways: the senior communities mentioned at the start of this chapter, the relevance of shows like *The Golden Girls* for helping women negotiate the aging process in relation to the media,[42] and the trend of "female foursomes" helped create shows that built on its successful model of a core group of women such as *Designing Women, Living Single,* and perhaps, most famously, *Sex and the City.*[43] The sitcom inspires drag performances,[44] fan Web sites such as *Golden Girls Central,*[45] the Kickstarter crowd-sourced *Golden Girls* coloring book (soon followed by an official Disney coloring book for the show), podcasts such as *Out on the Lanai,*[46] Lego versions of the girls' house, the Big Gay

Ice Cream Shop featuring desserts named after some of the starring actresses[47] and the Rue La Rue Café in Washington Heights, both in New York City, and innumerable social media accounts, likes, comments, tweets, and follows.[48] Hulu recently has begun streaming the show, ensuring the entire series is available to a whole new generation who are now binge-watching it[49] and becoming dedicated fans.[50] The "girls" and these fans strike a chord with all of us who feel traditional familial structures and normative ways of living are not adequate and that we must desire otherwise. This community experiment is steeped in utopia, a word that literally means the good place that is no place. But the utopia of *The Golden Girls* was someplace, and that someplace was Miami, Florida, and in viewers' hearts.

Many people have dreamed—myself included—of living together with their best friends, sharing secrets, lives, loves, and losses, and having late-night chats over delicious goodies. Many of us want to have "the girls" for real friends, to pull up the fifth seat at their kitchen table, to dream and reminisce with them. I remember watching *The Golden Girls* with my grandmother when I was growing up in the 1980s and 1990s, and how, when I caught a glimpse of the girls' "house" on Disney's backlot tour during a high school senior class trip to Disneyworld in Florida, my excitement over this sight was baffling and indecipherable to my fellow classmates. I remember watching the show with my graduate school friends as I was earning my doctorate in the 2000s and 2010s. I still watch it when I need a pick me up, when I'm feeling "magenta," when I want to laugh, or love, or smile. The girls have shaped our beliefs about friendship, family, and community; taught us that life could and should be otherwise. In so many ways, we have invited the "girls" into our hearts, homes, and communities, drawing inspiration from them about our ideal way of living. We feel with Dorothy (who utters these words as she parts with the other women in the series finale) "that these are memories that I'll wrap myself in when the world gets cold, and I forget that there are people who are warm and loving." We too recognize that "it's been an experience that I'll always keep very close to my heart."[51]

NOTES

1. Marianne Kilkenny, "Return of the Golden Girls: How Seniors Are Creating Community," *US News & World Report*, June 6, 2012, http://health.usnews.com/health-news/health-wellness/articles/2013/06/20/return-of-the-golden-girls-how-seniors-are-creating-community.

2. Tara Bahrampour, "A New Generation of 'Golden Girls' Embrace Communal Living as They Get Older," *Washington Post*, June 15, 2014, https://www.washingtonpost.com/local/a-new-generation-of-golden-girls-embrace-communal

-living-as-they-get-older/2014/06/15/b3a67b30-edb3-11e3-9b2d-114aded544be
_story.html.

3. Golden Girls Network, http://goldengirlsnetwork.com/.

4. Marianne Kilkenny, "Are You a Good Fit for a 'Golden Girls' House?" June 6, 2012, http://www.womenlivingincommunity.com/are-you-a-good-fit-for-a
-golden-girls-house/.

5. Susan Harris, *The Golden Girls*, seasons one through seven, 1985–1992, NBC.

6. Susan Harris, *Golden Palace*, season one, 1992–1993, CBS. Another notable spin-off is *Empty Nest*, which showcased Estelle Getty for a few seasons. Susan Harris, *Empty Nest*, seasons one through seven, 1988–1995, NBC.

7. For an overview of some of the show's continued popularity, see Chapter 4, "What Makes the Girls So Golden?" in Jim Colucci, *Golden Girls Forever* (New York: Harper Design, 2016), 22–26.

8. Kim Vickers, "Aging and the Media: Yesterday, Today, and Tomorrow," *Californian Journal of Health Promotion* 5(3) (n. d.), 100–105.

9. John Bell, "In Search of a Discourse on Aging: The Elderly on Television," *The Gerontologist* 32(3) (June 1992), 305–11, doi:10.1093/geront/32.3.305.

10. Norman Lear, *Maude*, seasons one through six, 1972–1978, CBS.

11. Tracey Ross, "30 Years Later, 'The Golden Girls' Is Still the Most Progressive Show on Television: A Feminist Show, Portrayals of Aging, Gay Rights, Confronting Race, Disability Visibility, Fighting Poverty," *Medium*, September 8, 2015, https://medium.com/@traceylross/30-years-later-the-golden-girls-is-still-the-most
-progressive-show-on-television-b63aadd2edec.

12. Cynthia Fee, "Thank You for Being a Friend," *The Golden Girls* theme song, written by Andrew Gold, and released 1978.

13. Kathy Speer and Terry Grossman, "Take Him, He's Mine," *The Golden Girls*, season two, episode three, directed by Terry Hughes; aired October 11, 1986.

14. Josephine Ruggiero, "The 'Golden Girls': A Sociological Analysis of One Model of Communal Living for the 21st Century," *Sociology Between the Gaps: Forgotten and Neglected Topics*, 2(1) (June 2016), http://digitalcommons.providence
.edu/sbg/vol2/iss1/2.

15. Lynn C. Spangler, "A Historical Overview of Female Friendships on Prime-Time Television," *Journal of Popular Culture*, 22(4) (Spring 1989), 13–23, doi:10.1111/j.0022-3840.1989.2204_13.x.

16. Mitchell Hurwitz, Don Seigel, and Jerry Perzigian, "One Flew Out of the Cuckoo's Nest (Parts One and Two)," *The Golden Girls*, season seven, episodes 25–26, directed by Lex Passaris; aired May 9, 1992.

17. Barry Fanaro and Mort Nathan, "'Twas the Nightmare Before Christmas," *The Golden Girls*, season two, episode 11, directed by Terry Hughes; aired December 20, 1986.

18. Harriet B. Helberg and Sandy Helberg, "Foreign Exchange," season four, episode 24, directed by Terry Hughes; aired May 6, 1989.

19. Kevin Abbott, "That's for Me to Know," *The Golden Girls*, season seven, episode four, directed by Lex Passaris; aired October 12, 1991.

20. Jim Vallely, "Home Again, Rose: Part 2," *The Golden Girls*, season seven, episode 24, directed by Peter D. Beyt; aired May 2, 1992.

21. Jennifer A. Wagner-Lawlor, *Postmodern Utopias and Feminist Fictions* (London: Cambridge University Press, 2013).

22. Susan Harris, "The Engagement," *The Golden Girls*, season one, episode one, directed by Jay Sandrich; aired September 14, 1985.

23. Interestingly, Sophia's success on the show edged out another possible recurring character, Coco, the gay houseboy. See Colucci, op. cit., 7–8, 17–18, and 21; and Megan Garber, "When the Fifth *Golden Girl* Was a Man Named Coco," *The Atlantic*, September 14, 2015, https://www.theatlantic.com/entertainment /archive/2015/09/the-golden-girl-who-was-a-man-named-coco/405091/.

24. Kathy Speer and Terry Grossman, Winifred Hervey, Mort Nathan, and Barry Fanaro, "The Way We Met," *The Golden Girls*, season one, episode 25, directed by Terry Hughes; aired May 10, 1986.

25. Christine A. Berzsenyi, "The Golden Girls Share Signature Stories: Narratives of Aging, Identity, and Communal Desire," *Americana: The Journal of American Popular Culture (1900–Present)*, 9(2) (Fall 2010), http://www.american popularculture.com/journal/articles/fall_2010/berzsenyi.htm. Berzsenyi explores how storytelling establishes bonds not only among the four women but also among them and their viewing audiences.

26. Jeffrey Ferro and Fredric Weiss, "Three on a Couch," *The Golden Girls*, season three, episode 11, directed by Terry Hughes; aired December 5, 1987.

27. Barry Fanaro and Mort Nathan, "The Actor," season two, episode 14, directed by Terry Hughes, aired January 17, 1987; Winifred Hervey, "The Triangle," *The Golden Girls*, season one, episode five, directed by Jim Drake, aired October 19, 1985; Mort Nathan and Barry Fanaro, "Yes, We Have No Havanas," *The Golden Girls*, season four, episode one, directed by Terry Hughes, aired October 8, 1988; Jamie Wooten and Marc Cherry, "Journey to the Center of Attention," *The Golden Girls*, season seven, episode 18, directed by Lex Passaris, aired February 22, 1992.

28. Susan Harris, "Break-In," *The Golden Girls*, season one, episode eight, directed by Paul Bogart; aired November 9, 1985.

29. Susan Harris, "Sick and Tired: Part 1" and "Sick and Tired: Part 2," *The Golden Girls*, season five, episodes one and two, directed by Terry Hughes; aired September 23 and 30, 1989.

30. James Berg and Stan Zimmerman, "Adult Education," *The Golden Girls*, season one, episode 20, directed by Jack Shea; aired February 22, 1986.

31. Christopher Lloyd, "Second Motherhood," *The Golden Girls*, season one, episode 19, directed by Gary Shimokawa; aired February 15, 1986.

32. However, in many viewers and critics' eyes, Dorothy (Bea Arthur) is the glue that holds the show together, an opinion seemingly affirmed by the fact that it is literally her leaving the house/foursome to marry Lucas that ends the show (it was also her decision to leave the show in real life that ultimately ended the series). Similarly, her absence in the short-lived, relatively unsuccessful spin-off, *Golden Palace*, also validates her key role in the popularity of *The Golden Girls* (in fact, the two episodes she cameoed in, in *Golden Palace*, were the highlights of the short-lived series).

33. Christopher Lloyd, "The Artist," *Golden Girls*, season three, episode 13, directed by Terry Hughes; aired December 19, 1987.

34. IMDb, "The Artist," *The Golden Girls*, http://www.imdb.com/title /tt0589830/.

35. Wikipedia, *The Golden Girls* (season 3), https://en.wikipedia.org/wiki/The _Golden_Girls_(season_3).

36. Anne K. Kaler, "Golden Girls: Feminine Archetypal Patterns of the Complete Woman," *The Journal of Popular Culture* XXIV:3 (Dec.1990): 49–60. 52. doi:10.1111/j.0022-3840.1990.2403_49.x.

37. Ibid.

38. Wendy A. Burns-Ardolino, *TV Female Foursomes and Their Fans: Featuring The Golden Girls, Designing Women, Living Single, Sex and the City, Girlfriends, Cashmere Mafia, and* Hot in Cleveland (Jefferson, NC: McFarland & Co., 2016).

39. Colucci, op. cit., 24.

40. Jim Vallely, "Home Again, Rose: Part 2." Marlene S. Barr, a feminist science fiction scholar, discusses this episode in her preface, "*American Science Fiction;* or, 'What Happened to the Flying Cars?' Science Fiction/Millennia/Culture" (ix–xxi) to her book, *Envisioning the Future: Science Fiction and the Next Millennium,* (Middletown, CT: Wesleyan University Press, 2003), xix–xx. Barr asserts, "In a two-part episode, 'Home Again, Rose' (1992), the usual portrayal of feminist utopia in *The Golden Girls* becomes science fictional."

41. Eleanor Patterson, "The Golden Girls Live: Residual Television Texts, Participatory Culture, and Queering TV Heritage through Drag," *Feminist Media Studies*, 16(5) (September 2016), 838–51, doi:10.1080/14680777.2016.1149 087.838.

42. Dafna Lemish and Varda Muhlbauer, "'Can't Have It All': Representations of Older Women in Popular Culture," *Women & Therapy*, 35(3–4) (July 2012), 165–180, doi:10.1080/02703149.2012.684541.

43. Linda Bloodworth-Thomason, *Designing Women*, seasons one through seven, 1986–1993, CBS. Yvettee Lee Bowser, *Living Single*, seasons one through five, 1993–1998, Fox. Darren Star, *Sex and the City*, seasons one through six, 1998–2004, HBO. In fact, much of the scholarship that is out there on *The Golden Girls* is in relation to these other sitcoms.

44. Patterson, op. cit.; Colucci, op. cit., 49–51.

45. Golden Girls Central, http://www.goldengirlscentral.com/.

46. H. Alan Scott and Kerri Doherty, *Out on the Lanai: A Golden Girls Podcast.*

47. Colucci, op. cit.

48. Isaac Oliver, "Cheesecake for the Soul: A 'Golden Girls' Cafe Opens," *The New York Times*, February 18, 2017, https://www.nytimes.com/2017/02/18/arts /television/golden-girls-cafe-opens-in-washington-heights.html.

49. Hulu, "The Golden Girls," https://www.hulu.com/the-golden-girls.

50. Stacey Wilson Hunt, "The Golden Girls Creators on Finding a New Generation of Fans," *Vulture*, March 3, 2017, http://www.vulture.com/2017/03/the-golden -girls-creators-on-finding-new-fans.html.

51. "One Flew Out of the Cuckoo's Nest (Part Two)."

BIBLIOGRAPHY

Bahrampour, Tara. "A New Generation of 'Golden Girls' Embrace Communal Living as They Get Older." *Washington Post*, June 15, 2014, https://www.washingtonpost.com/local/a-new-generation-of-golden-girls-embrace-communal-living-as-they-get-older/2014/06/15/b3a67b30-edb3-11e3-9b2d-114aded544be_story.html.

Barr, Marlene S. *"American Science Fiction;* or, 'What Happened to the Flying Cars?' Science Fiction/Millennia/Culture." In *Envisioning the Future: Science Fiction and the Next Millennium,* edited by Marlene S. Barr, ix–xxi. Middletown, CT: Wesleyan University Press, 2003.

Bell, John. "In Search of a Discourse on Aging: The Elderly on Television." *The Gerontologist,* 32(3) (June 1992), 305–311, doi:10.1093/geront/32.3.305.

Berl, Rachel Pomerance. "Return of the Golden Girls: How Seniors Are Creating Community." *US News & World Report,* June 20, 2013, http://health.usnews.com/health-news/health-wellness/articles/2013/06/20/return-of-the-golden-girls-how-seniors-are-creating-community.

Berzsenyi, Christine A. "The Golden Girls Share Signature Stories: Narratives of Aging, Identity, and Communal Desire." *Americana: The Journal of American Popular Culture (1900–Present),* 9(2) (Fall 2010), http://www.americanpopularculture.com/journal/articles/fall_2010/berzsenyi.htm.

Burns-Ardolino, Wendy A. *TV Female Foursomes and Their Fans: Featuring The Golden Girls, Designing Women, Living Single, Sex and the City, Girlfriends, Cashmere Mafia and Hot in Cleveland.* Jefferson, NC: McFarland & Co., 2016.

Colucci, Jim. *Golden Girls Forever.* New York: Harper Design, 2016.

Fee, Cynthia. "Thank You for Being a Friend." *The Golden Girls* theme song, written by Andrew Gold, released 1978.

Garber, Megan. "When the Fifth *Golden Girl* Was a Man Named Coco." *The Atlantic,* September 14, 2015, https://www.theatlantic.com/entertainment/archive/2015/09/the-golden-girl-who-was-a-man-named-coco/405091/.

Golden Girls Central, http://www.goldengirlscentral.com/.

Hulu. *The Golden Girls,* https://www.hulu.com/the-golden-girls.

Hunt, Stacey Wilson. "The Golden Girls Creators on Finding a New Generation of Fans." *Vulture,* March 3, 2017, http://www.vulture.com/2017/03/the-golden-girls-creators-on-finding-new-fans.html.

IMDb. "The Artist." *The Golden Girls,* http://www.imdb.com/title/tt0589830/.

Kilkenny, Marianne. "Are You a Good Fit for a 'Golden Girls' House?" June 6, 2012, http://www.womenlivingincommunity.com/are-you-a-good-fit-for-a-golden-girls-house/.

Lemish, Dafna, and Varda Muhlbauer. " 'Can't Have It All': Representations of Older Women in Popular Culture." *Women & Therapy,* 35(3–4) (July 2012), 165–180, doi:10.1080/02703149.2012.684541.

Oliver, Isaac, "Cheesecake for the Soul: A 'Golden Girls' Cafe Opens." *The New York Times,* February 18, 2017, https://www.nytimes.com/2017/02/18/arts/television/golden-girls-cafe-opens-in-washington-heights.html.

Patterson, Eleanor. "The Golden Girls Live: Residual Television Texts, Participatory Culture, and Queering TV Heritage through Drag." *Feminist Media Studies*, 16(5) (September 2016), 838–851, doi:10.1080/14680777.2016.1149087.

Ross, Tracey. "30 Years Later, 'The Golden Girls' Is Still the Most Progressive Show on Television: A Feminist Show, Portrayals of Aging, Gay Rights, Confronting Race, Disability Visibility, Fighting Poverty." *Medium*, September 8, 2015, https://medium.com/@traceylross/30-years-later-the-golden-girls-is-still-the-most-progressive-show-on-television-b63aadd2edec.

Ruggiero, Josephine. "The 'Golden Girls': A Sociological Analysis of One Model of Communal Living for the 21st Century." *Sociology Between the Gaps: Forgotten and Neglected Topics*, 2(1) (June 2016), http://digitalcommons.providence.edu/sbg/vol2/iss1/2.

Scott, H. Alan, and Kerri Doherty. *Out on the Lanai: A Golden Girls Podcast.* Golden Girls Network, http://goldengirlsnetwork.com/.

Spangler, Lynn C. "A Historical Overview of Female Friendships on Prime-Time Television." *Journal of Popular Culture*, 22(4) (March 1989), 13–23, doi:10.1111/j.0022-3840.1989.2204_13.x.

Vickers, Kim. "Aging and the Media: Yesterday, Today, and Tomorrow." *Californian Journal of Health Promotion*, 5(3) (n. d.), 100–105.

Wagner-Lawlor, Jennifer A. *Postmodern Utopias and Feminist Fictions.* London: Cambridge University Press, 2013.

13

Cheers: Where Everybody Knows Your Name

Michael Katims

Michael Katims opens this chapter, "Cheers: Where Everybody Knows Your Name," with an autobiographical tale of learning to go "for one" in the cities of Paris and Cork. "Going for one," he soon discovers, refers to sharing a pint with friends in the local pub. Cut to Cheers *(1982–1993), the homey Boston bar "where everybody knows your name." Katims's reflections on the bar culture of his past sheds light on the deep fascination audiences had with* Cheers *throughout the 1980s. He argues that it is the characters' relatability and self-deprecating sense of humor that captured the imagination of a generation and inspired so many to search for a community of acceptance and understanding in their own local watering holes.*

In the early 1990s, around the time the series *Cheers* was winding down, I was living in Paris and scratching out a living using the only marketable skill I had—my native English. I hadn't yet written that sensational novel or game-changing screenplay that would allow me to live comfortably in the City of Lights and thumb my nose at the New York literary establishment and the entire entertainment industry. (Still haven't, but I haven't given up.) I couldn't find enough work as a translator, so I got a part-time job teaching English as a second language through an Irish-based company, catering to Europeans on the continent who needed to acquire English to succeed, mostly in international business and tourism.

After a misbegotten stint teaching basic comprehension skills to a group of likable but tongue-tied airline maintenance mechanics, the language school offered me a six-week gig on an immersion program in the city of Cork, Republic of Ireland, teaching conversational English to German bankers. I would be given a reasonable salary, an apartment, and a small stipend to cover meals and other expenses. Paris was emptying out for the summer and things weren't exactly going smoothly with my girlfriend, so I accepted. Hey, I needed the money.

The manager of the Cork branch of the language school was a bearded, bright-eyed Dubliner named Mark, only a year or two older than myself, who wore rumpled corduroy jackets and slightly mismatched socks. He found me a "flat" in the same building complex where he lived, in the Shandon section of town, in the shadow of the steeple of St. Anne's Church. It was a one-room studio with coin-operated electricity, bare wooden floors, a hot plate, an electric kettle, a worn-out armchair, a single freestanding lamp, and a sofa bed with a mattress that smelled vaguely of cooking oil. I loved it.

But I didn't spend much time there. That first evening, after my first six hours of grueling grammar lessons and vocabulary drills with junior executives from Deutsche Bank, I made a little dinner, showered and settled in for the evening with a good book. A knock came on the door.

"Yes?"

"Michael?"

"Yes, Mark?"

"Coming for one?"

"Huh?"

I hadn't packed a bathrobe so I pulled on my jeans and a sweater to open the door.

"Are you coming for one?"

"One what?"

Mark laughed. He thought I was being funny.

"You know," he said. "The pub."

"Oh. Listen, that's nice of you but I'm really beat. Maybe another time."

"Ah come on then, just one."

There was no way to say no. I was single, about 30, alone, sort of lost, and nearly broke. I was about to be changed forever.

Nowadays, if you ask a 30-year-old American, he or she likely won't remember much from the series *Cheers*. Born in the mid-1980s, that generation of TV watchers were mere children in 1993 when the series ended. Words and phrases like "sad" and "kind of depressing" keep cropping up as they recall watching, often with their parents, Sam and Diane, Woody, Norm, Cliff, Carla, Rebecca, and Frasier. But if you ask them if they remember any of the words to the theme song, the responses are surprisingly positive.

"I know some of that is wrong," says 30-year-old Ruth Hofheimer,[1] after quoting the refrain with almost letter-perfect accuracy:

> Sometimes you want to go
> Where everybody knows your name. . . .

Written by Gary Portnoy and Judy Hart Angelo for the series, the jingle struck a chord with millions of viewers. The same tandem had first proposed a theme featuring the lyric "People Like Us," but it was rejected by the network.[2] The network was right. The original lyric was excluding and would emphasize precisely the wrong aspect of the series. Cheers is a place where anyone can feel at home, not just "people like us."

Coupled with the brilliant opening credits sequence, the jingle—which also charted as a single—set the stage for the sitcom with arguably unrivaled effectiveness.[3] "Anyone who grew up with a TV in the 1980s," writes Stephen Coles for *Fonts In Use*, "would be familiar with the 60-second sequence."[4]

Conceived and designed by a specialized Los Angeles firm called Castle/Bryant/Johnsen, the opening credits begin with an exterior shot from across the street of the limestone Hampshire House mansion in Boston's Beacon Hill. A sign with the distinctive Cheers logo hangs outside beneath a red-and-white canopy. The entrance to the bar, the real-life name of which was Bull & Finch, is down a short flight of steps and behind a wrought-iron spike fence. A taxi and a black sedan whoosh past. A woman in white, carrying a shopping bag in one hand and a large handbag over her other shoulder, is about to cross paths with a man wearing flowery shorts and white socks up to his knees, walking in the opposite direction. So far, it's pretty standard stuff. But then a stroke of genius: the action freezes and a quick crossfade takes us back in time.

The same bar, the same red-and-white canopy, and even the same streetlamps—but now the passersby are wearing bouffant dresses, top hats, or derby hats, and a horse and carriage passes outside the bar. We move closer to the steps and then inside. A montage follows of drawings and retouched photographs of saloon and tavern patrons dating from approximately the 1880s to the 1940s. In each still illustration are recognizable and relatable characters in a moment of relaxation, celebration, communion, or seduction, drinks held high, eyelids drooping, collars open, skirts hitched up past the ankle, hats askew, and smiles all around.

Nothing in the series concept speaks of heritage or olden days. But the opening sequence ties the story in with something larger than the sum of its parts. It brings the audience along on a journey that transcends a single era, making it, in effect, timeless, eternally modern, and relevant. The message is clear: this place has always been here, it is yours, and it is a fundamental part of the American story. Sure, as the song says, "Making your way in the world today takes everything you got." But there is a place where you can be yourself, where you will be accepted for who you are, and liked despite your flaws, perhaps even, in part, *because* of them. There is a place where people will toast your triumphs and lament your latest defeat, where every pipe dream has value, regardless of whether it ever has a chance of coming true. There is a place where you don't need to be a celebrity to be remembered. You don't need money or power to be admired. You don't need to be an expert for your opinion to hold weight. That place has always been there. Your fathers and mothers gathered there. And their fathers and mothers before them. It will still be there for your children and grandchildren. Best of all, right now it is yours. Come on in and pull up a stool. Let me buy you a beer. Welcome to Cheers.

Mark took me to a pub where everybody knew his name and, and in a few hours, it seemed like everybody knew mine. Not much of a drinker, I nursed a single pint of Guinness stout for as long as I possibly could, then drank another in under five minutes after "last orders." I laughed and shared stories with a cast of characters ranging in age from 20 to 75. We stayed until closing time which, because of a nationwide battle against alcoholism, was mercifully early. I was in bed by 1:00 a.m., dog tired but slightly tipsy and still smiling. I'd learned a handful of new jokes, the chorus of a few old songs, and met some delightful and slightly desperate characters—women with tortured love lives, men who despised their wives, alcoholics who'd lost their jobs, civil servants who wanted to be actors. I left feeling I had been adopted. I was now a part of the life of that pub, and I would remain so, with or without Mark, for as long as I stayed in Cork. When evening rolled around, it was time for me to come along "for one." I was part of a community in a certain place and time.

Like the characters of Eugene O'Neill's *The Iceman Cometh*, each character in *Cheers* is living in a sort of insufferable holding pattern made halfway bearable by pipe dreams and self-delusion that form a part of their everyday reality, a large portion of which takes place in a local bar. Cliff (John Ratzenberger), the conspiracy-minded, know-it-all postman, proud civil servant and original thinker, always sits at the right hand of his friend, Norm (George Wendt), an overweight and often self-deprecating accountant. Stuck in a nowhere job and a nowhere marriage, Norm religiously occupies the corner stool, leaning over its classic brass railing and sipping from an endless brew. Carla (Rhea Pearlman), the wisecracking working-class waitress, has four kids to feed, a handful of no-goodnik ex-husbands, and no patience for pretentiousness or ostentation. Coach

Ernie Pantusso (Nicholas Colasanto), the punchy, ex-baseball coach and now bartender with a heart of gold, prone to malaprops and memory lapses, rounds out the original supporting cast. Each character is locked in a comic loop and relies on the support and recognition of the others to feel normal.

The leads are every bit as lonely and lost. Bar owner Sam (played by Ted Danson), a former professional baseball player, and Diane (Shelly Long), an attractive literature student and aspiring novelist with delusions of grandeur, provide the central dramatic tension for the series' first few seasons. Part of that tension probably stems from the fact that neither was the undisputed "star" of the show. Indeed, no other television pair has ever been so evenly billed, with scripts minutely calibrated to maintain balance. A carefully designed shared title card, one name lower left and the other upper right, made it impossible to read one name "over" or "before" the other.

Though it started out dead last in the ratings, *Cheers* eventually became immensely popular, with a viewership of more than 80 million by the time it reached syndication. More than 100 Emmy nominations, 26 wins, and ranked in the top-10 series for a decade, it is now widely considered one of network television's best and most artistically successful efforts. "You're asking me all these questions about . . . why it appeals to so many people," Danson told the *Baltimore Sun* when the series was ending in 1993, "and I don't know the answers."[5]

And it isn't easy to know why the series seems to reach beyond television and into the mainstream culture of an entire generation and beyond. It isn't only that people wanted to watch it—they wanted (and still want) *to be inside* it.

The Bull & Finch Bar, on Beacon Street across from the Boston Public Garden, soon changed its name to "Cheers" and licensed the logo from Universal Studios, so it could hang a sign outside just like the one on TV. The owners opened a T-shirt and memorabilia shop upstairs, accounting (at one point) for half of their $7 million annual gross, then added several souvenir shops around town.[6]

Host International, a subsidiary of Marriott, also licensed the name and logo for a string of airport lounges they were hoping to make less impersonal. They even created an animatronic pair named Bob and Hank, designed to resemble Cliff and Norm, who automatically started cracking jokes whenever a customer came close, drawing a lawsuit by Ratzenberger and Wendt.[7] "We have yet to open a *Cheers* bar that has not doubled the revenue that was being brought in in the previous space," Host company spokesman Richard Sneed boasted to the *Chicago Tribune* in 1990.[8] One explanation for the show's influence surely stems from its brilliant writing and, in particular, the ability of its creators—James Burrows, Les Charles, and Glenn Charles—to cull comedy and emotion from the characters' lucidity about their own hopelessness, foibles, or limitations. To varying degrees, the characters of *Cheers* know they're stuck and somehow they find humor in it. As Norm says, "It's a dog-eat-dog world and I'm wearing Milk Bone underwear."[9]

More than any other single element, the characters' sense of humor about themselves is what makes the series go. *All In the Family* invited its audience to laugh at Archie Bunker's limitations, misconceptions, and prejudices, and *Taxi* got guffaws from Louie De Palma's lust and avarice, but the jokes on *Cheers* are as often as not at the speaker's own expense. They are often *consciously being* funny, precisely because they are desperate, because they know they have no way out and are unable to change.

To begin with, Diane Chambers is fighting a losing war against the undereducated, unliterary, and uncultured world around her. She is keenly aware of how unbearable she can be, but she is on a mission and her mission is, in a way, the real premise of the series. At the conclusion of the pilot episode, she sits down with a couple at a corner table and introduces herself. Her speech and the resulting joke set the tone for the entire series:

> **Diane:** Hello, my name is Diane. . . . If anyone would have told me a week ago that I would be doing this, I would have thought them insane. When Sam over there offered me the job, I laughed in his face. But then it occurred to me. Here I am, I'm a student. Not just in an academic sense, but a student of life. And where better than here to study life in all its many facets? People meet in bars, they part, they rejoice, they suffer, they come here to be with their own kind. What can I get you?
>
> **Customer:** [thick foreign accent] Where is police? We have lost our luggage.[10]

Diane's faith in humanity is never vanquished, though she does come to terms with every grim reality, week after week, perhaps imperceptibly adjusting her sights a little lower as the years go by. She can spend an entire episode valiantly trying to convince Coach to give his future son-in-law a chance. By the end, she admits what is obvious to everyone else—the guy is "pond scum." But Diane somehow manages to draw a romantic conclusion— "Forgive my storybook mentality," she tells Sam. "Every woman has a Mr. Right, and it's a mistake to settle for anyone less."[11] Sam asks her to describe her own Mr. Right; when she's done, he teasingly points out that she has described herself.

Perhaps the most lucid character in the series is Sam Malone. His glory days are well behind him, and he is a recovering alcoholic who must serve alcohol all day to make a living. He remains an incorrigible philanderer, however, even though his legendary "little black book" is laughably out of date (and out of dates). "A lot of people might not know this but I happen to be quite famous,"[12] he tells new manager Rebecca when begging for a job at Cheers, the bar he used to own. Did he misspeak or is he trying to charm her with a bit of humor at his own expense? A little of both?

Woody Boyd (Woody Harrelson), the innocent farm boy from Indiana who replaces Coach Pantusso after actor Nick Colasanto's death, at times appears to be aware that he's not playing with the same cards as everyone else. "Do you believe in intuition?" Diane asks him. "No," replies Woody, "but I got a strange feeling that someday I will."[13]

So is he doing this on purpose?

Cliff Clavin knows he's a know-it-all. When Sam, looking for help with a stopped-up toilet, asks if anyone knows anything about plumbing, Cliff starts talking about the ancient Roman sewage system.

And perhaps the best illustration of this particular kind of humor, turning on the character's lucidity about his own shortcomings, is Norm Peterson. Take your pick of pithy comebacks as he enters the bar:

Coach: Norm, how's life?

Norm: Not for the squeamish Coach.[14]

Sam: What would you like, Normie?

Norm: A reason to live; gimme another beer.[15]

Coach: What's shakin', Norm?

Norm: All four cheeks and a couple of chins, Coach.[16]

The Cheers denizens are fat, or alcoholic, or snobby. They are washed up or bitter, hopelessly naïve or clueless. But they know it. And they are all keenly aware that the best part of their day is spent right there on a barstool, being honest about it, shirking responsibility, and ducking emotional confrontation. And because they are self-aware, we are on their side.

More succinctly put, the series never laughs *at* them, always *with* them. And that puts the audience in the same position as a stranger who has wandered into a pub in Corktown and been made to feel instantly at home.

Another facet of the writing surely contributes to its wide appeal, at least at the outset—the sexual tension in the primary story relationship. Though they both deny it, an undeniable attraction develops between Sam and Diane, a love–hate relationship between the folksy jock behind the bar and the loquacious, high-brow waitress who is only "passing through" on her way to better things. It is a consciously concocted Hepburn–Tracy rapport, and it seemed essential to the concept of the series, at least at first glance. But against all odds, *Cheers* outlived and outgrew that relationship, and one is tempted to say that it came to be about the life of the bar itself as much as about the characters inside it.

Now if you go to a neighborhood bar for 10 years, things are bound to change. And Cheers is no exception. Woody replaced Coach after Nick Colasanto died. Frasier Crane (Kelsey Grammar), a psychiatrist brought in as a potential love interest for Diane in season three, winds up staying on as a regular fixture in the bar, long after his relationship with Diane is over.[17] Lilith (Bebe Neuwirth), also a psychiatrist, is Frasier's girlfriend and then wife.

Most crucially, after Shelly Long decided to move on, the basic series dynamic changed. A large corporation buys the bar from Sam, who buys a sailboat and decides to travel around the world. But when his boat sinks, he comes back with his tail between his legs, begging for a job from the new bar manager, Rebecca Howe (Kirstie Alley). Although that relationship never quite provided the spark of the Shelly Long period, the role reversal, with Sam now the employee and the boss now a woman, made for some especially funny and relatable story lines.

The series proved to be as adaptable to real-life setbacks as any corner bar. Although the faces might change, the real enduring star is perhaps the bar itself and the illusion it provides—anyone could wander in and pull up a stool.

And that brings us to the most compelling reason for the series' success and perhaps the beginning of an explanation for why the series made people want to break the fourth wall and step inside their TV sets: almost every scene takes place *in public*. This sets it apart from family-based series like *The Honeymooners*, *I Love Lucy*, *Bewitched*, or *The Cosby Show* on the one hand, where the main set is in a couple's or family's living room, and workplace stories on the other hand such as *The Mary Tyler Moore Show*, *Taxi*, *WKRP In Cincinnati*, and *Murphy Brown*. The series creates a comic "family" of people who are not related and don't work together and, in that sense, it is a close relative (not to say forerunner) of such blockbuster comedy hits as *Friends* and *Seinfeld*.

Though the creators had been inspired by the short-lived but hit British sitcom *Fawlty Towers*, they had initially planned to place the action in a hotel or an inn in either Barstow or Las Vegas, but they eventually settled on the identifiably East Coast, red-bricked basement bar with brass and oak fixtures. They dressed the set with real and recognizable bottles, glasses on an overhead rack, faux Tiffany lamps, and so on. You could practically smell the place.

But it wasn't the realism of the set that mattered.

Cheers characters were both *at home* and *in public* at the same time. Indeed, that is the same operative principle behind the New York tavern of O'Neill's classic play *The Iceman Cometh*. Matters of the heart, political opinion, pipe dreams, and personal tragedy all go to the corner for a drink. Things come out, rumors circulate. Romance is kindled. People lose their livelihoods, land on their feet, get pregnant, die. In short, *life* happens in a bar. The writer can plausibly walk a new character on any time, for comic relief or to add thematic gravitas—no need to invent some tortured logic or improbable backstory. The door to the bar opens and in steps a new story.

Cheers was not the first comic series to make use of the local watering hole as a constant source of stories and jokes. In fact, Burrows' father, Abe Burrows, was the cocreator of an extremely popular radio series called *Duffy's Tavern*, written by and starring Ed Gardner, that produced hundreds of half-hour episodes between 1941 and 1951. Gardner's character, Archie, was the central figure and bartender, prone to malaprops delivered in a Brooklyn accent and unlucky in love. He's sort of like Carla, Coach, and Sam all rolled into one. But *Duffy's Tavern* functioned more as a variety show, with celebrity guests wandering in for a sketch or two to augment regular comic characters in the manner of *Rowan & Martin's Laugh-In*[18] or *The Carol Burnett Show*. So there wasn't much *Iceman* drama, and there was little of the reality found in *Cheers*.

During the few weeks I spent in Cork, I went to that pub pretty much every evening. Once I was invited to a party at a "pub mate's" home, a barbecue in the back yard. It was a fine evening, and everybody brought plenty of beer and alcoholic beverages. At about 11:30 in the evening, people started checking their watches. Finally, somebody said, "If we're going for one, we'd better hurry up." Within minutes, we were all back at the pub.

When I got back to Paris, I told my friend Mary, an Irish woman who worked at the language school, about my experience. She took me to a place in the Fifth Arrondissement called Finnegan's Wake, where French, Irish, English, American, German, and Austrian pub crawlers gathered most every night. I hooked up with a native New Yorker with a powerful singing voice, and the two of us worked up a repertoire of Irish folk songs we could perform, at first seriously and then, as the evening wore on, American-style spoofs to "take the piss." Brad and I were both keenly conscious of our own limitations as musicians and as people, and we put them on display, charming audiences of 20 and 30, three nights a week. The owners, bartenders, and Irish regulars got a kick out of us, and for years we were at the pub most evenings, drinking for free and singing "Wild Rover" with a Brooklyn accent.

Most of all, during that period in my life I knew I could go to Finnegan's any time of the day or night and there would be somebody there I knew and who called me Michael, somebody I didn't mind sharing a story with, or a joke, a half hour, and a beer. I could speak my mind, and somebody might just care what I thought. About music, literature, politics, or any other thing that crossed my mind. Looking back on it now, it's hard for me to imagine that I never saw how much like an episode of *Cheers* my evenings had become.

Finally, the inevitable happened. I met my partner and we had twins. Tom, the balding, kindly overweight Irishman who owned Finnegan's Wake, decided to sell the bar and retire. Maybe he bought a boat. Little by little, the faces changed, and one day when I stopped in to say hello I realized I didn't know anyone at all. The barmen had moved on, the customers were all French students, all at least 10 years younger than myself. It was over.

"I'm 45," Danson told the *Baltimore Sun* in 1993. "It's OK to be chasing around when you're 37. But when you're 45, it's kind of sad. . . . I'm spewing all these one-liners and I have no idea what I'm saying."

Of course, there is a limit to how much Cheers resembles a real-life bar. The most obvious of these is the effects of alcohol. No one at Cheers is ever stumble-down drunk, no one ever slurs his speech or blacks out. Everyone gets driven home even though they don't really need it.

Another difference with the real world, just as obvious, is that there is hardly anyone of color, anywhere to be seen. Once in a while, there is a brown face in the background. But there are no Hispanic or black characters on *Cheers*. Of course, one could argue that a corner bar in the Beacon Hill section of Boston at that time and place wouldn't be a likely place to meet an African American friend for a drink. Racist remarks and attitudes, however, are as absent from the series as people of color—and there is nothing realistic about that. *Cheers*, like many sitcoms of that period and before, asks us to suspend our disbelief and accept a world in which everyone is white. Though it's hard to imagine that as late as the 1980s and 1990s NBC could get away with such a thing, recall that for a long time *Cheers* was paired in the Thursday night lineup with *The Cosby Show*. It's as if the network were saying, "Look, we know this is very white. But don't worry, the African Americans have their own, separate-but-equal, prime-time slot."

Perhaps the specificity that made *Cheers* so special also limited its scope, both geographically and over time. Though it was a hit in Britain and Ireland, the series was never especially successful on the continent. Italy carried it for a few years, with the translated title *Cin Cin!* and the Spanish tried a remake, complete with an adapted theme song, but only nine episodes were ever made.[19] In France, where *Friends* and *Seinfeld* found success, *Cheers* is virtually unknown. As relatable and true to life as it once seemed to 80 million Americans, Cheers was never able to find an audience in countries where millions spent hours every day in *troquets* or *barras*.

The series pretty much skipped the 30-year-olds, so one wonders if Sam and Diane can find a new audience among millennials. "Eventually, I got sick of hearing ads for Spotify Premium on Spotify Broke," blogs Jake Flores,[20] "so I turned the jazz off and just really watched the shit out of

Cheers." Though the bar has "no AC/DC Pinball machine or giant Jenga," Flores finds "soul" and "depth" in Sam's "Bruno Mars hair and Barrack Obama jeans," or Cliff who has "hair like the guy on the Pringles box." So maybe *Cheers* just skips a generation?

Chloe Kostman, 24, has never watched *Cheers*. A bartender and aspiring actress and singer, Chloe describes working in a neighborhood bar in Crown Heights, a place where people stop in for a drink on the way home, say hello, call each other by their first names.[21]

A spin-off called *The Tortellis* never really found an audience, and another one, featuring Norm and Cliff, never got off the ground. Although *Frasier* was a huge success, nothing about it—beyond the characters of Frasier and Lilith themselves—was similar to *Cheers*.

Sad to say, it appears that *Cheers* hasn't quite lived up to the promise of its brilliant opening title sequence—it isn't timeless after all.

One rather remarkable three-camera series that owed a lot to *Cheers* recently completed a stellar and highly successful 10-episode season. *Horace & Pete* is set in a neighborhood bar in Brooklyn that has been owned by the same family for generations. The series focuses on the bar's current owners and their regular clientele. Conceived, written, produced, and entirely financed by the remarkable comedic performer Louis C. K., the series also owes much to O'Neil's *Iceman*. Starring alongside its creator is Steve Buscemi and a stellar supporting cast that includes Alan Alda, Jessica Lange, Steven Wright, and Edie Falco. The opening sequence features graphics that evoke the bar's 100-year history. It's accompanied by an iconic theme song (written and performed for the series by Paul Simon, no less). It has an uncompromising respect for its lost and desperate characters, all more or less lucid about their plight, who come to the bar to drink, to express their frustrations and opinions, and to search for solace, camaraderie, and a little meaning in their lives.

There is no live audience, no laugh track, and practically no zippy one-liners—rather surprisingly given the undeniable comic prowess of the cast and writer. Though Louis C. K.'s frank, acerbic wit pervades each script, the closed-ended story of the 10-episode series has more in common with a Sophocles tragedy than with *Duffy's Tavern*. So although in some ways it is a descendant of *Cheers*, Horace & Pete's is not always an especially congenial place. In fact sometimes, it's downright creepy. (And that's what makes the show outstanding.)

So where can you turn?

You can still get a *Cheers* T-shirt at the former Bull & Finch bar at 84 Beacon Street in Boston, which is still called "Cheers." And you can still find all 11 seasons of *Cheers* available for download or on satellite stations and late-night television throughout the United States, England, and Ireland. Yup, Sam and Diane are still hanging around in the 1980s, waiting for you to stop in for a quick one any time you feel the urge. And that's a rather remarkable thing 30 years later.

Nowadays, I don't go much to the pub. But I do enjoy a nip of scotch when six o'clock rolls around, and I am increasingly aware of being stuck inside a comic loop. So where do I turn for a little camaraderie and conversation in a space that's at once public and intimate?

There is a place where you can air your own foibles without fear of ridicule, where you don't have to be an expert to publicly express your point of view about politics, where you can share your sorrow about losing a parent, your inability to find love and companionship, or your difficulty training your pet. There is a place where you can laugh and cry with friends and strangers alike, where anyone can enter at any time, where you can escape and find acceptance and maybe even a little compassion. It's a place where, for better or for worse, everybody knows your name. I'll meet you there later, all right? It's called Facebook.

NOTES

1. Ruth Hofheimer, e-mail message to author, March 3, 2017.

2. "People Like Us" was included on a Gary Portnoy EP album, 2013, of music written for the series; available on iTunes at https://itunes.apple.com/us/album/cheers-music-from-tv-series/id598179288.

3. "Those Were the Days," the theme from *All in the Family* comes to mind, as does "Love Is All Around" for *The Mary Tyler Moore Show*.

4. Stephen Coles, "Cheers Logo and Opening Titles," *Fonts in Use*, October 27, 2013, https://fontsinuse.com/uses/5067/cheers-logo-and-opening-titles.

5. David Zurawik, "Last Call for Cheers," *Baltimore Sun*, May 16, 1993, http://articles.baltimoresun.com/1993-05-16/features/1993136158_1_cheers-mary-tyler-moore-thick.

6. Dennis A. Bjorklund, *Toasting Cheers* (Jefferson, NC: MacFarland & Co., 1998), 3.

7. Jeffrey Toobin, "The Bench/The Case of the Cheers Replicants," *The New Yorker*, March 27, 2000.

8. Bob Greene, "Cheers and Make It a Double," *Chicago Tribune*, November 16, 1992, http://articles.chicagotribune.com/1992-11-16/features/9204130961_1_robots-bar-television-series-cheers.

9. *Cheers*, "The Peterson Principle," season four, episode 18.

10. *Cheers*, "Give Me a Ring Some Time," season one, episode one.

11. *Cheers*, "Coach's Daughter," season one, episode two.

12. *Cheers*, "Home Is the Sailor," season six, episode one.

13. *Cheers*, "Chambers vs. Malone," season five, episode 12.

14. *Cheers*, "Friends, Romans, and Accountants," season one, episode seven.

15. *Cheers*, "Behind Every Great Man," season three, episode 19.

16. *Cheers*, "Job," season two, episode 18.

17. The hit series *Frasier* was the only successful spin-off of *Cheers*.

18. Dick Martin of *Laugh-In* got his start as a writer on *Duffy's Tavern*.

19. María González, "Telecine cancela 'Cheers' oficialmente," *¡Vaya Tele!*, November 24, 2011, https://www.vayatele.com/ficcion-nacional/telecinco-cancela -cheers-oficialmente.

20. Jake Flores, "A Millennial Reviews: 'Cheers' Chronicles a Sad Time Before Bars Had Giant Jenga," *Observer*, May 3, 2016, http://observer.com/2016/05/a -millennial-reviews-cheers-chronicles-a-sad-time-before-bars-had-giant-jenga/.

21. Interview with Chloe Kostman, March 20, 2017.

BIBLIOGRAPHY

Bjorklund, Dennis A. *Toasting Cheers*. Jefferson, NC: MacFarland & Co., 1998.

Flores, Jake. "A Millennial Reviews: 'Cheers' Chronicles a Sad Time Before Bars Had Giant Jenga," *Observer*, May 3, 2016.

González, María. "Telecine cancela 'Cheers' oficialmente," *¡Vaya Tele!*, November 24, 2011.

Greene, Bob. "Cheers and Make It a Double," *Chicago Tribune*, November 16, 1992.

Toobin, Jeffrey. "The Bench/The Case of the Cheers Replicants," *The New Yorker*, March 27, 2000.

Zurawik, David. "Last Call for Cheers," *Baltimore Sun*, May 16, 1993.

14

Feeling Some Type of Way: Whatever Happened to *Murphy Brown*?

Monique Ferrell

It's surprising that a show that addressed as many issues as did Murphy Brown *(1988–1998) is so rarely seen or talked about today. After all, this is a show that played a significant role in the 1992 presidential campaign, something few other sitcoms (if any) have been able to claim. As Monique Ferrell argues in this chapter,* Murphy Brown *appeared in (and helped create) "a momentous time for American television." It was also a momentous time for America, extending from the end of the Reagan era almost to the start of the impeachment of Bill Clinton. The change in the country, especially in terms of willingness to address questions of sexuality and gender roles, was startling, and* Murphy Brown *was right there with it.*

Hip-hop culture has always provided us with gems—little "tell it like is" culturally linguistic pearls of wisdom. When American vernacular needed a new way to affirm that something *more* than righteous had been spoken, we were given "True dat." Who needs the extended form and fashion of "Hello. How are you? How have things been?" when one can simply say "S'up"? Don't get me started on the varied ways that a man can indicate his possession of a woman by using a plethora of evolving titles: dime, boo, shorty, wifey. In addition, a man can indicate how impressed he is with another man's woman by asking, "Yo', is this you?" And if you don't like a woman at all, you can always call her a "thot" (that hoe over there); the students in my gender studies course taught me that one. My classes are nothing if not interesting.

Recently, a new phrase has dominated our ever-evolving language infused by popular culture: "feeling some type of way." Translated from hip-hop lingo to standard English, it simply means that something or someone has agitated you. This euphemism can be applied to personal, professional, or political circumstances. When used, the term is an internal call to action that needs only one thing: a strong sense of resistance. Currently, my mental resistance has me reflecting on the notable absence of the once iconic *Murphy Brown*. If you are a feminist or a womanist—one who believes in the equal standing, development, and protection of real-life women across the globe and are equally concerned about depictions of women on our most popular social medium, television—but find that one of the most iconic characters of the 20th century has all but disappeared from the television landscape—you, like me, are probably "feeling some type of way."

As an examination of the American woman, the situation comedy *Murphy Brown* was a teachable moment for the medium of television and its consumer. *Murphy Brown* grappled with alcoholism, breast cancer, illegal drug usage, the political world, and abortion. But Murphy Brown the character became the embodiment of our collective conversations about our comfortability with women: sex and sexuality, beauty, aging, reproductive rights, marriage versus being single, career over love or marriage, and, most notably, the fight against systemic sexism. Both the series and its main character were firsts and took their respective places unapologetically alongside a host of televised female firsts. Firsts that made *Murphy Brown* possible.

Firsts matter.

Diane Carroll made her mark on television as a first with the series *Julia*. During the late 1960s and early 1970s, American audiences watched as widowed nurse Julia Baker navigated the world. America was embroiled in the Vietnam War and experiencing an unwavering push for racial equality by way of the civil rights movement; however, the often apolitical *Julia* still managed to reshape the critical lens through which we viewed the black woman by defying existing televised and cinematic archetypes of black women as housemaids or prostitutes. She was simply an American woman. Marlo Thomas was also a first. Her series, *That Girl*, focused on a 20-something woman leaving the safe and comforting surroundings of her parents' home to construct her version of womanhood and female identity. She supported herself and lived in an apartment that she paid for. Mary Tyler Moore of *The Mary Tyler Moore Show* was a first for seven seasons—long after *Julia* and *That Girl* had been canceled. A 30-something single woman, Mary Richards starts anew (professionally and personally) after being jilted by a boyfriend. The award-winning show is often regarded as one of the top series of all time.

These women—the characters and the actresses who portrayed them—are cinematic touchstones. In their own way, each redefined assumptions about womanhood—assumptions that were in desperate need of clarification. They also represent the long-standing generational conversations we have always had about women in relation to race, economic standing, personal power, and age. *Murphy Brown* is of this ilk.

From 1988 to 1998, the series focused on a single, working woman in her 40s at the top of her game as a journalist. Murphy was talented, smart, uncompromising, complicated, nuanced, unpolished, unapologetic, aggressive, and wonderfully imagined. In short, she was a badass. But Murphy was not perfect, and this is where the true genius of the series delivered for its audience, the reason it has earned its rightful place as one of the greats. It is precisely because Murphy was smart (quite often the smartest person in the room) and complicated that she often butted heads with those around her—namely, men, both on screen and in the real world. Women everywhere could identify, understanding how much of their selfhood was defined by the men of their respective worlds; they also appreciated the gentle tightrope women walk when they set out to find themselves. *Murphy Brown*, the show and the character, walked us through these gender-specific dimensions with precision.

The series, although funny, was no laughing matter. It tackled hard-hitting issues and at one point took on a sitting U.S. vice president. Because of historical moments such as this, not everyone always liked Murphy Brown, but she had everyone talking. And if that's the case, where is she? In "Why the Hell Can't I Watch *Murphy Brown* Online?" Annalee Newitz, buoyed by what she knew to be the true cultural impact of the series, wondered about the limited access to episodes: "It seems more relevant now than ever before. Why is a triumphant, well-written tale of a professional woman not being streamed on Netflix or iTunes or any other service for those of us with 1990s nostalgia? Hell, only the first season is available on DVD. Sure it's on TV in syndication in some markets. And yeah, there are torrents of a few seasons that you can download here and there. But shouldn't such an important show be available legally?"[1] David Lambert answers this plainly—no one was watching: "Poor sales have kept studios from investing time, money, and resources in DVD sets they don't see a huge demand for."[2] For some reason, the viewing public decided that the always iconic and sometimes controversial character had nothing more to say—perhaps nothing left to teach. But I beg to differ.

Allow me to share a moment from my life.

It was a week before final exams. I entered the newly renovated elevator with six students: two young men and four young women. The guys rested against the walls, seemingly exhausted. The young ladies were irate. Apparently, they were enraged about the status of their respective standings in their science class and were less than eager to sit for the pending final exam.

The villain in this scenario was their professor. In the time it took to ride down from the 11th floor to the ground floor, I heard teeth sucking and all manner of swearing while they collectively shared their most recent graded assignment. But it was the latter part of the conversation that threw me: "What is her problem?" one of the young women said. "Oh, I know what her problem is," offered another, the most offended of the four. "The bitch is old and thirsty.[3] She can't take looking at us. What is she, around 35 or 36? She's mad because it's not her turn anymore." I thought of my life. Thought of all that I had endured to obtain my degrees and to become a published author. I thought about my fight for professional success, measured by tenure and promotion, and then I thought about all of the workplace sexism and racism I'd encountered along the way. I hadn't realized that being a late "30-something" meant that it wasn't my "turn anymore." As a matter of fact, I had been laboring under the belief that I was just getting started. When we first meet Murphy Brown, she is 40. If she had been in that elevator, she would have said something. Her sass and wit were designed for that kind of moment.

Don't get me wrong. The show was by no means perfect. As fearlessly as is tackled issues of female identity, it was less courageous in other ways. Its central cast members were all white. It was all but absent in relevant discussions about racism and cultural diversity, xenophobia, or the LGBTQ community—social struggles that were pertinent then and have come to dominate our headlines even more so, especially after the 2016 presidential election. But I offer as a defense that *Murphy Brown* was not about the aforementioned social issues. The show was about women—one woman's struggle in particular. It was about what I experienced on that elevator. It was about how all women fight their demons—in whatever form they present themselves: restrictive archetypes, aging, and sexism—even substance abuse. Murphy's entire life was a response to her demons: the efforts to replace her, confine and conform her, soften her up so that she could be more palatable. It was a show about one woman's search for her personal truths and being comfortable with where those truths led her. Clearly, Murphy didn't fight every woman's battle, but fight she did.

MAKING MURPHY BROWN OR "BRING ME HEATHER LOCKLEAR"

Candice Bergen was not supposed to be Murphy Brown. Looking back, it is difficult to imagine the role could have gone to anyone else. Murphy Brown was always meant to be taken seriously—her presence and impact designed to be equally intentional and meaningful. At least that is what show creator Diane English wanted.

In her autobiography, *A Fine Romance,* Candice Bergen's extended chapter about her life while filming the series is titled "Murphy: Mike Wallace in a Dress." A funny title, yes. But this gender perception was indicative of a perceived flaw in the character that CBS executives took issue with. Even Bergen, who made the character beloved for so many years, could see the obvious: Murphy Brown was too much like a man. When you are a woman, behaving like a "man" or being perceived as unfeminine is unacceptable. But Bergen didn't care. After reading the script for the pilot, she remarked "There was something in the writing of Murphy that hooked me, as she eventually hooked many women. Is it that she was . . . who we wished we could be as women? Successful in a field dominated by men. Free of the need to please. Impolitic, impolite, yet in some weird way irresistible?"[4] *Murphy Brown* was the alternative to the proscribed identifying markers associated with "real" and expected womanhood. The episodes made us ponder, "Who are women really when no one is looking?" and "What are our personal truths about public perceptions verses private feelings?"

Diane English intentionally designed the show to upset the status quo:

> Murphy made her entrance stepping off the elevator at the offices of FYI, a nighttime magazine, after a month of rehab at Betty Ford. Did it have to be a *month at Betty Ford*? The network executives wanted to know. Why couldn't she be returning after a week at a spa? And did she have to be *forty*? Why couldn't she be *thirty* . . . and played by Heather Locklear? Diane, a committed feminist, pushed back: the whole point of Murphy was that she had crossed forty and was at the top of her profession but decidedly flawed, an alcoholic. [English] refused to let the network defang the show.[5]

However, the final word of the show's creator wasn't so final. Her "no" to the network was suddenly subject to negotiation. Less than impressed with Bergen's audition, the network president told English, "I don't think she can do it."[6] Bergen further recounts how English fought for her, stating,

> Diane English was convinced I could and so was I. Diane backs down for no man. She took the president back to his office and said . . . "I have as much invested in this as you do. We [Joel Shukovsky, her husband and creative partner at the time] are convinced she can do this and feel very strongly about casting her." He came out looking sheepish. Walking up to me, he stuck out his hand and said, smiling tightly, "Congratulations, Murphy." I had the job. Soon afterward, he was fired from the network. [7]

Both English and Bergen understood that to protect the integrity of the show, each would have to be just as resolved as men are allowed to be both personally and professionally. This tenaciousness gave us a beautiful fictionalized framework free of unwanted and unnecessary trade-offs. As such, when the elevator doors open to the offices of *FYI* in the pilot episode "Respect," we aren't witnessing an emasculating and castrating woman who wants to be a man, thereby replacing them; instead, Murphy represents what it means to be a woman without restriction.

OFF TO A GOOD START: THE FIRST SEASON

"I'm BAAAAA-AAACK!!!"[8] These are the first words uttered by Brown on exiting the elevator after battling chronic alcoholism. Mere minutes after meeting her newly hired producer, Miles Silverberg, she insults him, annoyed that a man—a young man nearly 20 years her junior—would be in charge of her career moving forward. "I'm sorry, Mr. Silverberg, if it appears that I'm being rude to you. It's just that I can't help thinking about the fact that while I got maced at the Democratic Convention of '68, you were wondering if you'd ever meet Adam West."[9] Next, she learns that substitute anchor, the attractive and younger Corky Sherwood, has become a regular part of the *FYI* team. She is now Murphy's immediate equal—without having done an iota of the work.

It should have been laughable. On the surface, Corky, the Southern belle, was the anti-Murphy in every way imaginable. She was a former Miss America. In truth, she was the runner-up, only crowned much later after the actual title holder becomes embroiled in a scandal. Comically, Corky takes herself seriously, but there is nothing serious about her nonexistent journalistic skills. But it doesn't matter, *FYI* viewership was up because of her.

Without her usual fallbacks of cigarettes and alcohol, in her office away from Miles and Corky, Murphy experiences a moment of vulnerability with the rest of her team. "Lately, I've been wondering what to do for an encore," she says.[10] To us, her office was representative of a life well lived, including trophies, plaques, and framed magazines with her face on each cover. And there she stood worried about an "encore." The best at what she did because of how she had always done it, Murphy returns to a world that does not want her—one that wants a new, unskilled, and younger version of herself. Without question, she was "feeling some type of way," but Miles, although intimidated by her, is also clear: things will be different.

In the second episode, "Devil with a Blue Dress on," Murphy and Corky arrive to work wearing the same dress. To make matters worse, while Murphy lays out the agenda for the day, her secretary swoons over Corky. Then Miles tells Murphy that she'll be sharing an important story with her rival.

The shared assignment is Miles's way of attempting to reign in the journalist who makes her interviewees sometimes sob or flee—or, in the case of "The Unshrinkable Murphy Brown" episode, die on the set. Corky, buoyed by the opportunity to work with the incomparable Murphy Brown, is excited. Murphy wants none of it and sends her out on a bevy of false leads. During a debriefing, while Corky rattles off several inane factoids about their story, Murphy realizes the novice had inadvertently stumbled across an important clue but had missed its significance. Murphy follows up and breaks the story.

Murphy Brown is back. Corky Sherwood who?

The newcomer handles the one-upmanship with grace, and, when approached by Murphy, now contrite and filled with the type of feminist guilt one can only feel after undermining another woman, Corky offers, "I missed the lead. That's the difference between you and me."[11] But Murphy cannot forgive herself. By sideswiping Corky, she creates two certainties: she is no longer the best and she is jealous of Corky. To make things right, she approaches her nemesis and agrees to share the live version of the backstory on *FYI*. Acknowledging Sherwood as an equal, she asks her to introduce the segment. Corky, however, continues beyond the introduction and claims the storyline as her own.

Afterwards, "the Belle" puts on her "aw shucks" Southern drawl, offers apologies, and sentiments about being carried away—promises it will never happen again. Murphy, elegant smile in place and head gently cocked to the side, channels Michael Corleone: "Do anything like this again and you're dead."[12] The threat continues with talk of "wet cement" and Corky's leftover "bits and pieces." The newcomer surrenders with a nod and a smile. Murphy returns the smile. The women retreat to their respective corners.

This episode shows how masterful the series would be at addressing the dual nature of sexist attitudes—both male and female. When Miles first approaches Murphy about "cooling" down her aggressive behavior, he is essentially arguing that the viewing public is not interested in seeing a woman behave "like a man." Frank Fontana was the show's "man on the street"—the gritty reporter. Jim Dial was the great patriarch who guided the show from segment to segment. The executives did not need Murphy as the "third man." Forcing the pairing of Murphy and Corky is an attempt at normalizing and softening Murphy Brown, revealing that she can "play nice" as a woman with another woman. She must, therefore, put the show first, not her career or genius. She must become smaller so that Corky can rise and share the spotlight with her for a turn and then inevitably fade away.

The viewing public, however, comes to understand that the assumptions made about Corky are also problematic. First, they assume she is pretty but not smart. Second, they assume her youth is somehow indicative of her not being experienced. Third, they assume it is her nature to want to topple Murphy Brown because all women are born to be rivals. While Corky is naïve, she isn't dumb. Her on-air take-back of the story is evidence of her shrewdness. It is Miles and the network executives who create the Corky Sherwood "style over substance" motif, thereby generating an unnecessary rivalry and triggering Murphy's insecurities.

Yet Murphy and Corky defy the stereotype. There is no catfight. Murphy does not march into management's office rattling off her resume and asking for Corky to be fired. Neither does Corky loudly proclaim that she is the new, fresh young face who stopped *FYI* from going over the ratings cliff, followed up by an equally vigorous call for the removal of Murphy Brown from the show that she helped to build. Instead, the two women quietly acknowledge they will not participate in the sexist game being played around them. They will not tear each other to pieces personally or professionally.

The show's content also allowed Murphy to address how women feel about sex, having a career, and married life by asking a question: can a single professional woman have it all? Enter Brown's ex-husband, Jake Lowenstein. The infamous leftist activist first appeared in "Signed, Sealed, Delivered" when he is faced with being interviewed by Murphy, his equally famous ex-wife on her Emmy Award–winning show. When they meet again, nearly 20 years have passed since they walked away from each other just five days into their marriage. During the interview, we all learn that the short-lived marriage ended because they wanted their careers more than love and are stunned when he asks Murphy to marry him again midinterview. It wasn't over for either of them.

For a brief moment, we're made to question whether this sitcom is going to be like every other show, reducing itself to the traditional coupling that equals "happily ever after." Is this the right lesson for Americans? For women? For little girls?

With the cameras off and the romance of the on-air proposal quieted by reality, it happens again. He wants her to follow him. After all, she can be a journalist "anywhere," he tells her. Murphy, however, wants to live the professional life that she designed, and this includes reporting at *FYI* in Washington, D.C. So she comes up with a compromise. As the marriage and their rekindling each lasted five days, she suggests that they meet every so often for "five glorious days filled with sex."[13] He agrees.

Sexual gratification and attachment without professional compromise? Done.

Soon after pondering the effects of her career on her love life, Murphy unexpectedly hears the call of her biological alarm clock. In "Murphy's Pony," a downtrodden fan abandons her small children at the *FYI* station shortly before Christmas. The mother's note declares that the journalist will be a better mother because she's smart and financially secure. When the eldest of the small children declares that Murphy is their new mother, she replies, "I can't be your mother. I don't like kids—that's why I don't have them."[14] But she takes them home anyway, fearful of what will happen to them in foster care and because it's Christmas *and* because she hears that alarm clock ticking. Before the episode ends, the mother returns, full of regrets—and so is Murphy. She is misty-eyed, and we know, even though there is no immediate answer, she is wondering if she has missed out on something.

This theme is echoed in "Baby Love," when Murphy is visited by a pregnant friend. The friend, also 40, tells her, "Don't miss this experience."[15] In this moment, Murphy is overcome and marveled by the life kicking away inside her friend. After the commercial break, we learn that she is considering sperm donation and that she wants her best friend and colleague, Frank Fontana, to be the donor. The plan is derailed once they are informed that they'll have a better chance at conceiving if they do so the traditional way. After some comedic slap-and-tickle attempts at intimacy, the two decide that conceiving isn't worth sacrificing their friendship. Furthermore, we learn that what Murphy wants is a baby, *not* a man.

And what do you do when a hit show's main character comes to that realization? Why, you keep pushing the envelope, thereby revealing there is nothing wrong with being in a stand-off with expected conventions, that opposition in life is acceptable, that inaction in the face of uncertainty isn't cowardice or female flakiness. It is, instead, realism and critical thinking made manifest and indicative of what can happen when a woman is allowed to choose herself every time.

PISSING OFF DAN QUAYLE

Turns out drawing the ire of the Vice President didn't take much at all—just a fictional pregnant single mother. The baby in question was a profound decision from its conception to the delivery and beyond: everyone had an opinion. Murphy's pregnancy was heralded as being a brave and brilliant statement on a woman's right to make decisions about her own body. At the same time, it was viewed as being representative of an accepted declining morality and the demise of family values in America:

> [T]he sophisticated professional woman played by Candice Bergen bears almost no resemblance to most real-life unmarried mothers. Murphy appears to be in her late thirties or early forties. In real life, the highest rate of unwed childbearing is found among teenagers. Murphy is white. In real life, the highest percentages of unmarried mothers are found among African Americans and Hispanics. Murphy . . . is economically secure. In real life, the majority of unmarried mothers are economically vulnerable. Fundamentally, the glamorization of unwed motherhood promotes a bold new idea in our culture . . . fathers are expendable.[16]

As Candice Bergen so eloquently stated, "Murphy Brown went from commenting on the culture to becoming embedded in it."[17]

Again, the show pushed boundaries. Murphy has sex with her on-again, off-again love interest, Jake Lowenstein. This time, however, the romantic interlude leads to pregnancy. Now what? Inserting itself in the culture wars, Murphy ponders abortion: "I know I have the right to make a choice. Women in this country still have a choice. At least I think they do. I haven't read the papers yet. I'm going to exercise my choice to have this baby."[18] The critics applauded, "The Monday night powerhouse deserves both high ratings and thank yous for brushing aside the politically correct and devoting an hour to abortion with both sense, sensitivity, and humor."[19] Still, more cultural pundits marveled at the significance of Murphy's pregnancy:

> Murphy is the star anchor of the fictional investigative news program [FYI], 42 and unmarried. Her predicament, coming after several pregnancies among high-profile real-life network newswomen, is only one of the latest examples of the ways in which the series blurs the lines between real and fictional characters.... According to Ms. English, Mr. [Don] Hewitt's much-publicized run-in last February with Meredith Vieira, the "60 Minutes" correspondent who was expecting her second child, inspired an exchange between Murphy and her boss, Gene Kinsella. [When] Murphy confirms that she is pregnant by her ex-husband and resists her boss's efforts at "damage control" (a shotgun marriage to Miles, her 27-year-old executive producer), Kinsella proclaims: "Brownie, I am corporate. I am responsible for a multi-million-dollar operation that does not thrive on taking risks. I don't see any choice but to take you off the air."[20]

Within the series, Murphy's pregnancy was comedic fodder. "My God, Murphy, it's a modern medical miracle,"[21] Corky teases. But what happened on the other side of the camera was no laughing matter. In the real world, male bosses were attempting to sideline the careers of professional women because of pregnancy. The art of the show imitated life, and it didn't stop there. Just ask former Vice President Dan Quayle.

While campaigning at a Republican rally for the 1992 reelection of the George H. W. Bush and Dan Quayle ticket, the vice president delivered what he believed to be an impassioned speech about the need for a return to an America that held at its core a belief in morality and family values. In illustrating his point, he said, "It doesn't help matters when prime-time TV has Murphy Brown—a character who supposedly epitomizes today's intelligent, highly paid, professional woman—mocking the importance of fathers by bearing a child alone and calling it just another lifestyle choice."[22] The birth of Murphy's baby was viewed by 38 million Americans, and quite a few of them wanted to know just what Quayle meant. Was he publicly criticizing single mothers? Advocating for abortion over bringing pregnancies to term? Absolving absentee fathers of their responsibilities? Was a woman not allowed to make a decision about procreation? Turns out, Quayle hadn't actually watched the program. Which means he spoke without knowing that Murphy's ex-husband wanted nothing to do with her pregnancy, that Murphy seriously considered abortion but decided against it, and that her job was jeopardized because she chose motherhood.

The show's answer to the political upheaval was precise. Both English and Bergen had created a multiple Emmy Award–winning ratings juggernaut; Quayle's response was indicative of its societal meaningfulness. How best, then, to make a fictional show about fictional politicians adequately respond to a real-life political ambush without making the show or its character look buffoonish? Even Bergen believed, "It was always a tricky balance to get Murphy to redeem herself by the end of every episode, not be too selfish or ego-driven, that was my mission. She was in danger of becoming a caricature—the man-eater...."[23] Their respective responses to Quayle delivered hard-hitting quotable lines. Diane English's public statement came first: "If the Vice President thinks it's disgraceful for an unmarried woman to bear a child, and if he believes that a woman cannot adequately raise a child without a father, then he'd better make sure abortion remains safe and legal."[24]

And then it was Murphy's turn.

The hour-long premiere of season five, "You Say Potatoe, I Say Potato," finds Murphy, a disheveled and exhausted new mother, surrounded by her well-meaning friends from *FYI*. Suddenly, Quayle's voice can be heard on the television in the background. In a calculated move, they made his words the center of the episode, thereby making both events (his speech and their response) real. Turnabout was fair play. An exhausted Murphy shouts Qualye's own words back at him, once again recontextualizing for the voting public during an election season.

> "Glamorizing!" shouted an unshowered Murphy.... "Frank, do I look glamorous to you?" "Of course not!" Frank shot back. "You look disgusting."[25]

Adding insult to Quayle's growing injury, Murphy brings single parents to a taping at *FYI* studios, where she addresses the vice president: "These are difficult times for our country, and in searching for the causes of our social ills, we could choose to blame the media, or the Congress, or an administration that's been in power for twelve years—or we could blame me."[26]

In a rap battle, this is what is known as the "mic drop."

THE FINAL CHAPTER—SAYING GOODBYE WITH MEANING

What does one do for an encore?

Despite being relevant and groundbreaking, for so many reasons and seasons, there was a concern that perhaps the influence of the series had waned after the show's journey into motherhood: "When the press starts referring to you as 'the veteran series Murphy Brown,' you have stayed too long at the party. We probably should have stopped after our fifth or sixth year, optimum for half-hour story lines, but we just kept things going."[27] Apparently, motherhood had diminished Murphy Brown:

> [I]ts original premise was gutsy. . . . In the process, she became an instant icon: a survivor, a plastic surgery refusenik, a Natural Woman. . . . Within a few seasons, though, that complex past evaporated and Murphy seemed merely in a perennial and inexplicable bad mood. Then, of course, there was the unwed-mother escapade, when Murphy, a stable, high-earning professional, decided to bear a child on her own, thereby becoming a pawn in the national debate on family values. . . . With the lines between fiction and reality beginning to blur, she used the bully-pulpit of her sitcom to offer a rebuttal. . . . Since then, Murphy Brown has become almost willfully conventional.[28]

And the pundits weren't alone in their summations about the sitcom, for, somewhere along the line, America stopped watching *Murphy Brown*, leaving her to die—literally and figuratively.

With this new reality in place, the show's creators decided to exit with ethos, pathos, and a lot of logos. And it did so, proving that a once 40-something, now approaching 50-something, American woman still had something important to say. In season 10, Murphy Brown was diagnosed with breast cancer. These substantial final episodes explored women's health, dignity through diagnosis and treatment, self-reflection, and fear. The viewers came home. They had to. In 1998, the leading cause of death for American women was the malignant neoplasm, the chief one being breast cancer.

Audiences were moved by the show's content, and Murphy once again inserted herself into the national conversation about illegal drug usage, palliative care, and the debilitating effects of chemotherapy treatment—namely, the weakness and nausea. It is Jim Dial, of all people, who comes to Murphy's aid. The straight-laced, virgin on his wedding night, ultraconservative patriarch of their team buys her some "weed." In this moment, we recall that he wanted her at *FYI* when male executives said "No." He nominated her for entry into the restricted club that forbade female membership. The man who affectionately called her "Slugger" would not see her brought low by her disease. It was a meeting of the minds between liberalism and conservativism, and love conquered all.

There was immediate controversy. The Clinton administration's so-called drug czar accused the show of "trivializing drug abuse," further stating that "marijuana [was] not medicine," and that the episode "did a great disservice."[29] The show, refusing to apologize, also featured real-life cancer patients and survivors as members of Murphy's fictional cancer-support group, allowing the sitcom to depict the radical changes of the female body as it fights to live. For Bergen, the season "carried a powerful message, which left a deep imprint on me. . . . The show was informative about the physiological effects of breast cancer."[30]

In the series finale, "Never Can Say Goodbye," Murphy gets the greatest interview of all: God. Whether inspired by the fear of dying or the exploratory breast surgery she endures, God shows up, and the two **women** have a long and comedic conversation. We know, then, that everything is going to be okay. The curtain falls on the show, and the cast took endless and tearful final bows before a grateful and equally tearful audience.[31]

Afterward, some writers were upset that the show's concluding episode was overlooked by the critics: "No media blitzkrieg. No secret scripts. No stakeout of the stars. . . . The sitcom that once steered the national debate . . . overshadowed by *Seinfeld's* closing episode."[32]

I understand the frustration. A woman determined to live on her own terms shook up the world. Suddenly, motherhood caused people to question her relevance, and then it takes illness—her "suffering"—to redeem her before the world. Her near death, not her accomplishments, makes her relevant again, and then she is written off the stage.

But there is a power in witnessing the momentous.

The season of *Murphy Brown* was a momentous time for American television; for the ever-evolving questioning woman could find parts of herself reflected within the series. And perhaps the deepest parts of herself felt safe and just a little more certain. And this was because of Murphy—who kicked, punched, and scratched at every wall set before her. Murphy, who sang Aretha Franklin's "Natural Woman" off-key and at the top of her lungs. When. She. Felt. Like. It. Murphy, the woman who turned "feeling some type of way" into an art form.

I am penning this for you and for the women who made you eternal.

NOTES

1. Annalee Newitz, "Why the Hell Can't I Watch Murphy Brown Online?" Gizmodo (blog), April 10, 2015, http://gizmodo.com/why-the-hell-can't-i-watch-murphy-brown-online-1697060751.

2. David Lambert, "Boy Meets World—Trade Mag Explains Why No More Seasons for Boy Meets World, Who's the Boss, Night Court, Airwolf, and More!" TVShowsonDVD.com, June 17, 2006, http://www.tvshowsondvd.com/news/Boy-Meets-World-/5678.

3. Slang for coveting attention that no one wants to give.

4. Candice Bergen, *A Fine Romance.* New York: Simon & Schuster, 2015, 94.

5. Ibid., 95.

6. Ibid.

7. Ibid., 96.

8. Ibid., 99.

9. Ibid.

10. *Murphy Brown*, "Devil with a Blue Dress On." Original airdate November 21, 1988, directed by Barnet Kellman (Burbank, CA: Warner Home Video, 2005).

11. Ibid.

12. Ibid.

13. *Murphy Brown*, "Signed, Sealed, Delivered." Original airdate December 5, 1988, directed by Barnet Kellman (Burbank CA: Warner Home Video, 2005).

14. *Murphy Brown*, "Murphy's Pony." Original airdate December 11, 1988, directed by Barnet Kellman (Burbank, CA: Warner Home Video, 2005).

15. *Murphy Brown*, "Baby Love." Original airdate December 12, 1988, directed by Barnet Kellman (Burbank, CA: Warner Home Video, 2005).

16. Barbara Dafoe Whitehead, "What Is Murphy Brown Saying? For Starters, That Unwed Motherhood Is a Glamorous Option," *Washington Post*, May 10, 1992, C5.

17. Bergen, op. cit., 142.

18. Dick Williams, "Murphy Brown and CBS Mull Abortion with Grace," *Atlanta Journal Constitution*, September 18, 1991, A11.

19. Ibid.

20. Neal Koch, "Everyone Has Advice for Murphy, Especially Real-Life TV Journalists," *The New York Times*, September 29, 1991, H33.

21. Bergen, op. cit., 143.

22. Joe Urschel, "Life in the Murphy Zone: Place Where Reality Ends and Fiction Begins," *USA Today*, 1992, 1A.

23. Bergen, op. cit., 143.

24. Peter Johnson, "Quayle: Murphy No Role Model," *USA Today*, May 20, 1992, A1.

25. Bergen, op. cit., 151.

26. Ibid., 143.

27. Ibid., 209.

28. Peggy Orenstein, "Show Tackles Issue of Breast Cancer: Murphy Brown Character Diagnosed with Disease," *The New York Times*, Section 2, September 28, 1997, 29.

29. William Goldschlag and Corky Siemasko, "Murphy Brown Going to Pot, Drug Czar Says," *Daily News*, November 6, 1997, 6.

30. Bergen, op. cit., 209.

31. Ibid., 210.

32. Janet Weeks, "Murphy Closes 10-Year Run and an Era," *USA Today*, 1998, 17E.

BIBLIOGRAPHY

Bergen, Candice. *A Fine Romance*. New York: Simon & Schuster, 2015.

Goldschlag, William, and Corky Siemasko. "Murphy Brown Going to Pot, Drug Czar Says." *Daily News*, 1997, 6.

Johnson, Peter. "Quayle: Murphy No Role Model." *USA Today*, May 20, 1992, A1.

Koch, Neal. "Everyone Has Advice for Murphy, Especially Real-Life TV Journalists." *The New York Times*, September 29, 1991, 2: 33.

Lambert, David. "Boy Meets World—Trade Mag Explains Why No More Seasons for Boy Meets World, Who's the Boss, Night Court, Airwolf & More!" TVShowsonDVD.com, http://www.tvshowsondvd.com/news/Boy-Meets -World-/5678.

Newitz, Annalee. "Why the Hell Can't I Watch Murphy Brown Online?" *Gizmodo* (blog), April 10, 2015, http://gizmodo.com/why-the-hell-can't-i-watch -murphy-brown-online-1697060751.

Orenstein, Peggy. "Show Tackles Issue of Breast Cancer: Murphy Brown Character Diagnosed with Disease." *The New York Times*, September 28, 1997, 2: 29.

Urschel, Joe. "Life in the Murphy Zone: Place Where Reality Ends and Fiction Begins." *USA Today*, 1992, 1A.

Weeks, Janet. "Murphy Closes 10-Year Run and an Era." *USA Today*, 1998, 17E.

Whitehead, Barbara Dafoe. "What Is Murphy Brown Saying?; For Starters, That Unwed Motherhood Is a Glamorous Option." *Washington Post*, May 10, 1992, C5.

Williams, Dick. "Murphy Brown and CBS Mull Abortion with Grace." *Atlanta Journal Constitution*, 1991, A11.

15

It Still Matters: *The Cosby Show* and Sociopolitical Representation on Television

Jacqueline Jones

Today, the first question anyone must ask about The Cosby Show *is W. B. Yeats's "How can we know the dancer from the dance?" Bill Cosby has become so reviled that we risk forgetting that* The Cosby Show *(1984–1992) was not. In this chapter, Jacqueline Jones demonstrates the continuing importance of this series that brought the classic sitcom (down to its middle-class settings) into depiction of African American lives. By crossing over from a niche to a mainstream audience (the show's success was across the board), Cosby demonstrated that race and ethnicity do not have to be exclusionary in terms of audience reach. The possibilities of the genre that have been fulfilled since, therefore, owe a great debt to the show. Because of Cosby's personal problems, the show is rarely broadcast now, but that does not diminish the impact* The Cosby Show *has had on both television and American culture.*

In the 1980s, no other sitcom had a greater impact on American popular culture than *The Cosby Show* (1984–1992). Airing Thursday nights on NBC, the family comedy centers on the day-to-day activities of Cliff and Clair Huxtable and their five children. The Huxtables are an upper-middle-class African American family living in a brownstone in Brooklyn, New York. Cliff (Bill Cosby) is an obstetrician and Clair (Phylicia Rashad) a lawyer.

The couple's children are Sondra (Sabrina LeBeauf), a student at Princeton University, teenagers Denise (Lisa Bonet) and Theo (Malcolm Jamal-Warner), 11-year-old Vanessa (Tempestt Bledsoe), and five-year-old Rudy (Keisha Knight-Pulliam). *The Cosby Show* was created and developed by comedian Bill Cosby and is "an extension of his own experiences as a father."[1] In addition to starring in the sitcom, Cosby was involved in every aspect of its production—from picking the actors who played his family to script development and composing the music for its opening themes. By ensuring his vision of portraying a positive black family on television was fulfilled, Cosby intangibly linked his legacy to the objectives he set out to reach with *The Cosby Show.*

In many respects, *The Cosby Show* is an update on classic domestic comedies such as *Leave It to Beaver* (1957–1963) and *The Donna Reed Show* (1958–1966). Domestic comedies generally involve a character sharing a quandary with a family member who provides guidance that helps the character navigate a challenge. By the conclusion of the episode the predicament is resolved and the character has learned a moral or lesson. Sociologist Andrew Greeley suggests that comedies such as *The Cosby Show* are modern versions "of the morality plays of the middle ages because they treat their viewers to the solution of family conflicts and tension through 'paradigms of love.'"[2] Cosby updated this familiar format by minimizing the use of sitcom formulas and gimmicks such as catch phrases and one-liner jokes in favor of a "loose story structure and unpredictable pacing" that matched his personal style.[3]

The Cosby Show was America's top-rated program from 1985 to 1990 and was ranked in the top 10 for its entire run. Watched weekly by 60 million viewers, the sitcom assisted NBC in becoming the top-rated network for the first-time in its history.[4] Linda Fuller describes *The Cosby Show* "wielding such ratings power that the first pitch in the fifth game of the 1988 World Series . . . was delayed by a half-hour."[5]

Nevertheless, *The Cosby Show's* success was unexpected. In the early 1980s, the most popular shows on television were action thrillers and dramas such as *Magnum PI* (1980–1988), *The A-Team* (1983–1987), and *Dynasty* (1981–1989). Sitcoms rarely appeared on prime-time lineups, and marketing executives had declared them "dead."[6] Before *The Cosby Show* was picked up by NBC, two networks had declined because they deemed family comedy unlikely to succeed.

Shows featuring black families had never garnered such widespread crossover appeal with black and white audiences. As Lynn Norment remarks, *The Cosby Show* was a standout because it pointedly avoided "stereotypical blacks often seen on TV. There are no ghetto kids or maids or butlers wise-cracking about Black life."[7] Instead *The Cosby Show* provided viewers a universal feeling of familiarity and relatability. It produced a model family that viewers wanted to be part of or emulate.[8] Audiences were drawn to Cosby's intoxicating mix of comedy and authority. As Todd Klein put it, Cosby embodied "the mastery of stand-up comedy, the passion of a parent, the wisdom of Solomon."[9]

The Cosby Show's most notable achievements are twofold. First, it provided viewers a positive and nuanced representation of African Americans that had never been seen before on television. Second, *The Cosby Show's* success led to an influx of television shows in the late 1980s and 1990s featuring African American casts. Sitcoms such as *A Different World* (1987–1993), *Frank's Place* (1987–1988), *Roc* (1991–1994), and *Living Single* (1993–1998) built on the legacy of *The Cosby Show* by expanding and diversifying the range of issues, perspectives, and images representing African Americans on television. However, as the number of scripted television programs featuring black casts dwindled by the early 2000s,[10] more than 20 years after its run, *The Cosby Show* still remains the most iconic and positive representation of African Americans in popular culture for many people.

AFRICAN AMERICANS ON TELEVISION: FROM *AMOS 'N' ANDY* TO *THE COSBY SHOW*

Television is a form of ritual, a mythology that simultaneously captures, creates, and shapes our view of ourselves and others. Television offers cultural symbolism that reaffirms our existing social order and provides "a series of common shared experiences and images" that become a part of our collective traditions.[11] For most watchers, television is an act that blurs the lines between the real and unreal, concurrently mirroring what we believe to be reality while providing models of the reality we would like to see. For marginalized groups such as African Americans, television consequently both indicates and shapes societal attitudes and perceptions of the group. As cultural representations influence our perception of others, African Americans have long fought to see positive and diversified images of themselves on screen.

Prior to the 1970s, few African Americans appeared in lead roles on television. *Amos 'n' Andy* (1951–1953), a popular radio show in the 1930s and 1940s, was adapted for television to feature the first all-black cast on television. Unfortunately, *Amos 'n' Andy's* portrayal of African Americans maintained long-standing negative images of the group. Despite its popularity, CBS canceled *Amos 'n' Andy* after two seasons because of pressure from the National Association for the Advancement of Colored People (NAACP). In a 1951 bulletin, the NAACP contended that *Amos 'n' Andy* portrayed African Americans as clowns and crooks who were dumb, dishonest, and lazy. It also depicted "black doctors as quacks," black lawyers as ignorant and dishonest, and black women as "cackling, screaming shrews."[12] As the sole representation of blacks on television, the program was seen as too harmful to remain on the air. As Mack Scott points out, the pressure from the NAACP for positive images coupled with Southern white supremacists' refusal to accept images that weren't stereotypical, led television executives to shut out black actors from lead roles for more than a decade after *Amos 'n' Andy*.[13]

In the 1970s, a flurry of sitcoms featuring black casts emerged on television, including *Sanford and Son* (1972–1977), *That's My Mama* (1974–1975), *Good Times* (1974–1979), and *What's Happening!!* (1976–1979). Although these shows were incremental improvements on the portrayal of African Americans, they still featured characters acting like clowns or buffoons. With the exception of comedies such as *Julia* (1968–1971) and *The Jeffersons* (1975–1985), black sitcoms before *The Cosby Show* generally featured characters living in low-income neighborhoods. These comedies tended to emphasize perceived cultural differences between African Americans and other Americans from fashion, dialect, and music to politics, values, and personal aspirations. Shows such as *Good Times*, which was set in a Chicago public housing project, featured zany exaggerated plots and fueled the notion among television viewers that there are glaring disparities in the values, morals, and humor between black and white Americans.

The Cosby Show was an intentional response to 1970s black sitcoms. It attempts to counter negative images by stressing commonalities the Huxtables have with other (nonblack) families. Cosby, a proponent of color-blind humor, saw *The Cosby Show* as an opportunity to unify audiences: "I don't think you can bring the races together by joking about the difference between them. I'd rather talk about the similarities, about what's universal in their experiences."[14] *The Cosby Show* accomplished this by presenting a strong nuclear and extended family, with professional parents who stressed the importance of personal responsibility and education (particularly higher education). Cosby envisioned *The Cosby Show* providing positive images of African Americans that his race could be proud of while educating white Americans who were ignorant or misinformed about African Americans and their culture.[15]

Taking his mission seriously, Cosby hired Harvard psychiatrist Alvin Poussaint as a consultant to review scripts. Poussaint ensured that "'the family interactions [were] psychologically accurate, that the children act[ed] in age-appropriate ways, and that the show create[d] the feeling of a loving and caring family.' Guarding against stereotyping, sexism, racism, inconsistencies, and/or inappropriate behaviors, Dr. Poussaint [made] changes and suggestions" to scripts that would help the show meet these goals.[16]

The foundation of *The Cosby Show's* portrayal of a loving family was the visible affection characters show each other. Although it was common in domestic comedies for parents to exchange a peck on the cheek or for children to tell their parents they loved them, affection on the The Cosby Show was much more visible. Cliff and Clair, for example, are regularly seen engaged in long kisses that suggest to the audience that the couple's bond fuels the love they share with their children. In the episode "Play It Again Vanessa," Rudy walks into the living room and says, "Hi, daddy." Cliff responds, "Hi, Peaches" and gives her a kiss on the cheek. Rudy then asks "Are you mad at me?" Cliff, with a perplexed look on his face asks, "Should I be?" Rudy then explains: "This morning I got a kiss and a hug." Cliff responds "Okay" and proceeds to kiss and hug Rudy and then asks, is "that better?" Rudy emphatically responds "No!" Cliff asks, "What am I supposed to do?" Rudy responds that "when Mary Lopez's father kisses Mary, he says 'I love you, Mary.'" Cliff then kisses Rudy and says, "I love you, Mary."[17] In addition to demonstrating the level of intimacy between Cliff and Rudy, this scene also illustrates the intricacy in which small day-to-day interactions are featured on the sitcom. Although not necessary to advance an episode's plot, such exchanges are invaluable to the image of a loving, supportive family Cosby wanted to portray. They are moments that humanize the Huxtables in ways not previously seen on family sitcoms.

Although The Cosby Show sought to maintain an inclusive experience for all viewers, it still presented the Huxtables as a black family. The Huxtable's racial heritage is expressed through cultural markers such as Cliff's love of jazz music, the family's multigenerational tradition of attending the fictional historically black college Hillman, the anti-apartheid poster on Theo's bedroom wall, and Sondra choosing to name her newborn twins Winnie and Nelson.[18] Heritage is also signified through artwork, cuisine, and the show's multiple African diasporic guest stars, including Sammy Davis Jr., Lena Horne, Dizzy Gillespie, Tito Puente, Alvin Ailey, Miriam Makeba, and Stevie Wonder. In this way, The Cosby Show was able to introduce nonblack viewers to aspects of black culture they may not otherwise have been privy to.

In particular, episodes featuring Hillman College are poignant examples of the show's attempt to acculturate its audience. Historically black colleges are not often portrayed on sitcoms, and Hillman's integration on The Cosby Show brought to the forefront the history of racial segregation in America that spurred the creation of historically black colleges. Episodes featuring Hillman emphasize these institutions as academically rigorous and nurturing environments. Lastly, Cosby frequently challenged long-standing assumptions that historically black colleges are less rigorous than predominately white institutions. This is most prominently evident through family conversation about the value of attending historically black colleges and more subtly evident in small things such as the collegiate sweatshirts Cliff wears that feature institutions such as Meharry Medical College[19] and Princeton University equally.

The Cosby Show consciously chose not to directly confront racism or poverty, but one social issue it regularly addressed was sexism and gender equality. To an extent, the social climate of the 1980s demanded *The Cosby Show* address these issues. One reason cited for the decline of the sitcom by the early 1980s were social changes that challenged the utility of the nuclear family structure.[20] With stigmas around divorce and single-parent homes slowly dissipating and increasing numbers of women in the workforce, a sitcom about a nuclear family needed to account for how the familial structure was changing with the times. *The Cosby Show* met this need by presenting an egalitarian parental unit. Both parents are on screen cooking, cleaning, and actively engaging with their children. This division of labor best complemented the Huxtables' two-career household and suggests to viewers that an equal division of labor is the ideal model for marriage and family.

The egalitarian nature of the Huxtable household is most vocally articulated in the episode "Cliff in Love." An episode in which Sondra's boyfriend, Elvin. comes over to pick her up for a date. As Elvin waits for Sondra to emerge, Clair offers Cliff and Elvin coffee. Elvin is surprised by the offer and responds, "I'm sorry, Mrs. Huxtable, I didn't think you did that kind of thing." Clair asks "What kind of thing?" Elvin responds, "You know . . . serve." Clair, seeking clarification asks, "Oh, serve *him*. As in 'serve your man?'" She goes on to lecture Elvin asserting:

> I am not *serving* Dr. Huxtable. . . . That's the kind of thing that goes on in a restaurant. Now I am going to bring him a cup of coffee just like he brought me a cup of coffee this morning. And *that*, young man, is what marriage is made of. It is give-and-take, fifty-fifty. And if you don't get it together, and drop these macho attitudes, you are never gonna have anybody bringing you anything, anywhere, anyplace, anytime, *ever.*[21]

When sexism is challenged on *The Cosby Show*, female characters typically take the lead while Cliff silently demonstrates his agreement. In the preceding exchange, Cliff squirms and makes faces that suggest he finds Elvin's views objectionable. Such interactions also demonstrate that the Huxtable household is one in which women feel free to speak their minds and their words are taken seriously.

The Huxtables' modeling of gender equality also trickles down to their children. In the episode "Theo and Cockroach," Theo and his friend Cockroach are called out by Denise and Vanessa for using the objectifying terms of "burgers," "double burgers," and "deluxe burger with the works" to refer to women they find attractive.[22] Perhaps the strongest indication that the

Huxtable's modeling of gender equality is adopted by their children is found in Rudy. In conversations with her friend Kenny, Rudy routinely engages in discussions about gender roles. When Kenny, for example, explains that his brother "says a man has to wear the pants in the family. If he doesn't his wife will put on his shoes and walk all over him" and that if he told Rudy to marry him she would. Rudy replies, "No, I wouldn't, you have to earn my love."[23] In her exchanges with Kenny, Rudy asserts her intentions to grow up to be an independent woman unfettered by the confines of gender conventions. She symbolizes the hope that the next generation will be more evolved concerning gender.

THEY'RE JUST NOT BLACK ENOUGH

Although *The Cosby Show* has been praised for its gender politics, it has also persistently been critiqued for its representation of race. The show has been labeled by some as not being "black enough" because it lacks overt conversation concerning race and poverty and focuses on a middle-class family. Cosby's position has been that it isn't his duty "to make all the black social statements," and his show takes a classy approach to dealing with race by illustrating "life in the positive sense."[24] Criticism of *The Cosby Show* engages long-standing debates concerning respectability politics, the idea that the way African Americans dress or carry themselves will affect their ability to eradicate discrimination. It has long been thought that positive images of black Americans in the media will significantly contribute to changing other Americans' perceptions of the group. Cosby adheres to this viewpoint, and favorable assessments of *The Cosby Show* credit it with convincing Americans "to view blacks as human beings."[25]

Nevertheless, the argument could be made that when Cosby took on the task of single-handedly eradicating decades of negative images of African Americans he also became solely responsible for that image. As a result, Cosby had a duty to consider criticisms levied at his show. His choice to ignore such criticism resulted in some considering him arrogant.[26] Still, Cosby has a point that it is not his sole responsibility to make social statements for all African Americans. A show about one family can't comprehensively represent an entire group. In addition, it is also important to note that Cosby did demonstrate a commitment to addressing social issues affecting African Americans through *A Different World*.[27] The sitcom's college campus setting allowed the show to provide characters of various economic backgrounds and values and to develop storylines on topics such as apartheid in South Africa, because activism and controversial discourse is an expected part of the college experience. *The Cosby Show* can't represent all facets of African American life, but its success made it possible for more programs with African American characters to appear on television. Shows that succeeded it such as *Roc* provided more diverse representations, including ones marked by class (the title character of *Roc* was a sanitation worker).

Another critique of *The Cosby Show* is that it isn't realistic or "black enough" because it represents the experiences of a middle-class African American family. Research conducted on television audiences have consistently cited that respondents holding negative views of *The Cosby Show* deem it unrealistic. Leslie Innis and Joe R. Feagin's interviews with 100 middle-class black viewers reported that some respondents questioned why the Huxtables never faced serious tragedy and thought it was unrealistic for one family to contain both a lawyer and a doctor.[28] These are valid critiques, but it is also likely that African American viewers place a higher burden on *The Cosby Show* to provide realistic images of African Americans than they would place on other shows because of the historical legacy of black images on television. Furthermore, scholars such as Patricia D. Hopkins have critiqued assessments of realism based on class. African Americans who accuse *The Cosby Show* of not being "black enough," Hopkins argues, suggest that authentic black experiences are rooted in being impoverished and uneducated, which is a stereotype. Speaking to her own background and experience, Hopkins asserts that "just because I was poor and from the working-class projects, culture was not denied to me: in fact, it was all around. Equating the poor with a lack of culture and then inextricably combining being poor and lack of culture with *authentic* blackness, I assert, negates *my* black experience."[29] Note that working-class African Americans were just as likely as their middle-class counterparts to watch *The Cosby Show*. Both groups believed the values and characteristics depicted on the show matched those within their own families and communities.

Some scholars have also challenged the claim that *The Cosby Show* educated and led white Americans to reassess their ideas about African Americans as Cosby had hoped. Researchers Sut Jhally and Justin Lewis conclude from interviews with white viewers that, though respondents have positive opinions of the Huxtables, they did not view them as a typical black family. White respondents viewed the Huxtables' success as unlikely for most African Americans. Jhally and Lewis conclude that "shows like *The Cosby Show* allow . . . a new and insidious form of racism. The Huxtables proved that black people can succeed; yet in doing so they also prove the inferiority of black people in general (who have, in comparison with whites, failed)."[30] Similarly, Henry Louis Gates Jr. argues that "as long as all blacks were represented in demeaning or peripheral roles, it was possible to believe that American racism was, as it were, indiscriminate. The social vision of 'Cosby,' however, . . . reassuringly throws the blame for black poverty back onto the impoverished."[31] Having positive images of African

Americans on television, Gates contends, has not changed African Americans' sociopolitical status in society. In other words, *The Cosby Show* proved that the idea that positive images lead to meaningful social change is false.

RESPECTABILITY POLITICS AND THE LEGACY OF *THE COSBY SHOW*

In the early years of *The Cosby Show*, Cosby stated that his goal was to demonstrate that African Americans have "the same kinds of wants and needs as other American families."[32] This was taken to mean that Cosby believed African Americans were the same as other Americans and that the respectability the Huxtables represent always existed among African Americans. However, by the mid-2000s, interviews, speeches, and the coauthored book *Come On, People: On the Path from Victims to Victors* (2007) suggested the comedian's views had changed. Cosby was now espousing the opinion that low-income African Americans were squandering the gains made by the modern civil rights movement. Furthermore, Cosby now seemed to believe that his revered status within the African American community and as the architect of a positive group image via *The Cosby Show* entitled him to direct wayward African Americans back onto a righteous path.

The most infamous articulation of Cosby's new views came during a May 2004 NAACP event commemorating the 50th anniversary of the U.S. Supreme Court decision *Brown v. Board of Education*. Known as the "Pound Cake Speech," Cosby chastised low-income African Americans for their low standards. Cosby argued that blacks held a 50-percent dropout rate from school and that the rest were in prison. Cosby cited a lack of parenting as the root cause of the issue: "I'm talking about these people who cry when their son is standing there in an orange suit. Where were you when he was two? . . . How come you don't know he had a pistol? And where is his father, and why don't you know where he is. . . . You can't keep asking that God will find a way. God is tired of you." Cosby went on to state that young black men were "going around stealing Coca Cola" and were "getting shot in the back of the head over a piece of pound cake." Cosby argued that white Americans were no longer the cause of injustice or socioeconomic problems in black communities. Poor behavior was now the root of these problems. Cosby concluded by stating that "the white man" was laughing at African Americans and encouraged African Americans to start parenting their children.[33]

Michael Eric Dyson is one of the most vocal critics of Cosby's recent views, writing a book-length response titled *Is Bill Cosby Right? Or Has the Black Middle Class Lost Its Mind?* (2005). Dyson argues that Cosby's comments were elitist and "ill-informed on the critical and complex issues that shape people's lives."[34] Indeed, key tenets of Cosby's appraisal of low-income African Americans are not supported by available data. As Adam Serwer outlines in his annotated version of the "Pound Cake Speech," in 2004 the dropout rate among African Americans was 13 percent, not 50 percent. Out-of-wedlock births and the rate of violent crimes among African Americans had also dramatically declined.[35] Critics of Cosby's message, much like critics of *The Cosby Show*, argue that his focus on respectability ignores current and historic institutional policies that directly affect African American poverty and educational achievement. Cosby's views about low-income African Americans had a marginal effect on the legacy of *The Cosby Show*. Although it did lead some long-time supporters to believe that even though the positive images portrayed in *The Cosby Show* were meant to help white Americans reassess their notions of blacks, in light of the views Cosby now espoused, *The Cosby Show* was also an endorsement of black respectability politics. The sitcom functioned as a means for Cosby to assert a self-appointed patriarchal role among African Americans, providing not simply an endorsement of concepts of black respectability but also a tutorial for wayward African Americans that would guide them toward bettering themselves and transcending the effects of racism.

Yet Cosby's recent stint as a public moralist greatly backfired. Although the allegations were not widely known to the public until 2014, the comedian had long been rumored to have sexually assaulted many women. Cosby's finger wagging eventually became the central argument used to call him out as a hypocrite and led to the allegations against him becoming public discourse. Allegations of Cosby's alleged sexual assaults became even more widely known in October 2014 when a video of African American comedian Hannibal Burress critiquing Cosby on stage spread virally on social media and was picked up by news outlets. In the clip, Burress states that he hates Cosby's smug "old black man public persona." Burress then imitates Cosby stating, "Pull your pants up black people. I was on TV in the eighties. I can talk down to you because I had a successful sitcom." Burress then retorts, "But you rape women Bill Cosby, so turn the crazy down a couple notches." Buress goes on to state, "I guess I wanted at least to make it weird for you to watch *Cosby Show* reruns." The clip ends with Burress instructing the audience to "google Bill Cosby rape."[36]

After the Burress clip went viral, more than 50 women publicly accused Cosby of sexual assault. As most of the alleged crimes took place as far back as the mid-1970s, they are well past the statute of limitations and cannot be criminally prosecuted. However, Cosby has been charged with felony sexual assault in Pennsylvania stemming from a case originally reported in 2004. The Montgomery County district attorney declined to prosecute

Cosby in 2005. As a result, his accuser, Andrea Constand, filed a civil suit against Cosby in 2006. Cosby gave a deposition as part of discovery in the civil suit (which was eventually settled out of court). In the deposition, Cosby acknowledges that in the 1970s he obtained (the now-illegal sedative) quaaludes to give to women he intended to have sex with. Cosby's deposition remained sealed for a decade until July 2015 when U.S. District Judge Eduardo Robreno granted the Associated Press's request to obtain it.[37] Montgomery County's current district attorney used information from the unsealed deposition to reopen the criminal investigation and on December 30, 2015, formally charged Cosby with felony sexual assault. Despite numerous attempts to get the charges dismissed, Cosby stood trial in June 2017.[38] The jurors in the case deadlocked after six days of deliberation. The judge declared a mistrial, and Cosby was free to go. Whether Cosby is guilty or not, his deposition revealed that the comedian used illegal drugs to have sex with women outside his marriage. These acts were not in keeping with Cosby's moralistic persona and exposed Cosby as hypocritical.

Ever since the allegations against Cosby became widely known, Cosby has been tried in the court of public opinion and generally has been thought to be guilty. In 2015, 12,000 ticket holders requested refunds for two of Cosby's comedy shows in Denver.[39] A comedy special due to air shortly after the allegations first resurfaced was shelved by Netflix, and a development deal Cosby had with NBC to star in a new family sitcom was canceled. Reruns of *The Cosby Show*, which appeared on networks (with crossover appeal) such as TV Land, were taken off the air.[40] The television show *Family Guy* also aired an episode with a scene in which an alternative opening theme for *The Cosby Show* is shown with all female characters in the cast drugged.[41]

The Cosby Show's legacy has been greatly marred by the accusations leveled at Cosby. This stems from Cosby suggesting, from the title of *The Cosby Show* to his public comments, that he embodies his character, Cliff Huxtable. The general public had come to see Cosby and Cliff as one and the same. This fusion resulted in the public initially refusing to believe that the rumors about Cosby were true. Later, it also resulted in projects involving Cosby being shunned once public opinion changed. African Americans have been divided in their support for Cosby. Particularly on social media, supporters have said they don't believe the allegations leveled at Cosby. Many of these individuals assert that Cosby has been targeted because of his success as an African American male and particularly because he was able to change the perception of African Americans on television through *The Cosby Show*. Others have simply voiced a desire not to allow the allegations against Cosby ruin the legacy of *The Cosby Show*. These claims have equally summoned responses from African Americans on social media, blogs, and articles encouraging supporters to untangle their love of Cosby from the character he portrayed. The depth and diversity of African Americans' feelings surrounding the legacy of *The Cosby Show* were perhaps best captured when *Ebony* published a photo on its November 2015 cover of the cast of *The Cosby Show* with an overlay of broken glass, insinuating that the legacy of the show had been fractured. The cover quickly became controversial and fueled supporters' sentiment to defend both Cosby and *The Cosby Show*'s legacy.

As allegations against Cosby continue to play out, the future of *The Cosby Show*'s legacy remains unknown. What can be said is that the show made a major impact on television. Its groundbreaking ratings and the positive images of African Americans it produced is undeniable. Although claims that *The Cosby Show* improved race relations or changed white Americans' notions of African Americans are debatable, *The Cosby Show* is still considered by many people to be the most comprehensive and nuanced representation of black family life on television. No show since has portrayed or updated the congenial relationships between parents and children that were the hallmark of *The Cosby Show*. As such, despite current allegations against Cosby, *The Cosby Show*'s legacy is one many African Americans continue to be invested in protecting.

NOTES

1. Lynn Norment, "The Cosby Show: The Real-Life Drama Behind TV Show About a Black Family," *Ebony*, April 1985, 30.

2. Muriel Cantor, "The American Family on Television: From Molly Goldberg to Bill Cosby," *Journal of Comparative Family Studies* 22(2) (Summer 1991), 205.

3. Darnell M. Hunt, "The Cosby Show," Museum of Broadcast Communications, December 31, 2015, http://www.museum.tv/eotv/cosbyshowt.htm.

4. Linda J. Fuller, *The Cosby Show: Audiences, Impact, and Implications* (Westport, CT: Greenwood, 1992), 20, 22.

5. Ibid., 25–26.

6. Norment, op. cit., 28.

7. Ibid., 27.

8. Tom Werner, "*The Cosby Show*: An Inside Look," Seminar at Museum of Broadcasting, New York, NY, September 20, 1989. Tom Werner, executive producer of *The Cosby Show*, stated that people "respond to the love the Huxtables feel for each other. It doesn't feel artificial. They say they wish they were part of that family."

9. Todd Klein, "Bill Cosby: Prime Time's Favorite Father," *Saturday Evening Post*, 258(3) (April 1986), 42.

10. The decrease in the number of shows featuring African Americans after the early 2000s suggests its increase in the 1990s was reflective of networks capitalizing on a popular trend rather than signifying a firm commitment to diversify television.

11. Michael Marsden, "Television Viewing as Ritual." In *Rituals and Ceremonies in Popular Culture*, edited by Ray B. Browne (Bowling Green, OH: Popular Press, 1980), 124.

12. John Carman, "Wrestling with an Albatross: 'Amos 'n' Andy,'" *Electronic Media*, 21(35) (September 2, 2002), 12.

13. Mack Scott, "From Blackface to Beulah: Subtle Subversion in Early Black Sitcoms," *Journal of Contemporary History*, 49(4) (October 2014), 743. Not until 1965, when NBC cast Bill Cosby as the first African American lead in the drama series *I Spy* (1965–1968), did African Americans begin to receive significant parts in television series.

14. Richard Zoglin, "Cosby, Inc.," *Time*, September 28, 1987, 59.

15. Norment, op. cit., 30. Cosby clearly identified these objectives when he asserted, "I'm here because I am a human being [and] I want to show the happiness within our people. I want to show that we have the same kinds of wants and needs as other American families."

16. Fuller, op. cit., 69.

17. *The Cosby Show*, "Play It Again Vanessa," season one, episode eight, directed by Jay Sandrich, written by Jerry Ross, NBC Studios, November 8, 1984.

18. The twins' names have significant political implications as it is a reference to South African activists (and subsequent president) Winnie and Nelson Mandela.

19. See "Quick Facts," Meharry Medical College, http://www.mmc.edu /_modules/events/didyouknow2.html. Meharry is the leading producer of African American PhDs in biomedical sciences.

20. Susan Horowitz, "Sitcom Domesticus: A Species Endangered by Social Change," *Channels of Communication*, 10 (September–October 1984), 22. Susan Horowitz argues that in light of "diverging life-styles, and the splintering of both the television audience and the nuclear family, the sitcom must adjust to the viewers' new realities."

21. *The Cosby Show*, "Cliff in Love," season two, episode four, directed by Jay Sandrich, written by John Markus, NBC Studios, October 17, 1985 (emphasis added).

22. "Theo and Cockroach," *The Cosby Show*, season two, episode 15, directed by Jay Sandrich, written by Thad Mumford, NBC Studios, January 30, 1986.

23. "The Visit," *The Cosby Show*, season four, episode 16, directed by Regge Life, written by John Markus, Carmen Finestra, and Gary Kott, NBC Studios, January 21, 1988.

24. Norment, op. cit., 29–30.

25. Leslie B. Inniss and Joe R. Feagin, "*The Cosby Show*: The View from the Black Middle Class," *Journal of Black Studies*, 25(6) (July 1995), 696.

26. See Norment, op. cit., 30.

27. *A Different World* is a spin-off of *The Cosby Show* set at Hillman College.

28. Inniss and Feagin, op. cit., 699.

29. Patricia D. Hopkins, "Deconstructing *Good Times* and *The Cosby Show*: In Search of My 'Authentic' Black Experience," *Journal of Black Studies*, 43(8) (2012), 958.

30. Sut Jhally and Justin Lewis, *Enlighten Racism: The Cosby Show, Audiences, and the Myth of the American Dream* (Boulder: Westview, 1992), 94–95.

31. Henry Louis Gates Jr., "TV's Black World Turns—But Stays Unreal," *The New York Times* (November 12, 1989), 40.

32. Norment, op. cit., 30.

33. Adam Serwer, "Bill Cosby's Famous 'Pound Cake' Speech, Annotated," BuzzFeed, July 9, 2015, http://www.buzzfeed.com/adamserwer/bill-cosby-pound -for-pound#.ybEaejdWd.

34. Michael Eric Dyson, *Is Bill Cosby Right? Or Has the Black Middle Class Lost Its Mind?* (New York: Basic Civitas, 2005), 2.

35. Serwer, op. cit.

36. Eye Sight, "Hannibal Buress Called Bill Cosby a Rapist During a Stand Up," YouTube video, October 29, 2014, 1:41, https://youtu.be/dzB8dTVALQI.

37. Mark Joseph Stern, "Why Bill Cosby's Court Statements Were Revealed," *Slate* (July 8, 2015), n. p., http://www.slate.com/articles/news_and_politics/juris prudence/2015/07/bill_cosby_quaalude_testimony_judge_eduardo_robreno _unsealed_drug_and_sex.html.

38. Maria Puente, "Bill Cosby's Latest Efforts to Get Criminal Charges Tossed Are Denied," *USA Today*, http://www.usatoday.com/story/life/tv/2016/11/16/bill -cosbys-latest-efforts-get-criminal-charges-tossed-denied/93963526/.

39. Kevin McSpadden, "1,200 Ticket Refunds Requested for Bill Cosby's Den- ver Shows," Time.com, January 22, 2015, n. p.

40. Although reruns of *The Cosby Show* were off the air for about a year, recently the African American serving network Bounce announced that it will begin airing reruns of the show despite criticism. See the Associated Press, "Bounce TV to Bring Back 'Cosby Show' Reruns," *Boston Herald*, http://www.bos tonherald.com/entertainment/television/2016/11/bounce_tv_to_bring_back _cosby_show_reruns.

41. See *Family Guy*, "Peter's Sister," season 14, episode six, directed by John Holmquist, written by Tom Devanney; *Fox*, November 15, 2015.

BIBLIOGRAPHY

Amos 'n' Andy. Created by Charles J. Correll and Freeman F. Gosden. CBS Televi- sion, 1951–1953.

Associated Press. "Bounce TV to Bring Back 'Cosby Show' Reruns." *Boston Her- ald*, November 15, 2016, n. p., http://www.bostonherald.com/entertainment /television /2016/11/bounce_tv_to_bring_cosby_show_reruns.

The A-Team. Created by Stephen J. Cannell and Frank Lupo. NBC Studios, 1983–1987.

Cantor, Muriel G. "The American Family on Television: From Molly Goldberg to Bill Cosby," *Journal of Comparative Family Studies*, 22(2) (Summer 1991), 205–216.

Carman, John. "Wrestling with an Albatross: 'Amos 'n' Andy,'" *Electronic Media*. 21(35) (September 2, 2002), 12.

Cosby, Bill, and Alvin F. Poussaint. *Come On, People: On the Path from Victims to Victors*. Nashville: Thomas Nelson, 2007.

Cosby, Bill, and Alvin F. Poussaint. "Pound Cake Speech." Speech given at the NAACP's 50th anniversary commemoration of the *Brown v. Topeka Board of Education* U.S. Supreme Court decision, Washington, DC, May 17, 2004.

The Cosby Show. Created by Bill Cosby. NBC Studios, 1984–1992.

The Cosby Show. "Cliff in Love." Season two, episode four, directed by Jay Sandrich, written by John Markus, NBC Studios, October 17, 1985.

The Cosby Show. "Play It Again Vanessa." Season two, episode eight, directed by Jay Sandrich, written by Jerry Ross, NBC Studios, November 8, 1984.

The Cosby Show. "Theo and Cockroach." Season two, episode 15, directed by Jay Sandrich, written by Thad Mumford, NBC Studios, January 30, 1986.

The Cosby Show. "The Visit." Season four, episode 16, directed by Regge Life, written by John Markus, Carmen Finestra, and Gary Kott, NBC Studios, January 21, 1988.

A Different World. Created by Bill Cosby. NBC Studios, 1987–1993.

The Donna Reed Show. Created by William Roberts. ABC Studios, 1958–1966.

Dynasty. Created by Esther Shapiro and Richard Alan Shapiro. ABC Studios, 1981–1989.

Dyson, Michael Eric. *Is Bill Cosby Right? Or Has the Black Middle Class Lost Its Mind?* New York: Basic Civitas, 2005.

Ebony, 71(1), November 2015.

Family Guy. "Peter's Sister." Season 14, episode six, directed by John Holmquist, written by Tom Devanney, Fox, November 15, 2015.

Frank's Place. Created by Hugh Wilson. CBS Television, 1987–1988.

Fuller, Linda J. *The Cosby Show: Audiences, Impact, and Implications*. Westport, CT: Greenwood, 1992.

Gates, Henry Louis Jr. "TV's Black World Turns—But Stays Unreal." *The New York Times* (November 12, 1989), 39–40.

Good Times. Created by Mike Evans, Norman Lear, and Eric Monte. CBS Television, 1974–1979.

Hopkins, Patricia D. "Deconstructing *Good Times* and *The Cosby Show*: In Search of My 'Authentic' Black Experience." *Journal of Black Studies*, 43(8) (2012), 953–975.

Horowitz, Susan. "Sitcom Domesticus: A Species Endangered by Social Change." *Channels of Communication*, (10) (September–October 1984), 22.

Hunt, Darnell M. "The Cosby Show." Museum of Broadcast Communications, http://www.museum.tv/eotv/cosbyshowt.htm.

Inniss, Leslie B., and Joe R. Feagin. "*The Cosby Show*: The View from the Black Middle Class." *Journal of Black Studies*, 25(6) (July 1995), 692–711.

The Jeffersons. Created by Norman Lear, Don Nicholl, and Michael Ross. CBS Television, 1975–1985.

Jhally, Sut, and Justin Lewis. *Enlighten Racism: The Cosby Show, Audiences, and the Myth of the American Dream*. Boulder, CO: Westview, 1992.

Julia. Created by Hal Kanter. NBC Studios, 1968–1971.

Klein, Todd. "Bill Cosby: Prime Time's Favorite Father." *Saturday Evening Post*, 258(3) (April 1986), 42–110.

Leave It to Beaver. Created by Joe Connelly, Bob Mosher, and Dick Conway. CBS Television, ABC Studios, 1957–1963.

Living Single. Created by Yvette Lee Bowser. Fox, 1993–1998.

Magnum P.I. Created by Donald P. Bellisario and Glen A. Larson. CBS Television, 1980–1988.

Marsden, Michael. "Television Viewing as Ritual." In *Rituals and Ceremonies in Popular Culture*, edited by Ray B. Browne, 120–124. Bowling Green, OH: Popular Press, 1980.

McSpadden, Kevin. "1,200 Ticket Refunds Requested for Bill Cosby's Denver Shows." Time.com (January 22, 2015), n. p.

Norment, Lynn. "The Cosby Show: The Real-Life Drama Behind TV Show About a Black Family." *Ebony*, April 1985.

Puente, Maria. "Bill Cosby's Latest Efforts to get Criminal Charges Tossed Are Denied." *USA Today*, http://www.usatoday.com/story/life/tv/2016/11/16/bill-cosbys-latest-efforts-get-criminal-charges-tossed-denied/93963526/.

"Quick Facts." Meharry Medical College, http://www.mmc.edu /_modules/events/didyouknow2.html.

Roc. Created by Stan Daniels. Fox, 1991–1994.

Sanford and Son. Created by Norman Lear. NBC Studios, 1972–1977.

Serwer, Adam. "Bill Cosby's Famous 'Pound Cake' Speech, Annotated." BuzzFeed, July 9, 2015, n. p., https://www.buzzfeed.com/adamserwer/bill-cosby-pound-for-pound?utm_term=.envRvqNRe#.wueymA1yV.

Scott, Mack. "From Blackface to Beulah: Subtle Subversion in Early Black Sitcoms." *Journal of Contemporary History*, 49(4) (October 2014), 743–769.

Sight, Eye. "Hannibal Buress Called Bill Cosby a Rapist During a Stand Up." YouTube video, October 29, 2014, 1:41, https://youtu.be/dzB8dTVALQI.

Stern, Mark Joseph. "Why Bill Cosby's Court Statements Were Revealed." *Slate*, July 8, 2015, n. p., http://www.slate.com/articles/news_and_politics/jurisprudence/2015/07/bill_cosby_quaalude_testimony_judge_eduardo_robreno_unsealed_drug_and_sex.html.

That's My Mama. Created by Dan T. Bradley and Allan L. Rice. ABC Studios, 1974–1975.

What's Happening!! Created by Eric Monte. ABC Studios, 1976–1979.

Werner, Tom. "*The Cosby Show*: An Inside Look." Seminar at Museum of Broadcasting, New York, NY, September 20, 1989.

Zoglin, Richard. "Cosby, Inc." *Time*, September 28, 1987.

16

"The Reagans Have Had a Very Bad
Effect on You": Neoliberalism and
Queer Possibilities in *The Fresh Prince
of Bel-Air*

Jessica Best

On its surface, The Fresh Prince of Bel-Air *(1990–1996) seems light-hearted enough. Will Smith, of DJ Jazzy Jeff and the Fresh Prince fame, plays a young man who is relocated from a rough neighborhood in West Philadelphia to live with his relatives in ritzy Bel-Air, California. Culture shock ensues. As Jessica Best explores in " 'The Reagans Have Had a Very Bad Effect on You': Neoliberalism and Queer Possibilities in* The Fresh Prince of Bel-Air," *this whimsical sitcom also allows viewers to "enter, engage with, and even challenge dominant national narratives that tell us who is accepted and who is excluded within mainstream U.S. culture," specifically in relation to race, class, gender, and sexuality. Best argues that* The Fresh Prince of Bel-Air *grapples with "what it means to be African American within the legacy of Reaganism and the rise of neoliberalism."*

The first television shows featuring black performers were based on radio programs reminiscent of minstrel performances from the 18th and 19th centuries, where African American performers enacted racial stereotypes to entertain white audiences. Such stereotypes included the servant, the "mammy," the criminal, and the deadbeat. Black performers were also restricted to comedic programs, which were considered a lower, more popular form of art. Shows such as *Amos 'n' Andy* (1951–1953) and *Beulah* (1950–1953) enraged black activists for embracing "stereotypical notions of blackness [that] would have a negative impact on the black community."[1] Though the humor in these comedic performances often spoke exclusively and in a subversive manner to black audiences, they were mostly funded by white network executives and written for white viewers.[2] Such power dynamics sparked debates over racial representation that continue to this day. Thus, from its inception, television became one of the key sites of cultural debate in the United States, where the loaded concepts of "whiteness" and "blackness" were played out. Though we often think of television as escapist entertainment, where we "veg out," relax, and enjoy ourselves, throughout the decades it has displayed and negotiated racial tensions and the meaning of blackness as a culturally contingent category (not as a fixed, essential identity) alongside other identifying factors such as class, gender, and sexuality.

Stereotypical representations of African Americans continued through the 1950s, 1960s, and 1970s with programs such as *The Nat King Cole Show* (1956–1957), *I Spy* (1965–1968), and *Julia* (1968–1971), creating non-threatening black characters who were contained within subservient roles. Indeed, these series "attempted to make blacks acceptable to whites by containing them or rendering them, if not culturally white, invisible."[3] In the 1970s, African American characters on shows such as *Sanford and Son* (1972–1977), *Good Times* (1974–1979), *The Jeffersons* (1975–1985), and *What's Happening!!* (1976–1979) aspired to and idealized the white, heteronormative, middle class.

However, the 1970s was also a time of change within visual media. Along with so-called blaxploitation films, television displayed large numbers of African Americans for home audiences, not only in sitcoms from white producers but also in successful African American–produced shows such as *The Flip Wilson Show* (1970–1974) and *Soul Train* (1971–2006), which became the longest running syndicated show on television. Although the African American television presence has continued to grow, it has not remained without its complications, and it is a useful endeavor to investigate where the sitcom allows us as viewers to rethink racial representation and its connections to gender and sexuality, national belonging, socioeconomic class, and consumer capitalism.

NBC's *The Fresh Prince of Bel-Air* (1990–1996), takes up categorical identifying factors that allow all of us to enter, engage with, and even challenge dominant national narratives that tell us who is accepted and who is excluded within mainstream U.S. culture. By looking at how this series engages with matters of race, class, gender, and sexuality, we can situate it not only within the history of television but also within the cultural histories of African American and LGBTQ+communities that work within and against Reaganism and neoliberal economics. Doing so can allow us to better understand our current moment and seek out the resonances of those who do not participate in mainstream culture, those who are not included within the dominant narrative, and those who do not fit into the categorical identifying features of race, class, gender, and sexuality but instead exist within the gaps.

Fresh Prince develops the life of teenager Will Smith, whose mother sends him from their lower-class home in West Philadelphia to live with his wealthy relatives, Aunt Vivian and Uncle Phillip Banks, in a mansion in Bel-Air, presumably to avoid street life in the inner city. *Fresh Prince* portrays black racial identity couched in heteronormativity and provides a model of success that directly aligns itself with American capitalism and the neoliberal agenda. Neoliberalism is the all-encompassing economic ideology that trickled down from the Reagan era and asserted itself into every aspect of American culture. The neoliberal mindset thinks only in economic terms, where everything from goods to people comes under the realm of the free market and profit (at any cost) is the ultimate goal. Such thinking attempts to absorb civil rights activism and minority cultures, making everything uniformly monetized and stripped of its resistant capabilities. However, the sitcom is more than just another mouthpiece for dominant culture, consuming even while portraying African American and hip-hop political and cultural identities.

Conducting a queer reading of this favored American sitcom allows us to investigate when Smith and other characters on the show have the potential to resist neoliberal culture. The word "queer" was reappropriated by the LGBTQ+community and became an area of academic interest in the early 1990s with the rise of queer theory. "Queer" rejects definition and celebrates the disruption of stable identifications such as "gay," "straight," "male," and "female." Indeed, scholars adopted the verb "to queer" as a way to investigate the gray areas between normal identity categories, allowing for new articulations of identity that disassociate from the norm and have the potential for resistance. According to queer scholar Eve Kosofsky Sedgwick, "queer" refers to "the open mesh of possibilities, gaps, overlaps, dissonances and resonances, lapses and excesses of meaning."[4] A queer reading therefore allows us to formulate possibilities for resistance within neoliberalism's incorporation of black identity politics, as it allows us to conceptualize individuals outside of traditional, Western stable identity categories based on race, class, gender, and sexuality. A contemporary queer reading of *Fresh Prince* allows us to illuminate our current race culture and its relation to dominant neoliberal ideology, creating connections over the past decades and offering new future meanings.

FROM REAGANISM TO NEOLIBERALISM

The effects of Ronald Reagan's social and economic policies pervade the United States and the global community today more than ever. Reaganism included social policies that invited Americans to return to "traditional values" and nostalgically invoked an imaginary utopic American past as one that was void of all societal ills purportedly caused by tense race relations, poverty, changing gender roles, and the emergence of a strong gay and lesbian civil rights movement. Playing on dominant white culture's basic fears, Reaganism rhetorically established white culture as the victim of so-called social ills, placing the blame on "blacks, Latinos, feminists, the poor, single mothers, gays and lesbians, and undocumented immigrants," and the social and economic policies that supported them such as affirmative action and welfare.[5] Reagan's social policies favored whiteness, heteronormativity, individualism, and wealth. Reaganism, as an economic policy, promoted corporate growth and unrestrained markets, the dismantling of the welfare state, increased privatization, a strong military, and private property.

After spending the 1960s and 1970s focusing on the workplace, childless couples, groups of friends, and single mothers, the sitcom returned to its 1950s themes of the nuclear family under the conservative resurgence that came with Reagan's election. The father became a prominent figure in 1980s sitcoms, and the most popular was *The Cosby Show* (1984–1992).[6] Not only did *Cosby* embody the heteronormative "father knows best" idyllic familial representation that Reaganism promoted, but also he and his family were examples of the model minority "that neoconservatives celebrated and presented both to counter the dependence of the underclass and to affirm their commitment to racial equality. These African Americans were just like whites, loyal to the ethos of capitalism and bourgeois individualism, and that loyalty rewarded them with the same middle-class privileges as whites."[7]

Reagan's legacy trickled down into the 21st century in the form of neoliberal economics, which are embodied in global institutions such as the World Bank, the International Monetary Fund, and the World Trade Organization. Neoliberalism has now become the "common-sense way many of us interpret, live in, and understand the world," and it includes rampant consumer culture, the deregulation and promotion of the free market with unrestrained wealth increases for the wealthiest Americans, increased privatization and social inequality, and a dismantling of the welfare state, along with neoconservative political policies that attempt either to assimilate or to dispose of people of color, the poor, immigrants, and those who identify as queer. A neoliberal state, furthermore, assumes that "individual freedoms are guaranteed by freedom of the market and of trade," and it "seeks to bring all human action into the domain of the market."[8] As the

1990s began, neoliberalism offered the American public a new rhetoric of "multiculturalism," inclusion, and "color-blindness," which continues into the 21st century with the discourse of a "postracial" America. The neoliberal model, instead of demonizing minority subjects, incorporates them through the rhetoric of inclusion or assimilation.[9] Instead of fighting against social and political movements, the neoliberal state creates new laws, brands, and logos so that political identities can be absorbed and rendered harmless.

NEOLIBERALISM, HIP-HOP, AND BLACK MALE IDENTITY

The Fresh Prince picks up where *The Cosby Show* left off in trying to grapple with what it means to be African American within the legacy of Reaganism and the rise of neoliberalism. Central to capitalist market forces and neoliberal politics during this time was the role of black male artists within the rise of hip-hop culture, which brought America's poor urban ghettos into the forefront. In the late 1980s and early 1990s, rap music often focused on "the increasing social isolation, economic hardship, political demoralization, and cultural exploitation endured by most ghetto poor communities."[10]

The other side of the hip-hop spectrum, "pop rap," appealed to American listeners in the early 1990s because it avoided racial politics and ghetto life and instead created light-hearted songs about suburban teenagers. Enter DJ Jazzy Jeff and The Fresh Prince, who emerged on the scene with their album *He's the DJ, I'm the Rapper* in 1988, on which the artists rapped humorously about various crises associated with being a teen. Will Smith and Jeff Townes's music, unlike the majority of hip-hop and rap music during the time, was devoid of social commentary and racial pride. According to cultural critic Michael Eric Dyson, such music "mean[t] the sanitizing of rap's expression of urban realities, resulting in sterile hip-hop that, devoid of its original fire, will offend no one."[11] Pop rap reinforced dominant heteronormative culture while allowing neoliberal culture to absorb black political identities, bringing them into the capitalist market.

Black masculinity within hip-hop and rap culture was taken to the extreme because machismo and the exploitation of women became prevalent. This version of black masculinity carried over from the black power movement, where race was often viewed as the most important identifying factor, and matters of gender and sexuality were either ignored or blatantly dismissed. This prioritization often caused "black (heterosexual) women's intellectual and community work [to become] marginalized, if not erased, [as] homosexuality was effectively 'theorized' as a 'white disease' that had 'infected' the black community."[12] Although black hip-hop artists critiqued white culture, many of them did so at the expense of other marginalized groups such as women and those who identify as LGBTQ+. Such hypermasculinity carried over into pop rap as black male artists such as Smith and Townes were compelled to replicate machismo and heteronormativity in order to be accepted into the genre and popular culture at large. Pop rap not only avoided critiquing the racial structures in America but also appealed to white, patriarchal, neoliberal society through the portrayal of rappers as alpha males and women as objects ready for consumption.

With his nonthreatening, humorous demeanor and his conformity to heteronormative black masculinity, Will Smith was the perfect entertainer for the African American sitcom to follow *The Cosby Show*. Like the Cosby family, he was a model minority—a wayward African American youth who was saved from the ugliness of urban ghetto life and placed on the neoliberal trajectory toward wealth, consumerism, and heteronormativity—at the expense of African American identity politics. From the show's pilot, Will's future path is paved for him as his Uncle Phil, played by James Avery, who was once an activist in the black power movement, instructs Will that he is living at their Bel-Air mansion in order to "work hard, straighten out, and learn some good old fashioned American values."[13] These are values that are clearly aligned with the white upper class, as Will discovers when he is chastised for acting too black at a dinner party with white neighbors at the Banks's residence. The Banks's ultimate goal is to symbolically have their other neighbors, the Ronald Reagans, join their dinner party—even though the Reagans had declined "the last [16] invitations," as Vivian Banks grievously laments. Indeed, it is clear right from the first episode that the role of the Banks's family is to absorb and thus render harmless Will's urban, lower-class version of blackness that reflects the black masculinity of hip-hop culture and not that of a (white) neoliberal paragon. Will consistently promotes the machismo of rap culture as he dates countless women, brags about his sexual conquests, and exudes an air of sexual prowess; indeed, he is the self-proclaimed "most handsome, the most intelligent, and unequivocally, the most flamboyant bachelor since Billy Dee."[14] The sitcom establishes this model of black masculinity as being of the past, as Uncle Phil explains to Will, "I grew up on the streets, just like you. Believe me; I know where I come from."[15] Uncle Phil's past activism in the black power movement is aligned with Will's current behavior, both of which are designated as an outdated model for blackness. Uncle Phil has seen the light from his past as a black power activist, as he states, "Now I have a family, and I choose not to fight in the streets. I have an office to fight from, . . . and I am not ashamed to write a big fat check for something I believe in."[16] His past identity politics is absorbed by the neoliberal model that he ultimately represents, where whiteness, money, heteronormativity, privatization, and state recognition are the current and future goals for blackness that will be achieved through individual effort, according to Reaganism.

Despite being a fish out of water, Will easily succumbs to the Reagan-inspired neoliberal model that the family represents. Throughout the sitcom's six seasons, Will works hard at jobs and school while purporting a hypermasculinity couched in heteronormativity and consumerism. He does this under the tutelage of Uncle Phil, Ronald Reagan's African American counterpart on the sitcom, who is there to instruct viewers along with Will on how to be a model (male) minority. Will still has his ups and downs, which is where the comedy of the show exists, but his trajectory on the neoliberal path is marked from the first episode, and this is what makes him successful—he is inherently nonthreatening to the dominant heteropatriarchal, neoliberal order.

GAY IDENTITY POLITICS, QUEERNESS, AND AFRICAN AMERICAN MASCULINITY

To find out where in *The Fresh Prince* the viewer can see African American identities that do not conform to neoliberalism's incorporation of minority identity politics—and may potentially resist it—we can invoke the tools provided by queer theory. As a discipline that provides a unique methodology, queer theory looks beyond all identifying categories that are considered "normal" in order to push at the spaces in between, revealing what may be hidden by dominant ideologies. This kind of theorizing allows us to look beyond neoliberalism's grasp because it incorporates minority identities and obscures that which is oppositional or queer, where "queer" refers to "the lapses and excesses of meaning when the constituent elements of anyone's gender, of anyone's sexuality aren't made (or *can't* be made) to signify monolithically."[17] In the case of the *The Fresh Prince*, or any popular media that seemingly aligns itself with dominant ideology, queer theory can be useful in determining if there are any possibilities for otherness, for difference, or for disaligning oneself with the neoliberal agenda, which, in the post-9/11 world of increasing privatization, state regulation, and the growing wealth of 1 percent of Americans, has become an unavoidable concern.

For the queer-minded viewer, it does not take a leap of the imagination to pinpoint a character on *The Fresh Prince* who does not comply with the normative models for black male masculinity that both Uncle Phil and Will expertly adopt—the "model minority" and the hypermasculine womanizer, respectively. Carlton Banks, played by Alfonso Rivera, Will's nerdy cousin, can never achieve the hypermasculine, woman-chasing machismo that Will naturally exudes, and for this he is constantly ridiculed by both Will's character and the sitcom at large. The show invites its viewers to laugh at Carlton's ineptitude at adopting a recognizable black masculinity.

Indeed, Carlton is read as white by his most prominent viewer and critic, Will, in the first episode of the series as the two cousins dress up in tuxedoes for a benefit dinner to which the Reagans were invited. Carlton prompts Will to get dressed, proclaiming, "Just wait till we come down to dinner in those tuxes. People may not think we're twins, but I bet they'll think we're brothers," a sincere comment to which Will jokingly responds, "I don't think you have to worry about anybody mistaking you for a brother."[18] In a humorous tone, Will instructs the audience in two important lessons that persist throughout the series: that Carlton can be read as white and that it is okay to make fun of his inability to adopt Will's version of black masculinity. In season three, as Uncle Phil remarks that Carlton is on his way to becoming the first black president, Carlton humorously responds with, "I'm black?"[19] This negotiation with blackness becomes a regular theme on the show, often taking a serious tone, for example, as Carlton states to Will in season one, "You always act like I don't measure up to some rule of blackness that you carry around."[20] Will's mocking of Carlton, as previously stated, is an assertion of the machismo and sexism that was part of rap culture during the 1990s and also part of a history of hypermasculinity within the African American community.

The sitcom does not invite us to dislike Carlton because of his failings; rather, his character often provides comic relief, and we enjoy snickering at his "feminine" ways. While the sitcom never labels Carlton as such, using a queer reading that pushes the boundaries of identity categories allows us to see that Carlton functions as the gay comic sidekick, who, next to the ultramasculine Will, is a legibly gay African American sitcom character.

In addition, although Carlton's femininity and awkwardness around women clues the viewer into the fact that he is "different," and his inability to grasp black male masculinity often makes us laugh, it is his adoption of whiteness that ultimately signifies his character as queer. For Halloween, Carlton paints his face white and puts lipstick on to become a vampire, a historical symbol of queer lust and desire that is tied to whiteness. Indeed, on seeing Carlton, Will remarks that he is "living out his fantasies."[21] Later, in season three, Carlton confesses that he played Maria in an all-boy production of *West Side Story* when he was 12.[22] During the 1990s, white, middle-class gay male identity politics became prominent on the neoliberal scene, following the gay and lesbian civil rights movement and the activism surrounding the AIDS crisis. Under the neoliberal model, identity politics are often incorporated into the system, where the goal becomes not to overthrow the establishment but to become part of it. White, middle-class gay male identity politics was swiftly incorporated to create what queer scholar Lisa Duggan calls "homonormativity," where those who identify as gay and lesbian focus on the nuclear family, state recognition of such rights as gay marriage, and lives based in consumption and consumerism.[23] TV shows such as *Sex and the City* (1998–2004), *Will and Grace* (1998–2006), *Queer as Folk* (2000–2005), and *Queer Eye for the Straight Guy* (2003–2007) featured white, middle-class gay men who fit the neoliberal model. Gayness in the 90s often went hand in hand with being a white, male consumer. Indeed, during the 1990s, television made explicit the historical trend that black queer scholar Roderick Ferguson discusses in which "sexuality as social construction becomes a way of announcing the assimilability—and thus normativity—of white middle-and-upper-class homosexuals as well as a means of excluding working-class and nonwhite queers on the basis of the inability to conform to normative ideals of American citizenship."[24] To be legibly gay, one must be a white, upper-class consumer because working-class queers and queers of color are ignored by dominant American neoliberal culture.

To be read as gay or queer within popular media, Carlton's character must adopt a white, upper-class masculinity. In this way, the television show allows Carlton to exude not Will's version of black male masculinity but the dominant gay male masculinity based on wealth and whiteness. In season two, Will and Carlton make a bet with Will's cousins, Hillary and Ashley, that the girls cannot accomplish the traditionally masculine chore of putting a bicycle together while the boys cannot design and sew a dress. Carlton is overjoyed at the traditionally feminine opportunity of making a dress but is specifically interested in the more upper-class role of designer as he envisions the dress with "a full smocking and smart pleat." After he and Will sew the dress, Carlton tries it on and models it for the viewing audience. Admiring himself in the mirror, he proclaims, "We're gonna win this bet, Will. I love the neckline, and the fabric's great [looking at himself in the mirror with a smile]. And the color really brings out my eyes."[25] Carlton's negation of the model of black masculinity offered by Will and his Uncle Phil and his adoption of white, upper-class values allow the viewer to see him as belonging to stereotypes surrounding white gay men in the 1990s—that they are feminine, middle-class consumers. Although this episode could be categorized as a comedic cross-dressing routine, it is queer in that Carlton already knows more about female fashion than Ashley, Hillary, and Will. He exhibits some secret knowledge about female attire that is unexpected but not all that surprising—neither to the other characters nor to the viewer. In this way, Carlton's character uses the stereotypical white, middle-class gay male identity to present himself as a preliminary legibly gay African American man on television.

Although Will Smith adopts Uncle Phil's model of black masculinity that conforms to neoliberal ideology while maintaining the remnant machismo of hip-hop culture, and Carlton functions as the sitcom's legibly gay character through his alignment with white gay male stereotypes that are recognizable through neoliberalism's consumer culture, it is DJ Jazzy Jeff, or "Jazz," played by Jeffery Allen Townes, who vocally recognizes and dismisses class hierarchies and consumerism, resists the norms for black masculinity through his constant failure at machismo, and commits to a homosocial relationship with Will, which is one of the key examples of successful coupling throughout the six seasons of the show.

The first time that Jazz appears on the show (season one, episode two), he walks through Uncle Phil's Bel-Air mansion with his mouth agape, carrying a boom box and staring at the splendor as though he is viewing a palace on Mars. Immediately, Jazz, who lives in a run-down apartment complex in Compton, resists Uncle Phil as a model of neoliberal success, as he slaps the hand that Phil holds out to shake, and proclaims, "Man, you loaded!" This begins Jazz's humorous resistance to both Will's and Phil's adoption of neoliberal ideology, calling them out on their wealth and privilege at every opportunity and thus questioning its normativity.

Some of the most memorable scenes in the sitcom occur when Uncle Phil throws Jazz out of the mansion, ejecting him from the neoliberal sanctuary in which he does not belong. In the same episode, Will asks Jazz to turn up the classical music that Phil is enjoying. Jazz starts spinning it, scratching the record with expertise, shocking the Banks family because they consider such skills to be part of lower-class African American hip-hop culture, from which they have progressed. It is in the next scene that Uncle Phil throws Jazz out of the mansion for the first time, but not the last, forcing Vivian to scold him, proclaiming, "You know, I think living down the street from the Reagans has had a very bad effect on you!"[26] Repeatedly throwing Jazz out of the mansion illustrates the Banks's rejection of Jazz's ability as a queer character to mock and resist their adoption of neoliberal ideology and all of the wealth, power, and privilege it entails.

Just as Jazz is rejected from the symbolic Bel-Air mansion repeatedly throughout the show, so too is he romantically rejected by Hillary, the Banks's eldest daughter and Bel-Air princess, signifying his inability to adopt the hypersexual black masculinity and machismo that the sitcom promotes. Because he does not participate in neoliberal advancement and does not have Will's womanizing qualities, it is clear to the viewer that Jazz will never display the normative black masculinity that might attract Hillary Banks, and Jazz's crush becomes another running joke in the show. However, this joke differs from the ones surrounding Carlton's feminization and adoption of whiteness because, though he always fails, Jazz never stops attempting to adopt this machismo. When Will and Jazz unsuccessfully go to the mall to find a girlfriend for their butler, Geoffery, Hillary exclaims, "Well what did you expect? You went to the mall with girl-away there," referring to Jazz. Will sticks up for his womanizer in training, claiming that Jazz is irresistible to women, to which Hillary snidely remarks, "Maybe during a blackout." At this point, Jazz attempts, once again, to hit on Hillary at an inopportune time and in an unappealing manner when he tells her, "I'd love to get ahold of you during a black out." She is clearly repulsed, and the scene ends with Uncle Phil throwing Jazz out of the mansion, showing Jazz's inability to adopt the kind of masculinity that Will exhorts, though not through lack of trying, and his literal ejection from the space of normative black male masculinity.[27] In this way, he becomes a character foil to Will, calling attention to the absurdity of defining black masculinity based on heteronormativity and an exaggerated sexuality.

In season one, episode seven, while Will is attempting a poem that will attract his latest female crush, Jazz proclaims that the line, "Let's go get some barbeque and get busy," always works for him, humorously revealing his model of black masculinity as one that does not align with hip-hop culture as he once again fails to find the right line to get the girl.[28] Jazz's humor further reveals that Will is conforming to normative behavior, trying to be someone he is not by writing a poem to attract another girl. Just as he retains the ability to question the Banks's neoliberal normativity, so Jazz as a queer character who does not fit into traditional models of black masculinity calls into question Will's adoption of heteronormative behavior.

Furthermore, Jazz is consistently portrayed as Will's sidekick on the show, his best friend, and the one person with whom a stable relationship is possible. Their friendship persists throughout the sitcom despite their continued differences in class, education, and future pursuits, creating homosocial bonding that the sitcom upholds as a model for all relationships because the two characters' heteronormative endeavors always fall apart.

This homosocial relationship is celebrated in season three, episode seven, which uses a video montage set to Dean Martin's "Everybody Loves Somebody" with Will and Jazz high-fiving and hugging on the beach; Will even picks Jazz up and twirls him around. The two of them are also shown in Paris, playing patty-cake and spinning while holding hands in front of the Eiffel Tower. Later in the episode, Jazz and Will have a fight that reads like a clichéd heteronormative breakup scene. Jazz, playing the role of the female, proclaims, "Oh, comes the dawn! My mother told me you was no good. I knew I shoulda listened to her. See, I promised myself I wasn't gonna cry!" Will is the taciturn male who chides, "C'mon Jazz." The scene ends with Will reassuring his male partner that "just cuz somebody moves away from the family, that doesn't mean they break up. That just means the family has to work harder to stay together." As the two men make up, they hug, and Jazz asks Will to throw him out of the house "for old times' sake."[29] In this way, the sitcom portrays the two men's relationship as that which goes beyond friendship and into a queer partnering in which the characters are so emotionally connected that they can imagine sharing a romantic traveling experience and engaging in the same arguments that a couple in a sexual relationship may have. In addition, this is a queer relationship because, just as Will throwing Jazz out of the mansion shows, Jazz will consistently reveal and question Will's normative behavior, allowing the viewer to do so as well.

In this way, *Fresh Prince* ultimately presents viewers with many interpretations of black masculinity in contemporary culture, providing counter identities to Will's heteronormative, hypermasculine persona. Carlton, one of the first legibly gay black male characters on television, uses whiteness like a code to signal to the knowing viewer his nonheteronormative identifications. Finally, Jazz functions as a queer character who tries and fails at heteronormative pairing and ultimately resists such coupling through his queer partnering with Will while also disrupting neoliberal consumer capitalist tendencies as displayed within the Banks's household. These multimodal black male identifications paved the way for contemporary television shows such as *Spin City* (1996–2002) and *Greek* (2007–2011). More recent shows have featured queer people of color in unprecedented numbers, such as *Empire* (premiered in January 2015), *The Haves and the Have Nots* (premiered May 2013), *Being Mary Jane* (premiered July 2013), and *Orange Is the New Black* (premiered July 2013), which features Laverne Cox as the first male-to-female transgender person of color to gain the spotlight in American culture. Indeed, Matt Kane, a program director at GLAAD (The Gay and Lesbian Alliance Against Defamation) stated, "It was only a few years ago that GLAAD's annual television reports found that gay black men were one of the most underrepresented groups on television, but the current influx of more diverse characters is a very promising sign."[30] Ahead of its time, *The Fresh Prince of Bel-Air* offers its queer-eyed viewers different options for black masculinity, which speaks to the cultural power of television not only to have the potential to reinforce problematic cultural categories but also to offer up to the viewing public new ways of living, loving, and being in the world.

NOTES

1. Christine Acham, *Revolution Televised: Prime Time and the Struggle for Black Power* (Minneapolis: University of Minnesota Press, 2004), 6.

2. Ibid.

3. Herman Gray, *Watching Race: Television and the Struggle for Blackness* (Minneapolis: University of Minnesota Press, 1995), 76.

4. Eve Kosofsky Sedgwick, "Queer and Now." In *Tendencies* (Durham, NC: Duke University Press, 1993), 4.

5. Gray, op. cit., 18.

6. Saul Austerlitz, *Sitcom: A History in 24 Episodes from I Love Lucy to Community* (Chicago: Chicago Review Press, 2014), 177.

7. Gray, *Watching Race*, 19.

8. David Harvey, *A Brief History of Neoliberalism* (Oxford, UK: Oxford University Press, 2005), 7 and 3, respectively.

9. Herman Gray, *Cultural Moves: African Americans and the Politics of Representation* (Berkeley: University of California Press, 2005), 107.

10. Michael Eric Dyson, *The Michael Eric Dyson Reader* (New York: Basic Civitas Books, 2004), 404.

11. Ibid., 405.

12. E. Patrick Johnson and Mae G. Henderson, "Introduction: Queer Black Studies/'Quaring' Queer Studies," *Black Queer Studies: A Critical Anthology*, edited by E. Patrick Johnson and Mae G. Henderson (Durham, NC: Duke University Press, 2005), 4.

13. "Pilot (The Fresh Prince Project)," *The Fresh Prince of Bel-Air: Season One*, directed by Debbie Allen (1991) (Burbank, CA: Warner Home Video, 2006), DVD.

14. "Clubba Hubba," *The Fresh Prince of Bel-Air: Season One*, directed by Jeff Melman (1991) (Burbank, CA: Warner Home Video, 2006), DVD.

15. "Pilot," op. cit.

16. "Those Were the Days," *The Fresh Prince of Bel-Air: Season Two*, directed by Rita Rogers (1991–1992) (Burbank, CA: Warner Home Video, 2006), DVD.

17. Sedgwick, op. cit., 8.

18. "Pilot," op. cit.

19. "Will Gets Committed," *The Fresh Prince of Bel-Air: Season Three*, directed by Shelley Jensen (1992) (Burbank, CA: Warner Home Video, 2006), DVD.

20. "72 Hours," *The Fresh Prince of Bel-Air: Season One*, directed by Rea Kraus (1991) (Burbank, CA: Warner Home Video, 2006), DVD.

21. "Some Day Your Prince Will be in Effect, Part 2," *The Fresh Prince of Bel-Air: Season One*, directed by Jeff Melman (1990) (Burbank, CA: Warner Home Video, 2006), DVD.

22. "Will Gets Committed," op. cit.

23. Lisa Duggan, *The Twilight of Equality? Neoliberalism, Cultural Politics, and the Attack on Democracy* (Boston: Beacon Press, 2003), 50.

24. Johnson and Henderson, "Introduction: Queer Black Studies," op. cit., 8.

25. "Granny Gets Busy," *The Fresh Prince of Bel-Air: Season Two*, directed by Ellen Falcon (1991) (Burbank, CA: Warner Home Video, 2006), DVD.

26. "Bang the Drum, Ashley," *The Fresh Prince of Bel-Air: Season One*, directed by Debbie Allen (1990) (Burbank, CA: Warner Home Video, 2006), DVD.

27. "Kiss My Butler," *The Fresh Prince of Bel-Air: Season One*, directed by Rita Rogers Blye (1990) (Burbank, CA: Warner Home Video, 2006), DVD.

28. "Def Poet's Society." *The Fresh Prince of Bel-Air: Season One*, directed by Jeff Melman (1990) (Burbank, CA: Warner Home Video, 2006), DVD.

29. "Here Comes the Judge," *The Fresh Prince of Bel-Air: Season Three*, directed by Shelley Jensen (1992) (Burbank, CA: Warner Home Video, 2006), DVD.

30. Karu F. Daniels, "More Gay Black Characters on TV Series These Days: 'Empire,' 'Being Mary Jane,' and 'The Haves & the Have Nots,'" *New York Daily News*, March 8, 2015, http://www.nydailynews.com/entertainment/tv/gay-black -characters-tv-article-1.2137944.

BIBLIOGRAPHY

Acham, Christine. *Revolution Televised: Prime Time and the Struggle for Black Power.* Minneapolis: University of Minnesota Press, 2004.

Austerlitz, Saul. *Sitcom: A History in 24 Episodes from I Love Lucy to Community.* Chicago: Chicago Review Press, 2014.

Daniels, Karu F. "More Gay Black Characters on TV Series These Days: 'Empire,' 'Being Mary Jane,' and 'The Haves & The Have Nots.'" *New York Daily News*, March 8, 2015, http://www.nydailynews.com/entertainment/tv/gay-black -characters-tv-article-1.2137944.

Duggan, Lisa. *The Twilight of Equality? Neoliberalism, Cultural Politics, and the Attack on Democracy.* Boston: Beacon Press, 2003.

Dyson, Michael Eric. *The Michael Eric Dyson Reader.* New York: Basic Civitas Books, 2004.

Gray, Herman. *Cultural Moves: African Americans and the Politics of Representation.* Berkeley: University of California Press, 2005.

Gray, Herman. *Watching Race: Television and the Struggle for Blackness.* Minneapolis: University of Minnesota Press, 1995.

Harvey, David. *A Brief History of Neoliberalism.* Oxford, UK: Oxford University Press, 2005.

Johnson, E. Patrick, and Mae G. Henderson. "Introduction: Queer Black Studies/'Quaring' Queer Studies." *Black Queer Studies: A Critical Anthology*, edited by E. Patrick Johnson and Mae G. Henderson. Durham, NC: Duke University Press, 2005, 1–17.

Sedgwick, Eve Kosofsky. "Queer and Now." In *Tendencies.* Durham, NC: Duke University Press, 1993, 1–22.

"72 Hours." *The Fresh Prince of Bel-Air: Season One*, directed by Rea Kraus (1991) (Burbank, CA: Warner Home Video, 2006). DVD.

PART 4

The Oughts and Teens

17

Nearly 30 Years of "D'oh!": The Animated Legacy of *The Simpsons*

Paul Cheng

A fluffy white cloud floats in the blue sky as we hear the angelic, choral "ahhs" of the title sequence opening to The Simpsons *(1989–present). The first animated sitcom in this volume,* The Simpsons *crosses genres and decades and is becoming the longest-running show on television (on course to beat out* Gunsmoke's *635 episodes before its contract is up in 2019). In "Nearly 30 Years of "D'oh!": The Animated Legacy of* The Simpsons," *Paul Cheng argues that the influence of the show is attributable to the following trifecta—its early role in the culture wars of the 1990s, its success as a prime-time animated series with decidedly adult content, and its postmodern sensibilities.*

If there has been any show whose cultural impact has been logged, dissected, and analyzed in the last 25 or so years, it is *The Simpsons*. The show began, in the creators' own snarky admission, as "a series of crudely animated shorts on the *Tracey Ullman Show*" and has evolved into a cultural juggernaut whose accomplishments now read like a series of check-off boxes: an entry in the *Oxford English Dictionary* for Homer's now iconic "D'oh!" Check. Use in college classes, including a popular two-unit class at the University of California Berkeley entitled "*The Simpsons* and Philosophy." Check. Lasting impact in terms of comedic sensibility seen in *The Family Guy, South Park*, and on TV sitcoms and comedy in general ranging from *The Daily Show* to *Modern Family*. Check. Application in discussing various cultural movements and philosophies via the show such as feminism and postmodernism. Check.

The Simpsons represents a grand feat in the television landscape: after 28 seasons, and more than 600 episodes, *The Simpsons*, which aired its first episode on December 17, 1989, holds the record as the longest-running scripted prime-time television show, knocking the venerable *Gunsmoke* off its perch. However, measuring the cultural impact of *The Simpsons* is potentially difficult because of its multifarious nature. After all, it is not only a family sitcom but also a parody of a family sitcom. It is also an animated show on network prime-time television although it is possible that such a distinction may not matter anymore in today's expanded viewing universe.

The impact of *The Simpsons* can best be summarized in three ways. First, the show's immediate popularity had an unexpected impact on the "culture wars" of the 1990s, reaching deep into culture at large and provoking a kind of nationwide backlash. Second, it proved that prime-time television animation is a viable format and medium. And third, with its postmodern sensibilities, the show has created a template for what prime-time television animation—indeed, what animation in general—has looked like on American television for nearly 30 years.

The Simpsons seemed to triumphantly herald the return of prime-time animation. As one newspaper article boldly announced in 1992, "thank Fox Broadcasting and the phenomenal success of 'The Simpsons' for the resurgence of prime-time cartoons."[1] Since *The Flintstones* had ended its run in 1966, animation had been ghettoized as mere children's entertainment, and *The Simpsons* defied those expectations, offering a witty, intelligent, and sophisticated cartoon for adults. In the years after its debut, *The Simpsons* has been accompanied on Fox's schedule at various times by several other undeniably successful animated shows: Matt Groening's own *Futurama* (1999–); Mike Judge's and Greg Daniels' *King of the Hill* (1997–2010); Seth McFarlane's trio of shows—*Family Guy* (1999–), its spin-off *The Cleveland Show* (2009–2013), and *American Dad* (2011–); and *Bob's Burgers* (2011–). Fox had not aired first-run live action comedies on Sunday nights since 2005, leading Fox to advertise its Sunday night schedule as "Animation Domination." The cable lineup offers even more variety, ranging from prime-time shows such as *Archer* (2009–) and, of course, *South Park* (1997–) to the Cartoon Network's block of Adult Swim programming. It would not be an exaggeration to say that the impact of *The Simpsons* is clear all across the television landscape.

However, in surveying this current crop of animated fare on both the networks and cable, three characteristics stand out. First, there is no shyness in exploring what would be considered "adult" subject matter, which ranges from social satire to the merely outrageous and at times even the scatological. Second, there is a marked increase in the use of surreal imagery or animated non sequiturs that often come quickly and furiously. Third and finally, there is a decidedly postmodern sensibility in the approach to humor with ample inside jokes and references, with a liberal sprinkling of parody, satire, and self-reflexivity, all forming a kind of postmodern pastiche in which "with the collapse of 'the high modernist ideology of style . . . the producers of culture have nowhere to turn but the past'" resulting in a kind of "cannibalizing" of the past.[2] This relative sameness is also one of the most enduring legacies and lasting impacts of *The Simpsons.*

The questions are, how did animation on television get here from there? What role did *The Simpsons* play in this transformation? The story begins on December 17, 1989, when the fledgling Fox network introduced what would become America's animated first family with the Christmas-themed episode "Simpsons Roasting on an Open Fire."

The Simpsons, of course, actually began its animated life two years earlier as a series of shorts on *The Tracey Ullman Show.* After this premiere and with its first regular episode in January 1990, *The Simpsons* quickly became a bona fide hit for Fox. In fact, Donick Cary, a writer and producer on *The Simpsons*, notes that "in a lot of ways, the Fox Network wouldn't exist without the longevity and the amount of viewers that *The Simpsons* has consistently brought."[3] The entry for the show on the Archive of American Television notes that "*The Simpsons* was a watershed program in the establishment of the FOX network."[4]

Though a ratings bonanza for the network, the show became much more. Only a year after the show's release, Harry Waters described the show as "a breakaway ratings hit, industry trendsetter, cultural template, and a viewing experience verging on the religious for its most fanatical followers."[5] All of this resulted from a genre that had not been seen in prime-time since *The Flintstones.* By the middle of 1990, *The Simpsons* had graced the covers of nearly every major newsmagazine of the time, including *Time, Newsweek,* and *TV Guide.* The breakout character in all this, Bart Simpson provoked something of a mania. "I'm Bart Simpson. Who the hell are you?" suddenly became popular on T-shirts.

"Bartmania" had a seemingly ubiquitous presence in the media and culture. In quick order, Bart became "more than just a beloved cartoon character; he was a cultural phenomenon."[6] Despite this massive popularity (or probably because of it), Bart quickly became a cause for nationwide moral panic with his smart-aleck remarks and anti-authoritarian attitude, "the dark side of Beaver Cleaver,"[7] if you will. Elementary schools all over the country banned Bart Simpson T-shirts bearing such signature catchphrases as "Underachiever and proud of it, man," "Don't have a cow, man," and the pithy "Eat my shorts, man." A school principal said, "the program is not a positive influence. It's making a cartoon hero out a boy we don't wish to have modeled at school."[8] *The Simpsons* and Bart in their animated dysfunction quickly became the poster children for all that was wrong with America, earning the ire of such "values spokespeople of the religious right"[9] as then-drug czar William Bennett. This moral panic over the show reached its zenith (or nadir, depending on your point of view) in 1992 when President George H. W. Bush weighed in on the show, solemnly pronouncing during his reelection campaign that he would make families "a lot more like the Waltons and a lot less like the Simpsons."[10]

The controversy over Bart Simpson reflected the decidedly adult sensibilities that distinguished the show from the beginning. "Simpsons Roasting on an Open Fire" centered on Homer's often sadness-filled attempts to provide his family with Christmas after he loses his holiday bonus from work and Marge is forced to use the Christmas fund to remove a "Mother" tattoo that Bart impulsively got. Several scenes relied on a strong sense of pathos in showing Homer's sorrow when realizing that he has no money to provide for a good Christmas for his family. One such moment has Homer going outside by himself only to witness his neighbor's Christmas display, unable to reveal to his family that he has lost his bonus after witnessing the beaming, expectant smiles of his children. Homer's only reaction is to hang his head in shame. Such a realistic story line seemed more akin to the working-class focused sitcom *Roseanne* (which had premiered the previous year) and was no doubt revolutionary then as a topic for a cartoon on American television. As one later reviewer succinctly asked, "How many animated Christmas specials can you name that involved foul-mouthed eight year-olds with tattoos, drunken mall Santas, and dog track betting?"

As time passed, Bartmania went the way of other fads, the moral panic engendered by the show faded, and the show itself settled into an easy groove. Bart's ubiquity in pop culture, however, wasn't solely because of the show itself. Rather, part of the phenomenal reach of the show resulted from calculated mass merchandising by Fox and its producers.

After the first season of the show, Fox "struck a deal with Mattel and [50] other product licensees, beginning a merchandising boom the likes of which television had not seen before."[11] As mentioned, part of Bart's appeal stemmed from his character as portrayed on the show: "brazen and obnoxious . . . he said all the things we wished we could say to the authority figures in our own lives—our father, our boss, or the Man in whatever form he took."[12] In considering the popularity of Bart Simpson among African American youths, Russell Adams of Howard University suggested that here, too, Bart's outsider status *is* his appeal: " 'there is a rowdiness and an unvarnished chutzpah on the part of Bart' " and that "these qualities speak well to many black youngsters who are growing up in a society that often alienates them."[13]

What this explanation ignores is one of the things that allowed Bart and his clan to be reproduced on everything from T-shirts to mugs to calendars: Bart Simpson is a cartoon. He is an eye-catching, easily reproducible image with a series of iconic characteristics: the yellow skin, the zigzag haircut. Likewise, each member of the family has an easily recognizable feature that allows for easy reproduction: Marge and her hair, Homer with his exaggerated five o'clock shadow, and so on.

Bart and his image became the subject of unlicensed T-shirts featuring Bart as everyone from "Malcolm X, Michael Jordan ('Air Bart'), Bob Marley ('Rasta Bart')" to even neo-Nazis."[14] Such variations were then almost impossible with a nondrawn figure. Also, as one street artist of the time noted, "Bart is so flexible, almost anyone can relate to him."[15] And it is this flexibility that extends beyond the personality and into the aesthetics of the character itself. Indeed, it has been argued that animation, "more than any other genre, could be logically exploited across a variety of retail outlets. Theme parks, toys, clothes, magazines, CDs, and musicals-on-ice are better suited for *Scooby-Doo . . .* than *Saved by the Bell*."[16] After all, one of the basic features of animation is what Paul Wells characterizes as its "plasmatic flexibility."[17] Derived from a term by coined by Sergei Eisenstein, the idea of animation's *plasmaticness* is its ability to resist fixed and stable forms, its inherent flexibility and freedom of expression to "dynamically assume any form."[18] Here the visual figure of Bart served as a template that was easily manipulated to become whatever he needed to be within the social and cultural sphere.

To use animation's inherent flexibility as a kind of metaphor, what *The Simpsons* suddenly offered were *possibilities*. All of a sudden, animation appeared to be a viable medium for prime-time television, and the other three networks at the time were quick to capitalize on what *The Simpsons* seemed to represent.

However, as successful as animation has seemingly become in prime-time, the noncable prime-time landscape is actually littered with failures. In fact, no other broadcast network besides Fox features an animated show in its lineup as of this writing, and no animated show airing on a broadcast network other than Fox has lasted more than two seasons. Some of the more notable shows that have come and gone include the following: on ABC, *Capitol Critters* (1993), *The Critic* (1994), and *Clerks: The Animated Series* (2000); on NBC, *Family Dog* (1993), *God, the Devil and Bob* (2000), and *Father of the Pride* (2003); on UPN and WB, *Dilbert* (1999–2000), *Mission Hill* (1999), *Baby Blues* (2000), and *The Oblongs* (2001); and on CBS, *Fish Police* (1993). Most have faded into obscurity, but some of them have found a brief resurgence, and a few such as *The Oblongs* and *Baby Blues* have appeared on cable outlets such as Adult Swim. All in all, though, the number of animated failures outnumber the successes in prime-time. A closer look at the three shows that came out most immediately after *The Simpsons* might help illustrate some of the reasons certain animated shows have succeeded and others have failed, often spectacularly. The year 1993 saw the debut of *Capitol Critters* on ABC, followed in February by *Fish Police* on CBS, and later in the year by NBC's *Family Dog*. Mike Scully has suggested that these shows failed because of poor development and writing: "so without a lot of thought to character or content, they [the networks] rushed all these show [sic] on air and the public rejected most of them."[19] Although this argument may seem a compelling explanation for the failure of these shows, Scully's analysis may be a bit reductive. After all, each of the three shows that debuted in 1993 had no lack of development time, animation pedigree, or high-powered talent. Rather, the problem with these shows was simply that they were not *The Simpsons*.

Capitol Critters was produced by superproducer Steven Bochco, who was responsible for such live-action legal dramas as *Hill Street Blues* and *L.A. Law*. The show sent up politics in a "heavy-handed social satire" following a family of rats who lived underneath the White House. Likewise, *Fish Police*, which was also produced by Hanna-Barbera, featured established actors such as John Ritter, Hector Elizondo, Ed Asner, and Jonathan Winters in a film noir send-up set underwater. Based on an independent comic book of the same name, *Fish Police* featured Inspector Gil fighting crime on the mean streets of Fish City. With its hard-boiled parody, innuendo-filled dialog, and mild language, the show was clearly aimed at an adult audience. To quote producer David Kirscher, "'It's a sitcom . . . not an animated kids' show.'"[20] Finally, *Family Dog* was executive produced by Steven Spielberg and produced by Brad Bird, who actually worked on *The Simpsons* throughout the 1990s and directed the critically acclaimed *The Iron Giant* and later the equally well-received Disney-Pixar movies *The Incredibles* and *Ratatouille*. *Family Dog* concerned the misadventures of a dog and put-upon suburban family but is actually told from the point of the view of the titular dog.

All three of these high-profile animated shows failed in spectacular fashion: *Capitol Critters* was at one point ranked 101 out of 120 shows in the Nielsen ratings and disappeared after seven episodes. *Fish Police* suffered a worse fate, going belly-up (sorry) after three airings. *Family Dog* lasted the longest, airing 10 episodes before disappearing from NBC's schedule.

These shows may have had fundamental problems in character and plot or maybe, as Kirschner suggests, *Capitol Critters* failed because of problems in tone where poor writing "seemed to [trap the show] in a world between adults and kids."[21] Another possible explanation for their failure has more to do with questions of genre and content rather than other production factors. To further explore this idea, keep in mind that *The Simpsons* itself remained, and in many ways it still firmly remains in the mode of the standard family sitcom. In fact, as a standard family sitcom, *The Simpsons* is remarkably successful.

Likewise, an even cursory comparison of three animated programs that have seen the greatest success after *The Simpsons* shows that they hew pretty closely to a formula that dominated the sitcom in the 1990s: a middle-class, sometimes working-class family dealing with various hijinks. These shows are *Family Guy, King of the Hill,* and the newest of the group, *Bob's Burgers.* Each show features a beleaguered, somewhat dim-witted father (Homer Simpson, Peter Griffin, Hank Hill, and Bob Belcher), the loving if often beleaguered mother (Marge, Lois, Peggy, and Linda), and, of course, the often offbeat and precocious children. (For example, it is fully possible to draw a direct line from overachieving Lisa Simpson to too-smart-for-family Meg Griffin to wise-for-her-years Tina Belcher.)

In this context then it seems no surprise that the three contenders to *The Simpsons* animated throne failed. What these three failed attempts did, with the possible exception of *Family Dog,* was move beyond this genre in unfamiliar ways. Like *The Simpsons,* the shows remained firmly grounded in satire and parody (*Capitol Critters* tackled political corruption while *Fish Police* played with film noir conventions), but they veered dramatically away from this essentially tried and true basic format. Perhaps the shows were ill conceived or lacked vision and development, but as previously mentioned their greatest crime may have been that they were *not The Simpsons.* If America was willing to open its heart to prime-time television, at the very least it still needed to look like something that they were already familiar with. Each of the producers behind these shows thought that the success of *The Simpsons* was because of its medium of animation. What they failed to recognize is that the success of *The Simpsons* was actually rooted in the genre: the family sitcom. So while *Family Dog* had the basics of the family sitcom, having the show built around a nontalking dog was perhaps too much of a stretch in the basic format of the genre.

Of course, the enduring legacy of *The Simpsons* is not just simply providing a new medium for a tried and true television genre; it has to do with what the show has allowed for in terms of animation in the United States. Initially, *The Simpsons* opened up what can be best described as *possibilities:* no longer relegated to the programming ghetto of Saturday morning cartoons or syndicated afterschool fare, the show offered America a new way not only to watch cartoons but also to think about what that term means. In fact, only five years after the show's debut, the 1994 launch of the Cartoon Network on cable, a network featuring *only* cartoons and animated fare, seemed to offer a chance for animation to have a more permanent home in prime-time and the realm of possibilities seemed only to expand.

But as much as the show created these possibilities, the quick failures of the shows immediately following *The Simpsons* foreshadowed a narrowing of those same possibilities as the years passed. In other words, as time progressed, instead of the scope and variety of animation continuing to open up, there was instead a foreclosing of what animation could be and what animation should do. What *The Simpsons* ultimately did was to so firmly establish a set of defining characteristics not just for adult-oriented animation but also for animation in general. This influence has been so strong that large swaths of television animation for both adults and children have a remarkable sameness to them.

As discussed earlier, *The Simpsons* created a way for adult topics and themes to be combined with animation. With its play on the conventions of the family sitcom, combined with sophisticated writing that featured satirical, parodoxical, and often self-reflexive humor, *The Simpsons* was clearly aimed at an "adult" audience that would recognize and understand references to *The Birds* or contemporary politics or Ayn Rand. As director Brad Bird notes, "my agenda almost as long I've been working professionally is to try and reinforce the idea that animation is not exclusively for kids. And . . . *The Simpsons* was a wonderful way to get on board a ship that was flying in the face of that."[22]

Indeed, the show's decidedly humorous take on the dynamics of family dysfunction is coupled with sophisticated satire and an often endless stream of "high-brow" references to obscure cultural and historical figures. After all, the show has featured such literary figures as Tom Wolfe and the notoriously reclusive Thomas Pynchon, who has actually appeared on the show twice, lampooning his own reclusiveness by being animated with a brown paper bag covering his face. Furthermore, he is portrayed as an aggressive self-promoter wearing a sandwich board proudly announcing "Thomas Pynchon's House" and standing in front of said house, which is lit by a gaudy neon sign announcing the same thing. As Simone Knox points out, these kinds of references presuppose "a high degree of media literacy in its audience" and offer the show's viewers "the pleasure of recognizing these references and working out 'hidden' jokes."[23] In short, the show helps its audience feel smart with its "overwhelming number of references [that] range from pop culture to poetry, politics, and literature."[24]

Considering the immense number of episodes of the show, it becomes both easy and difficult to find examples that illustrate what *The Simpsons* does with animation. Perhaps one of the best illustrations of the show's uncanny blend of adult-centered humor, surreal asides, and postmodern metahumor is the 15th episode from season 11 titled "Missionary: Impossible." The entire episode is built around an absurdist conceit: Homer reneges on a $10,000 pledge to PBS, and in his attempt to escape, he ends up as a missionary on a tiny island in Micronesia. This setup allows such surreal sequences as Homer being pursued down the streets of Springfield by a mob of PBS personalities, including Fred Rogers, who tells Homer, "It's a beautiful day . . . to kick your ass." We also see Yo-Yo Ma firing his bow from his cello strings, the Teletubbies with laser-firing head symbols, and even *Sesame Street*'s Elmo, who threateningly reminds Homer, "Elmo knows where you live." The episode even engages in casual blasphemy as Homer suddenly finds himself on the way to Micronesia and points out that "I don't even believe in Jebus" and then later, when he realizes there is no way out implores, "save me, Jebus!" Moreover, once Homer finds himself trapped on the island, he passes the time by licking toads, attempting to find one with hallucinogenic properties: he would try one, gasp "Ewww" when realizes he has the wrong toad, and then has his pupils dilate and shimmer when he finds one. From blasphemy to drug use, the episode quickly takes on topics that are often taboo on television in general. At the same time, with its PBS parody, the episode makes assumptions that there is an audience that not only watches the show but also would recognize Garrison Keillor.

The episode ends on a what can be described as a self-reflexive moment of metatextual understanding: the episode of Homer's adventures as a missionary is revealed to be a ratings stunt and part of an ongoing pledge drive for the Fox network itself, featuring a put-upon Rupert Murdoch, the head of Fox. The goal of the drive is described to keep "crude, low-brow programming" such as *Family Guy* on the air, and it ends with Bart pledging enough money that would save the network. When told of this, Bart replies, "Wouldn't be the first time." It is these metatextual moments that often distinguish the show. In this case, the show not only takes a dig at one of its most popular successors, *Family Guy*, but also cheekily points to its own initial success in saving the Fox network in the 1990s. In many ways, then, an episode such as "Missionary: Impossible" captures many of the elements that have driven the success of the show, but it also features the elements that have shaped television animation in the United States.

As much as Brad Bird celebrated the way in which *The Simpsons* brought an adult sensibility to prime-time animation, he is also quick to point out that "unfortunately, a lot of people have taken the wrong lessons from *The Simpsons* and just done the butt-crack jokes, and not picked up the smart ball."[25] Perhaps the two shows that best demonstrate Bird's claim of creators and programmers learning the "wrong lessons" are Seth McFarlane's *Family Guy* and Matt Stone's and Trey Parker's hit for Comedy Central, *South Park*, which is now the second longest-running animated series in the United States after—you guessed it—*The Simpsons*. Indeed, the shows have been described as "*The Simpsons*' disobedient stepchildren,"[26] and Matt Soller Seitz has described *Family Guy* as "a consistently ruder, funnier show that was nonetheless never as rich as 'The Simpsons,' and that looted Matt Groening's cartoon like a department store during a blackout."[27] Moreover, both McFarlane and Stone have acknowledged the influence of *The Simpsons* on their respective shows. As McFarlane notes, " 'Wow, these guys are opening up a whole bunch of new doorways for animation with some bite to it.'"[28] As Bird notes, however, adding "adult" to the equation often became equated with just pushing the boundaries of taste and shock in the manner of *Family Guy* and *South Park*. After all, the first episode of *South Park* not only introduced the foul-mouthed, bleeped-out swearing quartet that constitutes the show's main characters but also crudely animated and graphic sequences featuring anal probes and explosive flatulence. All this is in addition to the graphic and gruesome death of Kenny, whose death every episode became a long-running joke with the show.

Similarly, the *Family Guy* episode "Let's Go to the Hop" illustrates the way *Family Guy* both builds on what *The Simpsons* does and pushes it to the extreme that Bird references. In *Family Guy*, what is basically a throwaway gag, Homer licking hallucinogenic toads, becomes the whole focus of the episode in which Peter Griffin, on discovering a toad in his son Chris's pocket, goes undercover at the local high school to persuade the high school kids to stop by delivering a full-scale, big budget musical number in the style of *Grease* that expounds on the dangers of toad licking. The pop culture reference, like the adult theme is clear, but the way in which the episode takes a two-line gag from *The Simpsons* and blows it up to episode length serves as both an example and a metaphor for the way shows such as *Family Guy* build on certain aspects of *The Simpsons* legacy while leaving behind key elements. As Bird suggests, the topic is there, but often the intelligence is ignored or lost.

Moving beyond prime-time television, the influence of *The Simpsons* becomes readily apparent in the brief overview of some of the more popular animated shows. Clearly, while a show such as *Adventure Time*—the story of a boy named Finn and his magical dog, Jake, in a fantasy world—seems far removed from the middle-class domesticity of *The Simpsons*, the show is first and foremost characterized by its comic nature and often surreal imagery and popular culture references (specifically to video game culture). Likewise, Cartoon Network's *The Regular Show* about best friends who happen to be a talking blue jay and raccoon has been lauded for its "offbeat sense of humor with lots of randomness that makes its title both peculiar and hilarious"[29] Likewise, FX's *Archer* is foremost a parody of secret agent movies and delivers the same sort of crass, boundary-pushing situations and dialogue pioneered by *The Simpsons*. Although unique in their own styles and subject matter, when stripped to the core, these shows display the same elements pioneered on network television by *The Simpsons*, but they push that boundary in the way that only basic cable can.

Another key way to see the lack of diversity in the current crop of animation is to consider types of shows that at one point aired on such cable outlets as Nickelodeon and Cartoon Network but are no longer being produced and to explore the specific way in which the influence of *The*

Simpsons helped their subsequent demise. Ostensibly aimed at younger audiences, shows such as *Avatar: The Last Airbender* and its sequel series *The Legend of Korra*, as well as *Young Justice*, are rarities: action-adventure shows set in either fantasy settings or featuring superheroes with story lines emphasizing action and drama over comedy. Both these shows often featured serialized story lines that played out over several episodes, and the main characters often had to deal with such weighty issues as self-identity and death, themes that definitely skew older and could even be considered "adult." These shows were also visually different in their character designs: instead of the more exaggerated physical characteristics, the characters in these shows look more realistic, resembling actual human beings more than "cartoon" characters. *Avatar* enjoyed great success on Nickelodeon, but *The Legend of Korra* had a bumpier road; in fact, the last two seasons were not even aired on the network. According to a *Vanity Fair* online article, because of its "dark material . . . less-than-stellar ratings, an ill-timed leak of episodes, and any number of mysterious behind-the-scenes factors," the show was relegated to online access only for the end of its run. In short, "in its final seasons, *Korra* became too dangerous, too risky for Nick to air."[30]

Unfortunately, the well-received *Young Justice*, a superhero show based on characters appearing in DC Comics, didn't fare as well as *Korra*. Despite high ratings and strong critical response, *Young Justice* was canceled by the Cartoon Network after only two seasons. Its companion CGI series, *Green Lantern: The Animated Series*, fared even worse, lasting only one season. In fact, the creator of *Young Justice*, Paul Dini, expressed his frustration with the cancellation of the show by explaining that, in their attempt to capture younger male viewers, studios and networks are focusing on shows that appeal to "boys who are into goofy humor, goofy random humor."[31] This style of humor, which is a key part of *The Simpsons*, is not often present in these shows that focus more on action and adventure, but it is in abundance with shows such as *Adventure Time, Steven Universe*, and *The Regular Show*. Even though a show such as *Adventure Time* features longer stories, the focus is on the humor and its odd characters and not on the type of dramatic storytelling that is the focus of shows like *The Legend of Korra* or *Young Justice*. In short, *The Simpsons* may have paved the way for more animation across the board and brought animation to a mainstream audience in a new and spectacular way, but it also steamrolled shows that were not necessarily comedy driven and did not fit into its formula.

An interesting show that replaced *Young Justice* on the Cartoon Network lineup was *Teen Titans Go!*, which was also based on DC Comics superheroes; it demonstrates this narrowing in animation.

The interesting case of the evolution of the animated superhero show featuring the Teen Titans will illustrate some of the more lasting impacts of

The Simpsons on the aesthetics and format of current animated fare— mostly, the often surrealistic or absurdist asides coupled with the often knowing and winking self-reflexive references. The animated *Teen Titans* have actually had two incarnations on Cartoon Network. The first series premiered in 2003 and ran for five successful seasons before ending its run in 2006. The show offered a blend of superhero action and comedy, most often in the form of Japanese anime-inspired exaggerations to reflect the show's focus "on teenagers and more emotional things" in a kind of story-telling experiment. Despite these injections of humor, the show operated with pretty straightforward episode-length narratives as well as season-long story arcs that developed the main characters—Robin, Starfire, Cyborg, Raven, and Beast Boy—across several episodes and seasons. The show was considered both a financial and critical success in its five-season run. In fact, the show was originally planned for just four seasons; a fifth season was added because of the show's overall success. Arguably, part of the reason for the show's success that began as a superhero cartoon geared "more for 6–11 year-olds"[32] was its serial nature and the fact that the main characters developed and changed during its five-season run. In fact, the final episode of the series is named "Things Change," a title and episode that Murakami notes, "explains what the whole series is about."[33]

Fast forward to 2013, and the characters introduced in the original *Teen Titans* series reappear in a new series on Cartoon Network. *Teen Titans Go!* features the same characters voiced by the same actors as the earlier series, but instead of extended narratives with developed characters in story arcs, this second series is constructed around 10-minute comedic shorts with an emphasis on rapid-fire, absurdist, and at times surreal action with a healthy dose of postmodern self-reflexivity. Though featuring the same characters as the older show, each story line is self-contained with characters and situations reset in each short and little or no continuity between episodes. For example, in one episode titled "Burger Vs. Burrito," a simple argument between Beast Boy and Cyborg about which of the two titular foods is better erupts in a surrealistic feud between the two that includes musical interludes, an *Iron Chef* parody, and culminates in a final battle between *kaiju*-sized burger and burrito. In fact, a later episode titled "The Fourth Wall" illustrates the postmodern reflexivity that is much as a part of the show as its absurdist humor. In this episode the supervillain Remote Control reveals to the current group of Titans their existence as cartoons and shows them the previous run of the show to prove their fictional nature. Moments like these illustrate not only the chronological distance between the two shows but also the tonal, thematic, and aesthetic distances. This difference shows a move away from long-range character development and a kind of long-form narrative storytelling to basically clever gag writing in a superhero milieu.

In many ways, this element is also similar to *The Simpsons* in a moment best illustrated in the fifth-season episode "Homer Loves Flanders." Although *The Simpsons* ran 20-minute, episode-length narratives, there were seldom multiepisode serial-length arcs, and character change and development were not main features of the show. In this episode, Homer actually becomes close friends with his neighbor and archnemesis Ned Flanders. Near the end of the episode, a flabbergasted Bart asks Lisa, "I don't get it, Lis. You said everything would be back to normal but Homer and Flanders are still friends." However, in an epilogue subtitled, "The following Thursday, 8:00 p.m." (the show's time slot at the time), Homer again tells his nosy neighbor "to get lost," much to the relief of Bart and Lisa. This willful and knowing resetting of the show's status quo in terms of character points to the way in which the show assiduously avoided the type of story and character development of more traditional television shows. This is what animated shows like the original *Teen Titans* tried to emulate.

Note that the difference between the original *Teen Titans* and its later incarnation is not necessarily a change in the quality or a judgment about which is the "better" show, but whether it serves as an example of the kinds of animated programs that are possible in the longer-term wake of *The Simpsons*. In other words, the distance between *Teen Titans* and *Teen Titans Go!* illustrates the narrow band in which animated entertainment now operates.

Without a doubt, *The Simpsons* marks a revolution in animation. It made a network, scared the bejeezus out of a nation, filled scores of academic papers, changed the English language, and made cartoons cool for a whole new audience. It is also important to step back and look critically at the specific ways in which *The Simpsons* has changed both the perception of animation and its content and has told a much different story. Yes, cartoons can be cool for adults (some would say again, after the golden age of Warner Brothers animation), but what "cool" is has been narrowly defined. *The Simpsons* has done some amazing work, but it will take another show, as yet unmade and unknown, to really and fundamentally change what animation could be in America. But until then, we'll just keep on laughing for as long as we can.

NOTES

1. James Erndst, "'Toons Moving into Primetime, but Will 'Fish' Float?" *Hartford Courant,* February 28, 1992, http://archive.is/20120708155034/articles .courant.com/1992-02-28/features/0000205235_1_capitol-critters-fish-police -animation.

2. Matthew Henry, "The Triumph of Popular Culture: Situation Comedy, Postmodernism and 'The Simpsons,'" *Studies in Popular Culture*, 17(1) (1994), 91, http://www.jstor.org/stable/23413793, February 4, 2016.

3. John Ortved, *The Simpsons: An Uncensored, Unauthorized History* (New York: Faber and Faber, Inc., 2009), 115.

4. Matthew P. McAllister, "The Simpsons," Archive of American Television, http://www.emmytvlegends.org/interviews/ shows/simpsons-the, retrieved January 21, 2016.

5. Matthew Henry, "'Don't Ask Me, I'm Just a Girl': Feminism, Female Identity, and *The Simpsons*." *Journal of Popular Culture*, 40(2) (2007), 272, retrieved January 21, 2016.

6. Ortved, op. cit., 117.

7. Linda Shrieves, "Bart: A '90s Kind of Hero the Coolest Simpson Has Become America's Hottest Kid," *Orlando Sentinel*, May 4, 1990, http://articles.orlandose ntinel.com/1990-05-04/lifestyle/9005030077_1_bart-simpson-send-bart -simpsons-party, retrieved February 4, 2016.

8. Lynn Smith, "Twisted Simpsons Spark Mania Television," *Los Angeles Times*, April 24, 1990, http://articles.latimes.com/1990-04-24/local/me-366_1 _san-onofre-nuclear-plant, accessed February 4, 2016.

9. Ortved, op. cit., 118.

10. Ibid., 122.

11. Ortved, op. cit., 117.

12. Ibid., 118–119.

13. Michel Marriott, "I'm Bart, I'm Black and What About It?" *The New York Times*, September 19, 1990, http://www-lexisnexis-com.citytech.ezproxy.cuny .edu:2048/lnacui2api/api/version1/getDocCui?lni=3SJD-MGK0-0038-D05N& csi=6742&hl=t&hv=t&hnsd=f&hns=t&hgn=t&oc=00240&perma=true, retrieved February 4, 2016.

14. Ortved, op. cit., 121.

15. Marriott, op. cit.

16. Simone Knox, "The Triumph of Popular Culture: Situation Comedy, Postmodernism and *The Simpsons*," *Studies in Popular Culture*, 17(1) (October 1994), 80, http://www.jstor.org/stable/23413793.

17. Paul Wells, *Understanding Animation* (London: Routledge, 1998), 23.

18. Ibid., 22.

19. Nick Griffiths, "America's First Family," *The Times Magazine*, April 15, 2000, https://www.simpsonsarchive.com/other/articles/firstfamily.html, retrieved February 6, 2016.

20. Erndst, op. cit.

21. Ibid.

22. Ortved, op. cit., 284.

23. Simone Knox, "Reading the Ungraspable Double-Codedness of *The Simpsons*." *Journal of Popular Film and Television*, 34(2) (2006), 75, retrieved February 4, 2016.

24. Ibid., 75

25. Ortved, op. cit., 284.

26. Ibid.

27. Matt Zoller Seitz, "Will Future Generations Understand *The Simpsons?*" Salon.com, March 8, 2011, http://www.salon.com/2011/03/08/simpsons_pop_culture/.

28. Ortved, op. cit., 287.

29. Neil Lumbrad, review of *Regular Show*, seasons one and two (Blu-ray), Adult Swim, DVDTalk.com, July 6, 2013, http://www.dvdtalk.com/reviews/61279/regular-show-season-1-season-2/.

30. Joanna Robinson, "How a Nickelodeon Cartoon Became One of the Most Subversive Shows of 2014," *Vanity Fair*, December 19, 2014, https://www.vanityfair.com/hollywood/2014/12/korra-series-finale-recap-gay-asami.

31. Lauren Davis, "Paul Dini: Superhero Cartoon Execs Don't Want Largely Female Audiences," iO9.com, December 15, 2013, http://io9.gizmodo.com/paul-dini-superhero-cartoon-execs-dont-want-largely-f-1483758317.

32. "Five Seasons of Murakanime," by Nightwing, *TitansTower.com*, July 15, 2012, http://www.titanstower.com/five-seasons-of-murakanime/.

33. Ibid.

BIBLIOGRAPHY

Davis, Lauren. "Paul Dini: Superhero Cartoon Execs Don't Want Largely Female Audiences," iO9.com, December 15, 2013, http://io9.gizmodo.com/paul-dini-superhero-cartoon-execs-dont-want-largely-f-1483758317.

Erndst, James. "'Toons Moving into Primetime, but Will 'Fish' Float?" *Hartford Courant*, February 28, 1992, http://archive.is/20120708155034/articles.courant.com/1992-02-28/features/0000205235_1_capitol-critters-fish-police-animation.

Griffiths, Nick. "America's First Family," *The Times Magazine*, April 15, 2000, https://www.simpsonsarchive.com/other/articles/firstfamily.html, retrieved February 6, 2016.

Henry, Matthew. "'Don't Ask Me, I'm Just a Girl': Feminism, Female Identity, and The Simpsons." *Journal of Popular Culture*, 40(2) (April 2007), 272–303, retrieved February 4, 2016.

Henry, Matthew. "The Triumph of Popular Culture: Situation Comedy, Postmodernism and 'The Simpsons.'" *Studies in Popular Culture*, 17(1) (1994): 85–99, http://www.jstor.org/stable/23413793, retrieved February 4, 2016.

Knox, Simone. "Reading the Ungraspable Double-Codedness of The Simpsons." *Journal of Popular Film and Television*, 34(2) (2006), 72–81, retrieved February 4, 2016.

Lumbrad, Neil. Review of *Regular Show*, seasons one and two (Blu-ray), Adult Swim, DVDTalk.com, July 6, 2013, http://www.dvdtalk.com/reviews/61279/regular-show-season-1-season-2/.

Marriott, Michel. "I'm Bart, I'm Black and What About It?" *The New York Times*, September 19, 1990, http://www-lexisnexis-com.citytech.ezproxy.cuny.edu:2048/lnacui2api/api/version1/getDocCui?lni=3SJD-MGK0-0038

-D05N&csi=6742&hl=t&hv=t&hnsd=f&hns=t&hgn=t&oc=00240&
    perma=true, retrieved February 4, 2016.
Nightwing. "Five Seasons of Murakanime." TitansTower.com, July 15, 2012, http://
    www.titanstower.com/five-seasons-of-murakanime/.
Ortved, John. *The Simpsons: An Uncensored, Unauthorized History.* New York:
    Faber & Faber, 2009.
Robinson, Joanna. "How a Nickelodeon Cartoon Became One of the Most Subver-
    sive Shows of 2014." *Vanity Fair,* December 19, 2014, https://www.vanity
    fair.com/hollywood/2014/12/korra-series-finale-recap-gay-asami.
Seitz, Matt Zoller. "Will Future Generations Understand *The Simpsons?*" Salon.
    com, March 8, 2011, http://www.salon.com/2011/03/08/simpsons_pop
    _culture/, retrieved February 4, 2016.
Shrieves, Linda. "Bart: A '90s Kind of Hero the Coolest Simpson Has Become
    America's Hottest Kid." *Orlando Sentinel,* May 4, 1990, http://articles.orlan
    dosentinel.com/1990-05-04/lifestyle/9005030077_1_bart-simpson-send
    -bart-simpsons-party, retrieved February 4, 2016.
Smith, Lynn. "Twisted Simpsons Spark Mania Television." *Los Angeles Times,*
    April 24, 1990, http://articles.latimes.com/1990-04-24/local/me-366_1_san
    -onofre-nuclear-plant, retrieved February 4, 2016.
Wells, Paul. *Understanding Animation.* London: Routledge, 1998.

18

No Hugging, No Learning: *Seinfeld* between the Yuppies and Slackers

Kevin L. Ferguson

The sitcom most remembered from the 1990s has to be Seinfeld *(1989–1998). With its claim to be a "show about nothing," the series broke down barriers surrounding intent, morality, and message in the writing for television, broadening the canvas not just for sitcoms but also for dramatic shows (including the so-called reality genre). According to Kevin L. Ferguson in "No Hugging, No Learning:* Seinfeld *between the Yuppies and Slackers," the show that plays with the idea of wasted potential is more about detachment than about what could be. Americans are more and more removed from the subjects of their lives, by television and now social media, which reinforces the attitudes* Seinfeld *portrays. One cannot blame the show for that, however. It reflects (appropriate to its theme) like a mirror and does not change what it shows.*

Jerry gets paranoid about his girlfriend's past when her iPhone automatically connects to the Wi-Fi in Newman's apartment. Jerry's Twitter is hacked and people like "Hacked Jerry" better. George tries to get trampled on during Black Friday so he can sue, but everyone is polite. These scenarios are inventions of the parody Twitter account "Modern Seinfeld" (@SeinfeldToday), which asks "What if *Seinfeld* (NBC, 1989–1998) were still on the air?" The popularity of @SeinfeldToday—and competing accounts such as "Seinfeld Current Day" (@Seinfeld2000) and "Ancient Seinfeld" (@BCSeinfeld)—is both a testament to the cultural longevity of the show and a clue to how *Seinfeld*'s quirkily distinct brand of humor remains relevant even when removed from its particular 1990s cultural context.

Even though *Seinfeld* feels timeless today, a closer consideration of the show's cultural zeitgeist reveals how the show was very much an evolving product of its era, capturing a set of American cultural attitudes as the country shifted from the yuppie 1980s to the Gen X 1990s. These two generational stereotypes represent polarized views of young adulthood at the end of the century. Baby boom yuppies were reviled for their self-centered, flashy, and wealth-obsessed lifestyles, but Gen X slackers were portrayed as the opposite—unmotivated, aimless, and nostalgic. In this, *Seinfeld* is both a specific product of its decade and an outline for an "ambivalently observational" cultural perspective that continues to inform contemporary debate about millennials and social media.

Twenty-five years after its premiere, the show has not lost one bit of influence. In April 2015, the trade publication *Variety* was surprised by the video-on-demand company Hulu's "mammoth" decision to pay reported syndication rights of $160 million to carry reruns of the nine seasons and 180 episodes of *Seinfeld*.[1] The show remains relevant and popular today because we still live in a *Seinfeld* world, struggling to resolve the great problem left over from the American 1980s: how to reconcile middle-class demands for individualism with an increasingly pervasive populism. Popular media's 1980s obsession with defining an expanding baby boom middle class resulted in a flood of articles, television shows, novels, and popular films suggesting paradoxical ways for individuals not only to belong to a shared social group but also to stand out as unique individuals.

No television show of the time wrestled with that problem better than *Seinfeld*. Although most often discussed as either a knowing satire or a meta-postmodern "show about nothing," I instead relocate the show in the context of cultural arguments over two disputed "lifestyles" of the period: on the one hand the Reaganite yuppie, who is scorned for aggressive conspicuous consumption, and the ironic Gen X slacker on the other hand who is confronted with the hostile monotony of an increasingly corporatized world. The show's "no hugging, no learning" mantra appears to resist interpretation, allowing viewers to remain morally above the selfishly narcissistic characters, but it actually expresses how the characters in *Seinfeld* consistently straddle the yuppie and slacker perspectives: *Seinfeld* is a show about how a group of would-be yuppies turned slackers. Like 1980s yuppies, the show's characters obsess over the minutiae of consumerist material culture and how to get ahead at the expense of others; but like 1990s slackers, they only engage in superficial, aimless, labor-intensive forms of domestic philosophy. As a "postfamily" sitcom sitting between contemporaries such as *Cheers* (NBC, 1982–1993) and *Friends* (NBC, 1994–2004), the characters of *Seinfeld* particularly emphasize friendship over family through the relationship of four primary characters: the starring comedian Jerry Seinfeld (Jerry Seinfeld), ex-girlfriend Elaine Benes (Julia Louis-Dreyfus), neurotic best friend George Costanza (Jason Alexander), and eccentric neighbor Cosmo Kramer (Michael Richards). Thus, the show transforms over time from modeling how one might navigate a hyperconscious yuppie world into a more conservative investigation of how the lonely yuppie's mantra of selfishness ultimately resulted in the Gen X slackers' shared mode of resigned indifference. No hugging, no learning, just talking and talking and talking, yada yada yada.

A SHOW ABOUT SOMETHING

The most common misunderstanding about *Seinfeld* is that the idea it is "a show about nothing" should be taken seriously. Nothing could be further from the truth. In fact, early in season two, Jerry breaks up with his girlfriend simply because she enjoys a Dockers commercial that drives him crazy because it features men who stand around "talking about nothing" (episode nine, "The Phone Message"). Initially, at least for Jerry, talk about nothing on television was something to scorn. As a description of the show, the idea of a "show about nothing" was only popularized in *Seinfeld*'s breakout fourth season (1992–1993) when George and Jerry are asked to pitch a show to television executives (episode 43, "The Pitch"). Taken in the spirit of the show's blurring of fiction and reality, many viewers and critics took George and Jerry's pitch to simply be a fictionalized version of the pitch for *Seinfeld* itself. But as it becomes clear from this episode in which George monopolizes the meeting and shouts Jerry down, the "show about nothing" is really just George's bad idea pushed to comical limits. Although the "show about nothing" label stuck in the popular imagination, the misunderstanding comes by taking George's fanatical behavior seriously and seeing him as the mouthpiece for the show's intentions.

So, of course, the show is about *something*—but it is not something that would have been readily visible. Although viewers might expect a specific material object to be the main subject of the show as suggested by episode titles like "The Jacket," "The Phone Message," and "The Statue," the show instead takes subjecthood as its object. In other words, whereas earlier sitcoms also focused on individual psychology and their characters' relationship to their world, *Seinfeld* was unique in that it was produced during a time when such subjectivity was particularly fraught. *Seinfeld*'s first season appeared right when the newly fashionable idea of postmodernism had reached a saturation point in popular culture; the term, which exploded in critical discourse in 1984, was by 1989 widely used in popular magazines and on television. As a consequence, even though most viewers of *Seinfeld* would likely have had only an imperfect understanding of postmodernism as a theoretical term, they would have known that a larger cultural conversation was taking place arguing for postmodernism as a new cultural imperative—a historical break or rupture—that was supposed to wholly transform social interactions and lead to new ways of living.

Historian Michel Foucault, suspicious of this postmodern insistence on a divisive break with the past, describes the frightening consequence of contemporary self-analysis: "We have been taught throughout the 20th century that one can do nothing if one knows nothing about oneself."[2] His solution to this problem is to look beyond the basic imperative to "know oneself" and ask instead, "What should one do with oneself?"[3] How should we "govern ourselves" while being conscious that our bodies are the instrument of our actions and the place where these actions are performed? Although there is not the time and space here to pursue Foucault's historical analysis in depth, his account of the problem facing society can also double as a version of the two questions underlying nearly every episode of *Seinfeld*: How do our decisions about what to do with ourselves define us? How should we, as a consequence, act around others and ourselves? We see this active self-examination in George's effort to improve his life by simply doing the "opposite" of his natural instincts (episode 86, "The Opposite"), Elaine's realization that she becomes more stupid if she does not have sex (episode 143, "The Abstinence"), Jerry's inability to date the perfect girl because she acts too much like him (episode 134, "The Invitation"), or Kramer's move to Los Angeles after realizing he was only living "in the shadows" of Jerry's better life (episode 40, "The Keys"). Furthermore, the shift from knowing oneself to governing oneself explicitly underlies the series' most famous (and most Foucauldian) episode, "The Contest" (episode 51), in which the characters wager who can avoid masturbation the longest and thereby earn the title of "master of your domain."

Rather than "a show about nothing," a more accurate description might be "a show about people who mistakenly think they are living in a new ahistorical time of nothingness and as a consequence try to figure out how to behave." A pithier version of this is the catchphrase "No hugging, no learning," the unofficial motto of cocreator Larry David, who connects physical action with ethical behavior—just like Foucault. David's answer to the question "What should one do with oneself?" argues for a much more cynical version of self-governance than Foucault's ethical model. But David's desire to create a show in which characters do not learn simply means they will constantly need to renegotiate their behavior as culture changes around them. In other words, although characters fail to develop in meaningful ways across the series, the cultural shift around them makes them fail to learn in new ways and environments. Their anxiety over proper behavior in light of shifting cultural norms propels the confused observational ambivalence of the series. Thus, *Seinfeld's* Foucauldian structure allows us to more clearly see the characters' transition from yuppies to slackers: as they are continually forced to reflect on their behavior in a changing world, they move from trying to identify with others to withdrawing in patronizing superiority.

THE YUPPIE *SEINFELD*

At the time, *Seinfeld* was widely understood to be a show about yuppies. Jay McInerney, whose first novel, *Bright Lights, Big City* (1984), is the urtext of fictional yuppiedom, called *Seinfeld* the greatest sitcom ever, the *Citizen Kane* of sitcoms.[4] In addition to establishing *Seinfeld's* yuppie cred for an audience of *TV Guide* readers, the terms of McInerney's assessment themselves speak to the yuppie mentality that characters in *Seinfeld* also initially aspired to: the show cannot just be good, it has to be the "best ever"; it cannot be compared to other sitcoms, it has to be compared to *Citizen Kane.* McInerney admired *Seinfeld* because he liked its presentation of single 40-year-olds like himself. On the flip side, *The New Republic* editor Leon Wieseltier was simultaneously blasting *Seinfeld* as "the worst, last gasp of Reaganite, grasping, materialistic, narcissistic, banal self-absorption."[5] Social and television critic Maureen Dowd agrees: "The show is our Dorian Gray portrait, a reflection of the what's-in-it-for me times" that have been ruinously created by those "revolting" yuppies.[6]

These responses show just how polarizing the figure of the yuppie was at the time. Although the label of "yuppie" began in 1984 to describe a narrow demographic category of those "aged 29 to 35 who live in metropolitan areas, work in professional or managerial occupations, and have an income of at least $30,000 if they live alone," it soon became associated with a raft of negative social stereotypes about the cultural consequences of the larger, growing group of baby boomers in America.[7] Yuppies gentrified neighborhoods, fetishized expensive imported goods, demanded exotic foods, and consumed as conspicuously as possible. Yuppies exercised constantly, worked constantly, shopped constantly. Yuppies "live[d] on aspirations of glory, prestige, recognition, fame, social status, power, money, or any and all combinations of the above."[8] Over the decade of the 1980s, they became objects of mockery and then of hatred; by the mid-1990s, they simply became a permanent fixture of the cultural landscape: "anyone who brunches on the weekend or works out after work."[9]

The problem of yuppies at the end of the 1980s was a problem of numbers: as a subset of the burgeoning 30-something baby boomer generation, yuppies were in competition with a growing number of other yuppies to lead the most worldly, eclectic, consumerist, unique lifestyle they could. To stand out from the crowd, strategies for individualism became more pronounced, and Wieseltier's sense of grasping materialism more desperate. The sense of an individual cultivating a unique personal style by being selective (or "picky"), taste driven ("snobby"), and whimsical ("irrational") pervades *Seinfeld*'s first few seasons. Early in the series, the characters foreground their engagement with yuppie iconography: cantaloupes, real estate, stocks, chiropractics, mountain bikes, Apple computers, plastic surgery. What they eat, what they watch, what they wear all constitute a network of choices that locates them among—but also ideally distinguishes them from—their peers. For the show, yuppiedom is mainly seen in quirky, external manifestations of a desire to be unique; that is, physical objects that represent a character's longing to become a different person. For example, when Jerry is talked into wearing a pirate-inspired puffy shirt (episode 66, "The Puffy Shirt"), viewers can easily laugh at how the urgency of yuppie fashion results in people taking otherwise ridiculous ideas seriously.

Food is one theme that most obviously connects *Seinfeld* to yuppie behavior, which now has new choices and valences. Although Jerry proudly displays his cereal collection and Kramer is constantly raiding his refrigerator, one key location, Monk's Café, provides a consistent opportunity for the characters in earlier seasons to anguish over the yuppies' new dietary rules: they must now not only be health conscious but also socially conscious. So, in episode three, "The Robbery," George looks at a menu and laments, "You can't have anything anymore," ruling out eggs, coffee, french fries, BLTs. He considers the eating habits of earlier generations: "I go to visit my grandparents [they're closing in on 100]: three big brisket sandwiches. I'm sittin' here with a carrot!" Next, in episode 13, "The Heart Attack," George sneaks a cucumber into Monk's to make his salad healthier, but before he can finish his meal, he has what he thinks is a heart attack (it turns out to just be his tonsils). The yuppie health food backlash sets in quickly, however. In episode 16, "The Chinese Restaurant," Elaine complains about the food Jerry offered her: "Healthy cookies. I hate those little dustboard fructose things." In the opening monologue of episode 17, "The Busboy," Jerry rejects another yuppie lifestyle label, the "foodie," characterizing them as constantly complaining about the quality of food unlike his own attitude of "Just eat it and shut up." Next, in that episode's first scene, this theme continues when George anguishes over pesto: "Why do I get pesto? Why do I think I'll like it? I keep trying to like it, like I have to like it." Pesto, which has suddenly appeared on the culinary landscape, represents for George an insurmountable barrier to acceptable yuppie eating habits. Luckily for him, by season four, yuppie eating practices are gone. And by season nine, eating has become truly perverse when George fetishizes eating pastrami on rye with mustard during a sexual encounter (episode 160, "The Blood").

More than just new generational anxieties over health, what marks these early versions of *Seinfeld* characters as yuppies is their debate over the social and ethical responsibilities surrounding food. Food is not just for nutrition; it is a stylistic marker of a political and ethical position. For example, in the first season's episode five, "The Stock Tip," Jerry must forgo his beloved tuna sandwich when Elaine objects over what he disparages as the "dolphin thing," alluding to popular news reports about dolphins trapped and dying in tuna fishing nets. For Jerry, "the whole concept of lunch is based on tuna," but to Elaine her choice of what to eat represents a larger ethical choice: "Can't you incorporate one unselfish act in your daily routine?" That Jerry switches to chicken salad instead of a vegetarian option shows the unnoticed hypocrisy in these firmly held food positions. In a later episode, "The Stranded" (episode 27), Elaine's false virtue is thrown in her face. She objects to the fur coat a woman wears at a party, who then calls Elaine a hypocrite after Elaine admits that she is a vegetarian but occasionally eats fish. As is clear in this scene, Elaine's yuppie outrage over wearing fur reflects a superficial sense of social consciousness and her failure to consider a lifestyle more fully consistent with her self-stated views. Elaine is defeated in this argument not because of the poor choices she makes (the woman could not care less what Elaine wears or eats) but because the woman is easily able to show that Elaine's yuppie morality is ultimately illogical. Seasons later, the moral yuppie has wholly abandoned her principles. In episode 168, "The Reverse Peephole," Elaine is horrified when her boyfriend wears a fur coat—but only because he looks ridiculous in it: "Eh, anti-fur . . . who has the energy anymore? This is more about hanging off the arm of an idiot."

FROM YUPPIES TO SLACKERS

In DVD commentary, Jerry Seinfeld suggests that *Seinfeld* is about the "gaps in society where there are no rules."[10] I acknowledge that the show developed into this but the first three seasons were more attuned to defining identity than examining appropriate rules of behavior. George's anxiety over pesto is an example of this; whereas pesto would be used in a gag about how to behave in later seasons (Kramer invents a new kind of pesto, George serves pesto to an allergic girlfriend, Elaine's boss requires her to sample all the pesto on the market), here pesto is simply a marker of the kind of person George is and the kind he wants to be: a pesto guy. Eating pesto is not an enjoyable activity or even one to have thoughts about; it is simply a requirement for being a certain kind of person. There are numerous similar examples of characters describing themselves reflexively in the show's early seasons: Jerry considers himself a "master packer" (episode three, "The Robbery") and a "kind man" and "great guy" (episode 24, "The Cafe"), while Elaine is proud to be the "queen of confrontation" (episode six, "The Ex-Girlfriend"). Icon Joe DiMaggio has a reputation as "a dunker" (of donuts, episode 18, "The Note").

The first episode of season two, "The Ex-Girlfriend" (episode six), concentrates the various ways characters think of themselves as types of people (rather than, as in later seasons, reflecting on what their behavior says about them). First is a telling exchange in which George encourages Elaine to confront a rude neighbor. Warming to the idea, she asks him, "Would you do that?" His response—"Yes, if I was a different person"— shows how much he sees behavior as an effect of identity rather than the other way around. Next, Jerry is imagining what will happen when he tells George that he is attracted to George's girlfriend, before concluding that he is blameless because he is a "nice guy." When Elaine arrives to describe her confrontation with the rude neighbor, an inspired Jerry embraces her "queen of confrontation" persona and tells George, who unproblematically accepts this turn of events and is genuinely surprised that he is not upset at Jerry. Because each character acts in accordance with the imagined behavior of a particular type of personal identity, they remain individually blameless and conflict is avoided.

As yuppie anxiety fades into Gen X ambivalence over the course of the show, however, later seasons make behavior more important than identity. This is clearly seen in one of the most popular episodes from the series, "The Opposite" (episode 86), in which George realizes that "if every instinct [he has] is wrong, then the opposite would have to be right." Rather than consider what kind of person he is, George simply must take note of and then reverse each of his natural actions. This outlandish (but strangely successful) scenario becomes more common as the series progresses; whereas earlier characters were concerned simply with fitting into a superficial cultural environment, later characters focus on controlling their actions in much more unnatural ways. Likewise, in episode 134, "The Invitations," Jerry falls madly in love with his doppelgänger; the twist comes when he finally realizes that despite their perfect similarities, he cannot be with her because he hates himself: "If anything I need to be with someone [who is] the complete opposite of me!" This conclusion depends on Jerry being profoundly unreflective of his life and reveals a transition from the earlier episodes' question of "How can I fit in?" to later episodes asking "What should I do with myself?" Philosopher Aeon J. Skoble discusses episode 86, "The Opposite," in particular when arguing that "the question 'What is the right thing to do in this situation?' is often examined via a consideration of 'what sort of person acts in such-and-such ways?'"[11] I argue that in the first three seasons of the show, the emphasis of this question is on characters being able to identify with and become the right "sort of person," whereas in later seasons the emphasis is on characters reflecting on how their actions have already made them become a certain sort of person. This shift aligns with arguments about how the yuppie of the early 1990s focused externally on conspicuous consumption and self-invention while the late-1990s Gen X slacker's nostalgia for a prewar time resulted in a sense of purposelessness and self-reflection. So, where the yuppie identifies with a set of behaviors and costumes outside of himself, the slacker examines themes of individuality and exclusion that are felt internally. A similar shift is seen in *Seinfeld*, such as in George's nonintuitive decision to do the opposite of his instincts. Motivated more by a fascination with behavior than with identity, George illuminates the show's shift from presenting characters trying to fit into superficial yuppie identity to characters who scrutinize and control their behavior in much more idiosyncratic ways.

Formal aspects of the show also changed to match this shift. One unique aspect of *Seinfeld* was its bookending and interruption of the show with clips of Jerry doing stand-up. Vestiges of an earlier concept in which Seinfeld explicitly discussed how comedians get material from their real lives, these interludes came to work as suturing devices to manage televisual flow (the sequencing of televisual elements to create a continuity), functioning as bridges between the show's often absurd narrative world and the mundane observational starting point for the social dilemmas the characters faced.[12] However, these stand-up interruptions become less frequent over the series and ended altogether during the seventh season. This matches a related shift over the course of the series in how tightly controlled the larger narrative world is. For the first three seasons, each half-hour episode focused on a single topic unrelated to previous episodes, usually requiring characters to help each other complete a task and usually concluding with a comedic twist undermining the characters' efforts or showing how their efforts had unintended effects. The show's early ethos was sarcastic, callous, and unhappy. In the fourth season, however, the show began featuring recurring plot lines and jokes, particularly around the in-show show that Jerry and George were working on but also extending to small catchphrases and items of clothing. Rewarding regular viewers and encouraging a form of water cooler fandom, the show's increasing ability to rely on viewers' knowledge of previous episodes was a sign not only of its popularity but also of its readiness to trade in earlier radical qualities for more conventional forms of long-term narrative.

This shift from the earlier, disconnected, episodes heavy with stand-up comedy to the later, more connected, concentrated episodes is a further clue to how the show gradually shifted from an uncomfortable negotiation of yuppie perspective toward a condensation of the slacker's shared ambivalence. The specific giveaway moment is episode 42, "The Trip (2)," the conclusion of a three-episode story line that bridged seasons three and four and the most strangely heartwarming episode of the entire series. At the end of season three, we saw Kramer move to Los Angeles to pursue acting after Jerry hurts his feelings by not trusting him with a set of house keys. The two-part premiere of season four finds Jerry and George visiting Los Angeles and meeting up with Kramer, who, despite being confused for a serial killer, seems perfectly happy. Back in New York at the end of the episode, the two are then shocked silent when Kramer surprisingly bursts into Jerry's apartment in his signature fashion. That no one makes a big deal of Kramer's surprise return shows how significant the reunion of normality is. This episode marks a transition from the show's willingness to be truly misanthropic and the beginning of the show's development of a consistent closed worldview around this group of friends. Although later episodes became more outré, such as the one that killed George's fiancé or the series finale when the four protagonists end up in jail, these plot points are overcompensation for the show's increasingly conservative tendencies. With the beginning of season four, *Seinfeld* became increasingly interested in a superficially quirky but ultimately more conventional point of view.

THE SLACKER *SEINFELD*

If plot lines from the first season revolve around late-1980s prototypical yuppie concerns—getting a better apartment (episode three, "The Robbery"), starting a new business (episode four, "Male Unbonding"), pursuing stock tips (episode five, "The Stock Tip")—then the last episodes of season nine show just how much our characters changed to reflect late-1990s Gen X slacker themes: low-wage menial jobs (episode 166, "The Strike"), fascination with nostalgic cultural objects (episode 162, "The Merv Griffin Show," and episode 174, "The Frogger"), and social alienation (episode 176, "The Puerto Rican Day"). Most demographers identify Generation X as those born between 1961 and 1981. The Gen X stereotype, furiously debated as soon as it was minted by Douglas Coupland's novel *Generation X* (1991), portrayed this new generation as overeducated but undermotivated.[13] Thus, in Coupland's novel we see youth with a shrewd understanding of global cultural and economic problems, but without a commitment to change or protest. Instead, the novel captures their world-weariness in a series of bumper-sticker slogans that acknowledge but do not reflect on central issues at the end of the millennium: "Quit Recycling the Past," "Shopping Is Not Creating," "Purchased Experiences Don't Count," "Plastics Never Disintegrate." In 1993, journalist Andrew Cohen described Gen Xers as "a Peter Pan generation afraid of adulthood, the 'lost boys,' and girls, of a generation gone slumming . . . a caravansary of down-and-out slackers . . . the doom-stricken Baby Bust behind the Baby Boom."[14] Gen Xers were slackers who moved back home with their parents, took mindlessly unsatisfying but not terribly difficult jobs, and talked nonstop about the big problems of the world. This description sounds a whole lot like the lives of Jerry, George, Elaine, and (somewhat) Kramer, who in later seasons move back home with parents (episode 66, "The Puffy Shirt"), work at jobs they are not even hired for (episode 137, "The Bizarro Jerry"), and, of course, endlessly yada yada yada (episode 153, "The Yada Yada").

Seinfeld's characters are clearly adults, but the show is more about friendship than family, although parents become surprisingly important in later seasons. This reflects tropes of the Gen X "baby boomerang," a supposedly new codependency between parents and their adult children who have had difficulty navigating a hypercompetitive, recession-driven world and thus must return home. Elaine's father is the subject of one early episode (episode eight, "The Jacket"), and Kramer's mother is briefly introduced in an episode in season six (episode 97, "The Switch"), but it is George and Jerry whose parents best demonstrate Gen X anxieties over the impossibility of true adult independence. Jerry's retiree parents were introduced early in the show, but they only come to play sustained roles in season four when they stay at Jerry's apartment during a two-part episode (episode 45, "The Wallet"). This episode, like all the ones with Jerry's parents, presents their relationship as conflicted primarily over Jerry's success in life: his parents are suspicious of his ability to make a living as a comedian, and he continually tries to prove to them that he is making money. In another two-part episode, "The Cadillac" (episodes 124 and 125), this theme is furthered when Jerry buys his father an expensive Cadillac to prove both his fidelity and his solvency. Jerry flies to his parents' home in Florida to deliver the gift, which naturally backfires: the Cadillac is seen by the other retirees as proof that Jerry's father is corrupt, and he is voted off the board of the homeowner's association and is so embarrassed he must move. In this case, the baby boomerang is presented as a catastrophe: the young adult with modern career path who returns to his parents to prove his success ultimately destroys their lifestyle. George has a similar narrative with his parents, who live in New York City. In episode 62, "The Handicap Spot," George agrees to become his father's butler in order to pay off a monetary debt he cannot afford. George's servitude is the inverse of Jerry's ability to give his parents expensive gifts, and his humiliation is reinforced four episodes later when he must move back home with his parents because he cannot afford rent. George's baby boomerang misery is compounded throughout that season when he becomes increasingly infantilized.

The economic reason for George's return home reflects a second Gen X attitude of the show, one especially seen in work-related themes in later seasons. Elaine has a succession of outrageous bosses and improbably finds herself advancing from copy editor to editor and then boss herself of a successful clothing catalog. Elaine's most Gen X job is when she is hired as a personal assistant at the beginning of season six, working for Mr. Pitt doing unimportant and unfulfilling tasks such as taking the salt off of his pretzels (episode 86, "The Chaperone"). Despite the trivial nature of this job, though, she and Mr. Pitt take it seriously. The comedy of Mr. Pitt is built around the changing nature of work: the show presents Elaine's work as comical but also as not all that unreasonable. At a stretch, we might read Mr. Pitt as an aging, demanding yuppie (he just wants to find the perfect pair of socks) and Elaine as the younger Gen X employee struggling to meet his impossible-to-sustain demands. Her next job at the J. Peterman catalog furthers the sense that Gen X labor is challenging mainly because it is socially eccentric: Peterman is as bizarre as Pitt, but his catalog is nonetheless seen as a purposeful and coherent object of work. When Elaine takes over for Peterman in season eight, she unsuccessfully tries to adopt weirdness as a brand (episode 135, "The Foundation"). Her failure indicates again a Gen X theme of competitive alienation in the workforce. On the other hand, George has the most traditional, office-oriented job, but we see him continually try to find ways to slack off at work—as in episode 152, "The Nap," in which he has a desk custom fit to hide a bed so he can sleep at work. Mirroring numerous media presentations of Gen X slackers, George comes off as a kind of role model for the contemporary labor force.

Scholar Martine Delvaux argues that despite its ambivalent name, the Gen X generation had a particular "need to talk about itself, to create self-definitions through the staging of acts of storytelling."[15] As a description of how Gen Xers process their world, this applies equally well to fiction like Coupland's *Generation X*, films such as *Clerks* (directed by Kevin Smith, 1994), and television shows like *Seinfeld*. In each, a group of friends feels detached from mainstream culture in a way that precludes any involvement other than observational talk: they are not bitter, political, or angry, just ambivalent, curious, and distanced. Likewise, media scholar Jonathon I. Oake suggests that "Generation X is more usefully defined as a spectatorship rather than as a group of individuals with common practices and rituals."[16] In other words, unlike the baby boomer who strives to identify with yuppie culture and practices, the Gen X slacker finds companionship by watching others. The final episode of *Seinfeld* emphasizes the slacker's observational ambivalence: after Jerry, George, Elaine, and Kramer stand by commenting on a robbery, the judge pronounces the four guilty for violating a good samaritan law that requires them to help others in trouble. That they videotape the event further supports Oake's argument that the "subcultural specificity of Gen X subjectivity revolves more around a unique relationship with media—particularly visual media—rather than a visual style (e.g., dress, music tastes, etc.)"[17] But the judge's sentence is not punitive so much as it simply enforces what was already the case: "I can think of nothing more fitting than for the four of you to spend a year removed from society so that you can contemplate the manner in which you have conducted yourselves." This is the slacker's sentence at the end of the 1990s, but it is not one that bothers the characters since it was already their life. When Jerry and George, sitting in a cell, have the same conversation about shirt buttons that they had in the first episode, the dark joke is that their previously promise-filled yuppie lives have instead devolved into the slacker's wasted potential.

The dark ending resonated because the show's later worldview was particularly worrying. Albert Auster describes the show's success in part because it was about things people can control—the small details of their lives—in a time that felt extremely out of control.[18] Elayne Rapping, in fact, sees *Seinfeld* as not much more than "a scary commercial message on behalf of the new economic system, in which most of us will have little if any paid . . . work to do, and the family ties . . . have become untenable."[19] Rapping channels Coupland when she sarcastically writes that shows like *Seinfeld* only serve to espouse "'mantras [like 'What, me worry?'] to get us through our pointless, postindustrial days."[20] She is right: "These pretzels are making me thirsty!" "No soup for you!" "Not that there's anything wrong with that." In her 1997 attack on the show, Maureen Dowd argues that "*Seinfeld* has progressed the way yuppies have, growing ever more self-referential and self-regarding."[21] Rather, I think what Dowd identifies is precisely the new trend of ironic Gen X detachment that *Seinfeld*'s characters are sentenced with in the finale. If Foucault is correct that a supposed postmodern cultural break has led to a renewed insistence on self-analysis, then *Seinfeld*'s finale shows how frightening this self-analysis can be for the Gen X slacker. We are how we behave, and although the show encourages active and obsessive self-examination, it presents the most cynical version of this possible. The transition in the show after the fourth season to longer plot lines, behavior-based rather than identity-based situations, and slacker themes reflects the larger cultural transition from yuppies to slackers. *Seinfeld*'s lasting success is a result of this generational shift, transforming yuppies into slackers and promoting an "ambivalently observational" cultural perspective only exaggerated in contemporary social media.

NOTES

1. Cynthia Littleton, "Hulu Sets Mammoth 'Seinfeld' Licensing Deal," *Variety*, April 28, 2015, http://variety.com/2015/tv/news/hulu-seinfeld-licensing-160 -million-1201483537/, retrieved September 25, 2015.

2. Michel Foucault, *Foucault Live: Collected Interviews, 1961–1984*, translated by Lysa Hochroth and John Johnston, edited by Sylvère Lotringer (New York: Semiotext[e], 1989), 318.

3. Michel Foucault, *Ethics: Subjectivity and Truth*, translated by Robert Hurley et al., edited by Paul Rabinow (New York: The New Press, 1997), 87.

4. Jay McInerney, "Is *Seinfeld* the Best Comedy Ever?" *TV Guide*, June 1, 1996, 14–22.

5. Quoted in Maureen Dowd, "Yada Yada Yuppies," *The New York Times*, May 14, 1997, A21.

6. Ibid.

7. "The Big Chill (Revisited), Or Whatever Happened to the Baby Boom," *American Demographics* (September 1985), 29. The terms "yuppies" and "baby boomers" are sometimes used interchangeably, but most observers consider the latter term to be more inclusive. *American Demographics* put the number of yuppies at 4.2 million, or 5 percent, of baby boomers. The U.S. Census Bureau defines the baby boom generation as those born between 1946 and 1964—thus viewers who would have been between 25 and 43 in 1989 when *Seinfeld* first aired.

8. Marissa Piesman and Marilee Hartley, *The Yuppie Handbook: The State-of-the-Art Manual for Young Urban Professionals* (New York: Long Shadow Books, 1984), 12.

9. Ibid.

10. "Inside Look" for "The Seinfeld Chronicles," *Seinfeld* (Columbia Tristar, 2004), DVD.

11. Aeon J. Skoble, "Virtue Ethics in TV's *Seinfeld*," in *Seinfeld and Philosophy*, edited by William Irwin (Chicago: Open Court, 2000), 176.

12. See Raymond Williams' introduction of the concept of flow in *Television: Technology and Cultural Form* (London: Routledge, 1990).

13. Jon D. Miller, "Active, Balanced, and Happy: These Young Americans Are Not Bowling Alone," *The Generation X Report*, 1(1) (2011), 1–8.

14. Andrew Cohen, "Me and My Zeitgeist," *The Nation*, July 19, 1993, 96. In a season six episode that aired in November 1994 (number 94, "The Mom and Pop Store"), Kramer comments on Jerry's extensive shoe collection, diagnosing him as having a "Peter Pan complex."

15. Martine Delvaux, "The Exit of a Generation: The 'Whatever' Philosophy," *The Midwest Quarterly*, 40(2 ((1999), 178.

16. Jonathon I. Oake, "Reality Bites and Generation X as Spectator," *The Velvet Light Trap*, 53(1) (2004), 83.

17. Ibid.

18. Albert Auster, "Much Ado about Nothing: Some Final Thoughts on *Seinfeld*," *Television Quarterly*, 29(4) (1998), 24.

19. Elayne Rapping, quoted in *Seinfeld, Master of Its Domain*, edited by David Lavery (New York: Continuum, 2008), 37.

20. Ibid.
21. Dowd, op. cit.

BIBLIOGRAPHY

Auster, Albert. "Much Ado about Nothing: Some Final Thoughts on *Seinfeld*." *Television Quarterly*, 29(4) (1998), 24–33.

"The Big Chill (Revisited), or Whatever Happened to the Baby Boom." *American Demographics* (September 1985), 29.

Cohen, Andrew. "Me and My Zeitgeist." *The Nation*, July 19, 1993, 96–100.

Delvaux, Martine. "The Exit of a Generation: The 'Whatever' Philosophy." *The Midwest Quarterly*, 40(2) (1999), 171–186.

Dowd, Maureen. "Yada Yada Yuppies." *The New York Times*, May 14, 1997, A21.

Foucault, Michel. *Ethics: Subjectivity and Truth*. Translated by Robert Hurley et al. Edited by Paul Rabinow. New York: The New Press, 1997.

Foucault, Michel. *Foucault Live: Collected Interviews, 1961–1984*. Translated by Lysa Hochroth and John Johnston. Edited by Sylvère Lotringer. New York: Semiotext(e), 1989.

"Inside Look" for "The Seinfeld Chronicles," *Seinfeld* (Columbia Tristar, 2004), DVD.

Lavery, David, ed. *Seinfeld, Master of Its Domain*. New York: Continuum, 2008.

Littleton, Cynthia. "Hulu Sets Mammoth 'Seinfeld' Licensing Deal." *Variety*, April 28, 2015, http://variety.com/2015/tv/news/hulu-seinfeld-licensing-160-million-1201483537/, retrieved September 25, 2015.

McInerney, Jay. "Is *Seinfeld* the Best Comedy Ever?" *TV Guide*, June 1, 1996, 14–22.

Miller, Jon D. "Active, Balanced, and Happy: These Young Americans Are Not Bowling Alone." *The Generation X Report*, 1(1) (2011), 1–8.

Oake, Jonathon I. "Reality Bites and Generation X as Spectator." *The Velvet Light Trap*, 53(1) (2004), 83–97.

Piesman, Marissa, and Marilee Hartley. *The Yuppie Handbook: The State-of-the-Art Manual for Young Urban Professionals*. New York: Long Shadow Books, 1984.

Skoble, Aeon J. "Virtue Ethics in TV's *Seinfeld*." In *Seinfeld and Philosophy*, edited by William Irwin, 175–182. Chicago: Open Court, 2000.

Williams, Raymond. *Television: Technology and Cultural Form*. London: Routledge, 1990.

19

Ellen: America's Coming Out Party

Laura Westengard and Aaron Barlow

*Ellen DeGeneres was already a household name in the late 1990s when her epony-
mous sitcom,* Ellen *(1994–1998), changed the television landscape with its landmark
two-part event, "The Puppy Episode" (April 30, 1997).* Ellen *was a popular sitcom,
and people recognized DeGeneres's comedic prowess, but it didn't make waves until
the show included a story line that involved* Ellen *coming out of the closet as a lesbian. Preceded by DeGeneres's own public coming-out announcement on the cover
of* Time *magazine, the country anticipated "The Puppy Episode" with intensely polarizing media hype. In "Ellen: America's Coming Out Party," Laura Westengard and
Aaron Barlow explore the impact that* Ellen*'s coming-out episode had both on television and the public understanding of coming out more broadly.*

We all knew it was coming. The rumor mills had been working overtime,
but we all knew the truth. From her appearance on *The Oprah Winfrey Show*
and a *Time* magazine cover story on April 14, 1997, we had already learned
that Ellen DeGeneres is gay; we knew that her character on her sitcom *Ellen*
would soon admit the same. It was just a matter of time.

Ellen, which ran from March 29, 1994 to July 22, 1998, was in its fourth
(and what proved to be its next to last) season when "The Puppy Episode"
aired on April 30, 1997, as a two-part show. The show is now viewed as having been groundbreaking, but was it?

In his book *The Celluloid Closet*, Vito Russo explains that Hollywood has
always included gay and lesbian characters in one way or another—from

their appearance as comedic "sissies" in the 1920s and 1930s to the miserable gay and lesbian characters of the 1960s who nearly always committed suicide to the mentally ill and often homicidal gay villains of the 1970s and 1980s. Homosexuality played a role in the popular media throughout the 20th century. The characters, however, were almost always ancillary and included for the voyeuristic thrill of the viewers rather than people treated with dignity and complexity.[1]

In the late 1970s, television shows were featuring gay characters in supporting roles, but their incidence was rare. "The Puppy Episode" aired almost 20 years after the *All in the Family* episode "Cousin Liz," another episode of a high-profile sitcom featuring questions of sexual orientation—and another show seen at the time as groundbreaking. "Cousin Liz" first aired on October 9, 1977, and deals with the situation of a closeted lesbian couple after one of them, a cousin to Edith Bunker, has died. Did it have much of an impact, for all of the notice it got? (By Hollywood writers, certainly: its script won an Emmy Award.)

At that time, awareness of the persecution and second-class legal status of gay Americans was finally beginning to seep into America's media consciousness (the episode appearing just a bit more than eight years after the Stonewall Uprising in New York City brought the cry for gay rights to public attention), but the American legal and cultural establishment still saw homosexuality as beyond the bounds of the law and polite conversation. The impact of the show itself was minimal.

In the early 1980s, *Love, Sidney* did feature a gay character in the lead role, but he never came out of the closet. Throughout the rest of the decade, gay characters would appear, but they were neither common nor central. Paradoxically, the lack of progress may have been the result of the growing awareness of the size and importance of the gay population in the United States through the immense tragedy of the AIDS epidemic. Suddenly, there was little funny about being gay—or being a gay character. It's no wonder that sitcoms of the time did not push against the cultural envelope around homosexuality, especially not through humor.

In the 1990s, things picked up a bit in terms of gay awareness on sitcoms; a lesbian wedding was even being depicted on *Friends* in 1996. Not until "The Puppy Episode" appeared in 1997, however, was there an explicitly gay lead character—one played, no less, by a now publicly gay star.[2] The episode, one of the most anticipated sitcom episodes in years, won a 1997 Peabody award; it was commended for "creating courageous and clever comedy with historic significance."[3] The episode also won two Emmy Awards.

The double-length episode was planned with a clear understanding of its potential significance. The creators were careful, and not simply because the ABC network was initially a bit reluctant to back the show, but because the desire was to convince, not bash:

The episode, which took pains to be as inoffensive about its coming-out storyline as possible, featured a cast of Hollywood stars including Oprah Winfrey, Demi Moore, Billy Bob Thornton, and Laura Dern as Ellen's love interest. It also included Jorja Fox as an uncredited extra and Gina Gershon in a cameo, and a number of lesbian celebrities, past and future. k. d. lang and Melissa Etheridge made appearances, and Leisha Hailey and Jenny Shimizu were both background extras.[4]

Though it may have seemed ahead of its time, there were soon hit shows, including *Sex and the City*, *Will & Grace*, *Two and a Half Men*, *30 Rock*, *Glee*, *Modern Family*, *Broad City*, and *Grace and Frankie*—among dozens of others—that featured gay characters in roles across the board and without concern.

In the late 1990s, things were breaking culturally in terms of attitudes of Americans toward homosexuality, but television seemed to be at least keeping up with societal attitudes even if it was not leading the way. This was a bit unusual. Normally, television lagged behind. In fact, it often seemed that the networks, at least, had to be dragged kicking and screaming into any new American cultural situation, and this had been going on for years.

In 2000, for example, when 10–13 per cent of the U.S. population identified as gay, only 2 per cent of characters in US sitcoms could be identified as such. . . . In 2011, by contrast, the Neilsen media research firm calculated that over a quarter of broadcast prime-time shows could be considered "LGBT-inclusive," with 3.9 percent of characters in comedy and drama identified as LGBTQ.[5]

The number of LGBTQ characters doubled in a decade. Though the total was still far below the percentage of gays in the general population, the increase was significant. What changed? Why was "The Puppy Episode" able to become a benchmark?

Part of the answer can be found in the episode itself, which was designed to be as unthreatening as possible to a broadly homophobic population. Sexuality itself is reduced and sex itself becomes, if not an afterthought, a secondary consideration to love—in conformity with heterosexual mythologies. The intent was to bring homosexuality into mainstream conceptions of relationships, not to change those conceptions or to provide alternatives. This is made quite clear in a session portrayed between Ellen and her therapist (Oprah Winfrey):

Ellen: I thought if I just ignored it, you know, it would just go away and I could just live a normal life.

Therapist: And what is a normal life, Ellen?

Ellen: I don't know. Normal. . . . I mean, just same thing everybody wants. I want a house with a picket fence, you know, a dog, a cat, Sunday barbeques, someone to love, someone who loves me, someone I can build a life with. I just . . . I just want to be happy.

Like most of the episode, this is constructed for the explicit purpose of normalizing homosexuality to make it acceptable, not to expand the bounds of "normal" to include homosexuality but bringing homosexuality within established expectations for American life.

Though "The Puppy Episode" was kept secret before it aired (the name was a deliberate attempt at misdirection), it did not attempt to present a surprise. Everyone knew it was coming, so it was not quite a surprise when Paige (Joely Fisher) yells to Ellen, who is dressing in the next room, "Ellen, are you coming out or not?" The tease had been going on; this was clear indication that it was almost over. The buildup, then, is not to the announcement, but to *how* it will be done, how Ellen will come to admit her sexuality to herself and her friends—and whether or not she will be able to act on her desires.

The episode stops short of the latter, in keeping with sitcom norms up to that time, norms of shoving explicit sexual actions to the background. This is even demonstrated through a lie Ellen tells before coming out: she tells her friends that she had spent the night before in great lovemaking with Richard, an old college friend in town for a visit. Of course, nothing of the sort had happened. The episode deals with personal discomfort associated with desire and not with network (and perhaps public) distaste for actual sex on sitcoms, even if behind closed doors.

Richard is a television reporter with a station in Pittsburgh who is in town with his producer Susan, with whom Ellen immediately forms a bond. The three split in the hotel where the visitors are staying, Ellen and Richard going to his room, Susan to hers across the hall. When Richard makes advances to Ellen, she leaves, running into Susan in the hall on her way back to her room with ice. In Susan's room which, they note, is exactly like Richard's room, they talk. Susan tells Ellen she's gay—and had assumed Ellen is, too. Ellen makes an even more scrambled flight out the door and back to Richard's room where she embraces him.

The next morning, Ellen regales her friends with tales of hot sex, but it is all lies, as she admits to her therapist. During the session, she admits that it was Susan she really "clicked with." Hearing that Richard is about to leave town, Ellen rushed to the airport, assuming Susan is leaving with him, but Susan tells her she is staying in town to finish up their story. After a struggle to say it, Ellen blurts, accidentally into an open microphone, "I'm gay."

After a dream about being in a grocery store where everything is loaded with overt signs about lesbianism, Ellen again speaks with her therapist and realizes that she has been suppressing her sexuality since junior high at the very least. On her therapist's advice, she decides to come out to her friends, starting with Peter, an out gay man. When Ellen cannot quite bring herself to tell the others, Peter accidentally outs her.

The possible relationship with Susan doesn't work out because Susan is in the eighth year of a relationship and has no intention of harming it, though she does come close to admitting an attraction for Ellen.

There is more to the episode than that, including the nature of the cast. Not only is the therapist played by Oprah Winfrey who was, at the time, playing something of the nation's therapist through her tremendously popular *The Oprah Winfrey Show*, but Susan is played by Laura Dern, who was a huge movie star at that time, having starred in the 1993 blockbuster *Jurassic Park* after a series of successful performances over the previous decade. Her then-boyfriend, Billy Bob Thornton, had just come from writing and acting in the Oscar-winning *Sling Blade* (which is used as part of the bonding process between Ellen and Susan in "The Puppy Episode") and makes a cameo appearance, as do model Jenny Shimizu, actresses Demi Moore (who was one of the highest-paid actresses of the time), Gina Gershon (who had played a lesbian role in the acclaimed 1996 film *Bound*), and Jorja Fox (then appeared on the hit TV show *ER*), and musicians k. d. lang, Melissa Etheridge, and Dwight Yoakam, all of whom were quite popular at the time, to say the least.

The point was that Ellen's coming out was not some freak occurrence but a natural part of an evolving American culture. The support shown by her friends was amplified by this greater circle, removing the action from the personal to the communal in the broadest sense, something signified in the show by Ellen's accidental "broadcast" of her first admission, "I am gay," at the airport. Significantly, the stars did not need to provide testimonials or make a point of their presence, they only needed to be there.

Though presented against the background of this star-studded cast, the show itself is subdued. The agonizing process of self-inspection that many people go through before admitting to themselves they are gay is reduced to a few lines. Coming out to family, one of the most painful experiences in way too many lives, is dismissed with a line, taking the action into the much more accepting arena of personal friends. What can be one of the most traumatic events of a lifetime becomes almost a case of "So, what's so special about that?" It becomes pedestrian, almost not worth noting. Yet it is clearly important, which is why it is essential to play these events out against the backdrop of an unusual and unusually famous cast.

The purpose of the show is not to delve into the psychological damage of closeted homosexuality or the dangers of coming out. It is to try to reduce that damage and diminish those dangers by making the coming out by a star character an event that can be presented with both humor and compassion—almost as "no big deal." But it is a big deal, and the show's creators know that, and they manage to negotiate the line between overdoing the presentation and reducing its importance.

That they succeed in this is one of the things that makes "The Puppy Episode" so significant. Before 1997, in most sitcoms that featured a homosexual character, there was almost a sense of "Look, we have a gay character on the show! Aren't we just so hip?" Since that time, though more and more sitcoms pride themselves on including LGBTQ characters, their appearance is becoming something of a standard—and becoming the normal that Ellen dreams of and that the coming-out episode is intended to promote.

Even if "The Puppy Episode" was not itself more responsible for an increased opening for gays in television (after all, *Ellen* was canceled the season after it aired) than "Cousin Liz" 20 years earlier, it did become something of a touchstone for people in the television industry who wanted to expand the breadth of topics and characters they could present. It also showed that it wasn't career suicide for an entertainer to admit forthrightly that she or he is gay (since *Ellen*, DeGeneres has been a staple on television, in her next sitcom and then as the host of a highly successful and long-term talk show). In a sense, it was in the right place at the right time, but the change it represents is nonetheless significant to the development of the sitcom over the succeeding 20 years.

COMING OUT AFTER *ELLEN*

On October 11, 1987, hundreds of thousands marched on Washington for lesbian and gay rights. We were in the middle of the AIDS crisis, which the Reagan administration was all but ignoring. Sodomy was illegal in many states, and those laws were being actively enforced. Gay and lesbian couples could not legally marry, and there were no protections for members of the LGBTQ community who faced discrimination in the workplace or elsewhere. The marchers angrily demanded that these issues be taken seriously by the federal government. They displayed the AIDS memorial quilt publicly for the first time, and the event inspired the creation of National Coming Out Day to be observed on October 11 each year.

When Ellen came out to her viewers 10 years later, the narrative of "coming out" was widely known and had taken root in the public imagination as an important milestone in gay life. To come out is not really a singular event. In a heteronormative culture, the default assumption is that any "normal" person is straight, so if LGBTQ people wish to be legible, they must constantly reveal their sexuality in different contexts throughout their lives.

At odds with this fact is the concept of the coming-out story—an emotionally laden, one-time event in which a person ceases to keep his or her sexuality private by announcing it to the world. The story generally follows a specific narrative: a person senses being fundamentally different from others at a young age, there is an interaction with someone of the same sex (usually in early teen years) that leads the person to discover he or she is gay, and the person hides this fact from others for a while and is unhappy being in the closet. Finally, the person decides to reveal his or her "true" self by publicly announcing his or her sexuality, usually to family and close friends, a revelation that involves a lot of trepidation because of the possible negative reactions from those the person cares about.

In the late 1990s, Jen Bacon proposed that coming-out narratives do a kind of rhetorical work by allowing gays and lesbians a "means of negotiating both individual and collective identity within a cultural context that emphatically marginalizes" anything outside of the heterosexual norm.[6] The standard coming-out narrative, however, does not account for the complexity of human sexuality and the impact of other factors such as race, culture, and class. It does not consider the various ways in which people negotiate the closet for safety and survival. Coming-out narratives are not necessarily a window into some more authentic version of the self, but in a reciprocal relationship both "describe a process of identity negotiation while simultaneously enacting that identity construction in their very performance."[7] In this respect, when Ellen comes out she is both *describing* a feeling about who she "really" is (but has been hiding from herself and world) and at the same time *creating* that story about herself.

In a similar reciprocal relationship, the show's famous coming-out plotline mirrored existing narratives about what coming out should look like, and it is also responsible for actually shaping the way we understand what coming out should look like. Once she has admitted to her therapist that she has only really "clicked" with one person in her life. The therapist asks, "And what was his name?" Ellen hesitatingly replies, "Susan." This interaction alone illustrates the heteronormative assumptions that LGBTQ people must constantly negotiate. Rather than make the point that coming out is a constant and lifelong burden resulting from the very structure of society, the episode instead implies that this misunderstanding is Ellen's to rectify as an individual. If she weren't in the closest, then her therapist never would have assumed that Ellen's love interest was a "he." Individual coming-out practices, in other words, place the impetus for change on individual LGBTQ people to make themselves visible (and therefore vulnerable) rather than on a myopic and monolithic cultural narrative based on assumptions about what it means to be "normal."

It is fitting that Oprah plays the role of therapist who coaches Ellen toward the discovery and proclamation of her true self. In her talk shows, television programs, and cable network, Oprah has become a spokesperson for authentic living. In an "Oprah's Life Class" video clip, Oprah features an interview with Ellen just after "The Puppy Episode" aired. She ends the brief video with the advice: "Ellen is an amazing and profound example of being able to step out of whatever is the lie of your life . . . and let yourself blossom in what is the fullness of your own truth."[8] Oprah as talk-show host praises writer and comedian Ellen for coming out just as Oprah as therapist encourages the character played by Ellen to tell her friends and family about her own "truth." The fictional sitcom narrative and characters cannot be separated from the larger cultural narratives and figures at work to construct and perpetuate what it means to be gay and what it means to "lie" about that identity.

After speaking with her therapist, Ellen decides to throw a coming-out party by inviting all of her closest friends to her home for cheese, chardonnay, and an "important announcement." To stage the coming-out scene as an invited gathering heightens its status as a one-time event, an expectation for the coming-out narrative that has since taken root in the cultural imagination. Even the Human Rights Campaign, the largest LGBT civil rights lobbying organization, joined in the hype during the initial episode airing by creating "Come Out with Ellen" party kits.[9] Ellen's coming-out story, while framed as a simple reflection of her discovered truth, also shaped the way America began to understand the structures of coming out itself.

The episode also provided a glimpse into the array of potential reactions that people might have to one's coming-out announcement. Once Ellen finally admits that she is a lesbian, each of her invited friends exhibits a different response to the news. Her openly gay friend Peter (Patrick Bristow) is excited and welcoming, as if her utterance was the secret word granting her instant entrance into a gay community (a joke that is repeated throughout the two-part episode). As part of the negotiation of "both individual and collective identity" associated with coming-out narratives, Peter immediately offers up his coming-out story to her in a return gesture of belonging. Audrey (Clea Lewis) is enthusiastically accepting, exclaiming that she thinks it is "super" and jumping up to give Ellen a hug. Paige (Joely Fisher) says she is supportive but shows a great deal of discomfort, hesitating to even touch Ellen. Spence (Jeremy Piven) immediately reframes Ellen's announcement to appeal to his straight male gaze, telling her insinuatingly, "If you ever want to bring a woman home, I'm cool with that. Very cool." Joe (David Anthony Higgins) is both caring and knowing, later revealing that he had bet the others that they were on their way to a coming-out party. The scene ends with them paying up.

The characters' reactions cover the gamut of possible *positive* responses to the news—there is no physical violence, Ellen is not kicked out of her home, she does not lose her job, and her friends do not abandon her. Although Ellen experiences some discomfort with her epiphany and its aftermath, the show casts her coming out as overwhelmingly positive, a party at which she gains new community, affirms existing friendships, and "blossoms" into the "fullness of [her] own truth" (to return to Oprah for a moment). The narrative structure offers a vision of coming out that has shaped our cultural understanding of the process in a way that simplifies its complexities and negates its risks.

Of course, there were negative reactions to the show itself. Advertisers pulled their sponsorship, Jerry Falwell publically called her "Ellen Degenerate," and "organizations associated with the religious right took out a full-page ad in *Variety*, calling the show 'a slap in the face to American families.'"[10] Even Ellen herself regretted the public reaction to the episode:

> It became bigger than I ever thought it would be. Bigger than I wanted it to be, and it overshadowed my talent. It overshadowed who I am as a person. It was only meant to be just being honest. And it became this snowball, this avalanche that just got bigger and bigger and bigger, and there was no stopping it and so it turned into people not liking me because they thought I was somehow political all of a sudden, and it was the last thing I wanted to do was to be political.[11]

It seems the coming-out experience for Ellen the writer and comedian was not as rosy as the coming-out experience of Ellen the sitcom character.

At the time, "The Puppy Episode" generated a kind of polarizing hype that Ellen never anticipated but that ultimately benefitted the network (as the saying goes, all publicity is good publicity). Though some companies withdrew their sponsorships and the ABC affiliate in Birmingham, Alabama refused to show the episode entirely, at the time the "audience was the third largest for a single series episode in the history of television."[12] Overall, the buzz generated by "The Puppy Episode" overshadowed the negative repercussions. Like the supportive coming-out party Ellen hosts for her friends, *Ellen's* "The Puppy Episode" was a kind of coming-out party for America. It changed the narrative of American culture (both within television and in LGBTQ politics), and perhaps it allowed us to step away from the historic refusal to feature thoughtful and developed narratives about LGBTQ characters on the screen.

Years later, Ellen DeGeneres was granted the Presidential Medal of Freedom, prompting President Obama to proclaim:

> It's easy to forget now, when we've come so far, where now marriage is equal under the law, just how much courage was required for Ellen to come out on the most public of stages almost 20 years ago. Just how important it was not just for the LGBT community, but for all us to see somebody so full of kindness and light—somebody we liked so much, somebody who could be our neighbor or our colleague or our sister—challenge our own assumptions, remind us that we have more in common than we realize, push our country in the direction of justice. What an incredible burden it was to bear, to risk your career like that. People don't do that very often.[13]

NOTES

1. Vito Russo, *The Celluloid Closet: Homosexuality in the Movies*, revised ed. (New York: Harper and Row, 1987).

2. Ellen DeGeneres, Mark Driscoll, Dava Savel, Tracy Newman, and Jonathan Stark, "The Puppy Episode: Part 1," *Ellen*, season 4, episode 22, directed by Gil Junger; aired April 30, 1997.

3. "Ellen: The Puppy Episode," Peabody Awards. http://www.peabodyawards .com/award-profile/elllen-the-puppy-episode.

4. Malinda Lo, "Back in the Day: Coming Out with Ellen," *AfterEllen*, April 9, 2005, http://www.afterellen.com/tv/34682-back-in-the-day-coming-out-with-ellen.

5. Andrew Stott, *Comedy (The New Critical Idiom)* (New York: Routledge, 2014), 147.

6. Jen Bacon, "Getting the Story Straight: Coming Out Narratives and the Possibility of a Cultural Rhetoric," *World Englishes*, 17(2) (1998), 250.

7. Ibid., 257.

8. "Oprah's Life Class: Ellen DeGeneres Stands in Her Truth," Oprah.com, http://www.oprah.com/oprahs-lifeclass/ellen-degeneres-stands-in-her-truth-video _1#ixzz4f6wGMXbS.

9. Lisa Capretto, "Ellen DeGeneres Reveals the One Side Effect of Coming Out She Never Expected," *Huffington Post*, October 24, 2015, http://www.huffington post.com/entry/ellen-degeneres-reveals-the-one-side-effect-of-coming-out-she -never-saw-coming_us_56291b73e4b0aac0b8fc0640.

10. Susan J. Hubert, "What's Wrong with This Picture? The Politics of Ellen's Coming Out Party," *Journal of Popular Culture*, 33(2) (1999), 31–36, doi: 10.1111/j.0022-3840.1999.3302_31.x.

11. Interview, "Ellen DeGeneres Reveals the One Side Effect of Coming Out She Never Expected," *Huffington Post*, October 24, 2015, http://www.huffingtonpost .com/entry/ellen-degeneres-reveals-the-one-side-effect-of-coming-out-she-never -saw-coming_us_56291b73e4b0aac0b8fc0640.

12. Hubert, "What's Wrong with This Picture?" 31.

13. Valentina Zarya, "President Obama Gets 'Choked Up' While Giving Ellen DeGeneres the Highest Civilian Honor." *Fortune*, November 23, 2016, http:// fortune.com/2016/11/23/obama-ellen-degeneres-medal/.

BIBLIOGRAPHY

Bacon, Jen. "Getting the Story Straight: Coming Out Narratives and the Possibility of a Cultural Rhetoric." *World Englishes*, 17(2((1998), 249–258.

Capretto, Lisa. "Ellen DeGeneres Reveals the One Side Effect of Coming Out She Never Expected." *Huffington Post*, October 24, 2015.

Hubert, Susan J. "What's Wrong with This Picture? The Politics of Ellen's Coming Out Party." *Journal of Popular Culture*, 33(2) (1999), 31–36.

Lo, Malinda, "Back in the Day: Coming Out with Ellen," *AfterEllen*, April 9, 2005.

Russo, Vito. *The Celluloid Closet: Homosexuality in the Movies*, revised ed. New York: Harper & Row, 1987.

Stott, Andrew. *Comedy (The New Critical Idiom)*. New York: Routledge, 2014.

Winfrey, Oprah. "Oprah's Life Class: Ellen DeGeneres Stands in Her Truth," Oprah. com, October 13, 2011.

Zarya, Valentina. "President Obama Gets 'Choked Up' While Giving Ellen DeGeneres the Highest Civilian Honor." *Fortune.com*, November 23, 2016.

20

Beyond Wedlock: Developing Romance in *Will & Grace*

Emily Mattingly

Throughout the 20th century, sitcoms carefully integrated narratives about sexuality—from the paternalistic lessons of romance dispensed by Ward Cleaver to the single adult sexuality of career-woman Mary Tyler Moore. Homosexuality has appeared in sitcoms over the years but usually for the purpose of generating a laugh. In "Beyond Wedlock: Developing Romance in Will & Grace," *Emily Mattingly points out that* Will & Grace *(1998 2006) was the first show to feature sustained story lines about gay characters and is credited with being partially responsible for the shift in U.S. views on gay marriage at the end of the 20th century. Mattingly explores how* Will & Grace *moves beyond the depiction of gay romantic monogamy to feature a variety of friendship structures that, in turn, lead to characters who do "not always perform proper aging by virtue of their friendship-centric lives."*

In May 2012, Vice President Joe Biden appeared on the longest-running American television program, NBC's political talk show *Meet the Press* (1947–present). The show's moderator at the time, David Gregory, pressed Biden on his official stance against same-sex marriage. Biden cautiously spelled out how his personal take on such unions now differed from federal policy. In hindsight, his comments made the Supreme Court's June 2015 ruling to strike down state bans on same-sex marriage seem like a pipe dream. He pussyfooted around the possibility of modifying federal laws defining marriage, emphasizing instead his "evolving" personal belief that all "loyal" couples deserve access to the same matrimony-based rights.[1] Biden asserted that his change of heart did not come out of left field, and he suggested that his newfound acceptance of so-called marriage equality was simply in line with a major shift in American social culture. His attitude shift reflected what he saw as a transformation in social consciousness.

What prompted this mass about-face? According to Biden, NBC's own *Will & Grace* (1998–2006), a sitcom credited with being the first TV series featuring sustained story lines about gay characters "probably did more to educate the American public than almost anything anybody's ever done."[2] For Biden, the show's social and historical significance boiled down to its making same-sex marriage palatable for mass consumption. He conflated palatability with visibility, a push for rights with a representational rite of passage. Although series cocreators Max Mutchnick and David Kohan welcomed Biden's high-profile review, they were not completely onboard with his suggestion that the series taught—or even aimed to teach— America about same-sex marriage's merits. During an appearance on *CBS This Morning* (2012–), Mutchnick noted that it's great if Biden came to the conclusion about these merits through watching the series.[3] At its core, though, Mutchnick clarified, the series is a meditation on friendships between gay men and straight women. Based on his own relationship with long-time friend Janet Eisenberg, the series is "a story we were living," not a case for same-sex marriage wrapped in sitcom packaging.[4] Kohan echoed this synopsis more than 10 years earlier when he recounted that inspiration for the show sprung from his confusion around this friend-ship's "romantic element."[5] This element muddled the distinction between friends and lovers in the name of bonding of all people, a gay man and straight woman. For Kohan, romance supplies the situation in this situa-tional comedy.

It's funny how a sitcom inspired by Mutchnick and Eisenberg's romantic friendship became twisted into the political poster child for state-sanctioned romances between men. Reducing *Will & Grace* to an educational touchstone about gay marriage overlooks its groundbreaking representation of a relational universe beyond wedlock. This sitcom is not *about* same-sex marriage, and its sole contribution to the sitcom genre is not its thin portrayal of married gay couples. Rather, the show pioneered territory within the genre through its depiction of romantic friendships between protagonists such as attorney Will Truman (Eric McCormack) and interior designer Grace Adler (Debra Messing). Of course, *Will & Grace* was not alone in its examination of friendship circles comprising mid-20- to early-30-somethings navigating urban singleness. A staple in the Nielsen rating system's top program list for half its run and a 16-time

Emmy Award winner, the series debuted during a televisual flashpoint when representing such circles began paying off big time. These circles supply young, white, educated characters armed with disposable incomes brought about by the urban economic boom in the 1990s and early 2000s access to intimacies divorced from the family. Popular contemporaries such as NBC's *Seinfeld* (1989–1998) and *Friends* (1994–2004) as well as HBO's *Sex and the City* (1998–2004) similarly offer images of characters whose primary relationships are not confined to the nuclear family's heterosexual romance. This romance is a sitcom staple and the primary stage on which the genre's comedy ensues. On this stage, courtship plots routinely drive story lines, and wedlocked or marriageable heterosexual couples assume the emotional spotlight. This spotlight creates a perimeter for experiences of true intimacy, relegating relationships outside this perimeter to supporting roles. The sitcom's serialization of courtship plots unfolds in what amounts to a sequence of sexual development. Intimacy grounded in heterosexual couples provides the emotional backbone for narratives that ultimately follow the sexual contours of chronological aging. The plotlines connecting these couples follow the plotlines of age organized around growing up and maturation. Passing through heterosexual developmental milestones such as marriage and parenthood, for example, means performing age correctly.

Sitcoms like *Will & Grace* examine the lives of characters whose friendships make topsy-turvy their relationships to age scripts. They navigate the courtship plot's periphery to examine characters who do not always perform proper aging by virtue of their friendship-centric lives. Navigating the periphery does not mean the series present worlds untouched by this plot. *Friends* is a great example of how friendship circles chocked with urban singles contain friends with benefits—benefits located in their couplings and other developmental achievements. This sitcom often traces these achievements within a friendship circle in unexpected ways—via a lesbian couple, for example. The first network series to depict lesbian nuptials, *Friends* offers the 1996 marriage between Carol Willick (Jane Sibbett) and Susan Bunch (Jessica Hecht) as a developmental reference point.[6] Carol becomes the first ex-wife of protagonist and core friend Ross Geller (David Schwimmer) after falling in love with her gym buddy, Susan. Though minor characters, Carol and Susan play a major role: they operate as the lesbian foil for straight coupling within the friendship circle. Finding true romantic love and passing through the marriage milestone together reinforces the couple and the courtship plot's importance as a rubric for measuring age-appropriate intimacies within the series. The couple functions as a comedic device to underscore what the show offers as thrice-divorced Ross's heterosexual shortcomings. Comedy gold within this context: not only does Ross divorce too many times, but also he's too young to be a divorcée. The series grounds its comedic timing in Ross's untimeliness or his inability to hit developmental milestones in timely and properly sustained ways.

The series showcases this untimeliness from the get-go when it introduces viewers to Ross in the pilot. When Ross arrives to the local coffee spot, Central Perk, his friends and younger sister, Monica Geller (Courteney Cox), comfort him as he grieves his first marriage's recent demise. Joey Tribbiani (Matt LeBlanc), the group's resident struggling actor, asks Ross how he neglected to realize Carol is a lesbian until now. Exasperated, Ross asks, "Why does everyone keep fixating on that?"[7] The live audience's giggles punctuate this rhetorical question, mocking his inability to enter into *viable* (i.e., uncomplicatedly straight) couplings with women. Ross declares his desire to be "married again" just as Rachel Green (Jennifer Aniston), the soon-to-be final member of the stylish clique, barges into the café. The scene is set for his wish coming true. Sporting an enormous wedding dress, she recounts how she just left her boring fiancé, wealthy orthodontist Barry Farber (Mitchell Whitfield), at the altar. She was led to the wedding chapel by pressure to marry a man who fits certain classed criteria for white respectability before she reaches a certain age. Rachel understands this age-based marriage market and, feeling there is time to couple with someone she actually desires, seeks respite from her suburban life on Long Island in the Manhattan singles scene. Rachel only knows one person in the city, Monica, her best friend from high school. Monica agrees to Rachel taking the second bedroom in her apartment as she sorts out her life. This domestic arrangement becomes the primary setting for the entire group's navigation of the marriage market's fringes. Hanging together in this space, they lock into a friendship that simultaneously delays and makes possible the inevitable: Ross and Rachel catching up with Carol and Susan. This foil's coupling creates an almost decade-long domino effect in which Ross overcomes his shortcomings by moving out of the friend zone with Rachel. Their long and tumultuous romance doesn't diminish the emotional core in the series—friendship. Instead, their relationship reinforces it, emphasizing the importance of romancing developmental rhythms in the context of broader constellations of long-lasting friendships. In these constellations, friends can become new lovers, and the best lovers are always old friends.

Will & Grace also glorifies old friends through a comedic examination of a circle living together in a world out of sync with heterosexual developmental rhythms. In *Will & Grace*'s version of New York City, the rhythms of first love, then marriage, and finally a baby in a baby carriage exist. However, the BFFs grow older in ways that put pressure on this rhythm by virtue of their friendship's anatomy. This anatomy doesn't develop into a romance—it is a romance. The pilot sets the scene for fleshing out this anatomy throughout the series, revealing how the characters hang together at the first of many developmental crossroads. This episode introduces important facts about Will and Grace: both are 30, reeling from recent breakups from people they thought were their respective forever lovers, and have known each other for nearly two decades.[8] They first meet 15 years earlier while attending Columbia University. In college, they date briefly before Will reveals to Grace he's gay during a semester break at her parents' upstate home. What happens after this revelation is a unique representational unfolding of possibilities for how and with whom you can age on TV. These possibilities manifest in a couple whose intimacies do not crescendo to sex and all of its attending developmental prospects (parenthood, for example). Where Will and Grace wind up together as they navigate their friendship is quite different compared to Ross and Rachel's happy ending. Their coupling is not the icing on the cake of intimacy, a romantic destination in their friendship's trajectory forward. Their coupling *is* intimacy.

Will and Grace hold nearest and dearest intimacies outside of those afforded by the wedded couple and their spawn. They are single throughout much of the series. Only, they are not: they are happily coupled via their friendship. They are what scholar Jennifer Doyle defines an "uncoupled" couple—a couple of friends whose affections belong "not quite to straight culture, not quite to gay and lesbian culture (although certainly more at home in the latter than the former)."[9] Put simply, their romantic pairing as a man and a woman doesn't quite fill heterosexual coupling's shoes. Rather, their "coupleness" exists in a cultural contact zone where friendship is a queer site of romance. They seduce each other with witty banter and kind gestures, refer to each other as soul mates, sometimes share domestic spaces, and take comfort in their relationship's durability. Will and Grace belong to each other. But their affections for each other do not belong to same heterosexual machinery of romantic coupling that drives characters like Ross and Rachel.

Their affections take the shape of what the series openly flaunts as a "fag–hag" coupling. *Will & Grace* deploys this friendship form whose very name is steeped in a history of homophobic insults and misogynistic slurs—"fag" and "hag"—to represent alliances between gay men and straight women. The series celebrates these fraught alliances and the term that frames them, infusing what often circulates as a two-syllable string of insults into a site of romantic comedy. In doing so, it examines a range of stereotypes located in this couple form. The central stereotype at play in the series is what Doyle tellingly describes in age-focused terms: an "insecure straight woman who retreats into asexual friendships with similarly stunted homosexual men."[10] Stunted growths. Developmental delays. Sexual underdevelopment. These romances suspend couples in asexual no man's lands, impeding moves toward true loves elsewhere. The series mines these stereotypes to breathe a new and complex life into this friendship form's representational field.

Romance may supply the situation in this situation comedy, but understanding this situation's comedy requires taking into account how the series narrates aging in the context of fag–hag coupling.

How *Will & Grace* mines fag–hag stereotypes attracted serious criticism. As much as the series was a prime-time darling and an enormous financial success, it was also a critical whipping boy. Even now, as the series continues its success in syndicated reruns and YouTube spin-offs like the 2016 hit "Vote Honey," it attracts major side eye.[11] Critiques of Will and Grace's whitewashed paradise of urban privilege untouched by HIV and AIDS are helpful for understanding the series' shortcomings as an artifact of what some call queer respectability.[12] Queer respectability is a term used to describe representations of LGBTQ+life in line with Joe Biden's push to, in theorist Michael Warner's words, "make the norms of straight culture the standards by which queer life should be measured."[13] Queer respectability makes straight norms like long-haul monogamy the measuring stick by which queer lives garner cultural and political value. The series fronts a general disinterest in taking to task such charges of respectability. Even so, painting the series as a sitcom solely designed to deliver laughs in the name of respectability flattens out how it straddles the gay-straight contact zones Jennifer Doyle describes. Reading how the series represents these zones straight up shortchanges its romantic vision of how fag–hag couples can age together in the sitcom format.

The series carves out a representational space for examining these contact zones with a sentimental eye. This sentimentality serves an important function: to bind the couples on the zones' frontlines. It is the series' emotional glue as the characters navigate the zones together over time. Binding these zones through images of sentimentality results in a romantic—albeit sometimes problematic—vision of fag–hag love. The sentimental hilarity organized around the eponymous couple's aging is what bothers Doug Wright most in his one-page series retrospective for *The Advocate*, "Was it Good for the Gays?"[14] Wright slams the series' sentimentality grounded in what he calls "a reassuring trope—a husband and wife in a marriage without sex."[15] He traces this trope back to the parallel twin beds featured in the sitcom classic *I Love Lucy* (1951–1957). Much like the chaste midcentury arrangements framing protagonists Ricky (Desi Arnaz) and Lucy (Lucille Ball), Wright suggests, Will and Grace are a castrated couple. True, Will and Grace share an asexual romance. The series even references *I Love Lucy* to explore this romance openly. Case in point: early in the first season, Grace becomes consumed by the thought that Will—who refers to himself as gay icon Ricky Ricardo—may be in the throes of a sexy affair with one of his clients.[16] This scenario references *I Love Lucy*'s 1954 episode entitled "Fan Magazine Interview."[17] In this episode, Lucy feels relief upon discovering that Ricky's potential paramour is *just* an old woman taking up his time with lengthy interviews for a popular rag. The supposed other woman's wrinkles and dowdiness appease Lucy. Business as usual commences after this revelation and the episode ends with the usual sentimental vision of chaste happiness on the heterosexual home front. What Wright overlooks is how *Will & Grace* breathes new life into this episode to offer the fag–hag romance as a sentimental epicenter. The series rewrites this *I Love Lucy* episode, in other words, to stage narrative acrobatics that put the husband–wife trope into conversation with fag–hag intimacies. It draws from this trope not to reproduce its heterosexual workings through Will and Grace but to shine a familiar light on the classic couple's depth of feeling through Will and Grace. The series amplifies this depth by reimagining a classic sitcom that serves as both a queer and straight pop cultural icon. With nostalgic hands, the series reworks the classic to stage an emotional world both within and beyond the classic sitcom couple.

In this way, the series calls on sentimental sitcom shticks to represent alliances between men and women that do not adhere to romantic norms and their attending tempos. Grace's fixations on Will rub against Lucy's obsessions with catching Ricky in an affair with a (young) woman. Feelings of sexual ownership and jealousy do not inform her fixation on the possibility that Will is in romantic clutches. Grace feels out of the information loop, sidelined in the story of Will's sex life. She feels betrayed by the possibility of Will not divulging information about himself to her. What bothers Grace most is the possibility that Will is not holding up his end of their intimacy bargain as a fag–hag coupling. Much like Lucy, Grace finds relief when she discovers that Will's meetings are with the eldest member of the couple's broader friendship circle, pill-popping socialite Karen Walker (Megan Mullally). Will's silence around these meetings simply reflects his maintenance of lawyer–client confidentiality with Karen. Karen recently started the process of divorcing her sugar-daddy husband, Stan, and came to Will for help. Also comforting: Karen is comfortably settled in her own fag–hag coupling with underemployed and infantile trickster, Jack McFarland (Sean Hayes), the circle's fourth and final member. Jack has been Will's friend since 1985 after encouraging him to come out to Grace, who knows Karen doesn't pose a threat to her primary relationship with Will. Grace's coupling is secure and primed for another episode. She no longer worries about growing older alone—her biggest fear during the episode. Will is there for her and her only. This easy, sentimental cleanup of melodramatic relationship blips gets under Wright's skin. And, ultimately, he blames the series' lack of political punch on the sitcom format itself. He suggests that sitcom genre presents nothing but breezy sentimentality. Any potentially subversive political statements in sitcoms are dead on arrival, he sneers, trapped in a coffin made of jingles promising consumptive fulfillment.

Wright confronts *Will & Grace* viewers with two difficult questions: What can you *do* with sitcom couples? What can the sitcom offer in terms of staging couples' lives together in serial form? The series engages these questions to pay homage to fag–hag couplings and their unique tempos. It reflects on these questions in the final season when a casting director informs Jack he finally landed a much-coveted lead in a sitcom.[18] This stroke of luck surprises the typically brash and charmingly shallow Jack, a sometimes actor who craves the spotlight. The first person he wants to tell about his casting: Karen. She's absolutely delighted for her "poodle" and can't wait to watch him realize his screen dreams. Jack's sitcom gig is a cheesy mess about a hypermasculine detective, Chuck Rafferty. It's made even cheesier and messier during the premiere when it showcases Jack's usual shrill and flaming glee dubbed over with an out-of-sync butchy voice. What he realizes as he watches the premiere: despite the dubbing, this still marks his big break into acting. What starts as a career tragedy ends in an opportunity via help from an ever-encouraging Karen. The episode filters Jack's realization through a self-reflexive lens, making clear the complexities of his queerness appearing on American television screens. Doubling back on this lens is the image of Karen, beaming with pride as she sarcastically exclaims on hearing Jack's dubbed voice, "And they say the sitcom is dead!" This verdict on the multicamera sitcom's fate segues into a scene in which Will—a handsome leading man who, unlike Jack, loathes the situational messes inherent in his sitcom life—finds out that his dad just died. Sitcom death encounters sitcom death. The phone call about his dad's passing rings in the background as he and Grace quarrel over a baby blanket in the apartment they've shared for nearly eight years. Will's upset because this blanket used to belong to him. His WASP-ified parents gave it to a pregnant Grace during a recent trip to their Connecticut home. Will interprets the gifting gesture as a blanket statement about his homosexuality. He thinks his parents assume he will not have children and that the gift will be at home with Grace.

Will's assumption about his parents is spot-on, but not necessarily in the way he initially imagines. Will keeps his parents at a distance, never expressing his interest in having children to them. They think children are not on his radar. Confronted by the blanket's new home, Will comes out to his parents from a second closet: one where the baby blanket should stay stowed away on a shelf for future use. Will tells his parents what he's only confided in the safety of the intimacy he shares with Grace: he wants a child. Will explodes when his dad states he feels "back in the gay minefield" of Will's first coming out. This emotionally charged minefield overflows with what his dad, George, imagines as political correctness bombs and trigger warnings.

Because of George's unexpected death, a sentimental exchange between a loving father and doting son never takes place. Will and Grace make amends over the blanket, though, confirming their commitment to the fag–hag couple form that binds them. No blanket can come between them. Their sentimental exchange raises their friendship to the status of kinship. Grace does not fill the familial hole George leaves; she simply stretches out further in her role as Will's romantic partner. Will may not have a tender closing moment with his dad, a bit of a tragedy in his life. He does, however, share a tender moment with Grace, and it's this moment that matters most. This moment doesn't simply reaffirm his bond with Grace, it also signifies his realization that the blanket will be woven into this expansive kinship network's fabric. He wants to help Grace raise her baby. He doesn't want to be the father per se, but he does want to forge ahead in creating a fag–hag coupling that brings parenthood into its relational fold. The sitcom may be in decline. Strange things like Jack becoming a macho TV star may unfold in their romance's background. One thing remains constant: Will and Grace's romance.

This sentimental break up to make up is not the first time Will and Grace almost lose it over love objects. Take, for example, an episode from the third season in which Will, Grace, Jack, and Karen pile into a car for a long road trip. Their destination: a posh civil union celebration at a picturesque chapel in the countryside.[19] At the center of this celebration are Joe and Larry, a posh gay couple who exist on the foursome's friendship sidelines. Before the ceremony, Grace hangs out in the designated gift area. She tries to track down the expensive gift—a kayak—Will bought weeks earlier. She assumes writing her name on the gift's attending card is no big deal. She assumes wrong. Will fronts his displeasure with Grace's mooching. The couple scuffles over the gifting issue in the chapel's entryway. Joe and Larry interrupt them midfight to ask a favor. They want Will and Grace to give a special reading together during the ceremony. They happily agree, flattered by the idea that Joe and Larry admire their coupleness. Once Joe and Larry exit stage left, Grace dives back into her petty attempt to write her name on the card. She doesn't understand why Will's so upset by the possibility of her name existing alongside his. Will's response to her confusion: "Because I don't want a wife." An awkward silence engulfs the couple. His discomfort stems from feeling confined in their relationship's developmental stasis. The ceremony envelops him in the evidence of gay men growing into the next developmental stage together—marriage. He confronts a feeling he's had for a while now but never expressed aloud: his relationship with Grace is simultaneously stagnant and moving forward into a territory he feels removes him from romantic potentials with men. His romance with Grace suspends him in an asexual no man's land and, in this moment, he wants to break free.

The scene following this tense interaction at the gift table features Will and Grace sitting in pews during the ceremony. The ceremonial rites take a backseat to their drama. In a pew near the front of the church, Grace turns back to Will and snarls, "I'm your wife? That's possibly the most vicious thing you've ever said to me." The obligation to read a speech about love and commitment to a packed room halts their fight in the pews—a fight centering on how their relationship doesn't give them what they feel they could experience in other coupling configurations. The carefully timed, back-and-forth speech reads as a straight couple saying vows as they lock into the family romance's ceremonial rhythms. An unscripted profession of love for each other punctuates the reading. Their exuberant ceremonial procession down the aisle adds layer on layer of matrimonial mimicry. This mimicry doesn't suggest that their fag–hag coupling is a sham marriage, a poor substitute for the real thing. Instead, it gives additional dimension to the particularity of their coupling. Their coupling doesn't fit the family romance's script. Going through most of the wedding motions doesn't signify a development from one sexual milestone straight to the next. These motions signify a deepening of their feelings for each while hanging together in their coupling's stasis. Larry and Joe awkwardly remind their friends that the celebration can't come to a close just yet—they're still waiting their turn.

The scene immediately following this reminder depicts Will and Grace eating cake. Mouths full, they reflect on their earlier fight. Will apologizes to Grace for policing the card and relates his hard feelings about the gift as such: "Chalk it up to my pre-mid-life crisis." Will drawing attention to his age as he articulates his hard feelings about coupling illuminates some of the series' temporal workings. These workings shape the sitcom's serialized sentimentality. Certain sentimental feelings tied to certain relationships are supposed to unfold at certain times. Will is aware of these times. As much as he loves Grace and wants to grow older with her, he mourns the possibilities he sees existing outside their relationship. This image of mourning tied to aging within the fag–hag coupling doesn't paint the duo as pathetic. The image breathes an emotional life into complexities often flattened by the fag–hag stereotype itself. Sentimentality remains the core feeling holding together the relationship. But the scene foregrounds how difficult feelings work alongside sentimentality to make their romance fleshy and rich.

The series finale is a sentimental tour de force in representing this complicated emotional life. Aging does all kinds of temporal acrobatics in the episode to ensure that old friends maintain sure footing as the series' emotional core. Maintaining this sure footing is not easy. The opening scene confronts us with a heated exchange between Will and Grace about their teenaged son being suspended from school. Much of the scene's humor stems from how Debra Messing and Eric McCormack don what Mary Zaborskis calls "age drag."[20] Put simply, age drag is a form of prosthetic aging that draws attention to how the body wears time. Age drag here helps Will and Grace make a temporal leap into this imagined future—a future in which they share a hypothetical son. McCormack wears makeup that maps his face with deep wrinkles, a toupee to cover the latex bald cap masking his hair, and a button-down shirt that snugly highlights his prosthetic pudginess. Messing exists in a parallel age drag universe: she wears similar makeup, a wig featuring a gray skunk stripe down the center of her otherwise auburn mane, and a tacky track suit that accentuates her fake bubble butt. Will and Grace's quibble about the teen's behavior soon turns into a tense meditation on their nil love lives, unfulfilling parental roles, and lack of style. They gave up important relationships when they were younger, the duo makes clear, to raise the son together. After their son hurls a snide remark about how these romantic sacrifices make him happy, Grace slaps him on the back of the head, setting off a Three Stooges–style slap fest. This fest ends when Will's toupee lands at his feet. He laments how he doesn't have time to "reglue" his hairpiece back on before guests arrive for a perennial *Will & Grace* ritual: game night. The son stomps out of the apartment, and Will and Grace share a parenting meltdown. Grace, never a character to pass up opportunities to get the last word in during fights, ends the brawl on a disdain-tinged note: "Time hasn't been kind to any of us."[21]

A knock interrupts Grace's reflection. Karen glides through the entryway as if she's walking on air. In this hypothetical future, she hasn't aged a day. She looks temporally suspended in her usual body, comically making clear as she stands in the living room that time—and help from plastic surgeons' skilled hands—has been nothing but kind to her. The only signs of aging Karen confronts are those she witnesses by proxy to Will and Grace. Karen is a manicured sculpture in what she wistfully calls "the wax museum" of Botoxed faces and tucked skin.[22] Jack soon appears to round out the core friendship circle. He takes center stage in front of his best gal pal as he puts a campy spin on the bridal march he hums aloud. He lifts a veil, revealing a George Hamilton–style spray tan and a too-white smile. His slightly wrinkled face beams as he proudly announces that he just got married. His new husband enters the frame seconds later: it's Kevin Bacon as himself, the actor Jack openly stalks for decades. Bacon, the apple of Jack's obsessive eye and the true man love of his life, stands in the living room as a testament to dreams coming true.

Kevin Bacon abruptly leaves the party to bandage a bleeding "Kyra Forever" tattoo he removed before walking down the aisle with Jack. The remaining guests—including Karen's former maid and now graying butch lover, Rosario (Shelley Morrison)—witness the saddest game night ever. The group plays a depressing round of a word association contest in which Will and Grace reference their crushed hopes and derailed life aspirations. In a hilarious turn of events, the couple wins the contest. The win proves they know each others' respective frustrations and unrealized desires all too well. Winning does not bring its usual satisfaction for the competitive couple. Will ends the match by telling Grace that she "ruined" his life. As this heavy word slips off his tongue, a narrative twist reveals itself: Jack's fantasy is actually Grace's nightmare. This word shakes a young and heavily pregnant Grace awake. She lies on the couch in the apartment she shares with Will, shaken by the terrible vision. What makes the dream so terrifying? How the image of ungraceful aging refracts through the prism of her relationship with Will. In the nightmare, the couple becomes haggard by their fag–hag relationship.

A series of temporal jumps, stops, and starts follows this nightmare. First jump: Grace's ex-husband and the father to her unborn child, Leo Markus (Harry Connick Jr.), unexpectedly appears at the apartment to redeem their broken relationship. Leo has been out the picture for awhile at this point in the series. Grace kicked him to the curb in the seventh season's finale after learning of his affair. He has no idea Grace is pregnant until he arrives. On seeing her belly, he confronts her with a proposition— be part of a future "gross old couple" with him. Grace accepts this proposal. Although we never see her fall out with Will, we know it happens. Will is suspicious of Leo. Specifically, he feels Leo can never be there for Grace the same ways he has over the course of their long relationship. The screen turns black, creating a narrative ellipsis right as Will walks in on Grace accepting Leo back into her life. The episode never explicitly depicts Will witnessing his fantasy to raise a baby together with Grace fade—it only shows the bumpy aftermath. The domino effect of Leo's proposal reveals itself in a two-year narrative jump forward. In this jump's first frame, Will sits comfortably in a domestic scene. He feeds who we come to find out is his toddler son, Ben, a child he conceives via a surrogate with his now long-time partner and self-proclaimed "old-fashioned homosexual," Vince (Bobby Cannavale).[23] Vince walks in on this scene just as Will laments to Ben that he no longer looks 25. It's Will's birthday, and he immediately asks Vince if Grace called to wish him well. Vince says she didn't before he reminds Will of something he keeps forgetting: "fate" binds him to Grace. It doesn't matter how much time passes between them. It doesn't matter that they haven't spoken in a while.

The episode visually pairs this gentle reminder with a cut to Grace in the apartment she shares with Leo and her own toddler, Lila. This cut suggests that Will and Grace live parallel lives. Right as Grace begins getting ready to take Lila to the zoo, Leo pleads with her to wish Will a happy birthday. He knows Will is her primary partner. He also knows not being with him is torturing her. An image of Karen and Jack sharing a bubble bath together as they scheme to fully recouple Will and Grace follows this plea. Bobbing together above the foam, the duo masterminds what Will later describes as "the dumbest version of *Parent Trap* ever." This trap works. But just when it seems Will and Grace will never again part ways, they do. They part for a few decades after kid obligations and other family matters happen. On the surface, they grow apart by folding into their respective familial rhythms with Leo and Vince, although these rhythms with the partners are as flat as the underdeveloped partners themselves. Leo and Vince function as supporting characters orbiting the fag–hag coupling. They are love interest props on a stage built for Will and Grace's romance.

The finale ends in a three-part vision of fag–hag togetherness. This vision uses age drag to imagine a future not wholly grounded in straight narratives of aging. The first of these future-leaning visions focuses on Karen and Jack spending a quiet evening together in the apartment they have now shared for 20 years. They silently read magazines together when Jack looks up to charm Karen by telling her she looks "good" and inquiring if she got "a little touch-up today." Of course she did. Jack looks much like he does in the finale's opening scene sans orange glow and blinding teeth. Karen looks exactly as she always does: youthful, Botoxed, fabulous. After babying an elderly Rosario who they call their "infant," Karen and Jack make their way to the piano to sing a duet of Nat King Cole's 1951 hit "Unforgettable." This scene sonically resonates their love for each other. The widescreen shot of their impeccable apartment frames this duet, inserting a new way to visualize aging into the sitcom's romantic archive. This heartfelt scene concludes with Jack and Karen rubbing bellies, their signature gesture of affection for each other throughout the series. This rub makes clear the series' investments in representing possibilities that rub against this sitcom archive—an archive in which dominant age scripts help develop scripts privileging the family romance.

The second scene of togetherness reaches deep into *Will & Grace*'s own archive to drive home these investments. In this scene, Will and Grace sit alone in their separate apartments as they chat on the phone and watch TV in the dark. Will and Grace wear age drag. Unlike in the opening scene, though, this drag is no nightmare. According to Grace, they "look good" for their age. The flickering TV screens highlight the lines on their faces as Will goes on about how glad he is that George Clooney is back on *ER*. This exchange mirrors the pilot's opening scene in which a 30-year-old Grace playfully asks Will if he's jealous of her having a boyfriend, Danny (Tom Verica). Without missing a beat, he responds, "Honey, I don't need your man. I got George Clooney."

This exchange is simultaneously familiar and strange. How it's familiar: Will and Grace bond over pop culture, TV, crushes, and quip. How it's strange: a verbal jab doesn't end the phone conversation. In the pilot, Will ends the call by noting he's not exactly a fan of Grace's then-boyfriend, Danny, a guy she leaves at the altar soon after the call ends. Instead of offering a critique, he offers an invite to meet up. Of all places, he wants to go to the same seedy dive bar they ended up at together in the pilot. This is the bar where they drank the night away after Grace showed up a hot mess in what was to be her wedding dress. This is the bar where their queer friendship read as a straight marriage to drunken eyes around them. These eyes saw Will and Grace as a properly coupled husband and wife. What the characters present, though: an uncoupled couple working through Grace's falling out from a developmental milestone. This is the bar where Grace made the following drunk "wedding" speech to Will: "To my Will. You are my hero and my soul mate. And, I'm a better woman for loving you." This is the bar where, after Grace made this speech, the duo kissed deeply and did—as they always do—coupling with a slant. This history at the bar is not lost on Grace, and she smirks nostalgically when she tells Will she wants to invite Jack and Karen along for the fun.

The final scene in the three-part vision puts the four friends at the visual center of the series—right where they belong. They stand at the bar together. They stand as a testament to long friendships whose relational contours shape their experiences of aging. Will interrupts their banter by making a quick toast to his family: his friends. Jack sighs, in classic Jack fashion, that the toast is "boooring." Karen follows his yawn by stating that the toast is "too real." She feels all the good, real feels—feels that confuse her. Will turns to his fag–hag comrades, smiles, and lovingly tells them that they haven't "changed a bit." It's all too easy to read this depiction of friendship as simply propping up the young hetero couple—Ben and Lila—who come to symbolize a kind of familial realness for Will and Grace. Their children met in college and are now engaged. Yes, Will and Grace will soon, through their children, become a "too real" family. But celebrating this supposed realness isn't the point in the series' closing scene. After Will's heartfelt toast, the camera closes in on the friends and then fades to black. They experience, through the blackness of the darkened lens, a collective shift in time. The bar fades back into view, following the friends' hands as they simultaneously place their empty shot glasses onto the bar top. The glasses aligned in a neat row, the camera moves up to the friends' busts above the counter. Their faces in full view, they appear as their 30-something selves. In the fade, their bodies make a temporal leap backward. They go back to a time before children and partners, a time when it was just them suspended in their own developing romance.

NOTES

1. "Biden Breaks Down Stance on Same-Sex Marriage," *Meet the Press*, NBC, May 6, 2012, http://www.nbcnews.com/video/meet-the-press/47312632#47312632, retrieved November 4, 2016.

2. Ibid.

3. "*Will & Grace*: Social Commentary or Just Entertainment?" *CBS This Morning*, CBS, May 10, 2012, http://www.cbsnews.com/videos/will-grace-social-commentary-or-just-entertainment, retrieved October 7, 2016.

4. Ibid.

5. Naomi Pfefferman, "Jewish and Normal? Oy!" *Jewish Journal*, September 6, 2001, http://jewishjournal.com/culture/arts/4792/.

6. *Friends*, "The One with the Lesbian Wedding," aired January 18, 1996 (Santa Monica, CA: NBC Studios, 2006), DVD.

7. Ibid., "The One Where Monica Gets a Roommate (Pilot)," aired September 22, 1994.

8. *Will & Grace*, "Love and Marriage," aired September 21, 1998 (Santa Monica, CA: NBC Studios, 2008), DVD.

9. Jennifer Doyle, "Between Friends." In *A Companion to Lesbian, Gay, Bisexual, Transgender, and Queer Studies*, edited by George E. Haggerty and Molly McGarry (Malden, MA: Blackwell, 2007), 326, 340.

10. Ibid., 332.

11. See Christopher Kelly's scathing "*Will & Grace* Changed Nothing," *Salon*, October 2, 2012, http://www.salon.com/2012/10/03/will_grace_changed_nothing/; and NBC's "Vote Honey," YouTube, September 26, 2016, https://www.youtube.com/channel/UCLem9J0NkphqGbIYX5_uZBw, November 4, 2016.

12. See Rahul Gairola's "Watching with Ambivalence," PopMatters, December 31, 1994, http://www.popmatters.com/review/will-and-grace; Todd Ramlow's "For Shame," PopMatters, December 31, 1994, http://www.popmatters.com/review/will-and-grace-060525; and Doug Wright's "Was It Good for the Gays?" *The Advocate*, May 9, 2006, 53.

13. Michael Warner, "Normal and Normaller: Beyond Gay Marriage," *GLQ: A Journal of Lesbian and Gay Studies*, 5 (1999), 123.

14. Wright, op. cit.

15. Ibid.

16. *Will & Grace*, "William, Tell," aired November 9, 1998.

17. *I Love Lucy: The Complete Series*, "Fan Magazine Interview," aired February 8, 1954 (Los Angeles: Paramount, 2007), DVD.

18. *Will & Grace*, "Blanket Apology," aired April 6, 2006.

19. *Will & Grace*, "Husbands and Trophy Wives," aired October 19, 2000.

20. Mary Zaborskis, "Age Drag," *WSQ: Women's Studies Quarterly*, 43 (2015), 115–129.

21. *Will & Grace*, "The Finale," aired May 18, 2006.

22. *Will & Grace*, "The Needle and the Omelet's Done," aired November 14, 2002.

23. *Will & Grace*, "Whatever Happened to Baby Gin?," aired May 11, 2006.

BIBLIOGRAPHY

Battles, Kathleen, and Wendy Hilton-Morrow. "Gay Characters in Conventional Spaces: *Will & Grace* and the Situation Comedy Genre." *Critical Studies in Media Communication*, 19 (2002), 87–105.

"Biden Breaks Down Stance on Same-Sex Marriage." *Meet the Press*, NBC, May 6, 2012, http://www.nbcnews.com/video/meet-the-press/47312632#47312632, retrieved October 7, 2016.

Castiglia, Christopher, and Christopher Reed. "'Ah Yes, I Remember It Well': Memory and Queer Culture in *Will and Grace*." *Cultural Critique*, 56 (2003), 158–188.

Davis, Glyn, and Gary Needham, eds. *Queer TV: Theories, Histories, Politics*. New York: Routledge, 2009.

Doyle, Jennifer. "Between Friends." In *A Companion to Lesbian, Gay, Bisexual, Transgender, and Queer Studies*, edited by George E. Haggerty and Molly McGarry, 325–340. Malden, MA: Blackwell, 2007.

Friends. 1994–2004. Santa Monica, CA: NBC Studios, 2006. DVD.

Gairola, Rahul. "*Will & Grace*: Watching with Ambivalence." PopMatters, December 31, 1994, http://www.popmatters.com/review/will-and-grace.

Hart, Kylo-Patrick R., ed. *Queer TV in the 21st Century: Essays on Broadcasting from Taboo to Acceptance*. Jefferson, NC: McFarland, 2016.

I Love Lucy: The Complete Series. 1951–1957. Los Angeles: Paramount, 2007. DVD.

Joyrich, Lynne. "Queer Television Studies: Currents, Flows, and (Main) Streams." *Cinema Journal*, 53 (2014), 133–139.

Kelly, Christopher. "*Will & Grace* Changed Nothing." *Salon*, October 2, 2012, http://www.salon.com/2012/10/03/will_grace_changed_nothing/.

NBC. "Vote Honey." YouTube, September 26, 2016, https://www.youtube.com/channel/UCLem9J0NkphqGbIYX5_uZBw, retrieved November 4, 2016.

Pfefferman, Naomi. "Jewish and Normal? Oy!" *Jewish Journal*, September 6, 2001, http://jewishjournal.com/culture/arts/4792/.

Pullen, Christopher. *Straight Girls and Queer Guys: The Hetero Media Gaze in Film and Television*. Edinburgh: Edinburgh University Press, 2016.

Ramlow, Todd. "*Will & Grace*: For Shame." PopMatters, December 31, 1994, http://www.popmatters.com/review/will-and-grace-060525.

Warner, Michael. "Normal and Normaller: Beyond Gay Marriage." *GLQ: A Journal of Lesbian and Gay Studies*, 5 (1999), 119–171.

Will & Grace. 1998–2006. Santa Monica, CA: NBC Studios, 2008. DVD.

"*Will & Grace*: Social Commentary or Just Entertainment?" *CBS This Morning*, CBS, May 10, 2012, http://www.cbsnews.com/videos/will-grace-social-commentary-or-just-entertainment, October 7, 2016.

Wright, Doug. "Was It Good for the Gays?" *The Advocate*, May 9, 2006. 53.

Zaborskis, Mary. "Age Drag." *WSQ: Women's Studies Quarterly*, 43 (2015), 115–129.

21

Ask and Tell: Ambiguity and the Narrative Complexity of *Sex and the City*

Kimberly Hall

A group of 30-something women navigate dating, career, and friendship in late 20th and early 21st century Manhattan. Sex and the City (1998–2004) aired on HBO and therefore offered something broadcast network sitcoms could not—sex. The adult content of the show, its focus on female experience, and its responsibility for the renaissance of the Cosmopolitan cocktail, often lead viewers to underestimate the show's complexity. In "Ask and Tell: Ambiguity and the Narrative Complexity of Sex and the City," Kimberly Hall moves beyond the show's content to examine its structure. Performing a narrative analysis to explore its reflexivity, performativity, and character deconstruction, Hall ultimately determines that Sex and the City strategically deploys its narrative structure to foster active forms of engagement among viewers.

Sex and the City premiered on the premium cable channel HBO on June 6, 1998. This timing is a critical fulcrum point between the dominance of network sitcoms such as *Seinfeld*, which aired the second part of its final episode on May 14, 1998, and the emergence of powerful cable dramas such as *The Sopranos*, which also aired on HBO, on January 10, 1999. This liminal space between two series focused largely on men, place, and genre seems to befit a series whose own position and legacy has been so fluid. The show about the sex and love lives of four professional 30-something women in Manhattan averaged 6.5 million viewers during its six-year run from 1998 to 2004, an undeniably strong showing for a premium cable series.[1] That popularity extended beyond its initial run, spawning lucrative syndication deals with two networks—TBS and E! The success of the series also translated into two spin-off films, *Sex and the City* (2008), which grossed more than $400 million worldwide, and *Sex and the City 2* (2010), which grossed more than $288 million worldwide. In addition, a backstory spin-off series, *The Carrie Diaries*, aired on the CW network from 2013 to 2014. *Sex and the City* was also the first cable series to win an Emmy Award, receiving the award for outstanding comedy series in 2001, and the series was nominated for a total of 158 awards, winning 48. By any quantitative measure, the show was an undeniable success.

Critically, however, the series fared quite differently, especially in comparison to the two series between which its pilot episode is sandwiched. *Sex and the City* is rated as the 40th best series of all time by *TV Guide* magazine; *The Sopranos* and *Seinfeld* are ranked numbers one and two, respectively.[2] Although the characters, the fashion, and the setting have all provided extensive fodder for journalists and scholars alike, recent critical reevaluations of the series question its feminine credibility, its overt consumerism, its lack of diversity, and the heteronormative endings celebrated in the finale and the films.[3] As *The Telegraph* cultural critic Tanya Gold summarily states it, "Sorry sisters, but I hate *Sex and the City*."[4] Even more nuanced recent analyses express a complicated assessment of the series. In Emily Nussbaum's 2013 article for *The New Yorker*, she laments the show's increasingly negative and undervalued legacy as a result of "the assumption that anything stylized . . . or funny, or feminine, or explicit about sex rather than violence, or made collaboratively . . . must be inferior."[5] Nussbaum compares the fading legacy of the series to the ascendancy of masculine focused series—both in front of and behind the camera—to the upper stratum of the television hierarchy.

The series focuses on four professional women living, working, loving, and especially having sex in Manhattan. The antihero protagonist, Carrie Bradshaw (Sarah Jessica Parker), is a columnist who writes about the trials and tribulations of adult love around the turn of the new millennium. And the fodder for her insights is derived not only from her own romantic entanglements but also from those of her three closest friends: public relations expert Samantha Jones, lawyer Miranda Hobbes, and gallery manager Charlotte York. In addition to providing striking modern female archetypes, *Sex and the City* also offers a rich visual spectacle. Instead of special effects and masterful action sequences, the camera lingers on enviable fashion, food, drinks, and the endless variety of settings offered by the city to which the series pays continuous homage.

It is the highly gendered nature of such spectacles that both earned the series its place in the cultural pantheon and tarnished its legacy. The two *Sex and the City* movies focus largely on that spectacle and the female fantasies it engenders rather than the narrative complexity and dynamic characters that gave the series weight and dimension. The franchise became a parody of itself, causing more recent critics such as television scholar Brett Martin to summarily dismiss the show as "a tourism campaign for a post-Rudolph Giuliani, de-ethnicized Gotham awash in money," and to slight its characters as "types as familiar as those in 'The Golden Girls': the Slut, the Prude, the Career Woman, the Heroine."[6] Despite the parallel cultural significance and popularity of *Sex and the City* and the critical darling, *The Sopranos*, which also aired on HBO during the same time period, Martin glorifies the "creative revolution" of a dramatic series focused on the intricacies of American masculinity, while relegating *Sex and the City* to the bargain bin of memory.

Still, despite the lack of critical kindness, the show has persisted and persevered in ways that demand a reconsideration of its influence and role in the "Third Golden Age of Narrative Television," as Martin has termed it, that it helped usher in.[7] Rather than demanding a renewed interest in its cultural relevance, however, this chapter considers its formal construction as a way of reviewing the series and arguing for its place as one of the most influential sitcoms of all time. Perhaps one reason why it has been so easy to write off the show and its legacy is the insistent scholarly focus on its cultural cache, which has always been largely gendered and somewhat ephemeral. Like any series, such affective resonance is doomed to fade unless the formal structure of the series can support a deeper viewing engagement that transcends temporal specificity. So rather than rehashing what the series is about, this chapter will consider how it makes meaning through a narrative analysis. This transition is in line with more recent television scholarship, which analyzes television by way of a reading of its medium-specific techniques.

Television scholar Jason Mittell terms this the "poetics" of television and argues that the significance and influence of a show depends on its narrative complexity.[8] In a similar vein, although Martin slights the series, he does concede that *Sex and the City* "helped pave the way for the revolution by establishing HBO as a destination for distinctive original programming" by acknowledging that it was part of a critical group of sitcoms that pushed "the definition of what had been previously thought possible on the medium [of television]—even if those boundaries had, by the nature of comedy, been easier to push."[9] Martin suggests that, although this complexity deserves recognition, it is also easier to achieve in sitcoms because the rules of the genre are different. As scholars such Brett Mills make clear, however, sitcoms have incredibly rigid conventions: "to be *too* different is to cease to be a sitcom at all."[10] *Seinfeld* has been critically hailed precisely because it was able to produce narrative complexity within those rigid conventions. *Sex and the City* wasn't bound by many of the same conventions as broadcast sitcoms because it aired, commercial free, on a premium subscription channel, so the challenge was reversed: to make the series recognizable as a sitcom while retaining the quality production on which HBO had built its brand and setting it apart as offering a unique and authoritative take on the sitcom. It navigated this challenge by developing a unique narrative structure that both adheres to and reflexively engages those norms and their transgression.

In this chapter, I argue that *Sex and the City* pioneers a sophisticated reflexive narrative by continuously calling attention to the constructed and performative nature of television through moments of deconstruction of Carrie's identity within the diegesis of the series. Through the voice-over narration of Carrie's column, the series develops an intimate, autobiographical, and often unreliable framing that encourages active forms of engagement.

DECONSTRUCTING CARRIE

One of the elements of complex television, as Jason Mittell notes, is a form of narrative sophistication that reveals—and revels in—television as a production by foregrounding an "operational aesthetic" marked by a high degree of self-consciousness and explicit reflexivity.[11] Rather than relying on elaborate visual special effects, the operational aesthetic enthralls through the creation of a narrative spectacle that reminds viewers that their enjoyment of a series is predicated on both the narrative world of the series, its diegesis, and the relationship between that world and its status as a produced cultural discourse that exists beyond the strict run time, its extradiegetic nature. Mittell defines this as "a formally aware baroque quality in which we watch the process of narration as a machine rather than engaging its diegesis."[12] This operational aesthetic allows viewers to engage in a form of double watching in which one is absorbed by the world within the show while appreciating how that effect is made possible by the construction of the show. In the case of *Sex and the City*, this operational aesthetic is achieved diegetically by humorously reminding viewers that "Carrie Bradshaw" is a performative construction that blurs the boundaries between fiction and reality.

One of the most consistent ways in which the show achieves this is through the long-running gag of the ad for Carrie's "Sex and the City" column displayed on the side of a New York City bus. "Carrie Bradshaw knows good sex*"—the ad intimates to passengers, pedestrians, and the camera in the title credits for *Sex and the City*. The horizontal billboard spans nearly the length of the city bus, and stretched out across this distance is an oversized photograph of Carrie, holding up her head with one hand as if returning the gaze of a lover. In the photograph Carrie wears "the naked dress," so named because its pale nude tones mirror the tones of her skin, creating the illusion of nudity as she gazes out at her viewer from a crumpled bed. The postcoital connotation is direct and deliberate: the setting, her clothes, her slightly mussed hair, and beckoning gaze all reinforce the idea that Carrie Bradshaw not just knows but also experiences good sex. Despite this consistency, the tagline reminds us that the picture is not fully cohesive. There is an asterisk at the end of the tagline that completes the statement at the bottom of the photo. Beneath Carrie's artfully angled legs—"*and isn't afraid to ask"—the addendum whispers to us. This unusual addition suggests both that Carrie isn't afraid to ask *for* good sex, and that she isn't afraid to ask *about* good sex. The blurring of the line between her role experiencing sex and writing about sex is deliberately separated by a full-frontal portrait of Carrie staring out at the viewer of the bus, and by extension, the viewer on the other side of the television screen. Carrie at one point describes herself as a "sexual anthropologist," digging and uncovering the truth about the sex lives of professional 30-something Gothamites. Her weekly column, as the asterisk suggests, revels in the details of the sex lives of her friends and acquaintances. But as her authorial presence and the overtly autobiographical rhetoric of the photograph strongly asserts Carrie also possesses this knowledge through direct experience.

Other scholars such as Kim Akass and Janet McCabe have similarly read this moment in the series as one of heightened reflexivity that calls the viewer's attention to the humor and doubling of reality and social construction, but they have neglected to attend to the significance of the text and textual production within the series.[13] This dynamic is significant, as the ad on the side of the bus suggests, because the series is essentially about experience and interlocution as it informs Carrie's column. The ad on the bus doesn't just call attention to Carrie as both an image and a reality—although it certainly does that, too—it asserts that Carrie's public image afforded by her role as a writer continually disrupts and challenges Carrie's self-construction.

The title credits end with the bus splashing water on a blissfully unaware Carrie as she is walking through the city, who then gazes about her in dismay. In this final humorous moment, Carrie Bradshaw the image reminds Carrie Bradshaw the person—and viewers—that Carrie's image literally circulates throughout the city as a constructed and often unruly image that exceeds the author's control.

The idea that Carrie Bradshaw is a constructed character and that such a construction is both collaboratively authored and problematic is highlighted in the first season episode that focuses on how the infamous bus photo was created. In "Secret Sex," the episode opens with the photo shoot that produces the photograph that ends up on the side of the bus: "Two weeks ago I had my picture taken," Carrie's voice-over informs us as the various scenes of a busy photo set are interrupted by a series of quick takes in which the short cuts are synchronized with the sound of a shutter snapping.[14] The quick black shots suggest a camera aperture opening and closing as we see Carrie during a variety of poses for the photo shoot. "It was the promotional photo for my column, scheduled to run on the side of a bus," Carrie informs the viewer in voice-over, calling attention to the title sequence that had just ended. Although Carrie outwardly seems to be enjoying the photo shoot, she tells viewers, "I had misgivings, which were somewhat mollified when they told me I could keep the dress." The highly sexualized nature of the photo shoot causes Carrie to question whether or not her image as an author will contradict her reality as an author, presenting her with a momentary moral dilemma that is quickly solved by the promise of free fashion. This short, tossed-off line is quite revealing of Carrie's character as well as the larger moral framing of the series. The complexity of sexuality is foregrounded in the photo shoot for Carrie's bus ad. In the opening scene, Carrie both owns her sexuality and sometimes laughingly shies away from it as when she breaks into a goofy grin and covers her face. This simple gesture, juxtaposed with the quick shots of her confidently displaying her sexuality for the photo shoot complicate any easy summary of her sexuality. She is both confident and coy; the quickly cut scenes bring these two sides of her personality into approximation.

The final shot of the scene zooms in on Carrie as she looks laughingly off camera toward, presumably, the photographer. After a brief laugh, she slides her hand across her throat in the gesture for "cut," suggesting not only that the photo shoot is over but also that she has a great deal of agency within the shoot—she is authoring her own image by controlling the conditions of its production. So while the overt sensuality of the shoot could suggest that Carrie is simply objectified by her status as a single, sexually desirable woman, her moments of humorous disruption, and her final gesture of ending the shoot also demonstrate that she understands this performative construction and takes an active role in its production. And by revealing the process by which the central image of the title credits is created, the series connects the diegetic and extradiegetic levels of the series.

This playful narrative engagement with engaged viewing extends further into the photo shoot scene. In addition to the iconic bus ad image, the scene includes quick shots of Carrie posing nearly nude on a stool with a black laptop open in front of her, seemingly for just another potential shot for the marketing campaign for her column. This image is significant, however, because this exact shot is the photo used as the publicity still for the series before its release and during its first season. Any viewer familiar with the ad for the series is rewarded with the double level of engagement the brief shot provides. That moment of recognition also provides a narrative disruption that deconstructs the neat division between the world of the series and a recognition of the series as a constructed world.

Photography often serves this blurring function within the series, suggesting that the image of Carrie Bradshaw often hilariously challenges her authority as an author; although her words and voice dominate the narrative frame of the series, images of Carrie within the series show how precarious that control really is. Later in the "Secret Sex" episode, Carrie decides to throw a celebration for her bus ad by meeting her friends on Fifth Avenue to watch the first bus with her ad drive by. This public revelation of the definitional image of Carrie—the very image that graces every title credit for the length of the series and thus reminds viewers again and again of this juxtaposition—is anticipated as a moment of triumph for Carrie. After flaunting the rules and sleeping with a man she refers to as "Mr. Big" on their first date earlier in the episode, she expects that witnessing her mirror image as a powerful, sexual woman will erase the feeling that she has been made less powerful by succumbing to her desires. But at the moment when the bus finally rolls by, everyone gasps when they first see the image; a giant penis has been drawn in white near Carrie's mouth on the photograph, insinuating that she is about to perform oral sex. Rather than revealing an empowered woman, the satirical graffiti instead suggests that Carrie has been revealed as a sexually promiscuous woman and thus must be mocked. No one says anything in the moment, and Carrie covers her mouth and looks down in embarrassment, much as she did at moments in the photo shoot. In a voice-over she correlates her behavior in the bedroom with a kind of public shaming that will circulate throughout the city: "I wore the dress, I slept with him too soon, and now I'm on a Fifth Avenue bus with a penis on my head."

Carrie believes the graffiti is some sort of karmic retribution for flaunting sexual norms. The ad continues to play this role throughout the series, a way to remind the viewers that Carrie's constructed public image often differs greatly from the more honest and intimate view that viewers are granted. In the season four episode titled "Ring a Ding Ding," Carrie decides to take the bus to save money, having just been turned down for a home loan because she wasn't "a desirable candidate," as the loan officer gently tells her.[15] As the bus arrives, it reveals the infamous ad of Carrie, prompting a woman waiting next to her to ask, "Why do you need to take the bus if you're on the bus?" highlighting the irony that Carrie is both financially irresponsible and a minor celebrity.

In addition to the persistence of the troubling bus ad, photographs of Carrie continue to disrupt the integrity of her public and private identity. In "They Shoot Single People, Don't They?" Carrie is thrilled to be photographed for a *New York* magazine piece on the fabulous single life. When Carrie oversleeps after a long night of partying, she arrives late and hungover to the photo shoot. She is rushed onto the set for "test photos" taken before the ministrations of hair and makeup. When the issue is released, Carrie is horrified to see her "test photo" shot on the cover: her hair is stringy and bedraggled, her face looks gaunt and shadowed by dark circles under her eyes, which gaze blankly back at the camera while she holds a cigarette. The title has been changed to "Single and Fabulous?" The punctuation change seems to interrogate Carrie's own self-perception.

This theme continues in the season five episode "Cover Girl" in which Carrie's columns have been turned into a book, a significant plot turn because the series itself is based on Candace Bushnell's "Sex and the City" columns that were eventually turned into a book of the same name.[16] This move again blurs the diegetic and extradiegetic worlds of the series, again for comic effect. When she is presented with the cover art for the book, Carrie gasps in horror and surprise. The photo-collaged image of Carrie presents her nude, hailing a cab on the city's streets. The image recalls both the overt sexuality of her bus ad and the startling vulnerability of her *New York* magazine cover. Carrie eventually convinces the editors to allow her to create a cover that features a single and less sexualized photograph—but not without difficulty. Carrie fights with Samantha over what outfit she should wear for the shoot; she questions the public relations expert's choice of revealing lingerie in favor of a more polished and fully clothed look in keeping with her everyday attire. Although Samantha correctly suggests that public images of Carrie are successful because they, like her column, are so sexualized, Carrie resists this expert advice in favor of an image of her own creation that challenges such as easy assumption.

These moments of conflict and miscommunication surrounding the production of Carrie's public image highlight the tension between Carrie's agency as an author and her lack of agency as a figure. And because this tension always involves information or images from the extradiegetic levels of the series, they continuously disrupt the cohesive diegesis of the series. Like the question mark at the end of the *New York* magazine title, the production of Carrie's public image through photography reminds viewers that such constructions are always performative and often unreliable. Like the questions with which Carrie always ends her weekly column, these moments of humorous disruption seem to ask: "Carrie Bradshaw?"

"WHAT'S SEX GOT TO DO WITH IT?"

Despite the unruly circulation of Carrie's public image, one constant of the series is her narrative authority—conveyed through the use of voice-over—which presents itself as a narration of Carrie's weekly column. Television scholar Stefanie Hoth has explored the importance of voice-over as a narrative strategy in female-focused television series, but what makes the voice-over distinctive in *Sex and the City* is that its authority is uncertain because of Carrie's reliance on the interrogative mode.[17] The narrative follows a distinct pattern in which a difficult scenario is introduced, typically surrounding mores of sex and love, and transitions into a scene of Carrie alone in her apartment, reflecting on the quandary the opening scenes present. This scene of reflection ends with a close-up of Carrie's laptop screen as she frames that challenge as a question that will be attended to but not necessarily answered over the course of the episode. This structure allows for a multiplicity of perspectives as differing and sometimes conflicting answers are offered by the three other primary characters. Question such as, "Twenty-something women, friend or foe?" and "Are men just women with balls?" summarize the theme for each episode in a pithy query. This structure provides both hallmark sitcom setups but also a showcase for Carrie's keen social insight and quick wit by homing in on the key issue. It also calls attention again to the text of the infamous bus ad for Carrie's column, which aligns her narrative authority in her fearless ability to ask important questions about love and sex.

Cultural theorist Esther Fritsch argues that Carrie's writing is little more than gossip but that the show uses this narrative structure presents gossip as "a way of knowing" that displaces Carrie's authority as sole arbiter of knowledge while underscoring the authenticity of the stories she recounts for viewers.[18] By relating details of events that she could not possibly have witnessed, Carrie's narration becomes a faithful retelling for the viewer. And yet she doesn't just document these events, she shapes them into a larger connected narrative by way of her crystallizing questions. The use of the question, however, doesn't always promise an answer; by embracing both the repetitive formula of posing the question and foreclosing any possibility of a final answer, the series presents an open-ended mode of narration that makes room for the viewer. This intimate engagement with the narration is extended in two different ways: through the use of direct address early in the series and through the sustained visual setup of Carrie's moments of writing.

As Jason Mittell explains, complex television calls attention to the narrative norms of television by upending them: "Complex narration often breaks the fourth wall, whether through visually represented direct address . . . or more ambiguous voice-over that blurs the line between diegetic and nondiegetic . . . calling attention to its own breaking of convention."[19] Mittell's argument is not that such techniques equate to complex television because they are unique but because they call the viewer's attention to the narrative structures that make the illusion of television possible. Such reflexivity allows a television series to layer diegetic and nondiegetic narratives, creating a split yet shared understanding of the show's complex modes of making meaning. *Sex and the City* uses these two devices, breaking the fourth wall and the voice-over, in a manner similar to other sitcoms, but it also establishes unique conventions that set it apart.

In sitcoms such as *The Office* and *Parks and Recreation*, characters break the "fourth wall" by speaking directly into the camera and thus directly to the viewer, disrupting the narrative illusion that the characters are being observed without their knowledge. When the fourth wall is intact, viewers occupy an omniscient position: all-seeing and all-knowing but without being seen or being known in return. When the fourth wall is breached, the viewer becomes directly involved in the narrative flow of the show, calling attention to the fictional wholeness television presents: the position of the camera in the fourth wall allows viewers to observe situations to which they would never otherwise be privy. By calling attention to the camera's presence by addressing it directly, the diegetic and nondiegetic constructs of the show collide, collapsing the boundary between the show's narrative world and the world of production and making visible the performative relationship the characters bear to the camera. In *The Office*, for example, this device was narratively framed by the premise that the series was the result of a years-long documentary by an unseen crew, a premise itself disrupted in the ninth season episode "Customer Loyalty," when one of the crew members breached the fourth wall in reverse to come to Pam's aid.[20]

In *Sex and the City*, the narrative construct is similar but used primarily to allow for a polyvocality that could potentially be foreclosed by the dominance of the voice-over. Samantha, Charlotte, and Miranda all play a large role in providing alternative perspectives, but the breach of the fourth wall allows minor characters such as the "Modelizer" in season one to speak directly to the camera, adding dimension and shape to that episode's diegesis. During the first and part of the second season, after Carrie would ask that week's burning question via voice-over, the following scene would feature short shots of other characters, some known and some unknown, answering Carrie's question from their own perspectives.

Carrie herself also breaches the fourth wall, but often to complicate rather than answer driving questions. In "Secret Sex," the central plot line revolves around Carrie's first date with Mr. Big and her debate about whether or not she should sleep with him. This question spools out to involve the three other primary characters—Miranda, Samantha, and Charlotte—who debate what the "rules" are for when you can sleep with a man. As Carrie dashes out of the apartment wearing the naked dress from the photo shoot, she breaks the fourth wall and speaks directly to the camera to confess, a technique the show employs heavily throughout the first season but eventually phases out. Inside the apartment, Carrie tells her friends that she's only going to dinner and that she's not going to have sex with Mr. Big. But after leaving her apartment, in the hallway she looks directly into the camera and states, "The truth is, I was dying to sleep with him. But isn't delayed gratification the definition of maturity?" She raises one eyebrow, cocks her head and smirks into the camera before walking off toward her date. This quick scene rehearses Carrie's complex moral logic from the photo shoot. Wearing the same dress and using the same facial features, Carrie's camera confessional reveals that even though she understands and tries to obey the strong social mores that dictate women's public behavior, she is equally in tune with her desires—for beautiful clothes, for sex, for validation. And because the confession ends with a question mark, this scene also recalls the *New York* magazine cover—"Single and Fabulous?"—as well as the tagline from her bus ad—"Carrie Bradshaw knows good sex* . . . * and isn't afraid to ask." This recurring ambiguity brings into juxtaposition Carrie's position as an authority on social norms and her challenges to those norms through her role as interlocutor. By asking about others and about the validity of norms such as maturity and delayed gratification, she exists in a perpetual cycle of self-interlocution—highlighted by the show's narrative structure—where her knowledge is either reaffirmed or challenged by her insatiable desire to question that knowledge, crafting her not as a stable archetypal female character but as a complicated and changeable heroine.

Although the direct address was phased out by the end of the second season, Carrie's use of questions continues in her columns and, by extension, her voice-over, which is framed as the narration of her weekly column. Indeed, one of the touchstone scenes of the series presents Carrie alone in her bedroom with her laptop, typing out the words that she's simultaneously reading aloud. In these scenes, Carrie is often in more casual or intimate clothing than she wears on the street, and she is often smoking, suggesting an intimate and relaxed atmosphere in which the viewer is allowed to see the process of her textual production.

Strikingly, these scenes are more revealing and intimate than any scene of Carrie engaged in sex. Her sex scenes are a series of short, quick suggestive shots that cut rapidly from Carrie's face to illustrative shots of feet sticking out from sheets or hands clasped on a headboard. These are scenes that visually suggest intimacy while revealing nothing specific about the act itself. Carrie's scenes of writing, on the other hand, linger on each moment of the creation process. The scenes typically begin with long pan-in shots that take the viewer from a distant framing to a tight close-up of

Carrie's face, which is often comically contorted or elegantly wistful as she either grimaces at her laptop screen or gazes into the distance, searching for the very words that are being narrated in her own voice. These visual cues echo the uncertainty revealed in the final shot of these scenes: the close-up of Carrie's laptop screen as she types out the framing question. Carrie is always alone when she writes and often breaks away from friends and lovers, claiming she has a deadline, and it is only the viewer who shares these vulnerable and productive moments with her. And although the series phased out the direct address to the camera, in many ways this premise is retained in spirit by allowing the viewer to witness over and over again the process of production by which the series is narrated.

Critics such as Ashli Dykes have analyzed the connection between the voice-over and female dialogue, but her analysis doesn't engage the construct of the voice-over as a narration of Carrie's column, a fact to which the show continually calls attention.[21] On the other hand, while Jonathan Bignell makes the connection between the textual production foregrounded in the series and the textual production of feminine discourse in women's magazines, his analysis doesn't account for the fact that Carrie's text is primarily autobiographical and observational and thus highly reflexive, a fact foregrounded by her interrogative mode.[22] These two overlooked factors: the significance of the voice-over as narration, and the importance of that narrative as highly reflexive are important because they foreground the operational aesthetic of the series. In other words, they repeatedly call the viewer's attention to the fact that the show is a constructed narrative that reflects on its process of creation. In its celebration of asking the question rather than answering it, *Sex and the City* attempts to multiply rather than foreclose its own narrative possibilities. And by creating a direct intimacy between the creation of the question and the act of viewing, the series suggests that any real answers must be provided by viewers themselves.

CONCLUSION

A careful close reading of the show's formal complexity is important for the series and perhaps overdue because it attends to the very technique by which it makes meaning: narration. The consistent use of voice-over reminds viewers at every moment that Carrie makes sense of her world and makes it public through the process of narration. The show is essentially a retelling of her column, and through that retelling we are reminded that the series does not offer an unimpeded view into the diegetic world; it is instead mediated and shaped at every moment by Carrie's narrative voice. The significance, and unreliability of this mediation is foregrounded by the diegetic creation of Carrie's photograph, which always causes moments of heightened awareness of the performative construction of Carrie as a character and by extension the construction of the series itself as a fictional world. Such a framing reminds us that narration is both the function of meaning making within a diegetic world and the externally imposed structure of a series that is the result of a process of selecting, shaping, and editing. As columnist and character, author and subject of photographs, interlocutor and confessant, Carrie is thus both an internal narrator and an external author of the world she gives us access to. The series relies on the disruption of these roles as the source of some of the show's most consistent humor, as in recurrent references to Carrie's ill-fated bus ad: the series continually reminds us that her authoritative role as a narrator is unstable and deconstructable. The show's complexity lies in its ability to establish and disrupt its own narrative norms, rewarding a form of engaged viewing that has become the contemporary hallmark of significant television. Although the legacy of the series may still include a question mark, it is the acceptance of that question mark as a fundamental premise of the series that erases any doubt of its importance and influence.

NOTES

1. Ron Simon, *"Sex and the City,"* in *The Essential HBO Reader,* edited by Jeffrey P. Jones and Gary R. Edgerton (Lexington: University Press of Kentucky, 2008), 194.

2. Bruce Fretts and Matt Roush, *"TV Guide Magazine's* 60 Best Series of All Time,"* *TV Guide,* December 23 (2013), http://www.tvguide.com/news/tv-guide -magazine-60-best-series-1074962/.

3. Monika Bartyzel, "Girls on Film: The Forgotten Legacy of *Sex and the City,"* *The Week,* February 21, 2014, http://theweek.com/articles/450525/girls-film -forgotten-legacy-sex-city.

4. Tanya Gold, "Sorry Sisters, but I Hate *Sex and the City,"* *The Telegraph,* May 21 (2010), http://www.telegraph.co.uk/culture/film/7746119/Sorry-sisters -but-I-hate-Sex-and-the-City.html.

5. Emily Nussbaum, "Difficult Women: How *Sex and the City* Lost Its Good Name," *The New Yorker,* July 29, 2013, http://www.newyorker.com/magazine /2013/07/29/difficult-women.

6. Brett Martin, *Difficult Men: Behind the Scenes of a Creative Revolution* (New York: Penguin, 2013), 58.

7. Ibid., 8.

8. Jason Mittell, *Complex TV: The Poetics of Contemporary Television Storytelling* (New York: New York University Press, 2015), 18–19.

9. Ibid., 12–13.

10. Brett Mills, *The Sitcom* (Edinburgh: Edinburgh University Press, 2009), 55

11. Mittell, op. cit., 42–43.

12. Ibid., 44.

13. Kim Akass and Janet McCabe, "Ms. Parker and the Vicious Circle: Female Narrative and Humor in *Sex and the City*," in *Reading Sex and the City*, edited by Kim Akass and Janet McCabe (London: I. B. Tauris, 2004), 177–198.

14. *Sex and the City*, "Secret Sex." Written by Darren Star, directed by Michael Fields. HBO, July 12 1998.

15. *Sex and the City*, "Ring a Ding Ding." Directed by Alan Taylor, written by Amy B. Harris. HBO, January 27, 2002.

16. *Sex and the City*, "Cover Girl." Directed by John Coles, written by Michael Patrick King and Judy Toll. HBO, August 11 2002.

17. Stefanie Hoth, "The Female Voice in Sex and the City and Desperate Housewives: Voice-Over Narration in Contemporary American Television Series," in *Gendered (re)vision: Constructions of Gender in Audiovisual Media*, edited by Marion Gymrich, Kathrin Ruhl, and Klaus Scheunemann (Gottingen, Germany: Bonn University Press, 2010), 79–102.

18. Esther Fritsch, "Serial Gossip as Theme and Narrative Strategy in *Sex and the City*," in *Narrative Strategy in Television Series*, edited by Gaby Allrath and Marion Gymnich (London: Palgrave Macmillan, 2005), 162–164.

19. Mittell, op. cit., 49.

20. *The Office*, "Customer Loyalty." Directed by Kelly Cantley, written by Jonathan Green and Gabe Miller. NBC, January 24, 2013.

21. Ashli L. Dykes, "'And I Started Wondering . . .': Voiceover and Conversation in *Sex and the City*." *Studies in Popular Culture*, 34(1) (2011), 49–66.

22. Jonathan Bignell, "Sex, Confession and Witness," in *Reading Sex and the City*, edited by Kim Akass and Janet McCabe (London: I. B. Tauris, 2004), 161–176.

BIBLIOGRAPHY

Akass, Kim, and Janet McCabe. "Ms. Parker and the Vicious Circle: Female Narrative and Humor in *Sex and the City*." Pp. 177–198 in *Reading Sex and the City*, edited by Kim Akass and Janet McCabe. London: I. B. Tauris, 2004.

Bartyzel, Monika. "Girls on Film: The Forgotten Legacy of *Sex and the City*." *The Week*, February 21, 2014, http://theweek.com/articles/450525/girls-film -forgotten-legacy-sex-city.

Bignell, Jonathan. "Sex, Confession and Witness." Pp. 161–176 in *Reading Sex and the City*, edited by Kim Akass and Janet McCabe. London: I. B. Tauris, 2004.

Dykes, Ashli L. "'And I Started Wondering . . .': Voiceover and Conversation in *Sex and the City*." *Studies in Popular Culture*, 34(1) (2011), 49–66.

Fretts, Bruce, and Matt Roush. "*TV Guide Magazine's* 60 Best Series of All Time." *TV Guide*, December 23, 2013. http://www.tvguide.com/news/tv-guide -magazine-60-best-series-1074962/.

Fritsch, Esther. "Serial Gossip as Theme and Narrative Strategy in *Sex and the City*." Pp. 153–167 in *Narrative Strategy in Television Series*, edited by Gaby Allrath and Marion Gymnich. London: Palgrave Macmillan, 2005.

Gold, Tanya. "Sorry Sisters, but I Hate *Sex and the City*." *The Telegraph*, May 21, 2010, http://www.telegraph.co.uk/culture/film/7746119/Sorry-sisters-but-I -hate-Sex-and-the-City.html.

Hoth, Stefanie. "The Female Voice in Sex and the City and Desperate Housewives: Voice-Over Narration in Contemporary American Television Series." Pp. 79–104 in *Gendered (Re)visions: Constructions of Gender in Audiovisual Media*, edited by Marion Gymrich, Kathrin Ruhl, and Klaus Scheunemann. Gottingen, Germany: Bonn University Press, 2010.

Martin, Brett. *Difficult Men: Behind the Scenes of a Creative Revolution*. New York: Penguin, 2013.

Mills, Brett. *The Sitcom*. Edinburgh: Edinburgh University Press, 2009.

Mittell, Jason. *Complex TV: The Poetics of Contemporary Television Storytelling*. New York: New York University Press, 2015.

Nussbaum, Emily. "Difficult Women: How *Sex and the City* Lost Its Good Name." *The New Yorker*, July 29, 2013, http://www.newyorker.com/magazine/2013 /07/29/difficult-women.

Simon, Ron. "*Sex and the City*." In *The Essential HBO Reader*, edited by Jeffrey P. Jones and Gary R. Edgerton. Lexington: University Press of Kentucky, 2008.

22

The Office: Broadcast Television in the Digital Era

Leah Shafer

A knowing look into the camera lens, an extradiegetic interview, an embarrassed pause as a character considers what to say next with the camera's presence in mind— these are rare occurrences in the world of sitcoms but common practice in the world of The Office *(2005–2013). Notably,* The Office *popularized the single camera, documentary-style format and therefore shifted the landscape of millennial television. In "The Office: Broadcast Television in the Digital Era," Leah Shafer situates* The Office *within the technologies and practices of the digital era, emphasizing the show's meta-awareness, relationship to surveillance, and challenge to "authenticity" as reflections of a uniquely 21st century shift in the television industry more broadly.*

According to hotel-review Web site tripadvisor.com, Schrute Farms is a popular vacation destination. More than 1,000 reviews have been written about the rustic bed and breakfast, with commentary about the smell of manure, the creepy hosts, and available activities such as butter churning and grave digging ("We dug until we saw hooves").[1] Though Schrute Farms has garnered more reviews than "many major Manhattan hotels," a blurb at the top of the page notes that "this fictional place doesn't really exist."

The listing for Schrute Farms was initiated by the writing staff of the NBC sitcom *The Office* as an extension of a plot in the episode "Money" in the show's fourth season. The beet farm B&B, of course, is the home of

Dwight Schrute, the prickly oddball who serves as the catalyst for many of the program's wackiest story lines. In an interview, *The Office*'s show-runner Paul Lieberstein said, "We thought it would be fun [to set up the fictional site], but then we didn't think about it anymore."[2] The show's fans, however, did not stop thinking about it and have continued to write fictional reviews of the fictional B&B long after the series' final episode. Fan enthusiasm for keeping the joke running attests not only to their ongoing investment in the NBC sitcom but also to the ways in which *The Office* universe has transcended conventional sitcom spaces and practices, making it an example of the ways TV exhibition, style, and fan practices have shifted in the digital era. In this chapter, I situate *The Office* within the rapidly changing landscape of television in the first decade of the 21st century.

The Office tells the story of a group of coworkers at the Scranton, Pennsylvania, branch of a small paper company, Dunder Mifflin. This office has been selected to be the subject of a documentary, so each episode is shot as if by a documentary crew. The show's distinctive look features candid, surveillance-style cameras moving among office coworkers. These sequences are intercut with "talking head" interviews in which the characters comment on the action in the other scenes. Hearing directly from the characters makes the idiosyncratic characters the generative force of the show's comedy, which is observational and character based. Dunder Mifflin's employees look like a random sampling of middle Americans, and much is made on the show of the company's location in an anonymous office park in the depressed Rust Belt town. Their non-Hollywood looks and diverse ages, races, genders, sexualities, and personalities are showcased by the talking head interviews as well as the intimacy and ideological lures of the show's single-camera visual language.

The distinctive mockumentary style of *The Office* developed as a result of labor, time and cost-saving decisions made by its cocreators, Stephen Merchant and Ricky Gervais. Gervais developed a buffoon character "more or less to entertain people down the pub," and Merchant's enthusiasm for the character led the two to develop a 20-minute short film for BBC Television that featured Gervais's character named David Brent as a blunt, blustery, and inappropriate paper company manager.[3] The short was filmed in a real office where Gervais had once worked. Because Merchant and Gervais had little time and tiny budget to create the short, their adoption of the documentary style was utterly pragmatic. As Merchant recalls,

> We only had a camera crew on the day, so we decided to do it that way because it would forgive any kind of dodgy lighting or noise or clunks, and just meant we could do it a lot quicker. We also realised that if we interviewed the character we could get more stuff in the can without lots of lengthy set-ups.[4]

When the BBC decided to make a pilot of the program, Merchant and Gervais insisted that the documentary style be central to the program because, to their minds, much of the show's humor came from observing people responding when they know they're on camera. The banality of the situation and the set would be undercut by this pervasive self-awareness and would open space for the awkward but ultimately devastating humor of the everyday that is a program hallmark.

The show was a sleeper hit in the United Kingdom. Merchant and Gervais created the memorable office staff's characters and plots by drawing inspiration from popular American situation comedies of the 1990s (such as *Seinfeld* and *Friends*), while pushing the envelope on those conventions and plotlines by staging them as a character-driven mockumentary. This hybrid approach resulted in a situation comedy that was familiar enough to draw in audiences but different enough to create an entirely new look and feel for the form. In 2005, Greg Daniels, who built a career working on *The Simpsons* and *King of the Hill*, decided to adapt the program for U.S. audiences. Daniels's plan was to maintain the look of the UK series as well as the basic characters and style while shifting references and cultural attitudes to those typical of middle America. The American show was popular with critics (and fans of the UK version) during its initial season, but not until season two did the show start to become a U.S. phenomenon after the writers and producers further Americanized the program by foregrounding the Jim and Pam romance and smoothing some of Michael Scott's rough edges.

The first few moments of the show's U.S. credit sequence set the scene for the program's visual and narrative obsessions and strategies. It can be read as a capsule history of the decline of American industry; for the descent of paper as a crucial technology is central to the program's pathos. It can also be read as a television-friendly contextualization of the program's relationship to the history of the American situation comedy. In the opening shot of the sequence, we see a camera zoom out from a 19th-century paper mill, then we're shown a visibly cold and gray street in downtown Scranton, then the camera rolls past a sign saying "Scranton Welcomes You: Embracing Our People, Our Traditions, Our Future." The following shot, which begins occluded by a tree and fence, tracks to the left to reveal the Dunder Mifflin loading dock sign. Though viewers are thus welcomed, they are quickly rebuffed by two visual obstructions to the Dunder Mifflin building. We can see in the opening sequence gestures toward the credit sequences of significant American situation comedies like *Maude* or *The Jeffersons* with their literally forward-moving introductions to the location of the story and emphatic indexical representation of location as central to character and story line. Where in *The Jeffersons*, for example, the camera draws the viewer from the impoverished inner city to a distinctive upper class high rise, the sequence in *The Office* locates the viewer within a depressed and obstructed postindustrial landscape and dreary workspace crammed with banal objects and furnishings.[5] We can see a reflection of the program's primary comic strategies in this pattern of invitation and rejection, dynamism and banality. This shifting appears throughout the program, particularly in the frequent movement between representational and presentational moments forged by the frequent talking head interviews. The tension between lure and rebuff is central to the show's comic tension and its ability to forge comic moments through metacommentary. The theme music, however, serves as a counterpoint to the program's affective strategy of keeping its audience ever locked into a push-and-pull relationship to its characters, location, and narrative threads. The song begins simply and adds musical elements at the introduction of each character. It shifts from a simple piano tune to a raucous rock song and back again to the piano tune at the end of the sequence. The undercurrent of affective entertainment suggested by the theme's crescendo also reflects a key strategy used by the show in which sentimentality offers a recurring counterpoint to sardonic meta-awareness.

When the camera moves in to the office, we are introduced to the program's main characters. Each new person is introduced doing his or her job as the camera restlessly moves around the scene in a manner that suggests the use of a Steadicam. Further, each actor's short introductory sequence is intercut with images of everyday office activities such as photocopying and a water cooler bubbling, and those intercut images further reinforce the program's emphasis on the everyday. The show is most explicitly about the interpersonal relationships of the coworkers at Dunder Mifflin, but those relationships are formed by the location and its inherent pathos. The restless dynamism of the camera movement is visually met by the intentionally depressing, gray, cold, and banal images of Scranton, and the montage aesthetic of the sequence's introductions and obstructions is mirrored in the series' mockumentary style and comic structure. Though the program embraces a *verité* style and revels in its ability to make its audience cringe and feel unmoored, it is nevertheless invested in narrative resolution and affective lures.

The series has several major story arcs—Michael's career, Jim and Pam's relationship, Dwight's struggle for power and recognition by Michael, and the effect of the rising and falling economy on the paper company's management and ownership—but the series mostly delights in constructing story lines for its beloved cast of misfits that are deeply absurd and only nearly imaginable as real-life situations. As such, the construction of the identities of the employees is central to understanding the series investments and story lines. Michael Scott, regional manager of Dunder Mifflin Scranton, is abrasive, narcissistic, and absurd. His infantile relationships and sociopathic need for attention underlie the program's initial emphasis on being a show about the claustrophobic horrors of the modern American workplace. Michael's inappropriate behavior repeatedly destabilizes the work environment and catalyzes many of the absurd scenarios that characterize the show's mordant humor. Actor Steve Carrell's deadpan earnestness, narcissism, and cluelessness serve as a foil to the series' overall strategy of offering interviews that gesture toward the other characters' ability to be self-aware. The other characters' reactions to Michael's obtuseness form much of the show's comic energy and social commentary.

The Office features transcendently sharp writing, performances, and direction. Much of the humor on *The Office* is cringe inducing and awkward, but at its core it is affectingly sentimental. It's a particularly American interpretation of the workplace experience, which reflects the neoliberal fantasy that surveillance is a benign consumer feature meant to give us insights into our interpersonal relationships, particularly those with the people who are our bosses. The surveillance-style camera models for the viewer an identificatory impulse that evokes a feeling of freedom and possibility that is not being experienced by the people at Dunder Mifflin. This dynamic allows the series to resist and reframe the brittle relentlessness of the British version for an American audience. *The Office*'s emphasis on the creation of a community of oddballs reflects the affective pleasures of earlier workplace sitcoms (like *Taxi* and *Cheers*), but the mockumentary device, with its talking head confessionals, gives the spectators' sentimental attachments to the characters a veneer of "truthiness" that is ultimately a lure toward normalizing a surveillance state and minimizing the ill effects of that surveillance state's systematic elevation of narcissistic and ineffective bosses to the detriment of the community.[6] As such, the series is brutal but imbued with an urgent (and divisive) sentimentality. This seemingly benign brutality mixes with the series' anarchic energy—both visually and in its more manic broad comedy—to model a new televisual aesthetic that has been widely adopted by broadcast, cable, and premium sitcoms.

In its earliest seasons, the show is primarily focused on situations arising from the staff's attempts to deal with Michael's delusions of grandeur and deeply unsettling lack of professional boundaries. As the series progresses, interpersonal relationships, romances, and internecine squabbles over employment status begin to form significant story lines, especially after the departure of Michael Scott. For the most part, this is a character-driven show that emphasizes its reality look and everyday location to make the most of the mockumentary's reliance on talking head confessionals. It's through these "real" glimpses into the characters who populate the office that we find the show's most urgent truthiness. Michael's closest work associates are Dwight Schrute and Jim Halpert. Dwight, an even more broadly written lampoon than Michael, is a rigidly bizarre ass-kissing rube who delights in irritating and frustrating his colleagues with his iron-clad commitment to his demented version of the rule of law. Jim is a smart, handsome, and disaffected prankster whose contentious relationship with Dwight and unrequited love for receptionist Pam Beasly form major story lines in the series. Pam is sweet, acerbic, and knowing: it's clear from both her central placement in the office work space (the receptionist's desk) and her central place in Jim's heart that she is meant to serve as the emotional core of the show.

The sales staff includes Phyllis, a middle-aged woman who went to high school with Michael Scott; Stanley, a cantankerous middle-aged African American man prone to ignoring Michael's directives; and, later in the series, Andy "The Nard Dog" Bernard, a foppish brownnoser with an Ivy League degree and anger-management issues. The accounting staff is made up of bumbling, overweight, and clownish Kevin; uptight, cat-loving scold Angela; and ironic, fastidious Oscar, who is eventually outed as a gay man. In accounts payable work two of the show's most outrageous characters: the lewd alcoholic Meredith and shady sociopath Creed.[7] The office annex includes a motley band of characters: frustrated jerk Ryan the temp; immature ditz Kelly Kapoor; and Toby, the feckless HR rep. (This particular group happens to be played by *The Office's* writing and production staff members B. J. Novak, Mindy Kaling, and Paul Lieberstein, so their placement in the annex is strategic in keeping them off screen much of the time: it allows them to work their other jobs on the production crew.) They're the emotional center of the show, but neither Pam nor Jim are particularly likable people. Their incessant mockery and pranking of their coworkers is funny but ultimately models a callous, ungenerous, and cruel sensibility. The rest of the staff, played by talented character actors, are several steps away from being loveable. They represent diverse segments of the American population, but their diversity is more frequently played for humiliation than for inclusivity. The show's mockumentary style, with its gestures toward "reality," invites us to enjoy the banality and cruelty visited on this population and to laugh at rather than with them.

The Office's presence on U.S. television from 2005 to 2013 reflects significant material shifts in the television industry during the late 20th and early 21st centuries, chiefly the deregulation of markets, the attendant industrywide embrace of international coproductions and format adaptation, and the transition to digital format with the attendant change in viewer and fan dynamics. The industrial structure of the U.S. television industry shifted significantly in 1995 with the expiration of the FCC's Financial Interest and Syndication Rules (fin-syn). The fin-syn rules had legislated a division between television studios and television networks by prohibiting CBS, NBC, and ABC from owning prime-time TV series aired on their channels. With the expiration of fin-syn came an era of significant mergers, centralization, and technological changes. One effect of these mergers was the increase in network ownership of individual TV properties.

Because networks were now free to capitalize on TV programs beyond using them to gain advertising revenue, there followed a significant rise in the import and export of programs and program formats across national boundaries. The post–network television era, as this moment came to be called, is characterized in part by the transnational flow of program formats.[8] In the transnational flow of *The Office*, we can see examples of this fundamental industrial change. As media scholars have noted, there is a debate about whether this shift signals "cultural or media imperialism on one hand [or] cultural or media globalization on the other."[9] In the importation and exportation of *The Office* we see an example that serves both sides of the debate. The program format, title, style, and basic set of characters from the UK version of *The Office* was imported to the United States, and the U.S. version has been syndicated to more than 80 countries, including, with fitting irony, the United Kingdom. The format for the show has been broadly licensed as well. Nationally specific versions have been produced in France, Germany, Canada, Chile, and Israel, and licenses to create a local version have been sold to Brazil, Russia, and China.

Another significant industrial change to the U.S. television industry that affected the run of *The Office* had its roots in technological change. The transition from analog to digital signals, which was mandated by the Digital Transition and Public Safety Act of 2005, shifted the labor conditions for *The Office*'s writing staff. One effect of this transition, which boosted the wireless broadband spectrum, was an increase in the digital streaming of television programs to devices such as laptops, tablets, and smartphones as well as the practice of "binge viewing" made possible by these new interfaces. *The Office*'s embrace of the affordances of the digital turn is driven by the show's writers, producers, and directors and its massive fan base. In this way, we can read *The Office* as a formative example of the ways that convergence culture reflects the production conditions of postmillennial television. The industrial shift to digital formats created new exhibition spaces for *The Office* content, particularly paratextual content like webisodes, Web sites, and DVD extras. Executive Producer Greg Daniels was keen to explore the possibilities offered by this shift in exhibition practices, so he urged his writing staff to create material that might not be included in the 22-minute network broadcast but could be shared via digital platforms such as Web sites, online video, DVD extras, and so forth. As an article in *The New York Times* noted at the time,

> *The Office* is on the leading edge of a sharp shift in entertainment viewing that was thought to be years away: watching television episodes on a computer screen is now a common activity for millions of consumers. . . . [10]

A related effect of the transition to digital streaming was the 2007–2008 strike by members of the Writers Guild of America (WGA).

At issue in the strike was writers' compensation for content that was exhibited via DVD and through new media formats such as streaming, straight-to-Internet content, Internet downloads, video on demand, and programming for smartphones. In 1985, the WGA had negotiated a residual payment for content that was distributed via VHS tape, but this negotiation did not cover new media distribution. With the rapid rise of new media distribution and exhibition mechanisms, members of the WGA realized that a significant source of income from their work was being withheld from them, so they entered into negotiations with the Alliance of Motion Picture and Television Producers (AMPTP). NBCUniversal, the distributor for *The Office*, is a member of AMPTP.

When these negotiations broke down, WGA members, including the staff of *The Office*, went on strike. In a moment of metacommentary typical of the series' contrarian conceptual pose, the writing and producing staff made an online video to talk about the fact they were not getting paid for the online videos they were making for the series. The video "The Office Is Closed"[11] features the writing and producing staff standing in a picket line and talking about why they're on strike. In the video, coexecutive producer Mike Schur says, "You are watching this on the Internet. A thing that pays us zero dollars." He goes on to contextualize the issue by discussing a series of webisodes that his staff wrote for the NBC Web site. He says, "The whole writing staff wrote them . . . and eight or nine of our series regulars acted in them. And they were all put on NBC dot com and they sold ads . . . and we actually won a daytime Emmy for those webisodes." Mindy Kaling pipes in to amplify the point: "and no one was compensated for it." *The Office*'s significant market share and fan base resulted in more than 1 million viewers watching this video about labor conditions on network television. The strike, which began on November 5, 2007, ended on February 12, 2008. Though the WGA did not feel it was an unqualified success, the writers were able to negotiate for a percentage payment on the gross from digital distribution, a concession that was prescient in its appreciation of the way that television exhibition modes would shift in the 21st century.

A further significant shift in television modes in the emerging digital era is the rise of fan-produced content. The vast resources of Dunderpedia,[12] a fan-produced *Office*-related wiki space, offer an excellent example of the type of transmedia storytelling that is common to the early digital age. Dunderpedia, which has more than 1,000 individual entries, exists because fans of *The Office* were moved to generate content, participate in collaborative online communities, and produce and promote paratextual information about the series. When viewer attention is fragmented by a previously unimaginable wealth of programming options, the development of affinity groups around innovative paratextual extensions helps TV series maintain an audience in the competitive climate of the postnetwork era. The collaborative, do-it-yourself nature of the fan-produced wiki site that attempts to classify and chronicle the dimensions of Dunder Mifflin attests to the way that *The Office* extends its reach beyond the network grid and offers a useful illustration of the shifts in fan behavior typical of the digital era.

The Office's mockumentary format creates a visual language that gives the show great latitude to make metacommentary while delivering conventional workplace situation comedy characters and plots. The first decade of the 21st century saw the rise of so-called reality television, and the visual grammar of that type of programming reflects its status as what Gerald Mast calls "an unstable designation."[13] Mast uses that phrase to refer to the form's "cross-generic" format, its fusion of contrivance and the "serious intent" of the documentary.[14] This combination of truth claim and fiction is destabilizing—it undermines the authority of the documentary style and reframes fictional narrative as a kind of reality. That lack of stability can be seen in the mockumentary's visual language. The visual language of the mockumentary style emphasizes handheld cameras, a single-camera look, the frequent erasure of the fourth wall, and a general restlessness in both camera movement and editing. This style is, of course, a fundamental shift away from the three-camera system and flat lighting style typical of U.S. situation comedies since *I Love Lucy*. Not only does this change mark a shift away from visual conventions that served as industrial and aesthetic cornerstones for almost 50 years, it also marks a shift toward a different conception of the "reality" being portrayed. This reality effect is heightened on *The Office* through its stylistic emphasis on the everyday and its embrace of unconventional casting.

One might say that part of the charm of 20th century situation comedies was their cheerful lack of authenticity: in them we saw colorful spaces that were created specifically to foreground situations and characters and the contrivance of those situations and characters. The reality claims made by the character-driven mockumentary mode are quite different. When we see Michael Scott address us directly, or when we watch the camera quickly pan from a conversation between Dwight and Jim to Pam's amused reaction to that conversation, we are watching a program that associates the camera's eye with the eye of a cameraperson whose work is associated with truth claims. The program's hybrid format and mockumentary style encourages viewers to form affective connections with its ironic depictions of "American banality."[15]

Twenty-first-century viewers would be visually savvy enough to recognize that the visual language of the documentary camera suggests that what is happening on screen is *real*. This emphasis on reality is, of course, a reflection of the era's embrace of reality television. That embrace is itself a reflection of the increase in actual reality of post-9/11 surveillance culture. On *The Office*, this nod to the complex politics of 21st-century living opens a space for satire and irony while retaining a structure that invites viewers to forge emotional connections to its characters and situations.

The Office's mockumentary format also signals its embrace of surveillance camera aesthetics as "the new, most culturally prevalent form of objectified communal belief."[16] On *The Office*, the surveillance look foregrounds its commitment to offering metacommentary on representation. This winking commentary allows *The Office* to adopt an ironic pose and performs a knowing gesture to a knowing audience, and this is extremely pleasurable. The show tells us that it knows we know that Michael Scott is a jackass. That reassurance is intended to draw the audience, to show it's in on the joke. In the absence of a laugh track, this gesture toward the audience's ability to read televisual codes serves an indexical function—it "uses debates about the nature of performance and representation within the media for its comic material."[17] It also reinforces sociopolitical norms that normalize the intrusive culture of self-surveillance and the unsettling rise of truthiness typical of post-9/11 America.

The idea that a group of people would thoroughly acquiesce to the constant presence of a documentary crew in their work and personal lives is a given on *The Office*. When audiences form emotional attachments to the characters on *The Office* or when they laugh knowingly at the awkwardness of the ways that the program violates previous cultural norms about the division between public and private, their affection and laughter tacitly acknowledge and embrace the presence of this ever-present surveillance team.

An illustrative example of this dynamic can be seen in episode one of season two of the series. This short sequence is lyrically evocative of the show's central preoccupation with surveillance used as a comic device. Early in the episode, we see Pam, Kelly, and Phyllis laughing about something written about Michael on the bathroom wall. The sequence begins with a jump cut from a talking head with Michael in his office to a Steadicam shot of the bathroom door filmed through the venetian blinds on the door to the annex. In the sequence, we see Meredith leave the women's room, Dwight enter the women's room, and Phyllis chases Dwight out of the room. As they argue, we see them framed between two walls of windows with blinds. The profusion of doors and windows and blinds through which this brief exchange are seen acts as a literal foregrounding of the camera's ability to open up a space for the viewer within the "reality" of the office. The blinds serve as a visual metaphor: they show viewers that they're looking through a window and what is happening on the other side of that window, and they still manage to suggest that we are not seeing everything we could be seeing. Further, this moment suggests that the characters peopling the space are as keen to hide and to unmask the social and emotional undercurrents of their interpersonal relationships as the cameras that share those relationships with us are. It's also a scene that plays the violation of social norms (spiteful graffiti, invasion of privacy) as fodder for laughter and community.

In this brief sequence, the movement between hiding and revealing is accessible through the visual metaphors of the doors, windows, and blinds as well as the literal movement of the camera across a plane that opens and closes to reveal the action beyond. The following sequence engages this same set of conventions while unpacking a story line that is more conventionally shot and represents one of the program's core narrative arcs: the romance between Jim and Pam. In its first season, *The Office* cleaved more faithfully to the alienating cringe humor of its British predecessor. In an attempt to boost ratings, the second season began to tone down Michael Scott's abrasiveness and foreground more conventional American sitcom conventions: the will-they-or-won't-they story line of Jim and Pam mirrors the Sams and Dianes and Rosses and Rachels familiar to American audiences. As such, this first episode of the second season relies heavily on Jim and Pam for its emotional payoff.

This sequence, which sets up the episode's narrative resolution, employs radically subjective camera movement to indicate to the viewers the connections they should be making between Pam and Jim's story lines. Immediately after the scene when Phyllis confronts Dwight for peeping in the women's bathroom, the camera cuts to a television screen in the conference room. On the screen we see Michael, Jim, Pam, and Roy, Pam's fiancé. The TV is playing a moment from the previous year's Dundie Awards ceremony when Pam was awarded a Dundie for "longest engagement." The sequence also suggests that the program itself is deeply invested in cultivating an affective connection between the viewers and the Jim and Pam romance. As soon as the initial shot is established, the camera zooms rapidly toward the TV screen so that Jim and Pam largely fill the frame. In the recording, we see that both Pam and Jim are upset by Michael's insensitive award. After we see something like a glance exchanged by Jim and Pam, the camera cuts away from the TV screen to Pam's horrified face watching the screen. The camera focuses restively on Pam's face as she registers her mortification, glances toward the camera, and then looks down.

The camera, which has not stopped moving, then pans quickly away from Pam, through the door to focus—blurrily at first—on Jim, who, seemingly unaware of the camera's eye on him, looks deeply upset by this turn of events. Jim then intervenes in Michael's plan to use this same joke at the Dundies, and later in the episode we see that Jim's plan leads to Pam feeling so grateful and happy that she drunkenly kisses Jim. This first kiss between the two becomes the germ of the story arc that sustains the series through its final season. It's also a potent example of the way that conventional sentimentality is manipulated by the mockumentary style's visual codes so it can model for viewers affective identification with characters whose mortifications and manipulations at the hand of an ineffectual narcissist are made to look like freedom.

Borrowing its single-camera mode from the increasingly dominant reality-TV style and its mordant look at middle-class mores from its British counterpart, *The Office* exemplifies crucial shifts in the generic, stylistic, and industrial trends of postmillennial television. It's an adaptation and an international coproduction. It's a cross-generic fusion of mockumentary, romantic comedy, and workplace sitcom. It's an Internet-ready, rapid-fire producer of catchphrases, paratexts, and fan-produced content. *The Office* is broadcast TV's response and antidote to reality television: one of the last great gasps of NBC's "Must See TV." It's a whip-smart, formally rigorous, devastatingly funny sitcom that offers viewers behind-the-scenes staging and awkward silences instead of a laugh track. Its acerbic interpersonal dynamics, fly-on-the-wall observations, and candid confessional interviews mark both a bittersweet return to irony after 9/11 and a cynical and ultimately dangerous cultural acceptance of surveillance culture. It's the sitcom that brought TV into the digital era.

NOTES

1. TripAdvisor, "Schrute Farms," http://www.tripadvisor.com/Hotel_Review -g52842-d730099-Reviews-Schrute_Farms-Honesdale_Pocono_Mountains _Region_Pennsylvania.html.

2. Stuart Miller, "For a B&B That Doesn't Exist, the Online Reviews Keep Coming," *The New York Times*, March 28, 2010, http://www.nytimes.com/2010/03/29 /business/media/29tripadvisor.html, retrieved March 13, 2016.

3. Walters, Ben, *The Office* (London: British Film Institute, 2006), 7.

4. Ibid.

5. The sequence also offers a gesture toward the program's status as an adaptation: both the British and U.S. versions end with the same graphic image of anonymous signage.

6. The term "truthiness" is borrowed from satirical television personality Stephen Colbert, who coined the term in reference to arguments that feel right even though they have no basis in factual reality.

7. As the series progresses, other characters begin to filter in as additions or replacements. A series of cast changes, additions, and reintroductions followed Steve Carrell's departure from the program after season seven. The series features

several recurring characters, each as idiosyncratic and verisimilarly absurd as the next. Notably, lovable Darryl from the warehouse, who becomes an upstairs worker; Erin, the quirky new receptionist who becomes a love match for Andy; and Gabe, who is brought in as a corporate mole when ownership of Dunder Mifflin shifts.

8. The term "post-network era" comes from the work of Amanda D. Lotz, who coined the term as a way to discuss the effects of television's technological shifts in the era after the primacy of the big three networks. See Amanda D. Lotz, *Television Will Be Revolutionized.* New York: New York University Press, 2007.

9. William M. Kunz, "Prime-Time Island: Television Program and Format Importation into the United States," *Television & New Media*, 11(4) (July 2010), 310.

10. Brian Stelter, "Serving Up Television Without the TV Set," *The New York Times*, March 10, 2008, http://www.nytimes.com/2008/03/10/technology/10online.html, retrieved March 13, 2016.

11. Available at https://youtu.be/b6hqP0c0_gw.

12. Dunderpedia is found at http://theoffice.wikia.com.

13. Jelle Mast, "New Directions in Hybrid Popular Television: A reassessment of Television Mock-Documentary," *Media Culture & Society*, 31(2) (2009), 231.

14. Mast, op. cit., 231–232.

15. Eric Detweiler, "'I Was Just Doing a Little Joke There': Irony and the Paradoxes of the Sitcom in *The Office*," *Journal of Popular Culture*, 45(4) (2012), 729.

16. Christopher Kocela, "Cynics Encouraged to Apply: *The Office* as Reality Viewer Training," *Journal of Popular Film and Television*, 37(4) (2009), 167.

17. Brett Mills, "Comedy Verité: Contemporary Sitcom Form," *Screen*, 45(1) (2004), 65.

BIBLIOGRAPHY

Banks, Miranda. "The Picket Line Online: Creative Labor, Digital Activism, and the 2007–2008 Writers Guild of America Strike." *Popular Communication*, 8(1) (2010), 20–33.

Detweiler, Eric. "'I Was Just Doing a Little Joke There': Irony and the Paradoxes of the Sitcom in *The Office*." *Journal of Popular Culture*, 45(4) (2012), 727–748.

Kocela, Christopher. "Cynics Encouraged to Apply: *The Office* as Reality Viewer Training." *Journal of Popular Film and Television*, 37(4) (2009), 15–22.

Kunz, William M. "Prime-Time Island: Television Program and Format Importation into the United States." *Television & New Media*, 11(4) (July 2010), 308–324.

Mast, Jelle. "New Directions in Hybrid Popular Television: A Reassessment of Television Mock-Documentary." *Media Culture & Society*, 31(2) (2009), 231–250.

Miller, Stuart. "For a B&B That Doesn't Exist, the Online Reviews Keep Coming." *The New York Times*, March 28, 2010, http://www.nytimes.com/2010/03/29/business/media/29tripadvisor.html, retrieved March 13, 2016.

Mills, Brett. "Comedy Verité: Contemporary Sitcom Form." *Screen*, 45(1) (2004), 63–78.

Stelter, Brian. "Serving Up Television Without the TV Set." *The New York Times*, March 10, 2008, http://www.nytimes.com/2008/03/10/technology/10online .html, retrieved March 13, 2016.

TripAdvisor. "Schrute Farms," http://www.tripadvisor.com/Hotel_Review-g52842 -d730099-Reviews-Schrute_Farms-Honesdale_Pocono_Mountains _Region_Pennsylvania.html, retrieved March 13, 2016.

Walters, Ben. *The Office*. London: British Film Institute, 2006.

23

Black Lives Matter: Even in *The Boondocks* World

Julian Williams

It's quite likely that the vast majority of Americans have never watched The Boon-docks (2005–2014). *Most may have never even heard of it. If television in the 1980s had to prove to itself that diverse characters could reach a mass audience, by the 2000s television was beginning to realize that it was now able to cater to niche audiences from a diverse menu. According to Julian Williams, "*The Boondocks *now acts as a map for developing the kind of stimulating commentaries that can be presented when a sit-com takes chances." The show, which lasted a mere four seasons over almost nine years, demonstrates that variety, not the similitude and conformity of television of earlier decades, is going to be the television order of the day for many days to come.*

If our eyes are seeing clearly, America's most consistent tradition has reap-peared. Apparently, the founding ideology of supremacy is back, resulting in oppressed groups feeling marginalized and targeted in many cases. To justify this tyranny, we simply have to look at the Texas state educational system, where newly pressed social studies books minimize—and some-times completely delete—discussions of slavery, Jim Crow, and the Ku Klux Klan. They also present a more simplified "states' rights"–friendly Civil War. Saving face over historical truths are matters of grave concern, espe-cially when charged with educating developing young minds. By contrast, our current community polemics are equally contentious. Over the last several years, based on recurring police shootings of unarmed black people and subsequent racialized protests, we are revisiting a continuous cultural conflict—the repeated ethnic battle that has become the norm on American sidewalks. As we go deeper into the 21st century, the questions we keep asking are head-scratching reactions to never-ending stories: "Why?" and "How did civil rights become the most important battle of the 21st century—again?" While we'd love to think that society has moved well beyond our "little" historical hiccups, the tensions remain, and they've returned to remind us that true equality is still a dream unfulfilled.

For black people, life has shifted from chains and public whippings to socioeconomic and educational gradualism—purposeful underservicing of communities that results in unemployment, internalized violence, and despair. These assertions have been the researched findings of sociologists, anthropologists, politicians, journalists, and, let's not forget, a wide range of those categorized as artists. Arguably, these brave women and men have often acted as the line in the sand, the keepers of historical records, the reminders of who we are—of who, if we are not careful, we'll revert back to.

Fortunately, for almost a decade, we had a champion who provided social commentary that was entertaining and mentally stimulating—one that poked fun at the social and political world that is forever entrenched in black and white. Initially armed with pen and pad, the mission of this culture critic was always clear: shock and awe. His weapons? Generational commentary fueled by the notion that only through the youth will we receive the raw and uncensored voice we so desperately need. His audience? Anyone willing to listen, especially a generation of young people now receiving "alternative" learning. His targets? The same as always: black and white people and their uneven culture war. His voice? Satire so bitter it was often like sipping vinegar through a straw.

America needed a young envelope-pushing folklorist to close the 20th century and lead us into the 21st. We needed a man to replate what Americans read and watch with smoldering irony and sarcasm; we needed a man willing to inspire us by taking up the mantle left by the literary bravery of Langston Hughes's Jesse B. Semple—the "simple" Harlem everyman of the 1940s who, along with his friends, taught black Americans about their connections to the world.

For us, his name was Aaron McGruder, and for many years controversy was his middle name.

MANCHILD IN A PROMISED LAND

For those who are unfamiliar, in 1996, McGruder developed a cartoon strip titled *The Boondocks* that focused on two African American brothers from the South Side of Chicago who live with their grandfather in the predominantly fictional white suburb of Woodcrest. The boondocks, aka Woodcrest, is a place where the boys at the center of the story brought citi-fied beliefs and teachings to a foreign and unwelcoming new home. For McGruder, this would be the perfect venue to express his views on every-thing questionable involving America. Plainly, *The Boondocks* was a comic strip that presented black viewpoints from a black man about how black people, especially black children, see the world.

Obviously, kids in comics asking probing questions isn't new. Political commentary in comics isn't new. Social perspectives from the mouths of babes or talking animals isn't new. In these areas, *The Boondocks* was often compared to Garry Trudeau's controversial and extremely successful *Doonesbury* comic strip. But unlike those who came before him, McGruder developed black people who had opinions based on their black experiences living in a racist white America.[1] Now this? This was new. To his credit, McGruder gave both sides of the hand when critiquing America. From the ineptness of the Bush administration and the invasiveness of the PATRIOT Act to the limited focus of Black Entertainment Television (BET) and the offensive nature of gangster rap,[2] no one was spared McGruder's opinions.[3]

This wasn't just a political comic strip. *The Boondocks* was, instead, the voice of a black man with something to say about a people who have been stereotyped to the point that their identity is both exaggerated and, to a large degree, purposefully projected as negative. Because McGruder had so much to share about so many things and jumped into the crowd apparently swinging on everyone within reach, he would soon be tagged as the "Angri-est Black man in America."[4] He frequently lampooned public figures and any legislative body he chose on any particular week. The comic "Free Huey World Report" and the annual "The Most Embarrassing Black People Awards" newsletters allowed McGruder to comment on his own people as scathingly as anything he ever said about white America.

In our modern society, the pressure to analyze an oppressed people and their stereotypes always must be more than just entertainment. For black people, every crime is personal to a people who are always the prime sus-pects. Every image shown is important when your humanity has been deval-ued. Every portrayal is scrutinized when the judgment is prejudiced, and the audience—black, white, and all people in between—has proven to be harshly judgmental.

In 2005, McGruder's vision on paper went live when he signed with the Cartoon Network's Adult Swim.[5] Television, as they say, would never be the same again. Many of the characters from the comic strip didn't transition onto the screen, but the ones who did would challenge "who can say what and why" on television forever. The standing of *The Boondocks* as a radical sitcom, one that moved the TV needle forward, is the result of its uncen-sored, unhinged examination of black life—one that put faces and voices to black life like nothing ever tried before. And let's not forget that the stars of the show, the brothers, are both voiced by a black woman, a pitch-shifting chameleon whose behind-the-scenes role makes for comedy gold.[6] Touching every aspect of being a people—culture, clothes, food, spirituality, language, music, history, displacement, and stereotypes—is exactly what McGruder planned to reveal. The gloves were off, and the quest to change the look and feel of situational comedy had begun.

For McGruder, the purpose of this show finally being seen and heard wasn't simply incendiary humor and personal insight. *The Simpsons* and *South Park* can entertain while offending without carrying the weight of white America. The same can't be said for a black man unveiling a black show in a society as divided as the United States. What must be understood is that resting on McGruder's shoulders was the raw unveiling of an oppressed ethnic group, not just the gut-punching imagination of a satirical artist looking through a particular lens. No, he was both the black creator and writer, so the way he displayed his genius required more—and was criticized more. As such, the legacy of *The Boondocks* is harder to discern.

The content was risqué. The episodes were outrageous. Even on Adult Swim, the more mature late-night–oriented cable network that generally targets an 18–34 male demographic, McGruder pushed the envelope. Barely blurred naked bodies appeared as frequently as any show featuring gratuitous nudity on HBO. The language was rated R and was generally offensive—who and why differed, but somebody was always offended. And the message was often fuzzy, frequently hidden in the madness created on screen. Although critics and criticism were disparate in their assessments during the show's four seasons,[7] it always excelled at being controversial.

The question is, "Was it worth it?" Did this show that poked fun at almost everybody and everything leave a legacy worth discussing or was it simply another short-lived sitcom that, oddly enough, lasted almost a decade? Did McGruder do enough to ensure we'll watch his brainchild 20 or 30 years from now? Did he open any doors? Does watching this cartoon merely provide inflammatory entertainment, or is it a bridge we can stand on, one that encourages us to view our history a little better?

The only way to really examine the impact and worth of this show is to dissect it. And the only way to dissect it is to watch every episode again. And again. The only way to comprehend the value of this sitcom is to look closely at the characters, the episodes, the hidden messages, and the provocative language. To judge *The Boondocks*'s merit as programming that not only reached the masses but also and more importantly produced content that will be relevant in the future, we have to determine what McGruder showed us. Did he reveal black people at their best and worst because he wanted us to see that all life, regardless of ethnicity, can be ridiculed to make the point that all stories and thereby all lives matter? Or was he trying to remind us that black lives actually matter in their own special way?

HUEY: THE ZEN WARRIOR

In the first episode, the Huey we meet is an extremely angry little boy. He is a self-described "revolutionary left-wing radical" who initially has little tolerance for those who don't share his cynical and well-read opinions on the world. Early on in season one, he disillusions his biracial neighbor anxiously awaiting the tooth fairy, informing her, "The truth hurts. The world is a hard and lonely place. And you know what else? One day you and everyone you know is going to die."[8] Like his creator, Huey says things that he believes will shock people. He is both one dimensional in his angry and righteous disposition and equally complicated given the fact that he is forever 10 years old. But whether intentional or a result of an ensemble broadcast on television as opposed to print, Huey changes.

In the beginning, Huey was the main character, much as in the comic strip, receiving most of the speaking parts. But as the show moved into season two, the other characters, especially Riley, would get just as much focus, if not more—leaving Huey as the serene conscience who no longer shouts his assertions but speaks low and calmly. Although his opinions are just as critical when the sitcom developed future story lines, they seem to be responses to those around him and not aggressive espousals meant to upset those who think differently. In season one, he functions as the narrator for almost every episode. By season three, Huey is still paranoid and still in tune with the world's lies, but he has clearly matured, a response to those around him becoming more irresponsible and more outrageous—particularly Riley, Grandad, and the anally retentive attorney, Tom Dubois, and his unsatisfied white wife, Sarah. As such, his opening and ending monologues are no longer expected standards. He is the only character to evolve in the series, and he does this by relinquishing his hold as "star" of the show. Instead, he becomes the brooding conscience, often functioning as a secondary character who is hyperfocused yet reasonable. And this is important because although everybody else is yelling and being wildly exaggerated, Huey acts as the responsible adult. As a matter of fact, as the seasons move on, Huey is virtually silent in many episodes. When this happens, he speaks with his large expressive eyes—eyes that see and understand things beyond his 10 years.

THE ART OF KEEPING IT REAL: DUALITY AND BEING YOUNG REEZY[9]

Riley Freeman also matures, but very differently. Alongside Huey, Riley is the live wire, embodying everything negative and unavoidable for a young black male who believes "being hood" is attractive. His offensive bravado makes audiences simultaneously laugh and shake their heads. Quite simply, Riley is funnier than Huey, so the series shifting its focus onto him makes increasing sense. He is a proud stereotype of blackness, encased in the shell of an eight-year-old boy. McGruder clearly understands that black children are perceived negatively, vilified, and often persecuted like no other ethnic group in America. As such, by incessantly stereotyping Riley, we are allowed to see him as he teeters between being seen as an adult, a chest-thumping "man" beyond his actual years, and an ignorant child. The people Riley chooses to align himself with allows McGruder to broaden his own contempt for black stereotypes, as well as analyze the continuing exploitation of black culture.

In "A Date with the Health Inspector," the audience is introduced to Gin Rummy (Samuel L. Jackson), alongside the previously established Ed Wuncler Jr. (Charlie Murphy)—white characters voiced by two of the most distinctive black voices in Hollywood. Rummy—who presents calm insanity when juxtaposed with Ed, who is equally insane but, to make him more extreme, has embraced all of the worst stereotypes of black culture—are the frequent sidekicks of the unsupervised Riley. For their part, they often encourage the more stereotypical beliefs held by their eight-year-old accomplice. With Huey narrating "Snitching: A Retrospective," we learn that when it comes to talking to the police, even as the victim, "It is no secret that black people are culturally inclined against snitching."[10] Reinforcing this in multiple episodes, Riley frequently repeats the credo of what he calls "street soldiers": real gangsters don't talk. And Riley is all about "keeping it real," even when Ed and Rummy steal Dorothy, his grandad's beloved car. At the end of the episode, even his bike, with its gaudy spinning wheels, is stolen by his so-called friends. As they ride away from the pursuing Riley, Rummy expresses his appreciation for Riley's unwavering code, shouting, "Thanks for not snitching!" followed by Ed addressing the utter ridiculousness of Riley's belief, as he mumbles, "Ya stupid muthafucka."[11]

Watching closely, we learn that Riley's behavior is often linked to his pain. As he explains to his neighbor, true believer Jasmine Dubois, his vendetta against Santa Claus, shooting various mall Santas with the pellet guns he and his brother frequently carry, is because Santa never came to the "hood" or responded to any of his Christmas requests in the past. Chasing another Santa through the mall, he screams, "You gon' pay what you owe, Santa!"[12] Watching episodes like this, we are reminded that Riley, no matter how gruff and aggressive and foul-mouthed he appears, is still a child—one totally vulnerable to the perceived rejection of a fictitious delivery man.

In Riley, audiences are presented a sensitive kid who is a budding artist juxtaposed with a homophobic alter ego who can't resist thumbing his nose at education and anything that doesn't reflect the most superficial aspects of living as a black male in America. No other sitcom ever tackled the reality of internal blackness to this degree. No writers dared; the fear of creating a modern-day minstrel show is the unspoken threat that still looms over sitcoms with black casts. But McGruder took the challenge on. With Riley, viewers are able to witness the walking, talking dichotomy of black need and desire versus the lure of everything stereotypically black. Because of this duality, and the fact that the negative lure is often more appealing to an eight year old, the brothers Freeman frequently don't get along.

THE NEVER-ENDING CONFLICT: BROTHER VERSUS BROTHER

By making the Freeman brothers polar opposites, McGruder has given us a sense of all-homes-normalcy while simultaneously exposing specific conflicts that trace back to the internal war within black culture that have existed since black enslavement: the educated versus the uneducated and the old versus the new (Huey being infinitely more mature). Their frequent battles come to a head in what Huey describes as their continuing "sectarian conflict," with the older brother constantly trying to prevent the younger from hanging with Ed and Rummy, who in one episode want to kidnap Oprah Winfrey. In the "Home Alone" episode, the boys fend for themselves while their horny grandfather sneaks off to Costa Rica. The hilarity of the younger sibling taking the money left for them to live on and going out and spending it without considering the consequences has been done before. But as their battle ensues, Huey exerts his "supreme authority" as the oldest and grounds Riley, tying his hands and sitting next to his bed all night, watching him like a prison guard. Set to a version of the somber theme song from the movie *Platoon*, Barber's "Adagio for Strings," the brothers, once Riley escapes, battle to what seems like the death, the responsible warden against the desperate inmate, fighting with fists and furniture and guns. At the end, pointing their weapons at each other, Huey breathlessly asks, "Why does it always have to end up like this?" Prepared to die as he has lived, Riley responds, "Cus you a bitch."[13] In this battle—even though Huey is older, smarter, and more skilled—there is no winner. Pulling the trigger simultaneously, the two—different paths, different mentalities, their futures as predictable as gray clouds—shoot each other at the exact same time. Here the unspoken opinion on how one can't survive without the other, about how black males can't win when divided, is buried in R-rated cartoon machinations. Intentional or not, for the discerning viewer, the substance of the episode—the ageless imposition of being "my brother's keeper" in the fractured black family—is a reminder of a common theme revisited.[14]

We must remember that his sitcom is a cartoon, so we are shown violent extremes that involve bloody injuries and hostile language that could never be shown on standard television shows with live-action casts. These brothers don't dress alike, they don't speak alike, they have no similar interests, and they have different types of friends.[15] Where Riley constantly seeks out bad influences who are usually older in years but somehow still his mental peers, Huey spends most of his time chasing behind his brother and making sure he doesn't drown when the ice cracks. And in future episodes, making Grandad's character sillier emboldens Riley as the older man's primary goals seem to be chasing after younger women and figuring out social media, thereby giving Riley a partner in crime and his principal enabler.

CIVIL RIGHTS LEGEND AND . . . A FOOL?

With Robert Jebediah Freeman, Grandad, we are presented with the disciplinarian,[16] the parental figure who, when not behaving sillier than the boys, claims to be a civil rights icon. He is the oral historian who often embellishes his role in history. Robert Freeman, his name functioning cleverly as a double entendre of what black males have been seeking since arriving—to be "free" and to be seen as "man"—is the keeper of the records, the interpreter of white America from a man who has fought oppression and now wants to be acknowledged and rewarded. Presented as a schemer always trying to con the system, he constantly explains that he does this because he wants reparations.

As the show's historian, we learn that Grandad marched with Martin Luther King Jr., was on the bus in Selma with Rosa Parks in 1955, flew missions with the Tuskegee Airmen, and refused to be nonviolent during a civil rights protest—an episode where the show actually questions the validity of nonviolence as a response to physical terrorism.[17] When he tells the story of their great, great, great, grandfather Catcher Freeman, the audience is privy to a comical take on the black enslavement, retold by the family sage, and challenged by the truth-seeking Huey, the action-prone Riley, and the resident self-hating racist Uncle Ruckus. No matter the comic elements presented, with Grandad, McGruder shows that the oral tradition as a historical teaching tool is alive and well in the black living room. What other sitcom ever did this? What other show dared? Grandad is a mocking commentary on fighting the good fight and demanding to be seen—alongside what it's like to age as a black man with so much to say and so few willing to listen.

"Don't Trust Them New Niggas Ova Der!"[18] Aka: A Continuing Teachable Moment

One of the most heavily criticized aspects of the show is the frequent, if not totally abused, use of the word "nigger." For his part, McGruder couldn't wait to get on television and flaunt it. In 2005, his take on finally having a medium where he could let the term fly was comparable to finding out that casual Friday attire is now allowed every day: "I think it makes the show sincere. . . . At a certain point, we all have to realize that sometimes we use bad language. And the N-word is used so commonly, by not only myself but also by a lot of people I know, that it feels fake to write around it and avoid using it."[19] Even in the interview, referring to nigger as the "N-word" seems awkward. Think about it—this horribly offensive term, which is rarely defined and is so casually used that only the most guilty liberal avoids saying it, is arguably the most popular cross-culture word in language. So much so, the term is actually said by not saying it, and by using the single letter followed by the word "word," it's deemed acceptable. Is there a more distinctive word in language than one recognized by only its first letter?

The word is used repeatedly in every single episode, functioning almost like a recurring cast member. As such, it's easy to believe, as many of his harshest critics do, that the show's creator did this frivolously. But when McGruder forces us to examine the term as a language tool immersed within a social context that seeks to affect us through the screen—again, it cannot be overlooked that this word is being used by a variety of the show's ethnically diverse characters, and all written by black writers—the result is powerful. Iconic sitcoms such as *Good Times*, *The Jeffersons*, and *All in the Family* used it occasionally, but these were shows about black life with black stars—or racist white characters reflecting the language of the day, developed and revealed to the world by mostly white writers and network executives. That understood, *The Boondocks*'s overuse of the word exposes us to lessons about it in a way that no other show has ever done before.

Early in season one, Huey explains in the opening voice-over, "Here's something black people have known for over a couple of hundred years: niggers are crazy." He goes on to explain that black people don't like to talk about "crazy niggers in public because white people may be listening."[20] Framing the episode in this way allowed McGruder to offer an in-depth commentary on entertainer R. Kelly's child-pornography trial and the resulting support he received from the black community because, according to the show, black people would rather excuse his bad acts than miss out on his next album. With battle lines drawn, the average R. Kelly fans— undereducated and angry[21]—are pitted against black scholars and academics, individuals who are frequently seen on television pushing the agenda for personal responsibility within the black community.[22] When interviewed by a reporter, one of the fans responds to the presence of the protestors, saying, "Fuck dem literal ass uppity niggas!" Again, McGruder presents part of the internal war that continues to divide the black community—the widening gap between the uneducated and the educated, as well as the resulting clash between lower- and middle-class sensibilities—and the insistence on giving those blacks who can sing or excel at sports a "pass" for illegal acts because of a history of white oppression—an excuse used all too frequently.

A "Nigga moment" is defined by "Webster's," according to Huey, as "the moment when ignorance overwhelms the mind of an otherwise logical Negro male . . . causing him to act in an illogical, self-destructive manner, i.e. like a nigger."[23] Huey goes so far as to explain that "A private nigga moment shames you. A public nigga moment shames the whole race"; this statement sums up perfectly the power of a negative term turned into action.[24] Only for an oppressed group can a word or event be that weighty. Only for a people hoping to be seen as different can one negative interaction affect everyone. On the surface, the show is doing exactly what black people have been leery of doing for generations, airing cultural secrets and personal dirty laundry in front of other cultures, most notably white people.

Huey goes on to explain that "this moment" is the third leading cause of death for black males "behind pork chops and FEMA."[25] As Huey explains in addressing the black-on-black violence that follows a "Nigga moment," "Some people are scared of zombies and vampires. But the thing that scares black people the most are niggas and nigga moments."[26] Both poignant and offensive, the "nigga moment" arc, which is revisited over four seasons, explains that every "moment" begins with "the nigger." Huey's voice explains that without this key element, "all you're left with is peace and quiet."[27] In the follow-up episode, "The Return of Stinkmeaner," the cantankerous character Colonel H. Stinkmeaner, who was actually killed by Granddad in the subsequent fight following their "moment," comes back for revenge. In this episode, Huey (McGruder) is at his best, informing us that the solution to a "nigga moment" is not violence but peace and harmony.[28] After it premiered, you can imagine in our politically charged landscape that some laughed. Many more frowned. But in "reacting," everyone was developing an argument for or against the accuracy of what was said; as such, everyone was thinking. In the world of sitcoms, morality lessons are the bread and butter of the shows; however, true introspection, which episodes like this one insist on, is rare.

When Grandad sues the school district over Riley's teacher calling him a "nigger," audiences are presented with *that* episode, the one that finally addresses the almost schizophrenic response that white people have to the way black people use the word. The teacher, Joseph Petto, when interviewed by the media, explains with cue cards that he thought he understood, based on studying rappers, how to differentiate between "nigga" and "nigger"—the first, he assumed, meaning buddy, the second the offensive term that should be unspoken by nonblacks. Mr. Petto's heartfelt explanation to the school board is a classic attempt to define the confusion caused by the highly repetitive use of the term that McGruder is so frequently admonished about. Mr. Petto explains that Riley uses the word so much, "I don't even notice it anymore." But it's the example he recalls to the school board that highlights the word's complexity: "Last week in lunch, Riley said to a classmate, 'Can a nigga borrow a french fry?' And my first thought wasn't 'Oh my God, he said that word, the N-word.' It was 'How is a nigga gonna borrow a fry? Nigga, is you gonna give it back?' "[29] He further explains, "My inside voice didn't talk like that before he got in my class." No other sitcom has ever presented such a wonderfully simplistic explanation for cross-cultural confusion, one that leads Mr. Petto to say with sincerity about his lack of understanding, "I need help."[30]

In the opening of season three, Riley describes himself to a documentarian as a "real nigga." This is the evolution of an eight-year-old boy who has grown over the course of five years, the time it took between McGruder's first and third seasons, into a more inappropriate eight-year-old boy—one who is proud to self-identify as an aggressive outsider within mainstream society. In the fantasy episode "Return of the King," Martin Luther King Jr.'s rant to a hip-hop crowd is the perfect summation of all that is contradictory about black people and the concept of black pride. After demanding that the crowd pay attention and stop dancing and patting themselves on the back and screaming "Will you ignorant ass niggers please shut the hell up!" King goes on to hold up a mirror to the hypocrisy of embracing and, at the same time, being offended by the word, listing the complex nature of both understanding and not understanding the term:

> Niggers are living contradictions; niggers are full of unfulfilled ambitions; niggas wax and wane; niggas love to complain; niggas love to hear themselves talk but hate to explain; niggas love being another man's judge and jury; niggas procrastinate until it's time to worry; niggas love to be late; niggers hate to hurry![31]

Having the word defined by Dr. King either enraged or confounded critics, who mostly seemed to agree that McGruder "push[ed] the slain civil rights leader into the swamp of self-loathing speech."[32] The point that the average viewer would miss the satirical message and only see and hear King saying the word repeatedly makes sense. The argument made by the USA Today's columnist, however, doesn't hold water:

> I doubt [the network's] [supportive] reaction would be the same if McGruder produced an episode in which former Israeli Prime Minister Golda Meir returned from the dead and repeatedly called a room full of Jews kikes . . . [or] a resurrected Cesar Chavez . . . called his people wetbacks.[33]

For the record, given McGruder's track record, both of these things, could definitely have happened on the show. True, the network probably would not have supported him, but what seems to be missing is the fact that there is no word as stigmatizing as "nigger" and that neither "kike" nor "wetback" are cross-cultural insults that their own people both self-identify with or have become so popular that non-Jews or non-Mexicans now incorporate them into every facet of popular culture.

Besides that, if you watched this particular episode and didn't think the Revered Dr. Martin Luther King Jr. calling a room full of his own people behaving badly "the ugliest word in the English language"[34] not-ready-for-prime-time arresting television—which has always been part of McGruder's mission—well, you probably don't think kitten videos are cute either. Add to this point the various ways this word can be used are endless: "Nigga technology," according to Rummy, is any "ignorant" technology like texting that doesn't plug into a printer. Why? Because, he says, "niggas never have anything to print."[35] Again, McGruder is providing adult humor that may have gone over the heads of many, the age-old joke that if you want to hide something from a black person, put it in a book—a ribbing that has usually been tossed out by educated blacks to undereducated blacks.

Funny? Depends. Offensive? Depends. Thought provoking? Definitely.

And then there is Uncle Ruckus, the recurring character who uses the word more than any other, a self-hating black man who claims to suffer from "re-vitiligo," a disease that makes him darker and darker. As a writer, to develop this character took courage. For Uncle Ruckus to be the break-out star that every lasting sitcom eventually has—the character that attains a sense of unexpected popularity, the one that viewers can't wait to see—is amazing, especially considering the fact that he is both physically unattractive and designed, at least on the surface, to be unlikable. The reason for his appeal is more complicated than the character of J. J. on *Good Times*, Florence on *The Jeffersons*, or Steve Urkel on *Family Matters*, all developed as supporting characters who became so essential to the success of every episode that a spin-off was always floated as inevitable.[36] They were second-ary players elevated to "star" status, personalities whose speaking parts provided the provocative quotes fans repeated the next day. But in the history of sitcoms, the concept of an Uncle Ruckus, is culturally hilarious because so many black people have that uncle who provides outrageous revisionist history in a way that is totally offensive while being equally comical. For Uncle Ruckus, this is done by using "nigger" as noun, verb, and adjective—a word that combines hate and casual camaraderie so seamlessly that it is confusing to any who haven't grown up with the diverse ways it can be applied.

The innovative nature of the show's writing, especially as it relates to using Ruckus remembering how the country has treated those deemed "niggers," comes from how McGruder and his team understand the importance of showcasing the timeless nature of the boomerang effect on history.

In a flashback to the 1957 trial of a blind black man accused of killing three white children with a Winchester rifle from 50 yards away, Uncle Ruckus screams, "Guilty, that nigga is guilty! . . . I don't need to deliberate. . . . I got the rope right here!"[37] America's eventual return to civil disruption under the heading Black Lives Matter, a movement that has inspired all oppressed groups to ensure that protesting becomes a 21st-century norm, is based on the long simmering prejudices of the country's past, which, as Ruckus reflects, are times that many people have never let go.

IT'S SO HARD TO SAY GOODBYE TO YESTERDAY[38]

Whether or not you like McGruder, you can't deny that what he developed from his own mind is a sitcom that, because of its nonelitist appeal, allows it to be both influential and insightful, an episodic teaching tool tackling issues in ways no one else ever dared. And not because it wasn't offensive, at times even vile, with language so obscene you often needed an urban, black people, hip-hop dictionary to keep up with the various ways language can impact conversations. And not because McGruder wasn't often unapologetically gleeful in his attacks on figures barely disguised or renamed.[39] Instead, *The Boondocks* is a testament to its creator's bravery and his indifference to making or maintaining friendships that didn't forward his clearly stated agenda: to be seen and heard, regardless of what anyone else thought.

On TV, black people presented the world with complex understandings of black life, a sitcom pushed to extremes never tried before, and then presented to an audience in dire need of witnessing it. How many other shows have disappeared for years, making loyal devotees wait, only to return again and again? Oddly enough, just as we had grown accustomed to waiting to see them come and speak on the latest events,[40] they were gone. Thankfully, they live on. The characters' images are forever silhouetted on the sides of blighted buildings, informing people that "black males were here." They are on posters. They are the urban faces printed on fliers in major cities across the world for various advertising campaigns. And for the diehard fans around the globe, they will live forever in the form of tattoos. Taken together, they have transitioned into their next lives as urban mythology, sketches that are so familiar they need no explanation.

With the country more racially divided than ever, *The Boondocks* now acts as a map for developing the kind of stimulating commentaries that can be presented when a sitcom takes chances. We've already seen ABC throw caution to the wind with its critical darling *Black-ish*, which has been heralded for making social commentary about black life in ways that haven't been allowed on prime-time network television since political correctness became the country's go-to response. This show—a comedic reflection of a black family with skin color issues, stereotypes versus perception, old versus new, financially secure yet conflicted in their mostly white environments—is constantly pushing that black people have unique stories and that black lives do indeed matter.

Sound familiar?

Whether acknowledged or not, the success of a show like *Black-ish* is because *The Boondocks* made us realize that comedy about cultures we've been taught to tiptoe around is funny to everyone when it's saying something.

Now isn't that the mark of greatness?

NOTES

1. "I think a lot of *The Boondocks'* success can be attributed to me growing up around white people. . . . If I didn't know white people so well, I would never be able to sell them angry black kids every single day. Old white people read the paper. I sell angry black kids to 20 million people a day, 30 million on Sunday." Michael Datcher, "Free Huey: Aaron McGruder's Outer Child Is Taking on America," *Crisis*, 110(5) (September 2003), 41–43.

2. Reginald Hudlin was a collaborator and executive producer of the cartoon and the 2004 comic novel *Birth of a Nation*. Their book asked the question, "Would we really care if East St. Louis seceded from the Union?" He was also president of BET from 2005 to 2008 and was lampooned as "Wedgie Rudlin" on two unaired episodes of the show. "Boondocks to BET: !*%#!." *Los Angeles Times*, http://articles.latimes.com/2008/jun/04/entertainment/et-boondocks4, retrieved January 1, 2016.

3. On several occasions, the comic strip was alleged to have gone too far. After 9/11, McGruder's comments on the Bush administration often resulted in suspensions by papers like the *Washington Post, Dallas Morning News,* and *Daily News*. It was dropped completely by *The Sun Herald* of Biloxi, Mississippi.

4. "No One Is Safe on 'The Boondocks.'" *USA Today*, October 31, 2005, http://usatoday30.usatoday.com/life/television/news/2005-10-31-boondocks_x.htm, retrieved December 26, 2015.

5. Distributed by Sony Pictures Television.

6. Actress Regina King does the voices for both Huey and Riley Freeman.

7. McGruder wasn't involved with season four in any way. In fact, the sitcom no longer introduced him as its creator or executive producer during the opening credits.

8. *The Boondocks*, "The Real," season one, episode eight (Culver City, CA: Sony Pictures Television), DVD.

9. His self-given hip-hop moniker.

10. *The Boondocks*, "Thank You for Not Snitching," season two, episode 18 (Culver City, CA: Sony Pictures Television), DVD.

11. Ibid.

12. *The Boondocks*, "A Huey Freeman Christmas," season one, episode seven (Culver City, CA: Sony Pictures Television), DVD.

13. *The Boondocks*, "Home Alone," season two, episode 10 (Culver City, CA: Sony Pictures Television), DVD.

14. This theme plays out with their extended black family as well, most notably between the trinity of proud Grandad, hateful Uncle Ruckus, and "White-like" Tom Dubois.

15. It is interesting that Huey doesn't seem to have any friends on the sitcom. His last peer connection on the show was the militant Cairo, who dissed Huey for abandoning Chicago and ended their relationship with a brutal headbutt in the episode titled "Wingmen."

16. After smacking Huey in episode one, Grandad only threatens Huey in future episodes, whereas Riley is actually beaten frequently.

17. *The Boondocks*, "Freedom Ride or Die," season four, episode 50 (Culver City, CA: Sony Pictures Television), DVD) was written solely by executive producer Rodney Barnes, who, alongside McGruder, is the often overlooked cowriter of 19 episodes in seasons one through three.

18. *The Boondocks*, "The Garden Party," season one, episode one (Culver City, CA: Sony Pictures Television), DVD). Uncle Ruckus warns the white guests with this song.

19. Mike McDaniel, "Boondocks Promises Animated Controversy," *Houston Chronicle*, July 20, 2005, http://www.chron.com/entertainment/article/Boond ocks-promises-animated-controversy-1517403.php, retrieved January 2, 2016.

20. *The Boondocks*, "The Trial of R. Kelly," season one, episode two (Culver City, CA: Sony Pictures Television), DVD.

21. In the background, supporters are seen carrying signs that read "We Luv Yu R Kelly" and "NOT GILLTEE!"

22. One protestor is an obvious characterization of Dr. Cornel West.

23. *The Boondocks*, "Grandad's Fight," season one, episode four (Culver City, CA: Sony Pictures Television), DVD.

24. Ibid.

25. Ibid.

26. *The Boondocks*, "Stinkmeaner Strikes Back," season two, episode 19 (Culver City, CA: Sony Pictures Television), DVD.

27. *The Boondocks*, "Grandad's Fight," op. cit.

28. *The Boondocks*, "Stinkmeaner Strikes Back," op. cit.

29. *The Boondocks*, "The S-Word," season two, episode 22 (Culver City, CA: Sony Pictures Television), DVD.

30. Ibid.

31. *The Boondocks*, "Return of the King," season one, episode nine (Culver City, CA: Sony Pictures Television), DVD. Note how the use of the term fluctuates between "nigger" and "nigga"; linguistically speaking, this is common in the black vernacular.

32. DeWayne Wickham, "Boondocks Steps Over the Line in Its Treatment of King," *USA Today*, January 31, 2006, http://usatoday30.usatoday.com/news /opinion/columnist/wickham/2006-01-30-boondocks_x.htm, retrieved December 15, 2015.

33. Ibid.

34. *The Boondocks*. "Return of the King," op. cit.

35. *The Boondocks*, "Lets Nab Oprah," season one, episode 11 (Culver City, CA: Sony Pictures Television), DVD.

36. "The Uncle Ruckus Movie" was McGruder's Kickstarter.com campaign seeking funding for a live-action film. He attempted to fund the $20-million venture to ensure no corporate backers would be involved. The pledges ended on March 1, 2013, with $129,963 having been raised.

37. *The Boondocks*, "The Trial of R. Kelly," op. cit.

38. Somber song that ends the black male coming-of-age movie *Cooley High* (1975); written by Freddie Perren and Christine Yarian, and performed by G. C. Cameron.

39. Characters such as Reverend Rollo Goodlove (representing Al Sharpton or Jesse Jackson); Winston Jerome and Ma Dukes (representing Tyler Perry as Madea); Ed Wuncler Jr. wearing his giant W medallion (representing George W. Bush); Gin Rummy (representing Donald Rumsfeld); Armstrong Elder, who helps Uncle Ruckus spread the "white Jesus" message (representing political commentator Larry Elder); Debra Leevil (representing BET chair Debra L. Lee); and Wedgie Rudlin (representing former BET president and friend Reginal Hudlin).

40. The show was off the air between seasons as follows: Season one ran from October 6, 2005, to March 19, 2006. Season two ran from October 2007 to March 2008. Season three ran from May 2010 to August 2010. Season four ran from April 2014 to June 2014.

BIBLIOGRAPHY

African American Literature Book Club. "Aaron McGruder," n. d., http://aalbc.com /authors/aaron.htm.

Barnes, Rodney. *The Boondocks: Animated Series*. "Freedom Ride or Die," season four, episode 50. Netflix.

"Boondocks to BET: !*%#!." *Los Angeles Times*, June 4, 2008, http://articles.latimes .com/2008/jun/04/entertainment/et-boondocks4, retrieved January 1, 2016.

Braxton, Greg. "Back to 'The Boondocks.'" *Los Angeles Times*, October 8, 2007, http://articles.chicagotribune.com/2007-10-08/news/0710080380_1 _boondocks-adult-swim-animated-show.

Brodesser, Akner. "Net Bashing 'Boondocks' Banned." *AdvertisingAge*, 79(5) (February 4, 2008), 6, http://adage.com/article/news/net-bashing-boondocks -banned/124786/.

Datcher, Michael. "Free Huey: Aaron McGruder's Outer Child Is Taking on America." *Crisis*, 110(5) (September 2003), 41–43.

McDaniel, Mike. "Boondocks Promises Animated Controversy." *Houston Chronicle*, July 20, 2005, http://www.chron.com/entertainment/article/Boondocks -promises-animated-controversy-1517403.php, retrieved January 2, 2016.

McGruder, Aaron. *The Boondocks: Animated Series*, seasons one through three (Culver City, CA: Sony Pictures Television), Netflix DVD.

McGruder, Aaron. *The Boondocks: Animated Series*. Various unedited episodes. YouTube.

"No One Is Safe on 'The Boondocks'." *USA Today*, October 31, 2005, http:// usatoday30.usatoday.com/life/television/news/2005-10-31-boondocks_x .htm, retrieved December 26, 2015.

Ryan, Maureen. "Creative Potential Not Yet Realized: Offensive Stereotypes in Animated 'Boondocks' Often Aren't Funny to Watch." *Chicago Tribune*, November 4, 2005, http://articles.chicagotribune.com/2005-11-04/features /0511040017_1_granddad-boondocks-comic-strip, retrieved December 12, 2015.

"Sharpton Criticizes 'Boondocks' for Showing King Saying the N-word." *USA Today*, January 25, 2006, http://usatoday30.usatoday.com/life/television /news/2006-01-25-sharpton-boondocks_x.htm, retrieved January 7, 2016.

Tyree, Tia. "Bringing Afrocentricity to the Funnies: An Analysis of Afrocentricity Within Aaron McGruder's *The Boondocks*." *Journal of Black Studies*, 42(1) (January 2011), 23–42.

Wickham, DeWayne. "Boondocks Steps Over the Line in Its Treatment of King." *USA Today*, January 31, 2006, http://usatoday30.usatoday.com/news/opinion /columnist/wickham/2006-01-30-boondocks_x.htm.

24

Broad City Scrambles the Formula

Robert Lestón

Broad City *(2014–present) got its start as a Web series. A cult favorite, the series was already popular before Amy Poehler decided to produce it as a cable series for Comedy Central. As such,* Broad City *exemplifies the indebtedness television holds to the Internet, even though television was the medium that came first. In "Broad City Scrambles the Formula," Robert Lestón explores how* Broad City *breaks the sitcom mold, eschewing the conservative and cyclical narrative structure of the traditional sitcom and thereby offering "a willingness to explore controversy and to cross identity, class, race, and gender boundaries."*

If we think about a typical sitcom, we can see the pattern: the show begins with the characters coming together in a situation, a joke or two is cracked, and the order that began at the outset is disrupted, causing the characters to be thrown into chaos. The rest of the show attempts to restore order. By the end, the underlying message is that problems can be solved, justice prevails, and mainstream values are upheld. Consider *Modern Family*. It is unique among mainstream programs because it features an outwardly gay couple, but its social awareness takes place merely at the level of representation, as though the show is trying to be a kind of mirror to America's demographic. Unfortunately, it represents gender, sexuality, and ethnicity in the most archetypal ways, depicting women in traditional roles, stereotyping Colombian culture, and depicting the gay men through heteronormative clichés about homosexuality, even holding a double standard by barely allowing something as innocent as a simple kiss between Cameron and Mitchell. Perhaps I'm being a little unfair. There are subtleties, after all. The more emotional, effeminate Cameron changes tires and used to play college football. Still, such nuances don't override the continual suppression of difference for the sake of conformity to mainstream white values and expectations.

Broad City doesn't follow these rules, though. Unlike shows like *Modern Family*, *Broad City* exemplifies a willingness to explore controversy and cross identity, class, race, and gender boundaries. The creators take considerable risk and walk the finest of lines to make funny, sometimes troubling comedy. Doing so can easily get them into trouble with critics, especially liberal ones with whom they most identify. Ultimately, however, *Broad City* is a show about all kinds of different "broads." It's a show about chicks who call each other "Dude" and hide weed from the police in their vaginas. It's about broadening the tried and true formula of the sitcom because that formula reinforces the status quo. It's about broadening the way we view women. And men. It's about broadening our concepts of drugs, race, ethnicity, sexuality, gender, class, and the economy. It's about broadening how we feel about whiteness as it manifests as both privilege and anxiety. It's about broadening the role of love.

LOVE AND CHEMISTRY

An emphasis on chemistry and love is at the core of *Broad City*. Ilana Glazer and Abbi Jacobson met at the Upright Citizens Brigade, the famous improv group that operates in the Lower East Side that has been used as a training ground for *Saturday Night Live*. They became friends and decided to do a Web series about themselves, which, as Jacobson has admitted, is 80 percent them, 20 percent exaggerations of themselves.[1] Amy Poehler was an instant fan and played an essential role in helping them get picked up by the Comedy Central television cable network. The final webisode features an epic run through the city of Abbi, Ilana, and Amy trying to get to their favorite bakery before it sells out its cookies. Poehler runs into a person carrying a box of oranges and falls, telling the women to run on. Poehler can't get up because there are "too may oranges" that were "too heavy" that she kept tossing on top of herself. When Ilana and Abbi get to the bakery, the cookies are gone and the show ends. But that wasn't the point of the show—it was their epic run through the city, filled with laughter, tragedy, and mischief.[2] There's no formula or story. As Poehler said about them in a *New Yorker* piece "The rule is: specific voices are funny and chemistry can't be faked. . . . There's something about them that's really watchable and organic and interesting. There aren't enough like them on TV: confident, sexually active, self-effacing women, girlfriends who love each other the most.[3]

Poehler's point about love is the key to the show's success. Given Ilana's notorious self-centeredness, it may seem surprising that she is primarily the one who most embodies this power. Typically seen as egotistical, libido-driven, promiscuous, a bad employee, and a girlfriend oblivious to the needs of her romantic partner, Ilana seems at first to be the antithesis of a loving person, but in actuality, she is in deep, committed love with her best friend, Abbi. At times she would like to see this love develop into something more romantic. She makes moves on Abbi occasionally (attempting stolen kisses, grabbing boobs out of nowhere, staring and commenting on Abbi's ass), but she is usually berated by Abbi for doing so. One running joke is Ilana's innocence and naiveté—she believes that her advances are an extension of her expression of genuine affection.

We see examples of Ilana's love for Abbi as early as in the webisodes posted on YouTube. One episode in the beginning of the second Web series stands out in particular: "Valentine's Day." This three-minute show passes with no dialogue until the concluding minute. We see Abbi and Ilana spending a typical New York winter day together—it's foggy, the skies are gray. They tour the city, beginning with the Staten Island Ferry and a ride to see the Statue of Liberty. A series of shots follows in which they hang out with street performers, pose to have their caricatures drawn, get into a snowball fight, snack on street food at Herald Square, shop, drink coffee at McDonalds, visit the museum of Jewish Heritage, get manicures, smoke a little weed, and finally enjoy the view of the skaters at Rockefeller Center from the street above. At the end of the day, Ilana looks over at Abbi and leans in for a kiss, where she is rejected by a frustrated Abbi, who says, "What the fuck. How many times do I have to tell you?" Ilana responds: "I was just trying to seal the night with a kiss. It was a really romantic day. It's Valentine's Day."[4]

In another scene from season two of the television series, Abbi is having her wisdom teeth pulled and Ilana appoints herself as the "keeper" of Abbi for the day. As Abbi is being sedated, Ilana says "Bye, Abbi. I'll see you when you wake up. And if you don't wake up, I'll still see you. . . ." Here the audio and video tracks switch to slow motion: ". . . cause I'm gonna kill myself and meet you in heaven or whatever."[5] The rest of the day is spent with Ilana attending to her every need, which, of course, goes awry primarily because of Ilana's attempts at being responsible for Abbi. What is considered "her best" might easily be construed as incompetence, but no one can deny the love Ilana feels. There are other moments throughout the series, but time and again, we see Ilana prioritizing Abbi over everything else.[6]

DO THE RIGHT THING

One of their most memorable webisodes is titled "Do the Right Thing" in homage both to rap group Public Enemy and Spike Lee's classic film of the same name. In this short of less than five minutes, Abbi and Ilana encounter creepy, cat-calling men as they go through their day, trying to do basic things like go to the bodega, make phone calls, or just walk down the street. At one point, they are minding their own business when they get hit on (yet again) by some threatening white dude bouncing a basketball: "New ladies on the block, I like it . . . bounce . . . bounce . . . bounce . . . you know what proportions are? You got the right proportions."

Their harassment has accumulated throughout the day, and they don't hold their anger in check: "What the fuck, dude. We are human beings. . . . Listen, we're people. You have to retreat us with resPECT. You are GROSS-ing me OUT! This is uncomfortable. Do NOT look me up and down. Gross. You small dick motherfucker." At this point they look directly into the cam-era. "Bullshit. Fuck this. Fuck you, man. FUCK you. Fuck YOU!"[7]

The scene rapidly dissolves into Ilana and Abbi dancing in front of a row of Brooklyn townhouses to Public Enemy's "Fight the Power," a track that also opened *Do the Right Thing*. Ilana is dressed as fly girl Rosie Perez, who did the opening dance sequence in the Spike Lee film in 1989. "*Broad City* is nodding to the aesthetic of this film," writes Philip Maciak, "to its sweaty picture of Brooklyn, to its swooping camera work, to its evocation of the tight social quarters of contemporary America, but it's also nodding to the way that even ridiculous, hyperbolic movement can be expressive."[8] The camera work echoes the cinematography and mood of Lee's film, but the sequence also highlights how language and commentary cannot express the emotional, raw power of music and dance. Their dance chan-nels years of frustration and aggression into a moving piece of art. It's Abbi and Ilana's unruly homage to Lee and Public Enemy, but Abbi and Ilana make it their own. "That was our best episode to date," commented Glazer. "It was huge for us."[9] Most people who talk about this early episode say it is one of their favorites and most powerful.

UNRULY WOMEN AND THE 1 PERCENT

Propriety trembled when Roseanne Barr sang "The Star Spangled Banner" before a San Diego Padres baseball game in 1990. The *Washington Post* called it "the most viral moment of the pre-viral age."[10] The singing was truly awful, perhaps the worst voice to ever sing the anthem at a public sporting event. (Barr sang it splendidly years later at a Little League game.) When she hit "rampart," it was as though she intentionally, defiantly let it shrill. The boos began and continued in progressive waves. When she hit the final "free," it was another shrilly, atonal, defiant shriek. She then grabbed her crotch, hawked a loogie, and spit.

After being rebuked by nearly everyone, including the president, columnist George Will, and opera singer Robert Merrill, Barr downplayed the event. A year later, though, she explained why she thought the performance bothered so many:

> It's because I'm a woman. And I was making fun of men and, you know, we have to remember, that's really dangerous. It still is. I really thought I was to that point in my career where I had broken all those barriers down and it served to remind me that it's still dangerous to be a woman who makes fun of men, or a woman who is funny, or a woman who does any social criticism, or a woman who has a brain, or a woman who has anything to say, or, you know, a woman period. . . . It's dangerous and frightening.[11]

We don't feel threatened or disgusted by Abbi and Ilana as so many were by Barr's performance, but Anne Petersen still places them into a tradition of comedic women who refused to be tamed by men or by expectation: Lucille Ball, Gilda Radner, Whoopie Goldberg, Melissa McCarthy.[12] Of course, each of these women challenges and expands the definitions of womanhood differently. Abbi and Ilana's unruliness primarily comes in the form of their sexual freedom, but it also comes from the "I don't give a fuck" attitude concerning propriety. Ilana describes herself as a "poop ninja" who spends her mornings at work napping in the bathroom stall. Sometimes Ilana craves "pink dick." Other times she flicks her tongue at black men walking down the street. She's also attracted to other women. When her boyfriend, Lincoln, asks her about the nature of their relationship, she tells him that its "purely physical." She and Abbi spend time guessing penis size at the basketball courts. "They're bad examples of womanhood," Petersen writes, "because they compromise our understanding of what a woman can or should act like."[13]

Petersen describes Ilana as being incompetent, irresponsible, solipsistic, and incapable of gauging how her decisions will hurt others, yet she is able to attract a mate, hold down her job, and "leverage" everyone around her. "Sound familiar?" Petersen asks. "That's because it's what a lot of white male (straight) privilege looks like: the ability to have no abilities and still survive in the world. Ilana's got swagger, and she uses that confidence to get what she wants—and that, far more than the weed smoking, is what marks her as transgressive."[14] Petersen goes on to place Abbi and Ilana as among the first women in the stoner tradition. I wouldn't disagree with Petersen's version of white male privilege, but one major difference between Abbi and Ilana and their stoner counterparts is that they are keen on systemic social oppression perpetuated by the ruling class to which so many privileged white males are oblivious.

Abbi and Ilana are a far cry from Jeff Spicolli, Bill and Ted, Harold and Kumar, or the Dude. In all of these cases, the stoner is equated with the slacker, men who refuse to leave childhood behind to enter the adult world of responsibility, finding more happiness in remaining perennial adolescents. To some small extent, Abbi and Ilana don't want to grow up, but their proximity to immaturity is more a function of their being in their 20s and their struggle to find a way to live as an adult meaningfully. The primary difference in comparing Abbi and Ilana to the stoner tradition is that their practical living situations require them to earn enough money to be able to continue to afford living in New York City. As Kate Aronoff has argued, what *Broad City* does extremely well is allow those within the millennial demographic that is the show's primary audience "to laugh at the situation the 1 percent has handed them."[15] Both Abbi and Ilana are employed. Abbi, who went to school to be an artist, is underemployed and works at a bougie gym named Solstice where she cleans up, the running joke goes, pubes and puke.

In the case of Ilana, things are more ambivalent. On one hand, she is clearly overemployed at her Internet startup called Deals, Deals, Deals. We have no sense how Ilana acquired her position, what her relevant skills are, or what the nature of her job is aside from making "deals," but we do know that her workplace behavior would undoubtedly get her fired from any real-world job. On the other hand, unlike her coworkers who express concern and even anxiety at keeping their techy jobs that have the negative consequence of contributing to the city's increasing gentrification, Ilana has enough wherewithal to know that the economic reality within which she's forced to participate is rigged:

Todd: Ilana, how come every time I e-mail you, I get an out-of-office reply that says you're in Mexico?

Ilana: Honestly, I do it to buy myself some time because I am so overworked. We all are. Today I got eight e-mails.

Todd: Speaking of that, you have to start using your company e-mail address.

Ilana: Why, Todd? So I can be another cog in your machine? What's my e-mail gonna be? "Business at the white man dot biz"? What's wrong with my personal e-mail?

Todd: It's "IlanaWexler @MindMyVagina.com." How do you not see that that's inappropriate? To remind every client immediately of a vagina?

Ilana: And a mind, dude.[16]

Their male counterparts refuse to grow up and become productive contributors to society; their stagnation is typically understood as a case of stunted mental and emotional growth. As such, the responsibility lies primarily with the shortcomings of the male characters, and remains at the level of the individual. For Abbi and Ilana, however, the responsibility for their underemployment and meaninglessness of their jobs takes place at the level of the social. It is not that they are failing to step up but that corporate America has failed them, and it is for this reason that *Broad City* is as good a vehicle as any for the post-2008 generation.

MISSING THE MARK?

Abbi and Ilana are often the butt of their own jokes, often embarrassing themselves in the process of attempting to offer some kind of social commentary on the economy, gender, race, and social class. It's this brand of commentary, this attempt to be critical of white heteronormative privilege that ruffles the feathers of some critics. Enter Rebecca Wanzo and Kyla Wazana Tompkins, two television critics of color who collaborated to write an article in the *Los Angeles Review of Books* titled "Brown Broads, White TV." If Abbi and Ilana are often the butt of their own jokes, then their indulgence in speaking on behalf of the abject explicitly effaces their own credibility on the show. Such self-awareness reveals that they know that they are not and should not be in a position of authority to speak on behalf of others. Even though they know they should not "go there," they do go there. This is a territory worth navigating and describing. This is also why more women scholars and critics of color such as Wanzo and Tompkins are needed. Although *Broad City* is often self-aware of its privilege, Wanzo and Tompkins help reveal the show's blind spots.

For instance, Wanzo makes an astute observation concerning the running joke of Abbi continually having to clean toilets. Abbi's work uniform is a T-shirt that says CLEANER. Despite her lack of experience and admitted lack of upper-body strength, she aspires to earn a T-shirt that says TRAINER. Whenever Abbi is wearing her work shirt and somebody notices (such as Jeremy, her neighbor love interest around whom she is jelly kneed), she tells them that the shirt is a "joke shirt" and that she's really a trainer, a lie that no one believes. One running joke is that Abbi must continually do a job that is obviously beneath her and that white middle-class woman should not have to clean toilets for a living, but Wanzo points out that double standard at work here: "some people spend much of their lives cleaning up after others. Many of them are working poor, working class, immigrants and people of color. So the show's joke relies on the idea that people who clean are not, should not be, people like Abbi."[17] It is true that the joke relies on the idea that the audience accepts without irony that those who clean up after others are people who are poor and of color, but when a middle-class white girl does it, it's seen as funny.

Wanzo's counterpart, Kyla Tompkins, draws our attention to another scene in which Ilana and Abbi are trying to raise money and Ilana steals office supplies from her place of work. The pair goes to an office-supply store and attempt to return the items. Rather than cash, they are given an in-store credit. Tompkins writes, "what got to me most of all was the memory of living like that in my teens and [20s]: on the financial edge . . . . It stressed me out! But for them, and for the audience, it's comic. And the thing is: it's only if you experience poverty or abjection as a state that you are going to move through, or that doesn't adhere to your own body or your value in the world, that you can find comedy in that."[18] Tompkins's point isn't far from Wanzo's—in particular, if you are a person who cleans toilets for a living or are poor and see no possibilities for getting a handle on your situation so that you can make a better life for yourself, you don't experience these jokes as humorous. Wanzo's and Tomkins' points are some that *Broad City* should take to heart, and maybe these points should come through the show with more force.

To their credit, *Broad City* displays a significant dose of awareness of white privilege concerning race issues. Although Tompkins may have been "stressed out" thinking about precarity and being in a state of poverty while Ilana was selling her goods back to the office supply store, Tompkins does not address the larger race joke that is at the heart of that scene. As they are standing in line to return the items, "What a Wonderful World" by Louis Armstrong is being played over the loudspeakers. Abbi comments on how much she likes the song, and Ilana, who is neither expert nor student on such issues, tells Abbi that the song is racist and a slave song.

> **Abbi:** It's not a slave song.
>
> **Ilana:** Yes, it is. It's widely known by the black community that "What a Wonderful World" is, like, a slave song.
>
> **Abbi:** Right, right, right, I totally forgot that you're, like, the voice of the whole black community.
>
> **Ilana:** It's a thing. Google it. It's in a Fugee's song. Wyclef's like, "and I think to myself." He's like angry about it.

As the argument continues, the line advances and Abbi says, "I feel like all we ever talk about is. . . ." They then come upon a young black female teller . . . "black people, and slaver . . . y."[19] The teller gives them a stare and shakes her head. Again, navigating difficult and sensitive terrain, the joke is designed less for laughs than to make everyone, regardless of race, feel uncomfortable. Abbi is speaking out of turn. Ilana realizes that she brought the issue up and positioned herself as an authority on being black in front of a black person. The teller has to endure two white girls talking about what they have never experienced. The audience watches from a distance and, I think it's safe to say, with some anxiety and discomfort.

Clearly, one of the running jokes with Ilana's character is that she thinks she can speak for those oppressed groups that she has no ability to speak for. In fact, there's a touch of Rachel Dolezal taking place with Ilana's character.[20] At the end of season one, Ilana puts on her bucket list that she would like to *be* Asian and that "if the technology ever allows for it, I'd actually love a crack at every race."[21] Speaking directly about Rachel Dolezal, Nicholas Powers takes 2008, the year of the financial crash, as the point when large numbers of mainstream society began to identify with minority social struggles. For Powers, whiteness is historically rooted in an American-style Aryanism, and its elevation as a category around the time of Bacon's Rebellion in Virginia in 1676 could only be achieved by denying those who didn't fit neatly into that category—Jews, Italians, the Irish, indigenous peoples, blacks, and so on. But whiteness is also about denying those things within oneself that do not fit the category of "civilized" culture (such as the unruly, the overly sexual, the wild). For Powers, the recent explosion of empathy and identification with blackness meant that whites could begin a process of coming back to themselves that they had historically "amputated." Powers argues that for years, white youth identified with black music and that globalization has allowed the appropriation of other cultures. Influences from Latin America, the Middle East, and Far East have begun to fill a sort of cultural emptiness in the white population. "Which is why Dolezal's passing as black was such a scandal," writes Powers.

> Her extreme act made visible what was already happening in popular culture. Contending with broken families, unemployment and precarious futures, a lot of white youth turn to black art to express their rage, hopelessness and maybe, redemption. And like Dolezal, identifying as black—however flawed that act may be—allows them to rediscover the most alienated parts of themselves.[22]

In this light, it's interesting to note Ilana's rituals when she masturbates. The sequence begins when she eats an oyster, and then we see a series of objects—lipstick, a candle, a photo of Janet Jackson in the background, and a particular set of large-hoop earrings that say "Latina." Sarah Mesle wonders what Ilana's fantasy is in this scene.

> *Broad City* is smart about race, but sometimes a little (more than a little?) perplexing. Ilana . . . always seems to be indulging in a fantasy of her own racial positioning. Whiteness, as she seeks to experience it, is grounded in

its very special appreciation of minority cultural richness. That's a little weird! Ilana's Latina earring (like, too, the brief shot of a taped-up Janet Jackson photo) gives us a shorthand for that fantasy and lets us know that the show is in on the joke.[23]

Both Powers and Mesle tell interesting stories, and some of this conjecture may well be true. One cannot deny, however, that, as Ilana and Dolezal show, a phenomenon is taking place in white culture by which an increasing number of whites want to identify with the struggle of all people, that they don't want to own the moniker of being the colonizer, the oppressor. Maybe it *is* a little weird, but as Abbi tells Ilana in another episode, "You know that you're so anti-racist sometimes that you're actually *really* racist."

These are all difficult and sensitive issues, but allow me to conclude by stating that what is quite desperately needed are comedy programs that are willing to take risks and are simultaneously supportive of all people being welcomed into the fabric of contemporary life. One might think of the show *Brooklyn Nine Nine* as a program that is hip on being all-inclusive. The show has a diverse cast. The chief is openly gay, but his lack of a sense of humor and the seriousness with which he takes his job is paramount to any of his other qualities. The show treats all members, regardless of ethnicity or sexual orientation, as equals. So, in some ways, as Allyson Johnson has convincingly argued, *Brooklyn Nine Nine* embodies the ideal that Ilana may be looking for. Unlike *Broad City*, however, the show shies away from navigating difficult terrain, treating everyone with an even hand. Although the show should be commended for its quiet, progressive nature, we also need shows like *Broad City* to jar us awake and make us remember that life, unlike sitcoms, doesn't follow easy formulas.

NOTES

1. Kate Story, "Comedy Central's 'Broad,' New Web to TV Plan," *New York Post*, January 13, 2014, http://nypost.com/2014/01/13/comedy-centrals-broad-new-web-to-tv-plan/, retrieved January 29, 2016.

2. Ilana Glazer and Abbi Jacobson, writers, "I Heart New York." In *Broad City* Web series, May 22, 2011.

3. Nick Paumgarten, "Id Girls," *The New Yorker*, June 23, 2014, http://www.newyorker.com/magazine/2014/06/23/id-girls, retrieved January 2, 2016.

4. Ilana Glazer and Abbi Jacobson, writers. "Valentine's Day." In *Broad City* Web series, February 12, 2011.

5. Abbi Jacobson and Ilana Glazer, writers. "Wisdom Teeth." In *Broad City*, Comedy Central, January 28, 2015.

6. Ibid.

7. Ilana Glazer and Abbi Jacobson, writers. "Do the Right Thing." In *Broad City* Web series, November 8, 2010.

8. Phillip Maciak, "Theses on the Dance Moves of Ilana Glazer." Los Angeles Review of Books, April 2, 2014, https://lareviewofbooks.org/essay/unruly-stoner -girl-makes-broad-city-radical, retrieved January 14, 2016.

9. Neil Drumming, "'Broad City' Co-Creators on Feminism, New York and Amy Poehler." *Salon*, February 14, 2014, http://bit.ly/1TrHOLW, retrieved January 29, 2016.

10. Geoff Edgers, "Roseanne on the Day She Shrieked 'The Star-Spangled Banner,' Grabbed Her Crotch and Earned a Rebuke from President Bush," *Washington Post*, July 23, 2015, http://wapo.st/1PDedt4, retrieved January 20, 2016.

11. In Kathleen Rowe, *The Unruly Woman: Gender and the Genres of Laughter* (Austin: University of Texas Press, 1995), 52.

12. I can't help but think of Joan Rivers, who was certainly perceived as unruly, but played into being a woman, as she said many times, "in a man's world."

13. Anne Helen Petersen, "The Unruly Stoner Girl: What Makes *Broad City* So Radical," *Los Angeles Review of Books*, April 2, 2014, https://lareviewof books.org/essay/unruly-stoner-girl-makes-broad-city-radical, retrieved January 14, 2016.

14. Ibid.

15. Kate Aronoff, "Why 'Broad City' Is the Perfect Comedy for the Student Debt Generation." *Yes! Magazine*, March 18, 2015, http://www.yesmagazine.org /happiness/why-broad-city-is-the-perfect-comedy-for-the-student-debt-generation, retrieved January 15, 2016.

16. Ibid.

17. Rebecca Wanzo and Kyla Wazana Tompkins. "Brown Broads, White TV." *Los Angeles Review of Books*, March 16, 2015, https://lareviewofbooks.org/essay /brown-broads-white-tv, retrieved January 13, 2016.

18. Ibid.

19. Abbi Jacobson and Ilana Glazer, writers. "What a Wonderful World." In *Broad City*, Comedy Central. January 22, 2014.

20. Rachel Dolezal came to infamy when in June 2015 her white parents publicly stated that Dolezal was a white woman passing herself as black. She was president of the NAACP chapter in Spokane, Washington, for the year before she came to widespread media attention.

21. Ilana Glazer and Abbi Jacobson, writers. "The Last Supper." In *Broad City*, Comedy Central, March 26, 2014.

22. Nicholas Powers, "White Anxiety: Rachel Dolezal, Dylann Roof and the Future of Race in America," *The Independent*, June 30, 2015, https://indypendent. org/2015/06/white-anxiety-rachel-dolezal-dylann-roof-and-the-future-of-race-in -america/.

23. Sarah Mesle, "Getting Off," *Talking Points Memo*, March 5, 2015, http:// talkingpointsmemo.com/dear-tv/dear-television-broad-city-season-two-episode -eight-kirk-steele, retrieved January 27, 2016.

BIBLIOGRAPHY

Aronoff, Kate. "Why 'Broad City' Is the Perfect Comedy for the Student Debt Generation." *Yes! Magazine*, March 18, 2015, http://www.yesmagazine.org/happiness/why-broad-city-is-the-perfect-comedy-for-the-student-debt-generation, retrieved January 15, 2016.

Drumming, Neil. " 'Broad City' Co-Creators on Feminism, New York and Amy Poehler." *Salon*, February 14, 2014, http://bit.ly/1TrHOLW, retrieved January 29, 2016.

Edgers, Geoff. "Roseanne on the Day She Shrieked 'The Star-Spangled Banner,' Grabbed Her Crotch and Earned a Rebuke from President Bush," *Washington Post*, July 23, 2015, http://wapo.st/1PDedt4, retrieved January 20, 2016.

Maciak, Phillip. "Theses on the Dance Moves of Ilana Glazer." *Los Angeles Review of Books*, April 2, 2014, https://lareviewofbooks.org/essay/unruly-stoner-girl-makes-broad-city-radical, retrieved January 20, 2016.

Mesle, Sarah. "Getting Off." *Talking Points Memo*, March 5, 2015, http://talkingpointsmemo.com/dear-tv/dear-television-broad-city-season-two-episode-eight-kirk-steele, retrieved January 27, 2016.

Paumgarten, Nick. "Id Girls." *The New Yorker*, June 23, 2014,. http://www.newyorker.com/magazine/2014/06/23/id-girls, retrieved January 2, 2016.

Petersen, Anne Helen. "The Unruly Stoner Girl: What Makes *Broad City* so Radical." Los Angeles Review of Books, April 2, 2014, https://lareviewofbooks.org/essay/unruly-stoner-girl-makes-broad-city-radical, retrieved January 14, 2016.

Powers, Nicholas. "White Anxiety: Rachel Dolezal, Dylann Roof and the Future of Race in America." *The Independent*, June 30, 2015, https://indypendent.org/2015/06/white-anxiety-rachel-dolezal-dylann-roof-and-the-future-of-race-in-america/.

Rowe, Kathleen. *The Unruly Woman: Gender and the Genres of Laughter* (Austin: University of Texas Press, 1995), 52.

Story, Kate. "Comedy Central's 'Broad,' New Web to TV Plan." *New York Post*, January 13, 2014, http://nypost.com/2014/01/13/comedy-centrals-broad-new-web-to-tv-plan/, retrieved January 29, 2016.

Wanzo, Rebecca, and Kyla Wazana Tompkins. "Brown Broads, White TV." *Los Angeles Review of Books*, March 16, 2015, https://lareviewofbooks.org/essay/brown-broads-white-tv, retrieved January 13, 2016.

25

"This Is What Happens When They Let Men Marry Men": Assimilative Politics and Liberal Identity in *Modern Family*

Laura Westengard

Much about Modern Family *harkens back even to* I Love Lucy: *one of the main couples in each consists of an Anglo American and a Latina or Latino. The plots of both shows concern misunderstandings within friends and families, and the lives reflected are those of successful middle-class Americans with middle-class values and expectations. But that's not all there is to the newer show. In this chapter, Laura Westengard shows how* Modern Family *has built on a solid American sitcom base and succeeded in moving its genre forward—ironically, by showing that even LGBTQ characters can regress into American stereotypes without losing their now-public sexual personae. By advocating for the assimilation of its LGBTQ characters, the show both creates new constraints and opens up new vistas as the sitcom moves into its new charted and uncharted waters.*

In 2013, ABC's tremendously popular sitcom *Modern Family* aired an episode after California's Supreme Court overturned Proposition 8, a state constitutional amendment banning same-sex marriage. One major story line running across several seasons of the series is the partnership, adoption process, engagement, and marriage of gay characters Mitchell and Cameron. In "Suddenly Last Summer" (season five, episode one), Mitch and

Cam receive the news that they can now marry in their home state and immediately begin to plan elaborate proposals for one another.[1] When Cam announces the news to Mitch's cranky, homophobic father, Jay Pritchett, and his sexy Latina trophy wife, Gloria, Jay and Gloria's infant child immediately spits up, setting into place a running gag in which the baby seems to have inherited Jay's homophobic impulses. "He just needs some time to get used to the idea," Jay says. Adorable hilarity ensues as Mitch and Cam compete to propose before the other one gets a chance, ruining both of their romantic plans and causing Jay to opine "We never had these problems. This is what happens when they let men marry men." The baby spits up. "That cannot be a coincidence," he states dryly.

Neither Mitch nor Cam succeed in carrying out their planned romantic proposals. Instead, the episode concludes with a simultaneous proposal as Mitch and Cam work together to repair a flat tire on the side of the road. They find themselves under the stars, both on one knee in front of the blown tire. They each look into the other's eyes, and without even having to speak the question, simultaneously whisper "Yes." Marriage equality achieved.

In 2006, years before *Modern Family* aired its celebration of marriage equality, a group of LGBTQ scholars and activists came together to draft "Beyond Same-Sex Marriage," a statement cautioning against the single-focus fight for same-sex marriage taking shape in LGBTQ leadership groups such as the Human Rights Campaign (HRC). On the surface, same-sex marriage seemed like an obvious step toward equal rights for all U.S. citizens, but this group of scholars took the somewhat surprising position that the fight for marriage equality could do more harm than good for community members who were already living in diverse household and family structures beyond the "narrow confines of marriage."[2] If the fight for same-sex marriage is won, they argued, "many individuals and households in LGBT communities will be unable to access benefits and support opportunities that they need because those benefits will only be available through marriage," a result that will "disproportionately impact poor, immigrant, and people-of-color communities."[3] Instead, they proposed a "more flexible set of benefits and options" by "separating basic forms of legal and economic recognition from the requirement of marital and conjugal relationship."[4]

Since the U.S. Supreme Court ruled in 2015 that states cannot stop and must recognize same-sex marriages, this debate may seem resolved. After all, the most visible and powerful LGBTQ organizations fought for and won a victory celebrated by LGBTQ folks and allies across the country. However, the argument in "Beyond Same-Sex Marriage" is worth revisiting as the LGBTQ community increasingly assimilates into the traditional understanding of marriage and family, granting privilege to those who accept and have access to these normative structures and values. Indeed, HRC's fight for marriage equality produced precisely the results predicted in "Beyond Same-Sex Marriage." The emphasis on monogamous couples and nuclear families sanctioned by the state through marriage has shifted the LGBTQ movement's focus from the liberationist politics of early LGBTQ activism to an adoption of what Lisa Duggan calls "homonormativity," or "a politics that does not contest dominant heteronormative assumptions and institutions, but upholds and sustains them, while promising the possibility of a demobilized gay constituency and a privatized, depoliticized gay culture anchored in domesticity and consumption."[5]

The fight for marriage equality rested on a platform that was remarkably traditional, lacking the queer radicalism of past LGBTQ activism, and it also garnered unprecedented support from non-LGBTQ allies. Marriage equality was a rights-based cause that was not threatening to liberal-minded folks, and straight allies rallied behind marriage equality because it fostered a narrative that bolstered their sense of themselves as liberal and progressive while stopping short of threatening the structures of the state that privilege heteropatriarchal norms of marriage and family. In other words, marriage equality could make liberal allies feel good about themselves without fundamentally disrupting the status quo that privileges their lifestyle.

Indeed, *Modern Family* introduces Mitch and Cam in their very first scene of the pilot episode (season one, episode one) as invested in domesticity and prone to solving political and rights-related problems with their purchasing power.[6] As Mitch and Cam walk down the aisle of an airplane with their newly adopted baby from Vietnam, they are simultaneously excited about their new nuclear family and insecure about their status as gay dads. Mitch overhears a woman saying to her travel partner, "Look at that baby with those cream puffs." Immediately incensed that someone would label the gay couple "cream puffs," Mitch jumps to his feet to chastise his fellow passengers with a well-rehearsed and heavy-handed speech. "Hear this: love knows no race, creed, or gender. And shame on you, you small-minded, ignorant few—" Cam interrupts Mitch's monologue with a gesture toward the baby holding a pastry, "Mitchell! She's got the cream puffs."

The joke undermines Mitch's righteous indignation at a perceived slight and implies that his impulse to recognize and publicly denounce homophobia is paranoid, unnecessary, and foolish—his activist impulse now demobilized with the advent of his entry into the domestic contract. Cam immediately attempts to smooth over his partner's gaffe by passing him the baby and placating their fellow passengers with a gift: "We would like to pay for everyone's headsets." This gesture moves the couple away from public activism that challenges oppression head on and firmly into the realm of privatized "domesticity and consumption." All while maintaining the liberal fantasy that Mitch's reaction is an outdated reflex, a remnant from the homophobia of days past that no longer has relevance in a society that allows gay men equal access to heteronormative institutions such as marriage and adoption.

Many critics have pointed out that *Modern Family's* portrayal of a same-sex couple pursuing marriage and family on network television is groundbreaking, and it is certainly true that sitcoms have come a long way since Ellen DeGeneres caused an uproar by scripting her character's coming out in a 1997 episode of *Ellen*.[7] Many critics also argue that the coming-out plotline in *Ellen* spelled its demise (it was canceled later that year). JCPenney, Chrysler, and Wendy's refused to advertise during *Ellen*'s coming-out episode, and "Jerry Falwell, Pat Robertson and other members of the evangelical community" spoke out against her, even calling her "Ellen Degenerate."[8] Ron Becker explains that the backlash was high profile and vocal; the "Conservative Media Research Center took out a full-page ad in *Variety* (signed by Pat Robertson, Phyllis Schlafly, and Jerry Falwell) imploring ABC/Disney to rethink 'this slap in the face to America's Families.'"[9]

Almost 20 years later, the public has received *Modern Family's* treatment of gay characters much more positively. In fact, *The Atlantic* points to *Modern Family*, in part, for shifting public perception around gay marriage, noting a wave of "people crediting their newfound sympathy toward gay people to *Modern Family*."[10] The show's depiction of the gay couple placed alongside the other nuclear family structures in the show implies that their challenges and successes are no different than those encountered by the other married couples in the family.

Depicting this admittedly "tame" pair has also directly influenced networks' willingness to take a chance on adding gay story lines to other shows, and "today there's unprecedented diversity in representation of sexuality on television, as shown in programs like *Empire* and *Orange Is the New Black*."[11] If viewers have expressed any misgivings about the depiction of gay characters on the show, it is that they are not demonstrative *enough* in their affection for each other. In 2010, viewers began a popular Facebook group called "Let Cam & Mitchell kiss on *Modern Family*!" *Huffington Post* contributor Waymon Hudson echoed the group's dismay that the "show completely neuters and desexualizes its gay couple." ABC responded:

> Cameron and Mitchell are a loving, grounded, committed, and demonstrably affectionate couple and have been from the beginning of the series. It happens that we have an episode in the works that addresses Mitchell's slight discomfort with public displays of affection. It will air in the fall and until then, as Phil Dunphy would say, everyone please chillax.[12]

Indeed, "The Kiss" (season two, episode two) did highlight the couple's lack of visible intimacy, blaming it on Mitch's idiosyncratic aversion to public displays of affection.[13] However, the kiss most prominently displayed in the episode was between Mitch and his father, Jay, in a mutually uncomfortable display of parental affection. The kiss between Mitch and Cam appeared as a quick, easily missed, and still desexualized peck in the background of the scene.

This instance highlights the series' apprehension around issues of gay sexuality, and it also perfectly illustrates its general orientation in relation to viewer discomfort. The show is willing to go only so far to highlight its own liberal tolerance for "modern" family dynamics—and it takes credit for its progressive stance—but it refuses to challenge its audience members in any meaningful way.

In a reflection of the homonormative investments of the marriage equality movement and its allies, *Modern Family* offers a comforting return to traditional values while buttressing viewers' self-perception as progressive and tolerant. Rather than offering a depiction of gay life that questions normative assumptions about relationships, family life, and privilege, Mitch and Cam's relationship instead offers viewers a white, wealthy, monogamous couple invested in neoliberal values regarding property ownership, private sexuality, nuclear family, and material wealth. In addition to embodying a rigid homonormativity, Mitch and Cam dogmatically police queerness within the series in ways that not only shape them as characters but also shape audience perceptions about "appropriate" homosexuality. Although the show's explicit themes concern multiculturalism and progressive politics, *Modern Family* implicitly demonstrates a rigidly policed assimilative politics reinforced though stereotypes about race, class, sexuality, and gender.

ALL IN THE MODERN FAMILY

Created by Steven Levitan and Christopher Lloyd, *Modern Family* portrays a blended, extended family with all of its endearing foibles and squabbles. Its pilot episode aired in 2009, and the critically acclaimed family sitcom is now in its ninth season. When it began, no one knew the impact this show would have on the television landscape. An early review in *Variety* praised the "smart, nimble, and best of all, funny" show but showed some concerns about the show's ability to "find a sizable audience."[14] Their concerns were unfounded. By 2011, the *Los Angeles Times* credited *Modern Family* alone for reviving the sitcom via "the 'Modern Family' effect" and "spearheading the recent renaissance of comedy on TV."[15] Indeed, this sitcom has received awards from all facets—from Golden Globes to Emmys to Gay and Lesbian Alliance Against Defamation (GLAAD) Media Awards and even a Peabody.

The show follows three related nuclear families, all of whom live in a wealthy suburb in Southern California. Jay Pritchett (Ed O'Neill) is the patriarch, an older, wealthy white man who has married a much younger Colombian wife, Gloria (Sofia Vergara), and heads a household with Gloria's preteen son, Manny (Rico Rodriguez). In season four, Gloria and Jay have a baby together, adding an infant to their multigenerational home. Jay's slightly uptight daughter, Claire (Julie Bowen), is married to the goofy, techie real estate agent Phil Dunphy (Ty Burrell). She begins the series as a stay-at-home mom and later takes on a job at her father's successful closet company. Claire and Phil have three teenage children: clueless Luke (Nolan Gould), brainy Alex (Ariel Winter), and worldly Haley (Sarah Hyland). Finally, we have the long-term gay partners, Mitchell (Jesse Tyler Ferguson), a sensible lawyer, and Cameron (Eric Stonestreet), a flamboyant Midwesterner. The season one pilot episode highlights Mitch and Cam's adoption of a daughter from Vietnam, Lily (played by infant twins Jaden and Ella Hiller in seasons one and two and later by Aubrey Anderson-Emmon). The three nuclear families have a close relationship with each other; they live in the same town, spend weekends and holidays together, distribute hand-me-downs, grant mutual babysitting favors, and even vacation together. Though the characters are not without their conflicts, each episode resolves with a heartwarming reconciliation and a recognition that love and mutual care are the bedrocks of the extended family dynamic.

Modern Family certainly conforms to the traditional situation comedy format in that each self-contained episode includes set of recurring characters, a premise, a conflict, and a resolution. Mintz explains that "the most important feature of sitcom structure is the cyclical nature of the normalcy of the premise undergoing stress or threat of change and becoming restored."[16] The generic desire for the return to a normalcy once disrupted speaks to the sitcom's conservative core. By definition, the genre only creates discomfort in order to resolve it, ultimately undermining any potential for radicalism and offering instead "a dense reduction of social desire in [22] minutes of typecasting and driven dialogue."[17] In this respect, *Modern Family* is a classic sitcom.

However, the show has taken on an updated twist by deploying a "single-camera, documentary-style format" in which the characters are periodically interviewed by an off-screen presence and are clearly aware of the cameras filming their lives. This stylistic choice is perhaps best known in the hit series *The Office*, but it is "more of a nod to 'This Is Spinal Tap' and Christopher Guest than 'The Office,' Mr. Levitan insists."[18] In addition to its documentary conceit, the show has also come to be known for its strategic product placement, use of social media, and integration of technology into the story lines.

Though heightened product placement and liberal politics may seem gesture to a new frontier of modern television, these investments also reflect the history of classic situation comedy. Hamamoto explains that since the emergence of television sitcoms in the post–World War II era,

> the commercial system of television has successfully packaged and marketed the affirmative aspects of democratic culture such as freedom, equality, community, autonomy, self-determination, planning, and popular control. Unfortunately, the commercial system of television has helped to confine the affirmative aspects of domestic culture to the private sphere organized around domestic life.[19]

So even though *Modern Family*'s position of tolerance around issues of multiculturalism and sexual orientation gestures toward liberal ideals of freedom and equality, the extent to which the show can push these boundaries is limited by the even greater investment in commercial profit. An interesting note is that the show's fans see and criticize the crass consumerism of its product placement (reflected in a sense of disillusionment at a season one plot revolving around Phil's desire for the new iPad), but they are less quick to critique the confinement of the show's politics to the individual and the domestic realm.[20]

ASSIMILATIONIST POLITICS AND ALLIES

Since the rise of LGBTQ activist movements in the 1970s, LGBTQ politics has been split between assimilationist approaches (advocating for inclusion within existing social structures) and radical approaches (advocating for the disruption and redefinition of existing structures). By the 1990s and early 2000s, the assimilationist approach dominated the public face of LGBTQ activism. Powerful lobbying groups such as the HRC, legal defense groups such as Lambda Legal, and media advocacy groups such as GLAAD worked to increase the LGBTQ presence in politics, legislation, and media and advocated for the inclusion of gays and lesbians to serve openly in the military, increases in hate-crime legislation, and access to same-sex marriage. All of these campaigns, however, were designed to grant LGBTQ community members access to existing institutions and structures replete with systemic limitations and biases. Julie Mertus notes that assimilative identity politics do not reflect or represent the variety of sexual identities that exist both in the United States and globally. Indeed, mainstream organizations' cooptation of LGBTQ rights discourse guided by the claim that "gays and lesbians are as 'normal' as heterosexuals" erases the multiplicity and fluidity of those who are, in fact, different from the norm. She adds that "participation in the status quo can go only so far for those who seek radical transformations of the social construction of sexuality and gender and of patterns of oppression in general."[21]

This assimilationist approach, however, has done much to generate wide-spread support for LGBTQ politics. Patrick Grzanka, Jake Adler, and Jennifer Blazer note that straight "ally" activism has become more visible in recent years in alignment with the marriage equality fight, and they outline several of the criticisms around LGBTQ ally politics, including the charge that allies enjoy "the political privileges of having socially celebrated 'awareness' without any of the risks of actual social marginality" and that allies "may feel that they are beyond reproach because they have honorably chosen to position themselves in solidarity with stigmatized groups."[22] Their study concluded that "straight allyship represented a form of identity choreography" in which allies construct an understanding of themselves "anchored in personal, self-reflected narratives about identity" adding that their interview subjects "consistently indicated that being an ally feels rewarding when received positively by the LGBT community and other allies" but that "some participants actively avoided situations where their activism might be challenged or disregarded; some even expressed concern with being considered queer."[23] In other words, allyship reinforces the ally's identity as progressive and invested in fundamental privileges such as justice, civil rights, and patriotism. To persist in activist practices, however, an ally must receive positive external feedback and avoid situations where their self-perception is challenged or their privilege is threatened.[24]

The assimilationist politics of the marriage equality movement struck the perfect balance to support ally identity formation by offering a liberal and progressive cause without fundamentally threatening straight allies' structural privileges. As a result, the movement saw an unprecedented amount of ally support. It was a feel-good movement. *Modern Family* walks the same line, and it also feels good to its viewers because it bolsters their liberal identity while reinforcing the traditional values and beliefs that ultimately maintain the hegemonic status quo.

WHAT IS "MODERN" ABOUT *MODERN FAMILY*?

As previously mentioned, Mitch and Cam's household could be described as "tame." They are a two-parent nuclear family. Mitch works outside of the house, and Cam is predominantly a homemaker, later working as a music teacher and high school football coach. They live in a condo they own, drive a Prius, and have one adopted daughter. As soon as they are able, they marry. It is their sexuality alone that functions as the single nontraditional aspect of their family life, and indeed the show goes to great lengths to desexualize them, normalize their gay family, and bring them back into the folds of tradition. Andre Cavalcante argues that the show constitutes the couple as "'normal,' rational, and responsible" through "anxious displacements," or the "*over*loading of negatively codified social differences and symbolic excess onto figures and relationships that surround LGBT . . . characters."[25] Cavalcante points out that *Modern Family* does this primarily though the depiction of racial excess associated with the nonwhite members of the extended family, primarily Gloria and Lily, and the peripheral characters of color such as gardeners and pediatricians with whom Mitch and Cam interact.

Indeed, in relation to Mitch and Cam's "normal" household, the family that emerges as most "modern" is the one that includes Gloria, an immigrant. The jokes at the expense of Gloria's excessive Colombian heritage—replete with over-the-top sexiness, exaggerated accent and malapropisms, and dramatic mannerisms—are seemingly endless. In addition to the gay marriage proposal plot, "Suddenly, Last Summer" features a plotline in which Manny is nervous to take a trip alone to visit family in Colombia. Jay is concerned and takes it on himself to encourage Manny to bravely face his fears, but his motivation is less than noble. Jay explains in an aside to the camera, "If he doesn't go to Colombia, Colombia comes to me. It's happened before." The camera cuts to an airport scene in which Gloria runs to greet a seemingly endless parade of loud, brightly bedecked relatives descending the airport escalator, arms piled high with homemade food and babies. Cut to Jay's horrified face. In this scene, Gloria is positioned as an unassimilated immigrant, more closely aligned with her embarrassingly un-American relatives than with the family she married into. Her difference, emphasized through racist stereotypes about Latin American culture, is acceptable only within the subdued, wealthy suburban household where she functions as sexy Latina trophy wife. When Colombia threatens "to come to" Jay, however, he is willing to go to great lengths to avoid interaction with those he deems unappealingly and excessively foreign.

Reading the Jay and Gloria family alongside the gay marriage narrative, Mitch and Cam's quiet, traditional approach to family life and romance appears comforting and normalized. They are not the characters who need to be contained; instead, it is Gloria and her relatives who function as the threat to respectability. These paired narratives in "Suddenly, Last Summer" reflect the show's limited progressive politics. Although it welcomes liberal viewers to share in Mitch and Cam's entry into the institution of marriage, the show goes to great lengths via "anxious displacement" to normalize Mitch and Cam in contrast to Gloria's racial and ethnic excess. Like the assimilative politics of marriage equality activism, the show's narrative structure makes viewers feel good about their tolerance for gay assimilation, but it does little to challenge preconceived assumptions about the primacy of marriage or the superiority of white, middle-class American behaviors and values. In fact, it uses subtle white supremacy to soothe any anxieties that viewers might have about gay marriage by reinforcing traditional and conservative racial hierarchies.

One could write a book on *Modern Family*'s casual racism. Not an episode goes by that doesn't include jokes at the expense of a character of color through which the white characters can define themselves as progressive-minded, well-meaning, yet adorably flawed white folks whose casual racism is cast as unexceptional and who are consistently redeemed in each episode's resolution. The show invites audience identification with the show's main characters who mirror the core demographic: wealthy suburbanites. In fact, the "wealthy suburbs around the nation's big cities . . . have mostly average TV-viewing habits but are [15 percent] more likely to tune in."[26] As wealthy suburban professionals, the characters in *Modern Family* exhibit blind spots not only in relation to race but also to class. The class status of the families is taken for granted. There is no overt discussion of their wealth, with the exception of Jay, who frequently comments on how all Gloria's purchases are made with his money. The grandeur of the family homes, their brand-named cars, access to the newest techie gadgets, and international vacations are all integrated into the plotlines as unremarkable and average.

The story line that receives some attention to class, however, involves the upward mobility of Mitch and Cam. As they are ushered into the mainstream, Mitch and Cam not only assimilate into the institution of marriage but also increasingly accept normative neoliberal values around property ownership and family life. In "Grill, Interrupted" (season six, episode 19), Cam receives a small inheritance, and he and Mitch decide to use it to expand their home by purchasing the condo above theirs.[27] In a parallel story line, Claire and Mitch reveal that their father loaned both children down payments for their existing homes, a privilege of property ownership through inherited class status that has gone unmentioned in the previous five seasons of the show. Claire and Mitch decide to offer to pay Jay back for the loan, an offer that requires Mitch and Cam to give up the inheritance check and their dreams of expanded home ownership, but as entitled children they are shocked when Jay actually accepts their offer. Rather than spending the inheritance on Cam's initial flamboyant and irresponsible (read "queer") purchase of a fur coat for Lily, Mitch (via his familial class entitlement) instead values homeownership and, even more important, family duty. Although it might not be Cam's first instinct, the two work together to gradually shift their position into the normative mainstream. This scenario perfectly reflects Lisa Henderson's observation that "in the class project of queer media visibility . . . comportment, family, and modes of acquisition are the class markers of queer worth, pulling characters and scenarios toward a normative middle."[28]

Indeed, as we watch Mitch and Cam's relationship develop over the seasons, it becomes clear that they define their gay sexuality via rigidly policed norms of decorum, especially around public sexuality. For Mitch and Cam, sexuality is strictly private and monogamous; public displays of gay sexuality are cast as tacky and shameful. In "Las Vegas" (season five, episode 18) the adult couples of the extended family take a trip to stay in three adjoining rooms on the Excelsior level of the Mandalay Bay Hotel in Las Vegas.[29] When they arrive, Mitch runs into his ex-boyfriend, Langham (Fred Armisen), who is celebrating his upcoming marriage with an extravagant bachelor party weekend. As Cam's gaze lingers on the poster for the male strip troupe known as "The Kilty Pleasures," Mitch affirms that they do not participate in such tacky and immature activities:

> **Mitch:** We are not participating in any of this.
>
> **Claire:** They're very judgy about bachelor parties. I offered to throw them one, and I got a whole lecture.
>
> **Mitch:** We're 40. We have a child. We've been together for 10 years.
>
> **Claire:** That's the one.
>
> **Mitch:** It's just not who we are anymore.

In alignment with what Jack Halberstam calls "straight time," or the heteronormative temporal structures and expectations that mark success and maturity via norms of reproduction and family life, Mitch and Cam define their sexuality as private and sedate, structured not by desire but by the longevity of their relationship, monogamy, and parenthood.[30]

Though the couple outwardly rejects the public display of gay desire in the bachelor party context ("We will be maintaining our dignity in the spa, thank you"), Cam is tempted by the flamboyant excesses of the "Bananas and Cabanas" pool party at which "the most creative speedo wins tickets to 'The Kilty Pleasures.'" Taking advantage of their separate spa treatments, Cam sneaks out to attend the pool party, a behavior that is cast as embarrassing and shameful regression to immature gay sexuality, one dominated by public displays of identifiable gay behavior and desire rather than by the elite and sedate space of the spa. The shamefulness of public sexuality is punctuated later in the series when, during a family therapy session in "Clean Out Your Junk Drawer" (season seven, episode eight), Mitch cautions Cam to avoid discussing anything "too personal" and "For God's sake, no bedroom stuff."[31] Later, it is Mitch, not Cam, who blurts out "It's been a month since we played with each other's pogo sticks," and in horror at the public admission of their sex life (or lack thereof), has an emotional breakdown, exclaiming "Oh my God!" and burying his head in the curtains in abject shame. These comic moments imply that both Mitch and Cam are actively working against their gay "instincts" to contain and conceal any overt indications of their sexuality and, through their good-faith effort, showing straight viewers that an assimilative gayness *should* be pursued and policed.

Throughout the series, Cam's flamboyance serves as a representation of the gay affect that comes naturally to those "born this way" (to parrot Lady Gaga's biological essentialism) but that must be retrained and contained to conform to the structures of appropriate gayness. As the comic foil to Mitch's "straight man," Cam's flamboyance allows the audience to laugh at the excesses of gay male behavior while maintaining a comfortable alliance with Mitch, a gay man who does not threaten straight liberal sensibility and acceptably voices the concerns and discomforts of straight allies around public visible gayness. Via his homonormative positionality, Mitch's embarrassment and manipulation of Cam's more flamboyant queerness operates as the cathartic voice of viewers, both hetero- and homonormative, who would welcome gay male sexuality only within the confines of normative bourgeois values and practices. Anything that disrupts or exceeds those norms must be contained or excised.

To this end, the show polices "gay behavior" via jokes about flamboyance and, more stringently, gender impropriety. In "The Bicycle Thief" (season one, episode two), Mitch is concerned that the other parents at a toddler play class will judge them for being gay and immediately criticizes Cam's sartorial choices saying, "Wow, paisley and pink. Was there something wrong with the fishnet tank top?"[32] Later he adds, "I don't wanna rub anyone the wrong way. Can you please just change your shirt?" During dance time, Cam anticipates Mitch's desire to modulate his visible gayness by cutting him off and saying, "Yes I know. Tamp down my natural gifts and dance like a straight guy." As in the Vegas episode, the dynamic between Mitch and Cam clearly illustrates Mitch's investment in gay identity that conforms to the norms of straight time and decorum, and though Cam's "natural" flamboyance is used as a temporary comic device, he too is generally willing to "tamp down" to serve the interest of their child. In their dynamic, audience members see gay identity as something naturally unruly but, in its most desirable form, dedicated to containing gay excess in the service of increasingly normative investments and behaviors. Mitch and Cam's self-regulation allows viewers to access the pleasure of laughing *along with* them about gay stereotypes without feeling guilty for laughing *at* gay stereotypes—a satisfying and confirming relationship for allies and assimilationists who consider themselves tolerant of homosexuality but are nonetheless invested in gay mainstreaming.

Many claim that *Modern Family* should get some credit for introducing America to complex, recurring gay characters who are lovable for their foibles. In "They Should Suffer Like the Rest of Us: Queer Equality and

Narrative Mediocrity," Kelly Kessler argues that a new crop of television shows is beginning to treat gay characters not as idealized special cases but as complex and flawed characters whose relationships are just as dysfunctional as any straight relationship. She notes that *"Modern Family* gives its gay adoptive fathers license both to develop and transcend stereotypes. They garner similar narrative time as their straight counterparts and project simultaneous images of stereotype and surprise."[33] In this new trend, Kessler highlights *Modern Family's* adoption of the HRC approach to equality via assimilation. Gay characters may appear more and more frequently on our television screens, but they do so not to disrupt or question the sitcom status quo.

This is not a revolutionary moment. Instead, the LGBTQ characters on the small screen, including *Modern Family,* offer a vision of liberal inclusion and tolerance without fundamentally disrupting any of the conventions, stereotypes, or values historically pedaled by sitcoms. In a reflection of the investments of the marriage equality movement, *Modern Family* makes its viewers feel good by bolstering their liberal self-conception while allowing them to rest comfortably in the knowledge that their deeper investments in the status quo will not be challenged. Perhaps more important, neither will their privileged social position.

NOTES

1. Jeffrey Richman, "Suddenly, Last Summer," *Modern Family,* season five, episode one, directed by James R. Bagdonas; aired September 25, 2013.

2. Katherine Acey et al., "Beyond Same-Sex Marriage: A New Strategic Vision for All Our Families and Relationships," Barnard Center for Research on Women, July 1, 2006, http://bcrw.barnard.edu/publications/nfs7/change/documents/Beyond Marriage.pdf.

3. Ibid., 2.

4. Ibid., 1.

5. Lisa Duggan, *The Twilight of Equality? Neoliberalism, Cultural Politics, and the Attack on Democracy* (Boston: Beacon Press, 2003), 50.

6. Steven Levitan and Christopher Lloyd "Pilot," *Modern Family,* season 1, episode 1, directed by Jason Winer; aired September 23, 2009.

7. Ellen DeGeneres, Mark Driscoll, Dava Savel, Tracy Newman, and Jonathan Stark, "The Puppy Episode: Part 1," *Ellen,* season four, episode 22, directed by Gil Junger; aired April 30, 1997.

8. Brinda Adhikari and Enjoli Francis, "Ellen DeGeneres Reflects on Coming-Out Episode, 15 Years Later," ABC News, May 4, 2012, http://abcnews.go.com /Entertainment/PersonOfWeek/ellen-degeneres-reflects-coming-episode -declaring-gay-15/story?id=16281248, retrieved October 6, 2016.

9. Ron Becker, *Gay TV and Straight America* (New Brunswick. NJ: Rutgers University Press, 2006), 166.

10. Spencer Kornhaber, "The 'Modern Family' Effect: Pop Culture's Role in the Gay-Marriage Revolution," *The Atlantic*, June 26, 2015, http://www.theatlantic.com/entertainment/archive/2015/06/gay-marriage-legalized-modern-family-pop-culture/397013/, retrieved October 6, 2016.

11. Ibid.

12. Waymon Hudson, "ABC's Modern Family: How 'Modern' Is Its Gay Couple?" *Huffington Post*, May 12, 2010, http://www.huffingtonpost.com/waymon-hudson/abcs-imodern-familyi-how_b_573508.html, retrieved October 6, 2016.

13. Abraham Higginbotham, "The Kiss," *Modern Family*, season two, episode two, directed by Scott Ellis; aired September 29, 2010.

14. "Modern Family (ABC; reviewed Sept. 20, 2009)," *Variety*, August 27, 2010, 48.

15. Yvonne Villarreal, "Thank 'Modern Family' for the Revival of the Sitcom," *Los Angeles Times*, October 30, 2011, http://articles.latimes.com/2011/oct/30/entertainment/la-ca-modern-family-20111030, retrieved September 12, 2016.

16. Lawrence E. Mintz, "Situation Comedy," in *TV Genres: A Handbook and Reference Guide*, edited by Brian Rose (Westport, CT: Greenwood Press, 1985), 114–115.

17. Lisa Henderson, *Love and Money: Queers, Class, and Cultural Production* (New York: New York University Press, 2013), 43.

18. Andrew Hampp, "Why Viewers and Marketers Are Loving 'Modern Family,'" *Advertising Age*, 82(15) (2011), 4.

19. Darrell Y. Hamamoto, *Nervous Laughter: Television Situation Comedy and Liberal Democratic Ideology* (New York: Praeger, 1989), 2.

20. The iPad-centric narrative of "Game Changer" (season one, episode 19; aired March 31, 2010) left many viewers feeling like Apple and ABC "had violated a social contract they had with the series by seemingly joining forces to impose a sales pitch into the narrative fabric of a beloved show purely for profit and marketing purposes." Kevin Sandler, "Modern Family: Product Placement," in *How to Watch Television*, edited by Ethan Thompson and Jason Mittell (New York: New York University Press, 2013), 257.

21. Julie Mertus, "The Rejection of Human Rights Framings: The Case of LGBT Advocacy in the US," *Human Rights Quarterly*, 29(4) (2007), 1064, https://www.jstor.org/stable/20072835?seq=1#page_scan_tab_contents.

22. Patrick R. Grzanka, Jake Adler, and Jennifer Blazer, "Making Up Allies: The Identity Choreography of Straight LGBT Activism," *Sexuality Research and Social Policy*, 12 (2015), 168, doi: 10.1007/s13178-014-0179-0, retrieved January 11, 2017.

23. Ibid., 177–178.

24. Glenda M. Russell, "Motives of Heterosexual Allies in Collective Action for Equality," *Journal of Social Issues*, 67(2) (2011), 383.

25. Andre Cavalcante, "Anxious Displacements: The Representation of Gay Parenting on Modern Family and the New Normal and the Management of Cultural Anxiety," *Television & New Media*, 16(5) (2015), 455 (emphasis in the original).

26. "Modern Family," *Advertising Age*, 83(16) (2012), 25.

27. Paul Corrigan, Brad Walsh, and Jeffrey Richman, "Grill, Interrupted," *Modern Family*, season six, episode 19, directed by James R. Bagdonas; aired April 1, 2015.

28. Henderson, op. cit., 34.

29. Paul Corrigan, Brad Walsh, and Bill Wrubel, "Las Vegas," *Modern Family*, season five, episode 18, directed by Gail Mancuso; aired March 26, 2014.

30. Jack Halberstam, *In a Queer Time and Place: Transgender Bodies, Subcultural Lives* (New York, New York University Press, 2005).

31. Steven Levitan, "Clean Out Your Junk Drawer," *Modern Family*, season seven, episode eight, directed by Steven Levitan; aired December 2, 2015.

32. Bill Wrubel, "The Bicycle Thief," *Modern Family*, season one, episode two, directed by Jason Winer; aired September 30, 2009.

33. Kelly Kessler, "They Should Suffer Like the Rest of Us: Queer Equality and Narrative Mediocrity," *Cinema Journal*, 50(2) (2011), 143.

BIBLIOGRAPHY

Acey, Katherine, et al. "Beyond Same-Sex Marriage: A New Strategic Vision for All Our Families and Relationships." Barnard Center for Research on Women, July 1, 2006, http://bcrw.barnard.edu/publications/nfs7/change/documents/BeyondMarriage.pdf.

Adhikari, Brinda, and Enjoli Francis, "Ellen DeGeneres Reflects on Coming-Out Episode, 15 Years Later." ABC News, May 4, 2012, http://abcnews.go.com/Entertainment/PersonOfWeek/ellen-degeneres-reflects-coming-episode-declaring-gay-15/story?id=16281248, retrieved October 6, 2016.

Becker, Ron. *Gay TV and Straight America.* New Brunswick, NJ: Rutgers University Press, 2006.

Cavalcante, Andre. "Anxious Displacements: The Representation of Gay Parenting on Modern Family and the New Normal and the Management of Cultural Anxiety." *Television & New Media*, 16(5) (2015), 454–471, http://journals.sagepub.com/doi/abs/10.1177/1527476414538525.

Duggan, Lisa. *The Twilight of Equality? Neoliberalism, Cultural Politics, and the Attack on Democracy.* Boston: Beacon Press, 2003.

Grzanka, Patrick R., Jake Adler, and Jennifer Blazer. "Making Up Allies: The Identity Choreography of Straight LGBT Activism." *Sexual Research and Social Policy*, 12 (2015), 165–181, doi: 10.1007/s13178-014-0179-0, retrieved January 11, 2017.

Halberstam, Jack. *In a Queer Time and Place: Transgender Bodies, Subcultural Lives.* New York: New York University Press, 2005.

Hamamoto, Darrell Y. *Nervous Laughter: Television Situation Comedy and Liberal Democratic Ideology.* New York: Praeger, 1989.

Hampp, Andrew. "Why Viewers and Marketers Are Loving 'Modern Family'." *Advertising Age*, 82(15) (2011).

Henderson, Lisa. *Love and Money: Queers, Class, and Cultural Production.* New York: New York University Press, 2013.

Hudson, Waymon. "ABC's Modern Family: How 'Modern' Is Its Gay Couple?" *Huffington Post*, May 12, 2010, http://www.huffingtonpost.com/waymon-hudson/abcs-imodern-familyi-how_b_573508.html, retrieved October 6, 2016.

Kessler, Kelly. "They Should Suffer Like the Rest of Us: Queer Equality and Narrative Mediocrity." *Cinema Journal*, 50(2) (2011), 139–144.

Kornhaber, Spencer. "The 'Modern Family' Effect: Pop Culture's Role in the Gay-Marriage Revolution." *The Atlantic*, June 26, 2015, http://www.theatlantic.com/entertainment/archive/2015/06/gay-marriage-legalized-modern-family-pop-culture/397013/, retrieved October 6, 2016.

Mertus, Julie. "The Rejection of Human Rights Framings: The Case of LGBT Advocacy in the US," *Human Rights Quarterly*, 29(4) (2007), 1036–1064, https://www.jstor.org/stable/20072835?seq=1#page_scan_tab_contents.

Mintz, Lawrence E. "Situation Comedy." Pp. 107–130 in *TV Genres: A Handbook and Reference Guide*, edited by Brian Rose. Westport, CT: Greenwood Press, 1985.

"Modern Family." *Advertising Age*, 83(16) (2012).

"Modern Family (ABC; reviewed Sept. 20, 2009)." *Variety*, August 27, 2010, 48.

Russell, Glenda M. "Motives of Heterosexual Allies in Collective Action for Equality." *Journal of Social Issues*, 67(2) (2011), 376–393.

Sandler, Kevin. "Modern Family: Product Placement." Pp. 253–261 in *How to Watch Television*, edited by Ethan Thompson and Jason Mittell. New York: New York University Press, 2013.

Villarreal, Yvonne. "Thank 'Modern Family' for the Revival of the Sitcom." *Los Angeles Times*, October 30, 2011.

Postscript

Laura Westengard and Aaron Barlow

As the American television sitcom enters its eighth decade, it is showing both its age and its youth. It constantly looks over its shoulder, reliving past glories both in reruns and derivative new shows. At the same time, it looks ahead to new venues and technologies, an audience now worldwide in ways it never was before, and the ability to address new topics in surprising and unexpected ways.

Perhaps it has always been so. Even at its birth, the sitcom was old, drawing not only from radio but also from traditions with roots deep in vaudeville, the Broadway theater, and even Hollywood. The early stars—including George Burns and Gracie Allen, William Frawley, Phil Silvers, and, of course, Lucille Ball—had learned their craft on stage or in media other than television. They brought with them the skills of the old days but adapted them quickly to the small screen where they discovered new possibilities and created a new craft.

Throughout its life, the sitcom has suffered the derision of serious artists. Even some comedians have avoided it (though fewer and fewer as time moved on). The sitcom was seen by many as stale even when it was new, and its constraints—from the half-hour format to the limitations of the small, black-and-white screen to network scolds who could pull the plug even on single lines to advertisers' concerns over controversy—too odious. Yet constraints can also foster creativity, and they have in just enough sitcoms.

Science-fiction writer Theodore Sturgeon is credited with Sturgeon's law, which goes something like this: so what if 90 percent of science fiction is crud? Ninety percent of *everything* is crud. This law applies to the sitcom, too: most of what appears is forgettable at best. Yet given the vast number of sitcoms that have appeared on American television over the past 70 years, huge numbers make up the memorable 10 percent. In this volume, we have culled that 10 percent down to a list of 25, a tiny part of even that. Many fine and influential shows have been left out—by necessity.

In 2015, there were "409 original scripted television series on broadcast, cable and online services, according to the research department of FX Networks."[1] That was almost double the number aired just six years earlier, and it continued to increase in 2016[2] and may for a few years more before reaching its peak. With comedies attracting a little more than 50 percent of adult audiences,[3] likely somewhere around half of the scripted shows broadcast are comedies, and a large percentage of those are sitcoms.

It is safe to say that the sitcom will continue to evolve and that shows seen as influential now will soon be forgotten as new issues and ideas eclipse the current. It is just as safe to say, however, that future shows will never have the impact of those of the past. At least, their impact will look different than that of past sitcoms. When there are so many possibilities addressed to such a wide variety of audiences, it is unlikely that any single one will have influence across the board. Perhaps, though, the increasing diversity of new media forms and the intimacies that new technologies foster will allow sitcoms to penetrate the public imagination in new and unanticipated ways. Sure, one show may never have the kind of singular influence that a sitcom like *I Love Lucy* has had, but the sheer volume and variety of contemporary media forms has the potential to influence more broadly.

This new landscape allows for a decentering of media power and control. Whereas television was once dominated by a few networks headed by a few powerful men, the future of television is developing from the ground up rather than the top down as people create Internet shows first as passion projects that are often later picked up for television and as cable networks broaden the scope of the allowable without the oversight of network censors. Ground-up freedom still only extends so far in the landscape of capitalism, however. All sitcom creators still depend on their advertisers for revenue harkening back to the early days of television corporate sponsorship. Perhaps we have not come so far after all.

The last episode of the third season of the Netflix show *Grace and Frankie* provides a good lesson about how we should view the future and a demonstration of what we draw from the past. Frankie has had a ministroke, and a CAT scan has revealed that she had suffered a much more major one a decade earlier, unbeknown to her. She is going to have to change the entire way she approaches life and has become rather depressed at the prospect. Grace is offered a ride in a hot-air balloon as a surprise by a suitor. Knowing this is something Frankie has always wanted to do, she asks her date if she could "borrow" the balloon. She and Frankie rise in it to the sound of "Who Knows Where the Time Goes," a song written by Sandy Denny in the 1960s. Significantly, whether or not the creators of the episode knew this, Denny died in 1978 of a brain trauma. At the time, it was assumed it happened because of a fall. However, she had been acting erratically since the birth of her daughter the last year and it is possible she had a series of undiagnosed strokes, and that the fall may have been caused by one. Its last verse ends with these lines:

So come the storms of winter and then the birds in spring again;

I have no fear of time.

The situation comedy has been through many cycles, its own spring coming, even though sometimes against expectations, and disappearing once again. It has survived and grown; it has no fear of time.

As long as there are broadcast venues, there will always be sitcoms. As long as there is social upheaval and difficult historical circumstances, there will always be a public need for release. Sitcoms provide a chance to escape the traumatic and mundane; and perhaps more important, they allow us to laugh at ourselves. By commenting on society's foibles and making light of the pressures of the everyday, sitcoms provide an escape. By returning to tradition, as so many do, sitcoms also provide many viewers with the comfort of the known, even as they ignore or marginalize the voices of others. Surprisingly, even those who can't find faces like theirs in the Bradys or don't see their experiences reflected in the Cleaver household have often still tuned in each week to watch the action.

Sitcoms have always walked the line between conservatism and nonconformity, but with the expansion of television media, we are beginning to see an expansion of who gets to write, create, and star in sitcoms. The proliferation of media venues has challenged what it means to be a "sitcom," making the term's definition unwieldy and productively so. As we move into the future, we hope to also see a proliferation of ideas about what is means to be "traditional," what stories are worth telling, and who gets to tell those stories.

NOTES

1. Koblin, John, "Business Briefing; 409 Original Scripted Shows on TV Represents Record," *The New York Times*, December 17, 2015, B2, https://www.nytimes.com/2015/12/17/business/media/how-many-scripted-tv-shows-in-2015-a-precise-number-and-a-record.html?_r=0.

2. McHenry, Jackson, "A Record High of 455 (a.k.a. Way Too Many) Scripted TV Shows Aired in 2016," Vulture, December 21, 2016, http://www.vulture.com/2016/12/record-455-scripted-tv-shows-aired-in-2016.html.

3. Scarborough, "Comedy Is a Favorite of the Top TV Genres," *Nielsen Local*, June 7, 2013. http://dialog.scarborough.com/index.php/comedy-is-a-favorite-of-the-top-tv-genres.

About the Contributors

AARON BARLOW specializes in American popular culture and has written several books for Praeger, including *Quentin Tarantino: Life at the Extremes,* and has edited *Doughboys on the Western Front: Memories of American Soldiers in the Great War* and the two-volume set *Star Power: The Impact of Branded Celebrity* for Praeger. He earned his PhD at the University of Iowa.

JILL BELLI, PhD, is Assistant Professor of English at New York City College of Technology, CUNY, and Co-Director of the OpenLab, the college's open-source digital platform for teaching, learning, and collaborating. Her interdisciplinary research focuses on utopian studies, positive psychology, happiness studies, writing studies, digital humanities, education, and pedagogy. Her current book project, *Pedagogies of Happiness*, explores the intersections of these fields. Recent publications include articles in *Kairos: A Journal of Rhetoric, Technology, and Pedagogy*; *Digital Culture & Society*; and *Composition Forum.*

JESSICA BEST, PhD, is an Assistant Professor of English at SUNY Adirondack. She earned her PhD in English from the University of California, Riverside, where she specialized in Queer Theory, American Literature, and Postcolonial Studies. She earned her MA in English from the University of York in England, where she studied South African literature and culture. Her current pedagogy focuses on helping students identify and dismantle systems of oppression within the United States.

PAUL CHENG received his PhD from the University of California Riverside. His dissertation, *Transpacific Identities in Film and Literature*, explores the intersection of the lived identities of Asian American subjects and film. The subject of his dissertation reflects his larger interest in the different types of crossings—from populations to capital to culture—that occur across the Pacific. Though his main areas of study included film, Asian American literature, and 20th-century American literature, in his publications and presentations at various conferences he has explored a wide range of interests that reflect his hobbies. These include work on comic books, video games, and film. He is currently an adjunct instructor at Mt. San Antonio College in Walnut, California, and California State University, Los Angeles, and lives in the suburbs of Los Angeles with his multigenerational family.

KEVIN L. FERGUSON is Assistant Professor at Queens College, City University of New York, where he directs writing at Queens and teaches digital humanities, film adaptation, college writing, and contemporary American literature. His book, *Eighties People: New Lives in the American Imagination* (Palgrave Macmillan, 2016), examines new cultural figures in the American 1980s.

MONIQUE FERRELL is a Professor of English at New York City College of Technology, City University of New York. She is primarily a writer of fiction and poetry. Both her teaching and writing focus on issues of womanism and feminism, race, (C)lass, gender politics, sexuality, and representations of sexual identity. Her poetry publications include *Attraversiamo* (NYQ Books, 2016), *Unsteady* (NYQ Books, 2011), and *Black Body Parts* (Cross Roads Press, 2002).

KIMBERLY HALL is an Assistant Professor in the department of English at Wofford College in Spartanburg, South Carolina. Her research and teaching areas include digital media culture and theory, autobiographical media, media history, and 19th-century British literature. Her publications include "The Authenticity of Social Media Performance: lonelygirl15 and the Amateur Brand of Young-Girlhood" in *Women & Performance: A Journal of Feminist Theory* and "Selfies and Self-Writing: Cue Card Confessions as Social Media Technologies of the Self" in *Television and New Media*.

JERRY G. HOLT is Associate Professor of English at Purdue University Northwest. He is a novelist and playwright whose newest work is *Ernie*, a play based on the life of war correspondent Ernie Pyle. His play *Rickey*, based on baseball guru Branch Rickey, will be presented at the Baseball Hall of Fame in 2018. He is also the recipient of a Fulbright Award, and will spend the 2017–18 school year teaching at the University of Bergen in Norway.

JACQUELINE JONES is an Associate Professor of English at LaGuardia Community College, City University of New York. She earned her PhD from the University of Massachusetts, Amherst, in African American Studies in 2010. Her research interests include 20th- and 21st-century African American literature and media studies, Black Women's Literature, and Literature of the Civil Rights Era. Publications include "We 'the People:' Freedom, Civics, and the Neo-Slave Narrative Tradition in August Wilson's Gem of the Ocean" (*Modern Language Studies*, Summer 2016).

MICHAEL KATIMS is a Brooklyn-born screenwriter and translator who has lived and worked in Paris for years. He worked with Roman Polanski to bring Yasmina Reza's play to the big screen in *Carnage*, with Jacques Perrin on the U.S. version of the documentary *Oceans*, with Nicolas Saada on *espion(s)* and with Elie Chouraqui on *Harrison's Flowers*. His many subtitling credits include Dany Boone's blockbuster *Bienvenue chez les Ch'tis (Welcome to the Sticks)*, Raymond Depardon's *Les Habitants*, and Claude Berri's adaptation of Zola's *Germinal*. He also translated Philippe Djian's novel *Elle*, published in the United States by Other Press.

MARTIN KICH is a professor of English at Wright State University's Lake Campus. He is the author of one book and has coedited another; he has contributed several dozen articles to professional journals, an equal number of chapters in books and essays in collections, and some 40 long articles and more than 400 shorter entries to literary and cultural reference books.

ROBERT LESTÓN is working on a book that studies autonomous communities and their relation to social movements. His work has appeared in *Configurations, American Book Review, Kairos, Enculturation, Electronic Book Review, Itineration, Atlantic Journal of Communication*, and other venues. He is also coauthor of *Beyond the Blogosphere: Information and Its Children* (2012) with Aaron Barlow. He is an Associate Professor of English at City University of New York, New York City College of Technology.

EMILY MATTINGLY is an Assistant Professor at the University of the Arts, where she is also the director of the First-Year Writing Program. She specializes in American culture and gender and sexuality studies. Her current book project examines how filmmakers, writers, and artists reimagine childhood to construct radical visions of aging. Emily earned a PhD from the University of California, Riverside.

STACIE McCORMICK received her PhD in English from City University of New York, The Graduate Center. She is currently an Assistant

Professor of English at Texas Christian University where she researches and teaches in the areas of 20th- and 21st-century American Literature, Black performance, body studies, and gender and sexuality. Her articles and reviews have appeared in *MELUS*, *Theatre Journal*, and the book collection *Imagining the Black Female Body: Reconciling Image in Print and Visual Culture*.

CYNTHIA J. MILLER is a cultural anthropologist specializing in popular culture and visual media. She is the editor or coeditor of numerous scholarly volumes, including the recent *The Silence of the Lambs: Critical Essays on Clarice, a Cannibal, and a Nice Chianti*. She serves as the series editor for Rowman & Littlefield's Film and History book series, National Cinema encyclopedia series, and Teaching History With . . . professional guide series as well as serving as editorial board member for the *Journal of Popular Television* and Bloomsbury's "Guide to Contemporary Directors" series.

LEAH SHAFER is an Associate Professor in the Media and Society Program at Hobart and William Smith Colleges where she teaches courses in television, advertising, and new media. Her work has appeared in: *Cinema Journal Teaching Dossier*, *The Journal of Interactive Technology & Pedagogy*, *Flow: A Critical Forum on Television and Media Culture*, *Teaching Media Quarterly*, and *In Media Res*. She also makes experimental documentaries.

TOM SHAKER has spent almost 30 years as a college professor, teaching courses in video and film production, media, music history, newswriting, sports announcing, and public speaking. He has taught at Northeastern University, Dean College, and Worcester Polytechnic Institute. He is the coauthor of *A Treasury of Rhode Island Jazz & Swing Musicians*, and his documentary film *Do It Man: The Story Of The Celebrity Club* is currently in postproduction. Shaker has hosted *The Soul Serenade*, a classic soul and funk show on NPR affiliate station WICN in Worcester, Massachusetts, for more than 10 years.

CHRISTINE TIBBLES McBURNEY was born and raised in Los Angeles, California, grew up in a television family, learned script structure from her father, George Tibbles, and sold her first script to *Love, American Style* at 20. She wrote for *One Day at a Time*, had countless scripts in development, and cowrote several documentaries with her producer and writer sister, Angela. She wrote songs and sang in her band, Undine and the Sireens. She paints daily and has participated in numerous art shows in Los Angeles. She is currently writing and illustrating a children's book and is working on a memoir about life in the world of music, art, and television.

A. BOWDOIN VAN RIPER is a historian whose research focuses on images of science and technology in popular culture. He has taught at Franklin & Marshall College, Kennesaw State University, and Southern Polytechnic State University, and he is currently Research Librarian at the Martha's Vineyard Museum. He is the author, editor, or coeditor of 14 books, among which are *Science in Popular Culture* (2002), *Teaching History with Science Fiction* (2017), and a series of essay collections coedited with Cynthia J. Miller, including *The Laughing Dead: The Horror-Comedy Film from* Bride of Frankenstein *to* Zombieland (2016).

LAURA WESTENGARD, PhD, is an Assistant Professor of English at New York City College of Technology, City University of New York. In addition to her publications on American literature and culture in journals such as *JNT: Journal of Narrative Theory*, *Steinbeck Review*, and *Assuming Gender*, Laura is pleased to have contributed a chapter on Lady Gaga's Gothicism to *Star Power: The Impact of Branded Celebrity* (ABC-CLIO/ Praeger). Her forthcoming monograph with University of Nebraska Press is titled *Gothic Queer Culture: U.S. Queer Communities and the Ghosts of Insidious Trauma*.

JULIAN WILLIAMS is the coeditor of several anthologies, including *Her Own Worst Enemy: The Eternal Internal Gender Wars of Our Sisters*. His latest coauthored publication—*Erotica, Intellect, and God-Like Transformation in Arthur Conan Doyle's Sherlock Holmes and Dr. Watson* is forthcoming. Using the pen name JL Williams, he is the author of the Emerson James mystery-detective fiction series. The first installment, *Legacies*, was published in 2016. He is currently working on its sequel, *Emerson James: The Death of Dreams*, which is due for release in 2018.

Index

DATE DUE

			PRINTED IN U.S.A.